高等学校经济与管理类教材 · 基础课系列

U0652150

国际结算 双语

主　编　杨来科　岳华

副主编　廖　春　徐世腾　闫云凤

华东师范大学出版社

· 上海 ·

图书在版编目(CIP)数据

国际结算:汉、英/杨来科,岳华主编. —上海:华东师范大学出版社,2012.5
应用型本科经管教材系列
ISBN 978 - 7 - 5617 - 9528 - 6

Ⅰ.①国… Ⅱ.①杨…②岳… Ⅲ.①国际结算－高等学校－教材－汉、英 Ⅳ.①F830.73

中国版本图书馆 CIP 数据核字(2012)第 097313 号

国际结算(双语)

主　　编　杨来科　岳华
副主编　廖春　徐世腾　闫云凤
策划组稿　蒋将
项目编辑　孙小帆
审读编辑　孟彬　蒋将
装帧设计　卢晓红

出版发行　**华东师范大学出版社**
社　　址　上海市中山北路 3663 号　邮编 200062
网　　址　www.ecnupress.com.cn
电　　话　021 - 60821666　行政传真 021 - 62572105
客服电话　021 - 62865537　门市(邮购)电话 021 - 62869887
地　　址　上海市中山北路 3663 号华东师范大学校内先锋路口
网　　店　http://hdsdcbs.tmall.com

印 刷 者　上海市崇明县裕安印刷厂
开　　本　787×1092　16 开
印　　张　22.25
字　　数　448千字
版　　次　2012年10月第一版
印　　次　2022年2月第五次
书　　号　ISBN 978-7-5617-9528-6/F · 207
定　　价　43.00元

出版人　王焰

(如发现本版图书有印订质量问题,请寄回本社客服中心调换或电话 021 - 62865537 联系)

前　言

随着中国对外开放进程的加快以及国际贸易地位的不断提升,我国的国际结算业务飞速发展。尤其是中国加入WTO之后,对国际结算人才的需求也急剧增长。国际结算作为一门研究国际间货币支付的学科,有其鲜明的特点和复杂性,不仅包含了很多英文术语和条款,又与国际商法和国际贸易法有紧密联系。因此,编写一本既能中英结合,又能将国际化与本土化结合的双语教材,是一项非常有意义又非常具有挑战性的课题。

本教材是写作团队精诚合作的结晶,书稿的编写分工如下:中文部分:第1—5章,杨来科、岳华;第6—8章,徐世腾、岳华;第9章,杨来科、廖春;第10—11章,闫云凤、岳华。英文部分:第1—3章,杨来科;第4—5章,廖春;第6—8章,徐世腾、岳华;第9章,杨来科、廖春;第10—11章,闫云凤、邹超。全书由杨来科负责统稿、定稿。

本教材是在岳华编写的《国际结算概论》(立信会计出版社,2003)和岳华、杨来科编写的《国际结算双语教程》(立信会计出版社,2007)的基础上而形成的。教材的编写参考了国际上一系列相关的最新法律规则以及研究成果,吸取了国内外最新教材的优点,在此对有关作者及出版单位表示衷心的感谢。另外,本书从最初的选题、策划,到最后的成稿、校对,离不开华东师范大学出版社蒋将女士的"催促"和鼓励,也离不开孙小帆女士的敬业、专业和细心帮助,在此一并致谢。

最后,由于水平有限,加之时间仓促,本教材一定存在很多缺点和不足,希望读者能够多多包涵,并提出建设性的建议和进一步修改的意见。

编者
2012 年 5 月

目　录

中 文 部 分

英 文 部 分

中文部分

第一章　导　论

★ **学习目标**

掌握国际结算的基本概念、国际结算的发展及演变趋势、国际结算的相关国际法律及惯例。

★ **本章概要**

国际结算以国际结算中的票据、国际结算方式、国际结算中的融资、国际结算中的风险及其防范等为研究对象,是一门应用性、实践性很强的课程。本章主要概括性地介绍国际结算发展及演变的历史,国际结算的概念、内容,国际结算中的国际惯例规则等。

第一节 国际结算的基本概念

所谓国际结算是指不同国家之间发生的货币收付行为,即不同国家的当事人,不论是个人间的、单位间的、企业间的,或政府间的当事人因为商品买卖、服务供应、资金调拨、国际借贷,需要通过银行办理的两国间货币收付业务就被称做国际结算(International Settlement)。

根据引起跨国界货币收付的原因,国际结算分为国际贸易结算和非贸易结算。国际贸易结算(International Trade Settlement)是指建立在商品交易货款两清基础上的结算,又称为有形贸易结算,它和国际贸易的发生和发展、世界市场变化、国际运输、货损保险、电讯传递有着密不可分的联系。贸易结算业务复杂、金额巨大,在国际收支中是个重要项目,需要银行投放很大力量。国际非贸易结算(International Non-Trade Settlement)是指由国际贸易以外的其他经济活动,以及政治、文化等交流活动,例如,服务供应、资金调拨、国际借贷等引起的货币收付,又称为无形贸易结算。它们大多建立在非商品交易基础上,范围广、种类多,不需运出商品就可收汇。

在以往的历史上,国际贸易结算一度占据首要地位,结算金额远远高于非贸易结算。自20世纪80年代以来,由于国际上大量资金闲置,资本流动速度加快,非贸易结算额急剧上升,目前已数百倍于贸易结算额。但仅从国际结算学科的角度而言,无论是内容还是形式,国际贸易结算远比非贸易结算丰富得多,其重要性也非后者所能比拟。掌握了国际贸易结算的理论和操作原则之后,处理非贸易结算将不再困难。因此,本书的研究对象主要是国际贸易结算,以下简称之为国际结算。

第二节 国际结算的历史发展

国际结算是随着国际贸易的发展而产生和发展的。纵观国际结算的历史发展,可以发现三大特点:

一、从现金结算到非现金结算

公元前6世纪以前,随着社会分工、私有制、国家等的出现,已经孕育着原始的国际贸易。但当时的产品交换是以物物交换的易货贸易形式进行的,交易过程本身就完成了贸易结算,因而不存在国际结算这一概念。

从公元前6世纪到12世纪,货币已经产生,其作为交易媒介极大地便利了贸易的发展。当时世界各国的对外贸易都是采用黄金、白银、铸造硬币作为国际间的现金结算货币。随着国际贸易区域不断扩大,从地中海沿岸至大西洋沿岸,然后远及亚洲、非洲、美洲,遍布全世界。此时,采用现金结算的缺陷是显而易见的,现金结算不仅运送风险大,费用高,需要清点和鉴别真伪,而且结算费时,积压资金。于是以当事人的信用作担保的票据应运而生。利用这种信用工具,对国际间的债务债权,通过转账划拨资金或者互相抵消的办法进行结算,既减少了结算的费用,又节省了时间。尤其是银行的信用保证和融资作用,通过票据的使用得到了进一步的发挥。而票据本身功能的逐渐扩展,汇票、本票、支票的立法不断完善,使票据成为贸易结算的主要工具,相应地,票据结算也成为当代非现金结算最主要形式。

在现代社会中,一方面各国政府为了制止非法交易以及伪钞流入市场和逃税等行为,采取了各种法律和经济手段来限制现金结算;另一方面随着电子信息技术的发展,金融系统的电算化和电子货币的出现,进一步促使现金退出了流通领域。国际结算今后的发展趋势将是非现金结算和电子化结算。

二、从直接结算到间接结算

最初的国际贸易多在商人之间以"一手交钱、一手交货"的方式完成,因此商人在交易的同时即完成了款项的交割,属于商人之间的直接结算。买卖双方直接结算方式不适合国际间贸易,使用不同货币,处在不同的贸易和外汇管理制度之下,不可能办理面对面的买卖双方货款两清的直接结算,只有委托银行办理结算。银行有它自己的机构网点,或代理机构网点,设在买方或卖方驻地,它们经营买卖各国外汇或套汇的业务,它们了解各国贸易、外汇管制情况,因此贸易结算自然地分工到银行,从而使买卖双方集中精力开展贸易,货款结算则完全通过银行办理。卖方可将货运单据经银行寄出,索取货款,银行则配合收款。卖方也可自寄货运单据给买方,由买方经银行汇回货款。在办理结算业务的同时,银行向当事人提供信用保证,或以单据为抵押向当事人融通资金,从而在更大程度上介入了国际结算的全过程。

银行为了划拨资金的方便和办理其他异地业务,不但在海外设立分支机构,而且广泛地建立了海外代理行关系和账户关系。随着财务电讯系统的不断完善,在全球范围内形成了一个高效率的国际间账务清算和资金转移网络。

目前,被广泛使用的全球性账务清算和资金转移网络有三个:

(1) 环球同业银行金融电讯协会(Society for Worldwide Interbank Financial Telecommunication,简称 SWIFT)。这是一个国际性银行资金清算机构,总部设在比利时的布鲁塞尔。该协会为各成员银行提供专门的通讯和终端设备,形成了一个高速的电讯网络,每天 24 小时不间断运行,具有自动储存信息、自动加押或核押、以密码处理电文、自动分类文件等多种功能,并规定了电讯的标准化格式和统一的代码(货币、国别)。通过 SWIFT 传送,国际结算更为快捷和安全。SWIFT 是当今影响最大的国际清算网络。

(2) 纽约银行同业电子清算系统(Clearing House Interbank Payment System,简称 CHIPS)。这是一个收付美元的国际电脑网络,是由 100 多家设在纽约的美国和外国银行分支机构自愿组成的清算系统,其目的是联网办理银行收付业务。1981 年,纽约联邦储备银行为 CHIPS 开立了一个特别清算账户。在国际贸易结算中,发送美元收付指标时,只要注明客户和会员银行的编码,就可以当日完成结算。

（3）伦敦银行同业自动清算系统(Clearing House Automated Payment System,简称CHAPS)。这是继CHIPS以后,英国于1984年在伦敦设立的电脑收付系统,由12家清算银行通过8条信息通道与信息转换中心相接,CHAPS采用双重清算体制,所有商业银行,通过其开立账户的清算银行进行清算;每天营业结束时,清算银行之间进行双边对账和结算,其差额通过它们在英格兰的账户划拨来结清。

三、从按货物结算到按单据结算

当贸易商与运输商有了分工以后,卖方将货物交给运输商承运至买方,运输商将货物收据交给卖方,卖方转寄买方向运输商取货。海上运输继续扩大,简单的货物收据发展成为比较完善的海运提单,它起着货物收据、运输契约和物权单据的三种作用。由于提单有物权单据的性质,它把货物单据化了,交单等于交货,持单等于持有货物所有权。海运提单因此成为可以流通转让的单据(Negotiable Documents),便于转让给银行持有,让银行凭此向买方索取货款,或者当作质押品,获得银行资金融通。从而使原始的"现金交货"方式改变为"凭单付款"方式。

商品买卖合同中,卖方履行合同的义务是按期、按质、按量地发运货物,买方履行合同的义务是接收货物,按期如数支付货款。卖方履约的表示方法是,提供各种单证,如交来提单,以其签发日期证明按期发货;提交商检局签发的品质证书来证明按质发货;提供商检局签发的数量证书来证明按量发货。又如机器设备交易可凭海运提单、制造商证书、安装证书、验收证书等确定卖方已经履约,并通过对这些证书的审核相符就可决定付款给对方。

货物单据化、履约证书化为银行办理国际结算创造了一个良好条件。但制单、审单、传递单证等一系列工作消耗了大量的人力、物力和时间。于是,随着电脑和通讯事业的发展,EDI应运而生。

EDI是电子数据交换(Electronic Data Interchange)的简称,由于它取代了以纸张为载体的贸易文件,所以又称为"无纸贸易"。采用EDI是将标准化后的贸易单证和文件转换成电脑语言,利用电脑通讯技术进行处理和传递,接受方再把其还原成各种贸易单证和文件,从而替代了原来纸面文字的缮制、审核、传送、再审核、处理等一系列费时费力的过程,而且不会在重复内容上出现差错。采用EDI技术,简化了贸易的中间环节,降低了成本。EDI以其迅速、准确、安全的特点,创造了巨大的经济效益。它的开发和应用,将使国际结算的方式和手段更为准确和有效。

知识扩展

SWIFT 简介

SWIFT（Society for Worldwide Interbank Financial Telecommunication）又称"环球同业银行金融电讯协会",是国际银行同业间的国际合作组织,成立于1973年,

目前全球大多数国家大多数银行已使用 SWIFT 系统。SWIFT 的使用,为银行的结算提供了安全、可靠、快捷、标准化、自动化的通讯业务,从而大大提高了银行的结算速度。由于 SWIFT 的格式具有标准化,目前信用证的格式主要都是用 SWIFT 电文。

SWIFT 于 1973 年 5 月由来自美国、加拿大和欧洲的 15 个国家的 239 家银行宣布正式成立,其总部设在比利时的布鲁塞尔。它是为了解决各国金融通信不能适应国际间支付清算的快速增长而设立的非盈利性组织,负责设计、建立和管理 SWIFT 国际网络,以便在该组织成员间进行国际金融信息的传输和确定路由。从 1974 年开始设计计算机网络系统,1977 年夏,完成了环球同业金融电信网络(SWIFT 网络)系统的各项建设和开发工作,并正式投入运营。

该组织创立之后,其成员银行数逐年迅速增加。从 1987 年开始,非银行的金融机构,包括经纪人、投资公司、证券公司和证券交易所等,开始使用 SWIFT。目前该网络已遍布全球 206 个国家和地区的 8000 多家金融机构,提供金融行业安全报文传输服务与相关接口软件,支援 80 多个国家和地区的实时支付清算系统。

1980 年 SWIFT 联接到香港。我国的中国银行于 1983 年加入 SWIFT,是 SWIFT 组织的第 1034 家成员行,并于 1985 年 5 月正式开通使用,成为我国与国际金融标准接轨的重要里程碑。之后,我国的各国有商业银行及上海和深圳的证券交易所,也先后加入 SWIFT。

进入 90 年代后,除国有商业银行外,中国所有可以办理国际银行业务的外资和侨资银行以及地方性银行纷纷加入 SWIFT。SWIFT 的使用也从总行逐步扩展到分行。1995 年,SWIFT 在北京电报大楼和上海长话大楼设立了 SWIFT 访问点 SAP(SWIFT Access Point),它们分别与新加坡和香港的 SWIFT 区域处理中心主节点连接,为用户提供自动路由选择。

为更好地为亚太地区用户服务,SWIFT 于 1994 年在香港设立了除美国和荷兰之外的第三个支持中心,这样,中国用户就可得到 SWIFT 支持中心讲中文的员工的技术服务。SWIFT 还在全球 17 个地点设有办事处,其 2000 多名的专业人员来自 55 个国家,其中北京办事处于 1999 年成立。

SWIFT 提供全世界金融数据传输、文件传输、直通处理 STP(Straight Through Process)、撮合、清算和净额支付服务、操作信息服务、软件服务、认证技术服务、客户培训和 24 小时技术支持。

SWIFT 自投入运行以来,以其高效、可靠、低廉和完善的服务,在促进世界贸易的发展,加速全球范围内的货币流通和国际金融结算,促进国际金融业务的现代化和规范化方面发挥了积极的作用。

SWIFT 的设计能力是每天传输 1100 万条电文,而当前每日传送 500 万条电文,这些电文划拨的资金以万亿美元计,它依靠的便是其提供的 240 种以上电文标准。SWIFT 的电文标准格式,已经成为国际银行间数据交换的标准语言。这里面用于区分各家银行的代码,就是"SWIFT Code",依靠 SWIFT Code 便会将相应的款项准确的汇入指定的银行。

　　SWIFT Code 是由该协会提出并被 ISO 通过的银行识别代码,其原名是 BIC (Bank Identifier Code),但是 BIC 这个名字意思太泛,担心有人理解成别的银行识别代码系统,故渐渐大家约定俗成地把 BIC 叫作 SWIFT Code 了。环球同业银行金融电讯协会是一个由金融机构共同拥有的私营股份公司,按比利时的法律登记注册,由会员银行和其他金融机构协同管理。

　　(资料来源:1. 环球同业银行金融电讯协会组织网站 http://www.swift.com　2. 百度百科:环球同业银行金融电讯协会词条)

第三节　国际结算的法律、惯例和规则

　　由于现代国际结算业务的操作日趋成熟与规范,从而为各类结算的法律、惯例和规则的产生创造了条件,这些法律、惯例及规则的确立,更加明显地减少了结算业务中的不确定性,使各类结算方式具有普遍认可的明确含义,便于交易当事人作出合理选择,从而推动贸易发展。

一、国际法

　　(1)《联合国国际货物买卖合同公约》。该公约规范了国际货物贸易合同双方当事人的权利和义务,一般也适用于当事人在结算业务中的行为。

　　(2)联合国《国际汇票和国际本票公约草案》、《国际支票公约草案》。该两草案至今尚未经联合国成员国签署成为正式的国际公约。

　　(3)《日内瓦统一汇票、本票法公约》和《日内瓦统一支票法公约》。上述两个公约统称《日内瓦统一法》,有法国、瑞士、德国等大多数欧陆国家,以及日本、巴西等共 20 余国参加。该公约主要依据大陆法系的学理制定,故英美等国未参加。

二、国内法

　　各国的民法和商法,特别是票据法、银行法等单项法律法规,是调整国际结算当事人关系的主要依据。

　　我国有关国际结算的法律和法规有:

　　(1)《中华人民共和国票据法》(1995 年 5 月 10 日实施,2004 年 8 月 28 日修订)。

　　(2)《中华人民共和国外汇管理条例》(1996 年 1 月 8 日实施,2008 年 8 月 5 日修订)。该条例规定了人民币在经常项目下的有条件可兑换;对资本项目则采取严格的管理措施。

　　(3)中国人民银行制定的《结汇、售汇及付汇管理规定》。该规定对出口结汇和进口售汇等有关事项作了具体的管理规定。

三、国际惯例和规则

(1)《托收统一规则》(URC 522)及其评论(URC 500)。

(2)《见索即付保函统一规则》(URDG 458)。

(3)《跟单信用证统一惯例》(UCP 600)。

(4)《信用证项下银行间偿付统一规则》(1996)。

以上国际惯例均由国际商会制定,并得到世界各国和有关当事人的普遍承认和采纳,成为国际结算最重要的行为规范和法律基础。

(5)《国际保付代理惯例》(CIFC,1994)。由"国际保理商联合会"制定。

上述法律、惯例和规则促进了贸易和结算向规范化和标准化方向迅速发展。

知识扩展

国际商会

国际商会是为世界商业服务的非政府间组织,是联合国等政府间组织的咨询机构。国际商会于 1919 年在美国发起,1920 年正式成立。其总部设在法国巴黎。目前,国际商会的会员已扩展到 100 多个国家之中,由数万个具有国际影响的商业组织和企业组成,已在 59 个国家中成立了国家委员会或理事会,组织和协调国家范围内的商业活动。

国际商会的基本目的是为开放的世界经济服务,坚信国际商业交流将促进更大的繁荣和国家之间的和平。

国际商会主要职能有四个:(1)在国际范围内代表商业界,特别是对联合国和政府专门机构充当商业发言人;(2)促进建立在自由和公正竞争基础上的世界贸易和投资;(3)协调统一贸易惯例,并为进出口商制定贸易术语和各种指南;(4)为商业提供实际服务。服务包括:设立解决国际商事纠纷的仲裁院、协调和管理货物临时免税进口的 ATA 单证册制度的国际局、商业法律和实务学会、反海事诈骗的国际海事局、反假冒商标和假冒产品的反假冒情报局、为世界航运创造市场条件的海事合作中心和经常组织举办各种专业讨论会和出版发行种类广泛的出版物。

国际商会的组织机构包括:理事会、执行局、财政委员会、会长、副会长及前任会长和秘书长、所属各专业委员会和会员、会员大会,此外还设有国家特派员。国际商会现下属 24 个专业委员会及工作机构。

(资料来源:国际商会(International Chamber of Commerce),网站 http://www.iccwbo.org.)

第四节 国际结算中的银行汇兑

现代国际结算业务都是通过银行媒介来完成的,银行通过国际汇兑,即跨国的两地资金划拨,结清债务债权关系。因此,银行只有在全球范围内建立起资金划拨的账户网络,才能为客户提供不同结算方式的服务。

一、银行海外机构网络的构成

银行建立海外机构网络的方法，主要是通过投资及签订代理行合作协议等方式，近年来银行间的兼并也成为银行扩大业务网点的有效方法。由此形成的银行海外网络主要包括以下成员：

（一）分行(Branch)

国外分行是总行在东道国开设的经营常规银行业务的机构。分行的资本金全由总行提供，其资产、负债、收入、支出及利润、盈亏等全部包括在其总行的有关财务报表中。分行的主要管理人员都由总行委任，其经营方针与重要业务决策都由总行制定，因而在营运上受总行控制。此外，按照国际惯例，海外分行只是总行在东道国当地的派出机构，它与总行及其他姐妹分行属于同一个法人，被视为同一家银行。因此，总行不仅承担其海外分行的盈亏风险，还承担其他的责任风险，而分行有时也不得不承担由其总行引起的风险。

（二）代理行(Correspondent Bank)

代理行是指因签订代理行协议而与国内银行互相提供代理服务的国外银行。代理服务的内容涉及结算、融资、咨询、培训等诸多方面，在代理行协议上签字的银行互相成为对方银行在本国的代理行。在协议规定的业务范围内彼此提供金融服务。海外代理行本身是一家独立的银行，在经营、资金、盈亏、风险等各方面与国内银行没有任何关系，国内银行既不需要对对方银行投资，也不能控制对方银行的经营管理。双方只是出于拓展海外业务网点，为各自客户提供全球性银行服务的共同需要，经过友好协商签订协议而形成了互相合作的代理关系。这种代理关系也可能因对方银行的倒闭、经营有问题或政府的限制而中止。在每一个国际性银行的海外机构网络中，代理行的数量都占绝对优势，成为这一网络的主要成员。

（三）子银行(Subsidiary)

子银行也称为附属银行，是国内银行在国外按东道国法律注册成立的独立银行，是一个独立的法人机构。国内银行可能是该子银行的全资、独资股东，也可能占大部分股份，其余少部分股权由当地资本或其他外国银行资本掌握，因此，国内银行对该子银行有控制权，可以通过股东大会，董事会等方式控制该子银行的经营。但是，子银行本身是具有独立法人资格的银行，其日常业务必须按东道国法律规定办理。

（四）联营银行(Affiliate Bank)

联营银行也是按东道国法律注册成立的独立银行，具有独立的法人资格。国内银行对该联营银行有部分投资，因而占有部分股权，但不能达到控股比例，无法控制该银行的业务。

（五）代表处(Representative Office)

代表处是总行在国外开设的代表该银行的办事机构，但其本身不是银行，不能经营存、贷款等常规银行业务。代表处的作用是代表总行与东道国的客户、银行及政府管理部门保持联系，为总行搜集与介绍东道国的政治、经济、法律、银行业务等方面的信息，为将来开办分行做准备。

在银行的上述五种海外机构中,最主要的是分行与代理行,其中代理行又占了绝大多数。

二、代理行关系的建立

代理行协议是确立代理行关系的基础,其主要内容通常包括下列项目:

(一) 签署机构

代理行协议一般都由两家银行的总行签署。如果协议包括双方的分支行,应在协议中注明其名称、地址。

(二) 合作范围

代理行协议规定的合作内容主要是结算业务,例如汇款的解付与偿付、托收的提示与收款、信用证的通知与保兑等等。此外,还可以涉及其他银行业务的使用,如外汇交易、资金融通、资信调查与咨询等等,具体内容由双方商定。

(三) 账户设置

大多数代理行之间并不设置账户,如果有资金往来,可以通过各自的账户行划账。因此,代理双方应在协议中注明某种货币的各自的账户行及账号。

有些代理行之间会开设账户,称为账户行。这类账户通常是活期存款账户,又称往来账户。本国银行在外国银行开立的往来账户,在本国银行看来,称为"往账"(Nestro),常用外币开立。外国银行在本国银行开立的往来账户,在本国银行看来,称为"来账"(Vostro),常用本币开立。事实上,本国银行的往账,就是外国银行的来账。

(四) 控制文件

控制文件主要包括授权签字样本、密押及费率表三种。前两种用于鉴定代理行之间往来信函、电讯的真伪性,后一种用于计收提供服务应收的手续费。

1. 授权签字样本(Specimen of Authorized Signatures)

它是列示银行各级有权代表银行或各自部门签署文件的授权人员的签字示样的文件。代理行之间往来的书面文件,如信函、凭证、票据、协议等,都需带有相关人员的签字,收件行将文件上的签字与预留的授权签字样本核对无误后方能确定来件的真实性,否则应立即向文件记载的发件行查询以判断真伪。

2. 密押(Test Key)

由于以电报、电传等方式传递的电讯文件无法用授权签字鉴定真伪,发电行会按照事先约定的编码方法编制密押,由收电行按同种方法破译,并以破译所得信息与文件字面信息相吻合来确定电讯文件的真实性。密押没有固定的编制方式,但基本原理是相同的,即将电讯文件中有关日期、金额、币种等重要信息及其他有关项目按某种方式折算成一项数字而得,除了传统的电传用密押之外,还有一种 SWIFT 密押,专门于 SWIFT 文件。按照规则,代理行之间的 SWIFT 密押每半年更换一次。

3. 费率表(Schedule of Terms and Conditions)

它是银行承办各种代理业务的收费标准。代理双方应互换费率表,以便让对方了解收费标准。

三、国际汇兑中资金偿付

国际汇兑是将资金从一家银行调拨到国外的另一家银行。汇出资金的银行,称为汇出行;接受资金的银行,称为汇入行。偿付就是委托付款银行(汇出行)向代理付款银行(汇入行)划拨资金头寸以弥补其垫款的行为。根据银行间往来账户的设置情况,国际汇兑中的资金偿付方式有以下几种类型:

(一) 账户行直接入账

如果汇出行在汇入行开立了往来账户,即汇出行在汇入行开立了往账,汇出行可向汇入行发出授权借记的偿付指示:"请将汇款金额借记我行在你行账户"(Please debit the sum to our account with you),汇入行在借记账后,应寄出借记报单(Debit Advice)通知汇出行。

如果汇入行在汇出行开立了往来账户,即汇出行有汇入行开立的来账,汇出行在委托汇入行付款时,应先贷记汇入行的来账,在偿付指示中应写明:"作为偿付,我行已将汇款金额贷记你行在我行的账户"(In cover, we have credited the sum to your account with us),汇入行在收到贷记通知后,即按委托解付汇款。

由账户行直接入账的业务流程如图1-1所示。

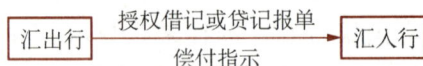

图1-1 账户行直接入账的业务流程

(二) 共同账户行转账

如果汇出行和汇入行之间并无往来账户,但它们在有关货币清算中心地的同一银行开有账户,该银行即为汇出行和汇入行的"共同账户行",则汇出行可以通过共同账户行将资金划拨汇入行,偿付指示中应写明:"作为偿付,我行已授权××银行借记我方账户并贷记你行在该行的账户"(In cover, we have authorized ×× bank to debit our account and credit your account with them),汇入行收到偿付指示并收到共同账户行发出的贷记报单后,即按照委托解付汇款。

由共同账户行转账的业务流程如图1-2所示。

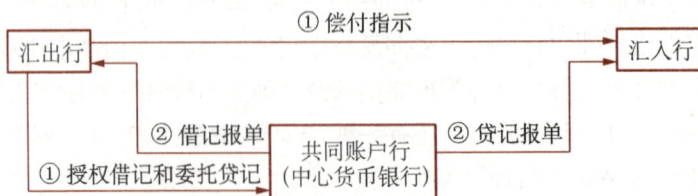

图1-2 由共同账户行转账的业务流程

（三）无共同账户行时的转账

尽管经营国际结算业务的银行，均在货币清算中心地的银行开有账户，但汇出行和汇入行所开立的账户可能在不同的银行，没有共同账户行，此时资金的划拨就会牵涉到 4 家以上的银行。由于经营国际业务的银行在货币清算中心的账户往往是在大银行，这些大银行之间，往往有账户行关系或至少也有共同账户行，此时汇出行必须掌握汇入行的账户行关系，进行查询核实，确定资金转移路线，偿付指示中应说明偿付路线，比如："作为偿付，我行已指示 A 银行将汇款金额付给你行在 B 银行的账户"（In cover, we have authorized A bank to pay the sum to your account with B bank）。典型的业务流程如图 1-3 所示。

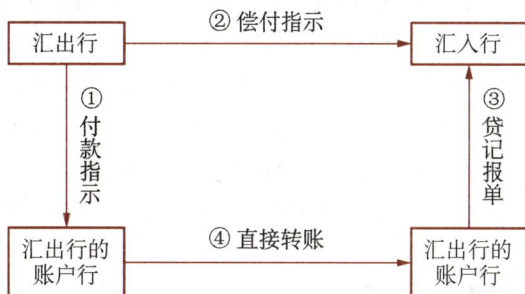

图 1-3　无共同账户行转账的业务程序

随着国际资金转移体系的不断完善，比如通过 SWIFT 汇款时，已不需要汇出行查核并确定资金转移路线，汇出行可直接委托其在货币清算中心的账户行，经过计算机网络以最合理和快捷的方式转入汇入账户行。

（四）中心汇票汇款——通过账户行入账的一种方式

如果汇票付款人是汇票所用货币清算中心地的银行，比如美元汇票的付款人为纽约的银行，英镑汇票付款人是伦敦的银行，这种汇票就叫中心汇票。中心汇票的付款银行一定是出票银行在货币清算中心地的账户行，因而，作为汇出行的出票银行无需划拨资金。该汇票相当于汇出银行给汇入行（付款后）的授权借记指示，付款行一见汇票就立即付款。而作为货币清算中心地的银行，通过票据交换机构进行清算十分方便，收款人当地的一般银行如买进中心汇票，只要直接寄往有关货币清算中心就可立即收款。对汇出行来说，在叙做票汇业务时，已收取了票款，而要等付款行付款时才从它的账上借记付出，可占用资金时间相当长，而通过中心汇票汇款则比较快捷。对汇入行来说，也省却了通知收款人的手续。因而票汇时大多采用中心汇票汇款。

中心汇票汇款流程如图 1-4 所示。

图 1-4　中心汇票汇款的流程图

本章案例 ■

国际结算方式与单据

国际贸易中,一个公司可以采用的结算方式是多样的,而且并非一成不变。以某跨国公司购买合同中的支付条款为例,可以选择以下几种结算方式:

1. THE SUPPLIER AGREES THAT THE BUYER WILL EFFECT PAYMENTS UNDER THE TERM OF T/T AGAINST RECEIPT OF B/L BY FAX.

2. HONG KONG SUPPLIERS AGREE THAT THE BUYER WILL EFFECT PAYMENTS UNDER THE TERM OF CAD(CASH AGAINST DOCUMENTS).

3. ONLY IN CASE OF NEW SUPPLIERS AND FIRST ORDER TO THEM, THE BUYER MIGHT AGREE TO EFFECT PAYMENTS UNDER L/C TERMS. THE L/C CHARGES ON THE BUYER'S SIDE WILL BE BORN BY THE BUYER AND THE L/C CHANGES ON THE SUPPLIER'S SIDE WILL BE BORN BY THE SUPPLIER. THE BILL OF LADING WILL BE MADE OUT TO ORDER AND NOTIFY THE BUYER.

4. IN CASE THAT THE SUPPLIER STILL INSIST ON L/C TERMS EVEN AFTER THE FIRST ORDER, THE SUPPLIER AGREE TO TAKE OVER ALL L/C CHARGES ON HIM AS WELL AS THE BUYER'S SIDE IN THOSE CASES WE REQUEST A BILL OF LADING...

关键词

国际结算、国际贸易结算、国际非贸易结算、SWIFT、EDI、代理行

思考题

1. 国际结算的概念、种类及基本内容是什么?
2. 国际结算的发展和演变的特征及趋势是什么样的?
3. 国际结算中主要涉及的国际惯例和法律有哪些?

第二章　票据概述

★ **学习目标**

　　掌握国际结算中票据的概念及性质,票据的作用及功能,国际上有关票据的法律体系。

★ **本章概要**

　　本章主要介绍国际结算中所使用的票据的性质及其功能,以及各国票据法的相关体系。通过本章的学习,可以为下面进一步了解和学习汇票、本票、支票等知识做准备。

第一节 票据的概念与性质

一、票据的概念

票据就是用以结清国际间债权债务的信用工具,它有广义和狭义之分。广义的票据泛指一切使用于商业交易中的物权证书(Document of Title),它代表对于商品的所有权或对资金的请求权,因此,提单、仓单、汇票、本票等都属于广义的票据;狭义的票据仅指代表资金请求权的物权证书,因此,只包括汇票、本票与支票三种。

作为一种物权证书,票据的转让可以带来物权的转让,但是不同的转让方式在转让手续与权利让渡的完整性方面是不同的。票据的转让有三种不同的方式。

第一种是过户转让,简称过户(Assignment)。过户在手续方面的要求是必须由票据转让人以书面形式告知票据债务人,使其了解票据转让事实,不因债权人更替而解除对票据受让人的债务。在权利让渡的完整性方面,按照财产转让的一个普遍原则,受让人权利不得优于转让人权利,因此,如果转让人权利有缺陷,受让人将受这种缺陷的影响而不获得票据的完整权利。通常采用过户方式转让的票据主要有股票、人寿保险单等。

第二种方式是交付转让,简称交付(Delivery)。交付与过户的区别在于转让票据时不需要对原债务人另作通知,只需要将票据交与受让人,或者在票据背面签字后交与受让人就可以完成转让,债务人对新的票据持有人仍有清偿的义务。但就权利让渡的完整性而言,交付与过户相同,即交付受让人的权利不优于其转让人。采用交付方式转让的票据有提单、仓单等。

第三种方式是流通转让,简称流通(Negotiation),又称议付、议让等。在转让手续方面,流通与交付一样,无需通知原债务人,仅凭交付或背书后交付即可。但在权利让渡方面,流通与过户及交付有实质性区别,即只要受让人善意地支付了对价,就可以获得充分完整的票据权利,即使转让人权利有缺陷,受让人亦不受其影响,因而,流通转让的受让人的权利可能优于转让人。在这里,善意与支付对价是两个重要的先决条件。所谓善意(Good Faith),是指诚实的行为,其判定要依具体情况而定,但一般而言,系指获得票据时没有偷盗、欺诈、胁迫等恶意行为,也没有有意或无意地忽视那些明显的应予以注意或应引起怀疑的情况等重大过失。所谓对价(Value),是指足以支持一份简单合约的价值,它可以是货物、劳务、资金,也可以是未清偿的债务。要求受让人支付对价,意味着无偿受让(如馈赠、继承等)的行为不构成流通。所以,只有受让人善意地支付了对价,就可以获得可能优于转让人的、充分完整的票据权利。

将票据概念与其流通性结合起来,可知流通票据是指以支付金钱为目的,可以流通转让的证券,由出票人签名于票据上,确定由本人或指定他人于一定的时间,无条件地向持票人支付一定金额。若约定由出票人本人付款,则是本票;若由他人付款则是汇票或支票。本章研究的票据是狭义的票据,即汇票、本票和支票。

二、票据的性质

票据是非现金结算工具,作为一种特殊证券,与其他类型的有价证券如股票、国库券、公司债券等不同,有其特有的性质,表现如下:

(一) 流通性(Negotiability)

正如前文所述,票据的流通性有两方面的特点:其一,票据凭交付或经背书后交付给受让人,即可合法地完成转让手续,而无需通知票据上的债务人。这与一般的债权转让不同。按民法原则,一般的债权转让必须通知债务人才能生效,否则,债务人在不知情的情况下,并不对受让人承担履行债务的责任。其二,票据流通中强调保护善意并支付了对价而获得票据的持票人,即受让人不受其前手权利缺陷的影响。这也不同于一般的权利转让。按民法原则,让与人只能把自己合法拥有的权利转让给他人。如果让与人所转让的权利不是他合法拥有的,或者其权利是有缺陷的,则受让人的权利同样是不合法的或者是有缺陷的,受让人的权利不能优于让与人。然而,在票据流通转让中,受让人的权利有可能优于让与人(受让人的前手),即倘若让与人的权利是有缺陷的,受让人出于善意并支付了对价,那么他将得到票据文义规定的全部权利。

(二) 无因性(Non-causative Nature)

票据是一种不要过问原因的证券,这里所说的原因是指产生票据上的权利义务关系的原因。票据的原因是票据的基本关系,它包括两个方面的内容:一是指出票人与付款人之间的资金关系;另一是指出票人与收款人,以及票据的背书人与被背书人之间的对价关系。从事实上看,任何票据关系的产生总是有一定的原因,例如 A 为出票人发出以 B 为付款人的票据,B 决不会无缘无故地成为付款人并同意付款义务,其中必有原因,其原因可能是 A 在 B 处有存款,或者 B 同意给 A 信贷等,这种关系就是所谓的资金关系。又如当 A 开出以 B 为收款人的票据,而 B 又以背书方式把该票据转让给 C 时,其中也必有原因,其原因可能是因为 A 购买了 B 的货物,需要开立以 B 为收款人的票据来支付货款,而 B 之所以要把该票据转让给 C。可能是因为他欠了 C 的债,这种关系就是所谓的对价关系。票据当事人的权利义务就是以这些基本关系为原因,这种关系称为票据原因。但是,票据是否成立,不受票据原因的影响。票据当事人的权利与义务,也不受票据原因的影响。对于票据受让人来说,他无需调查这些原因,只要票据记载合格,他就取得票据文义载明的权利,票据的这种特性就称为无因性,这种无因性使票据得以流通。

(三) 要式性(Requisite in Form)

票据的形成,从形式上看记载必要项目必须齐全,各个必要项目又必须符合规定,方可使票据产生效力。各国的票据法对这些必要项目都已作了详细规定,使票据文义简单明了,根据文义来解释票据,明确当事人的责权。

票据的要式性,有时也可说成票据是书面形式要件,即指票据从书面形式上包含的必要条件,符合票据法规定,它就是有效的票据。它的权利义务,全凭票据上的文义来确定,不需要过问票据基本关系的原因,这才有利于票据的转让流通,所以我们常说票据是要式不要因。

(四) 提示性(Presentment)

票据上的债权人(持票人)请求债务人(付款人)履行票据义务时,必须向付款人提示票据,才能请求付给票款。如果持票人不提示票据,付款人就没有履行付款的义务,因此,票据法需要规定票据的提示期限,超过期限,付款人的责任即被解除。所以票据付款,不同于信汇方式。采用信汇委托书付款,该委托书由汇出行寄给解付行,委托它解付汇款给收款人,解付行须通知收款人前来领取汇款。

(五) 返还性(Returnability)

票据的持票人领到支付的票款时,应将签收的票据交还付款人,该票据经正当付款即被解除责任而归还至付款人的档案,由于票据的返还性,所以,它不能无限期地流通,而是在到期日被付款后结束其流通。这也说明票据虽然可以模仿货币的功能,仍有它自身的局限性,一经付款,票据就不能流通了。

第二节　票据的作用

票据是信用经济发展的产物。作为一种信用工具,票据所特有的替代现金支付和流通、提供信用保障,以及融资和结算的功能,使得票据在国际结算和贸易融资业务中得到普遍应用。票据的作用主要体现在流通手段、支付手段和信用手段三方面。由于前文已对票据的流通性作了详细阐述,下面重点讨论票据的支付作用和信用作用。

一、支付手段

用票据代替现金支付,有着明显的省时、省力和安全的作用,持票人提示票据要求付款,受票人见票即付,或见票承兑,到期日付款。因此,票据是支付手段。

从单边的角度来看,使用票据可以避免携带、运送和清点现金的麻烦。从多边支付的角度来看,用票据可以抵销交叉的债务债权关系。比如,中国上海的 A 公司需向美国纽约的 B 公司支付 1000 美元,而 B 公司需向上海的 C 公司支付 1000 美元,则此时 B 公司可开出 1 张以 A 公司为付款人而以 C 公司为收款人的汇票,寄交 C 公司,由 C 公司凭汇票要求 A 付款。依此类推,国际间大量的债务债权关系,通过票据清算中心,互相抵销,从而得以迅捷、安全地完成多边支付即多边结算的业务。此外,票据作为支付工具,在一定程度上可以像现金一样流通,即只要债权人愿意接受,债务人可以将其所持有的票据转让给债权人以清偿其债务。

二、信用手段

票据的信用手段,是其最本质的作用,是其他各种手段的基础。

在国际贸易中,买卖双方同时一手交钱一手交货的情形很少发生,可能是一方先交货,也可能是一方先付款。这种权利和义务不能同时实现的交易是国际贸易,也是其他国际经济交易的主要特征。首先,履行义务的一方是债权人,而另一方则成为债务人,这种债权债务关系,在未发生之前,通过双方签订合同来加以规定和保障;一旦发生,则可以通过票据予以体现。我们把这种关系称为授受信用的关系。债权人提供了信用,而债务人则可以通过票据向债权人作担保,由于票据的无因性和流通性,票据上所体现的债权债务关系稳定而且单纯,因而它就成为一种相当好的信用保障凭证。比如,合同规定,买方在卖方发货2个月后付款,则卖方可出具1张远期汇票,在买方承兑后向其交货,买方在承兑后,即成为汇票的债务人,承担到期向汇票持票人付款的责任;卖方作为汇票的持票人,享有法律保障的债权,而且票据法对债务人的抗辩有所限制,如果卖方在汇票到期前已将汇票背书转让,则买方将无法以合同纠纷为理由对抗受让汇票的善意持票人。

持票人如果需要资金,还可以把所持有的未到期的票据以背书转让的方式换取现金,称之为贴现。贴现中持票人利用了承兑人和出票人的信用保证,再加上自己的信用,得到了资金融通。

第三节 票据法法系

票据的内容、票据行为,以及当事人的权利和义务,都由票据法加以规定。票据法具有强制性,票据的形式内容和票据行为都必须严格遵守票据法的规定,当事人不能另行约定。为了保障票据正常使用和流通,保护票据当事人的合法权益,各国纷纷制定票据法,重点是将票据流通规则制定为法律。

一、英国《1882年票据法》

英国于1882年颁布施行的《票据法》(Bills of Exchange Act)是起草人查尔姆(Chalmers)总结历来的习惯法、特别法,以及许多判例而编成的。该法共计97条,1—72条订立汇票全面法规,73—82条订立支票法规,83—89条订立本票法规。1957年另订立支票法8条,对于以前的支票法规作了修正和补充。

英国票据法的适用性较强,它的主要特点是:首先,从法律上保护票据的流通,它制订了一套完整的流通票据制度,使票据能够充分发挥流通工具的重要作用。其次,从法律上保护和发挥票据的信用工具和支付工具作用。再次,在银行处理大量的票据业务中,适当地保护银行权益,提高银行效率。故本书有关票据实务方面,较多地引用英国票据法的规定。

二、美国《统一流通票据法》

美国于1986年制订《统一流通票据法》(Uniform Negotiable Instruments Law)。它是起草人Crawford在习惯法和判例的基础上编写成的。1952年制订、1962年修订的《统一商法典》(Uniform Commercial Code)的第三章商业票据(Commercial Paper)中,对汇票、本票、支票和存单(Certificate of Deposit)作了详细的规定。美国的票据法是在英国票据法的基础上加以发展而成的。英国、美国及一些英联邦成员如加拿大、澳大利亚、印度、巴基斯坦的票据法均属英美法系。

三、《日内瓦统一票据法》

1930 年法国、德国、瑞士、意大利、日本以及一些拉美国家在日内瓦召开国际票据法统一会议,签订了《日内瓦统一汇票本票法公约》(Uniform Law for Bills of Exchange and Promissory Notes,1930),次年又签订了《日内瓦统一支票法公约》(Uniform Law for Cheques,1931)。这两项法律(一般合并称为《日内瓦统一票据法》)是比较完善的票据立法,由于英美未派代表参加签字,所以参加签字并遵守统一法的成员国家形成了大陆法系。

四、《国际汇票和国际本票公约》、《国际支票公约》

以《英国票据法》为代表的英美法系和以《日内瓦统一票据法》为代表的欧洲大陆法系之间在汇票必要项目的各方面大体相同,但也有些差异。

联合国国际贸易法委员会(United Nations Commission on International Trade Law)为了要消除两个法系的差异,于 1971 年成立国际流通票据工作组(Working Group on International Negotiable Instruments),并于 1973 年拟订了《国际汇票与国际本票公约草案》(Draft Convention on International Bills of Exchange and International Promissory Notes)和《国际支票公约草案》(Draft Convention on International Cheques)。经过十余年的讨论修订,于 1986 年 6 月 16 日至 7 月 11 日交联合国国际贸易法系委员会第 19 届会议审议,至 1987 年 8 月经上述委员会第 20 届会议正式通过,定名为《国际汇票和国际本票公约》、《国际支票公约》,并于 1990 年 6 月 30 日前开放签字,该汇票、本票公约共 9 章 90 条。

五、《中华人民共和国票据法》

我国的票据法虽然起步很早,但发展缓慢。早在 1928 年中华民国政府就颁布了《票据法草案》并于 1929 年实施。新中国成立后,1988 年实行了《银行结算法》这是第一个涉及票据的法律。但完整意义上的票据法是 1995 年 5 月 10 日正式公布,1996 年 1 月 1 日起生效《中华人民共和国票据法》。该法律在票据必须记载内容的规定上和《日内瓦统一法》相一致;有关票据权利的取得,则采纳了英美法系的立场,规定了应支付对价;并规定背书转让必须使用记名方式,提示期限大大缩短;不规定作成拒绝证书的时限,只允许银行出具本票等。

知识扩展

两大票据法法系的比较

英国于 1882 年颁布施行《英国票据法》,此后美国及大部分英联邦成员国,如加拿大、印度等都以此为参照制定本国的票据法,由此形成了英美法系的票据法。1930 年,以法国、德国等为代表的以欧洲大陆为主的20多个国家在日内瓦召开了国际票据法统一会议,并签订了《日内瓦统一汇票、本票法公约》。1931年,这些国家又签订了《日内瓦统一支票法公约》。两个公约合称为《日内瓦统一法》。此后,另有一些非大陆法系国家的票据法也参照《日内瓦统一法》制定本国的票据法(如我国的票据法)。由此形成了与英美法系不同的大陆法系的票据。

1982年,联合国国际贸易法律委员会公布了《国际汇票和国际本票公约(草案)》,设想将两大票据法体系统一在一个"公约"范围内,但因为签字国过少而未能推行。因此,在当今世界上,仍然是两大票据法体系并存的格局。两大法系国家的票据法各以这两个票据法为基础,并各自基本趋于统一。

1. 两大法系国家的票据法在立法体例上,表现为英美法系国家采用票据包括主义,大陆法系国家采用票据分离主义。如"英国法"在体例上采取三票合一的形式,并将本票、支票作为汇票的特殊形式加以处理(我国票据法类同于"英国法")。而日内瓦票据法则将三者区别开来,分别进行解释。

2. 在规定票据定义时,两大法系票据法有不同。"日内瓦法"中没有像"英国法"那样有严谨的文句对票据下定义,它只是规定票据的必要项目给票据下定义。

3. 票据是一种要式证券,"日内瓦法"尤为强调票据的要式性。所谓票据的要式性是指票据的格式和记载事项只有符合法律规定,才能产生票据效力,不依法定方式做成的票据不能产生法律效力,导致票据无效(我国的票据法也强调票据的要式性)。

在票据的必要项目方面:

(1)"日内瓦法"强调票据上要有票据名称的字样,即标明是汇票或本票或支票(我国票据法也有此规定)。"英国法"无此要求。

(2)在票据金额方面,两法都规定如大小写不一致,以大写金额为准(我国票据法规定,此种票据无效)。"日内瓦法"还规定,如果有两个大写不一致,以数额小的大写为准。

(3)关于票据的收款人抬头,"英国法"规定三种票据均可作记名抬头和来人抬头(我国票据法规定均不可作来人抬头)。

(4)关于出票日期,"日内瓦法"将此作为必要项目(我国票据法有相同规定)。"英国法"认为无出票日期,票据仍然成立。

在其他记载方面,两法也有一些不同规定。如"英国法"认为,出票人和背书人可用"免于追索"的文句来免除在票据被拒绝付款时受追索的责任。而"日内瓦法"认为出票人只能免除担保承兑的责任,而不能免除担保付款的责任(我国票据法认为此种责任不可免除)。

4. 票据的要式性除票据的格式、内容要符合要式,票据行为也是要式的。票据法对各种票据行为都有详细严格的规定。这样可以使票据纠纷减少到最低限度,从而保证票据的顺利流通。

(1)"英国法"规定,限制背书的被背书人无权转让票据权利。"日内瓦法"认为不得转让背书的票据仍可由被背书人转让,转让人只对直接后手负责,对其他后手概无责任(我国票据法同英国票据法)。

（2）票据权利的善意取得，应该包括取得票据时无恶意或重大过失。"英国法"对是否知道前手权利缺陷是以"实际知悉"为原则的。"英国法"认为，只有出于善意并付对价的正当持票人不受对抗。"日内瓦法"不强调是否付过对价（我国票据法同英国票据法）。

（3）票据应在时效内提示。"日内瓦法"规定，即期票据必须从出票日起1年内作付款提示；见票后定期汇票必须在出票日起1年内作承兑提示；远期票据必须在到期日及以后的两个营业日中作付款提示。"英国法"规定，即期汇票必须在合理时间内作付款提示；见票后定期汇票必须在合理时间内作承兑提示。远期汇票必须在到期日当天作付款提示（我国票据法规定，即期汇票自出票日起1个月内作付款提示，远期汇票自到期日起10日内作付款提示）。如果持票人未在规定时效内提示票据，那么他就丧失对前手的追索权。然而承兑人对持票人仍有付款责任。其责任时效"日内瓦法"规定为到期日起3年，"英国法"规定为承兑日起6年（我国票据法规定为到期日起2年）。

（4）作成承兑的时效，"英国法"规定付款人须在习惯时间内（24小时）作成承兑。"日内瓦法"规定2天内作成承兑（我国票据法3日内作成承兑）。

（5）"日内瓦法"规定付款人付款时不需要认定背书真伪。"英国法"规定付款必须认定背书真伪（我国票据法同英国票据法）。

（6）持票人遭到拒付时，根据"英国法"，只有国际汇票才必须由公证人作成拒绝证书。"日内瓦法"允许在汇票人或付款人破产时，以法院判决代替拒绝证书（我国票据法有相似规定）。

（7）"英国法"没有"保证"规定，"日内瓦法"允许"保证"票据（我国票据法同"日内瓦统一法"）。

本章案例 ■

平行贸易中票据的作用

假定美国的A公司向法国的B公司采购一批商品，价值为10 000美元，约定30天付款。同时，一家法国公司C公司向美国的D公司采购一批商品，价值也为10 000美元，约定30天付款。B公司与C公司之间存在业务关系，比如C公司向B公司出售商品或服务，或者C公司向B公司提供贷款。这是一个典型的平等贸易的例子。

票据产生之前，国际贸易采用的都是现金结算。在上述平行贸易的情况下，就会产生两个平行的现金流：一批现金从美国流向法国，另一批现金从法国流向美国。同时在B公司与C公司之间也会有大量的现金流入与流出。现金循环时间长，手续相对麻烦。在采用票据结算的情况下，则要简单快捷得多。

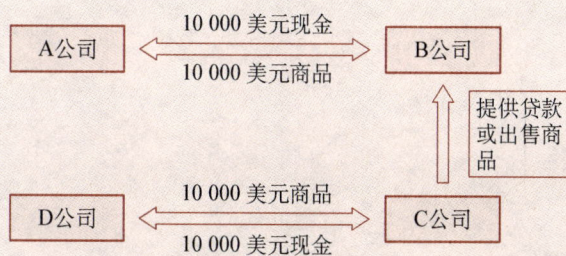

关键词

票据、过户转让、交付转让、流通转让、流通性、无因性、要式性、提示性、返还性

思考题

1. 什么是票据,它有哪些种类?
2. 票据的性质是什么?
3. 在国际结算中票据有哪些功能和作用?
4. 国际上关于票据的法律有哪些,它们有什么区别?

第三章　汇　票

★ 学习目标

　　掌握国际汇票的概念、内容及要项、汇票的当事人及其责任、汇票行为及其具体表示，汇票使用中的风险，以及汇票的融资功能。

★ 本章概要

　　汇票是国际结算中最重要的一种金融票据。汇票是出票人命令他人无条件付款的票据，其基本当事人有三人：出票人、收款人和付款人。汇票的记载内容包括必要记载项目和非必要记载项目。票据行为包括出票、背书、承兑、参加承兑、提示、付款等。汇票是一种支付工具，但也是一种融资工具。

第一节　汇票的定义与内容

一、汇票的定义

《英国票据法》关于汇票的定义是：A bill of exchange is an unconditional order in writing, addressed by one person to another, signed by the person giving it , reguiring the person on whom it is addressed to pay on demand or at a fixed or determinable future time a sum certain in money to or to the order of a specified person or to bearer. 中文意思是："汇票是一人向另一人签发的，要求即期、定期或在可以确定的将来时间向特定的人或其指定的人或来人，无条件地支付一定金额的命令。"

《日内瓦统一票据法》对汇票未下定义：只规定了汇票应记载下列事项：(1)"汇票"字样，所用文字应与该票据所用文字一致；(2)无条件支付一定金额的委托；(3)付款人名称；(4)付款时间；(5)付款地点；(6)收款人名称；(7)出票日期及地点；(8)出票人签名。

我国《票据法》对汇票的定义是："汇票是出票人签发的，委托付款人在见票时或者在指定日期无条件支付确定金额给收款人或持票人的票据。"

尽管各国票据法限定汇票的角度不同，但总的来看，对汇票概念的基本内容的规定是一致的，只是在一些具体项目的规定上略有差别。

二、汇票的当事人

(一) 基本当事人

汇票的基本当事人是指在汇票签发时即于票面载明的当事人，主要包括出票人、付款人及收款人。

1. 出票人(Drawer)

出票人是写成并交付汇票的人。出票人第一个在汇票上签名，是汇票的债务人，他以签发票据的形式创设了一种债权并将其赋予持票人，出票人本身也相应地承担起了债务。

2. 付款人(Drawee/Payer)

付款人是指由出票人在汇票中记名指定的、接受票据提示以进行支付的当事人。但是，出票人单方面的指定并不构成对付款人的约束，因为不能排除出票人对没有资金关系的当事人滥发票据的可能性。因此，为保护付款人正当权益，他完全可以自行决定付款与否，从这个意义上讲，"付款人"一词并不准确，严格地说，他只是接受票据提示的"受票人(Addressee)"。当然在正常情况下，付款人都会同意支付，要么立即付款，要么签字承诺在约定到期日支付，在这种情况下，付款人以签字形式承诺了出票人指定的支付义务，从而成为票据债务人。

3. 收款人(Payee)

收款人是第一个从出票人手中获得票据的当事人，也是基本当事人中唯一的债权人，其权利通常包括收款、转让，以及在付款人拒绝支付时向出票人追索。收款人通常是记名的特定当事人或其指定人,也可以是无记名的,在这种情况下任何持有该票据的人都可以是收款人。

(二) 其他当事人

其他当事人是指在除出票外的其他票据行为中产生的当事人。这些行为可能也同时涉及了基本当事人,但此时他们的身份已有所不同。

1. 承兑人(Acceptor)

承兑人就是在远期汇票上签字承诺付款的付款人。对于即期付款的汇票,不存在承兑的行为。若汇票不需承兑或尚未获得承兑时,出票人是第一债务人,也是主债务人。一旦出现承兑,则承兑人成为主债务人,而且该项主债务在票据失效之前不能撤销。

2. 背书人(Endorser/Indorser)

背书人就是指在票据背面签字并交付给他人的当事人。背书的目的是为了转让票据的一切权利,背书人是一个转让人。为了让受让人接受票据而不是直接要求现款支付,背书人必须让受让人相信付款人一定会同意支付。为此,背书人要以自身资信作保证,一旦出现付款人拒绝付款或拒绝承兑,背书人将同出票人一起接受受让人的追索要求。此外,背书人还须向受让人保证票据的有效性,以及他本人对票据拥有权利。因此,可以合法、有效地将票据权利转让给受让人。

3. 被背书人(Endorsee/Indorsee)

从背书人手里接受票据的当事人,可以被明确记名,也可以不记名。被背书人的权利与收款人相似,包括收款、转让、追索三方面。

4. 持票人(Holder)

持票人是指占有票据的当事人,可以是收款人、被背书人或执票来人。

《日内瓦统一法》没有对持票人作出分类,也没有提到关于对价的要求。我国《票据法》规定,除了税收、继承、赠予等情况外,票据的接受必须支付对价。英美票据法依据对价的支付情况,将持票人区分为一般持票人、对价持票人与正当持票人三种。

一般持票人的条件要求最松,可以不付对价,但其权利受限制程度也最大,尤其是可能因未付对价而被票据债务人否定其追索权。

对价持票人(Holder for Value)包括三种情况:(1)持票人本人支付了对价,如商品、劳务、货币资金。(2)持票人根据合约或法律对票据有留置权,那么在留置权金额内被视为对价持票人。例如,A将一张以其为收款人、面额为1000元的汇票抵押给银行,借得600元贷款,则银行对该汇票有600元留置权,对票据上的当事人而言,该银行是汇票600元部分的对价持票人。(3)持票人未付对价,但对价在先前任何时候已被付过,那么对承兑人和付过对价以前已成为票据当事人的各人而言,该持票人也视为对价持票人。例如,A签发一张汇票给收款人C,由B承兑后,C将其流通转让给D并收取对价,D随后作背书将汇票赠送给E。那么,对D而言,E不是对价持票人,但对A、B和C而言,E是对价持票人,因为他们都先于支付对价的D成为票据责任当事人。对价持票人的权利比一般持票人更大些。不存在未付对价因素的干扰,但是其权利仍有一定限制,尤其是要受到前手权利缺陷的影响。

正当持票人(Holder in Due Course),也称为善意持票人(Bona Fide Holder),是一种特殊的对价持票人,其构成条件有两个:(1)在票据形式方面,应该完整、合格,没有过期,也没有曾被退票(即拒绝付款或拒绝承兑)的记录。(2)在票据转让程序方面,持票人应善意地支付对价,并不曾知悉出让者对票据的权利有任何缺陷。按照英国立法的观点,正当持票人必须在流通转让中产生,由于收款人是由出票行为所确定,因而不能成为正当持票人;但美国的《票据法》则允许收款人成为正当持票人。

5. 保证人(Guarantor)

保证人是指对已经存在的票据债务进行担保的当事人。根据《日内瓦统一法》的规定,保证人既可以是非票据债务人,也可以是票据债务人。我国的《票据法》则规定保证人必须由非票据债务人充当。英美票据法对此没有明确规定,英国《票据法》中甚至连保证这一行为都没有提及。

保证人必须指明被保证人,可以是出票人、承兑人、或任一背书人。若未注明被保证人名称,则要视票据种类而定。如果是支票或本票,则以出(签)票人为被保证人。如果是已获承兑的汇票,则以承兑人为被保证人;若汇票未获承兑,仍以出票人为被保证人。

保证人的责任与被保证人责任完全相同。被保证人的票据债务在形式上有效时,不管其实质上是否有效,保证人责任都有效;若票据债务形式上无效时,保证人责任亦告解除。此外,持票人可以在被保证人未能清偿票据债务时向保证人请求清偿,也可以先于被保证人向保证人请求清偿,保证人都不能予以拒绝。一旦清偿了票据债务,保证人就可以向被保证人及其前手行使持票人应有的追索权。正当持票人的票据权利最为充分完整,可以不受前手权利缺陷的影响。

三、汇票的必要项目

汇票是一种要式证券,法律对汇票所记载的必要项目作了明确的规定。必要项目包括两种记载:一是必须记载事项,该类事项必须按法律规定在汇票上明确记载。另一种是相对应记载事项,该类事项如果记载在汇票上,就必须按法律规定记载;如果未记载在汇票上,则可以按法律规定来确定该事项的意义。

汇票的必要项目包括:(1)写明其为"汇票"的字样。(2)无条件的支付命令。(3)出票地点和日期。(4)付款时间。(5)一定金额货币。(6)付款人名称和付款地点。(7)收款人名称。(8)出票人名称和签字。

现将上述项目标明在附式 3-1 的汇票式样中。

附式 3-1

	Due 11th July, 20 _____
	(1)　　　(5)　　　(3)
ACCEPTED	Exchange for GBP 5000.00 Beijing, 5th April, 20 _____
12th April,20 _____	(4)　　　(2)　　　(7)
Payable Bank Ltd.	At 90 days after sight pay to C Co. or Order
London	(5)
For Bank of Europe,	The sum of five thousand pounds
London	(6)
signed	To Bank of Europe,　　　　　　　　(8)
	London.　　　For A Company
	Beijing
	(8)
	signature

现就必要项目分别说明如下：

(一) 写明"汇票"字样

汇票上注明"汇票"字样的目的在于与其他票据如本票、支票加以区别，以免混淆。如：Exchange for GBP4500.00 或 Draft for USD57 690.00。我国《票据法》和《日内瓦统一票据法》均规定为必须记载事项，《英国票据法》认为可以不写票据名称。从实际业务上看，写出票据名称可给有关当事人不少方便。

(二) 无条件的支付命令(Unconditional Order to Pay)

这一项目是汇票的基本性质，也是区别汇票与本票的首要标准。在没有标明"汇票"名称的情况下，就是根据这一项目来确认汇票。具体而言，包括三层含义：

1. 书面形式

汇票及其他票据都必须是书面形式，否则无法签字和流通转让。实务中使用的汇票通常都是在预先印刷好固定格式的空白汇票上经手写或打字填写的。

2. 支付命令

汇票所代表的是一种付款命令，因而必须用英语的祈使句，以动词开头，作为命令式语句。

> **范例**
>
> "Pay to A Co. or order the sum of one thousand US dollars. "
>
> "支付给 A 公司或其指定人金额为 1000 美元。"

3. 无条件性

这一必要项目并不要求在汇票上明示"无条件"字样，而是不允许在汇票上记载付款条件，因为汇票的付款必须是无条件的，不能以收款人履行某项义务或某种行为作为付款人付款的前提条件。比如，在汇票上表明："须待交付合格货物后才予以付款"或"从某批货物销售后所得款中支付"，这就是有条件的付款命令，这样的支付委托就不是汇票，将被视作无效汇票。

但是，在国际贸易中，往往在汇票中加注出票条款(Drawn Clause)，表明汇票的起源，这是允许的。

> **范例**
>
> "Pay to A Bank or order the sum of ten thousand US dollars. Drawn under L/C No. 12345 issued by X Bank, New York dated on 15th August, 20 _____ ."
>
> "支付给 A 银行或其指定人金额为 1000 美元。按照纽约 X 银行于某年 8 月 15 日开立信用证第 12345 号开立这张汇票。"

(三) 出票地点和日期(Place and Date of Issue)

出票地点应该与出票人的地址相同，《英国票据法》认为汇票未注明出票地点也可成立,此时就以出票人的地址作为出票地点,或者汇票交付给收款人由收款人加列出票地点。国际汇票注明出票地点,就应按照出票地点的国家法律来确定必要项目是否齐全,汇票是否成立和有效。各国采用行为地法律原则,即出票行为在某地发生,就以该地国家的法律为依据。

列明"出票日期"可起三个作用:

(1) 决定汇票提示期限是否已超过《日内瓦统一票据法》第二十三条、第三十四条分别规定的见票后固定时期的付款汇票,或见票即期付款汇票必须在出票以后一年内提示要求承兑或提示要求付款。

(2) 决定到期日。付款时间是出票日以后若干天(月)付款的汇票,就从出票日起算,决定其付款到期日。

(3) 决定出票人的行为能力。若出票时法人已宣告破产或清理,丧失行为能力,则汇票不能成立。

《英国票据法》认为,汇票未注明出票日期仍然有效,当它交付后,收款人应补加出票日期。

(四) 付款期限(Tenor)

汇票的付款期限有四种类型:

1. 即期付款汇票(Bills Payable at Sight/on Demand /on Presentation)

又称即期汇票(Sight/Demand Bill),是指持票人提示汇票的当天即为到期日,即期汇票无须承兑。若汇票没有明确表示付款期限者,即为见票即付的汇票。

2. 远期付款汇票(Time/Usance/Term Bill)

要求远期付款的汇票就是远期汇票。远期汇票的关键之处在于付款到期日的确定。常见的到期日确定方法有:

(1) 出票后定期(at a Fixed Period after Date)。如"30 days after date"(出票日后 30 天),或者"Two months after the date herin"(出票日后两个月)等等。这种汇票的出票日应记载明确,否则无法推算到期日。若出票日欠缺,按大陆法系与我国《票据法》规定,该汇票无效,但按英美票据实践,可由持票人补填,并按补填之日推算到期日。在国际贸易结算中,出口商通常开立以进口商为付款人的远期汇票来给后者提供短期商业信用,使用这种出票后定期支付的汇票可以帮助出口商控制赊销信用的期限,避免货款被长期占用。

(2) 见票后定期(at a Fixed Period after Sight)。如"At 90 days sight"(见票后 90 天),或者"Three months after sight"(见票后 3 个月)等等。要确定到期日,首先,要知道见票日,因此这种汇票需要作两次提示,第一次提示确定见票日;然后,根据此见票日确定的到期日作第二次提示以求支付。在第一次提示以确定见票日时,付款人可能会承兑,也有可能会拒绝承兑。若付款人承兑该汇票,就应注明承兑日期,并以此作为见票日。若承兑人未写明承兑日期,按英美票据法的规定,持票人可以补齐,即使补齐有误,只要不与出票日矛盾,就以补齐之日作为见票日。按照《日内瓦统一票据法》的规定,持票人应在适当时间内作出拒绝证书,以证明承兑日期未记。按照我国《票据法》规定,付款人应当在收到提示承兑汇票的 3 日之内承兑或拒绝承兑。因此,若付款人承兑但未记日期时,以这三天期限的最后一天为承兑日期即见票日;若付款人拒绝承兑,为确定到期日,持票人应请求公证机关作拒绝证书,并以拒绝证书出立日为见票日。

上述两种远期汇票,在确定到期日时,需要注意以下事项:

(1) 算尾不算头。凡规定出票日、见票日或特定事件发生日后一定时期付款的汇票,付款日的确定不包括开始之日而包括付款期间的最后一日。例如,见票后 30 天付款的汇票于 8 月 31 日获得承兑,则起算日应为 9 月 1 日,到期日为 9 月 30 日。同理,出票日或特定事件的发生日也不应计作起算日。

(2) "月"指日历月份。不考虑每月的具体天数,一律以相应月份的同一天为到期日,若当月无对应日期,则以该月最后一天代替。例如,出票后 1 个月付款的汇票注明出票日为 1 月 31 日,则到期日应为 2 月 28 日(若闰年则为 2 月 29 日)。

(3) 先算整月,后算半月,半月以 15 天计。如出票后 3 个半月到期的汇票以 7 月 25 日为出票日,则出票后 3 个月应为 10 月 25 日,再加半月(15)则到期日为 11 月 9 日。

(4) 凡汇票上仅记载月初、月中、月末者,分别指当月一日、十五日、最末一日。

(5) 若到期日恰逢周末或节假日等非营业日,则顺延到其后的第一个营业日。

范例

"见票后 90 天"(At 90 days after sight),见票日即是承兑日,如为 4 月 15 日的开头一天不算,即所述日不作起算日。

4 月 16~30 日	15 天	所述日之次日作为起算日
5 月 1~31 日	31 天	
6 月 1~30 日	30 天	
7 月 1~14 日	14 天	7 月 14 日末尾一天计算到期日是 90 天的最后一天,即第 90 天
	90 天	

此汇票到期日是 7 月 14 日,若 7 月 14 日恰逢假日,则到期日顺延至 7 月 15 日。

3. 定日付款汇票(at a Fixed Date)

指汇票正文中已经载明了付款到期日,无需再推算。此类汇票也称为板期付款汇票。

范例

"固定在 6 月 30 日付款"(On 30th June fixed pay to)。

---

4. 延期付款汇票(Deferred Payment Bill)

一般是指装运日/交单日/其他特定日以后若干天付款的汇票。

> **范例**
>
> "在出票日之后××天"/"在提交单据后的××天"或"其他指定日之后的××天"(At xx days after the date of (shipment)/(presentation of documents or other specified date)。

《英国票据法》没有订出"延期付款"期限,在实际业务上常见这种汇票,为了从票面就能算出到期日,出票人有时在汇票上加注提单/交单的具体日期,把它转变成说明日期以后若干天付款,还可以按照提单/交单的具体日期,填写为出票日期,把汇票变成出票日后若干天付款的汇票。

除以上四种期限外,凡是注明"在一个不确定日期付款"或是"在一个或有事件发生时付款"者,都不是汇票。

(五) 确定的金额(Certain in Money)

汇票票面所记载的金额必须确定,所谓"确定"是指任何人都可以计算出的金额,如有利息条款,则必须规定利率。《英国票据法》规定:有利息条款而未规定利率的汇票无效。《日内瓦统一法》规定:见票即付和见票后定期付款的汇票,出票人可规定利息条款并应载明利率,若未载明利率者,该利息条款无效,汇票本身有效。

1. 关于金额中的利息条款

计算利息,除了利率之外,还需知道计息天数,汇票上可以规定计息的起止日期,若票据上未说明计算天数的起止日期,按商业惯例,自出票日开始计算,直至付款日。

> **范例**
>
> 情况1:"支付给A公司的指定人金额为1000美元加上利息。"
>
> "Pay to the order of A Co. the sum of one thousand US dollars plus interest."
>
> 说明:由于没有注明利率,算不出"加上利息"是多少金额,按照《英国票据法》第九条规定,这张汇票不能成立。按照《日内瓦统一票据法》第五条规定"加上利息"视为无记载,汇票本身是有效的。
>
> 情况2:"支付给A公司的指定人金额为1000美元,加上利息按年率6%,从这张汇票出票日起算至付款日止,计算利息金额。"
>
> "Pay to the order of A Co. the sum of one thousand US dollars plus interest calculated at the rate of 6% per annum from the date hereof to the date of payment."
>
> 说明:此项利息条款注明利率,起算日和终止日就可算出利息金额。
>
> 情况3:"支付给A公司的指定人金额为1000美元,加上利息按年率x%计算。"
>
> "Pay to the order of A Co. the sum of one thousand US dollars plus interest calculated at the rate of x%."
>
> 说明:此项利息条款注明利率,没有起算日和终止日,可以接受。根据《日内瓦统一法》第五条,以出票日作为起算日,商业习惯以付款日作为终止日。

2. 关于汇率条款的几种情况

如果汇票上除了记载金额外,还记载了另一种货币作为支付货币,必须注明汇率。

范例

情况1:"支付给A公司的指定人金额为1000美元,折合成英镑等值货币。"

"Pay to the order of A Co. the sum of one thousand US dollars converted into sterling equivalent."

说明:因为没有注明折合的汇率,故折成英镑不是各方当事人能算出的相同英镑金额,不宜接受。

情况2:"支付给A公司的指定人金额为1000美元,按照现时汇率折成等值英镑支付。"

"Pay to the order of A Co. the sum of one thousand US dollars converted into sterling equivalent at current rate of exchange."

说明:表示按照"现时汇率"折成英镑,也即按照付款日当天的汇率折成英镑,则各方当事人都能按此算出相同的英镑金额,故可以接受。

3. 关于汇票金额的文字书写格式

汇票金额要用文字大写(Amount in Words)和数字小写(Amount in Figure)分别表明。如果文字与数字不符,以文字为准。实际做法多是退票,要求出票人更改相符后,再行提示要求付款。

(六) 付款人名称和付款地点(Drawee and Place of Payment)

付款人的名称地址必须书写清楚,以便持票人向它提示要求承兑或付款。特别是付款人为银行,它在某城市有两家以上的分支机构时,如果只写城市名称,不写街道及门牌号码,就会使提示汇票遇到麻烦。

付款人应与出票人是两个不同的当事人。如果付款人与出票人是相同的一个当事人,持票人可以选择把它当作本票或汇票看待。若当作本票看待,可以免去提示要求承兑,也让签票人自始至终处于主债务人地位。

《英国票据法》允许汇票开至两个付款人(A bills drawn on A and B is permissible),但是不允许开至两个付款人任择其一(A bill drawn on A or B is not permissible),因为这样的付款人是不确定的。

(七) 收款人名称(Payee)

汇票的收款人是汇票上记名的债权人。汇票上"收款人"的记载,通常称为"抬头",根据抬头的不同写法,确定汇票的可流通性或不可流通性。习惯上汇票只写收款人名称,不写其他地址(见《英国票据法》第七条解释)。汇票抬头有三种写法:

1. 限制性抬头

限制性抬头的汇票,不得转让他人。

范例

(1) 仅付约翰·戴维斯(Pay to John Davids only)。

(2) 支付约翰·戴维斯,不可转让(Pay to John Davids not transferable)。

(3) 支付约翰·戴维斯,在汇票其他处写有"不可转让"(Not transferable)字样。

2. 指示性抬头

指示性抬头的汇票,用背书和交付的方法转让。

范例

(1) 支付给 A 公司的指定人(Pay to the order of A Co.)。

(2) 支付给 A 公司或其指定人(Pay to A Co. or order)。

(3) 支付给 A 公司(Pay to A Co.)。

按照《英国票据法》第八条第四分条规定,第(3)种写法可以当作等同于"支付给 A 公司或其指定人"(Pay to A Co. or order)看待。

3. 来人抬头

《英国票据法》允许来人作为收款人,《日内瓦统一票据法》不允许来人作为收款人。有些国家票据法规定:凡票据上未记载收款人者,视作来人抬头。但《英国票据法》和《日内瓦统一票据法》都认为"收款人"非注明不可。来人抬头的汇票仅凭交付而转让,不需背书。

范例

(1) 支付给来人(Pay to bearer)。

(2) 支付给 A 公司或来人(Pay to A Co. or bearer)。

只要写上 bearer 字样,在它前面是否写有具体收款人名称,均视为来人抬头。

(八) 出票人名称和签字(Drawer and His Signature)

凡在票据上签字的人,就是票据债务人。换言之,他要对票据付款负责任,出票人在开出汇票时,首先要签字,承认自己的债务责任,汇票方可生效。收款人有了债权,票据随之成为债权凭证。如果签字是伪造的,或是未经授权的人签字,应视为无效。

出票人是个人,如果代理他的委托人签字,而委托人是公司、单位、银行、团体时,应在公司名称前面写上"For"或"On behalf of"或"For and on behalf of"或"Per pro."字样,并在个人签字后面写上他的职务名称,如:

For A Co. Ltd. , London

John Smith Manager

这样 A 公司受到个人 John Smith 签字的约束,而 John Smith 不是他个人开出的汇票,而是代理 A 公司开出汇票。

四、汇票的其他记载项目

汇票除了上述必要项目之外,还可以有票据法允许的其他记载项目。如:

(一) 担当付款人(Person Designed as Payer)

在汇票载明付款人后,再说明由第三者执行付款,该第三者称为担当付款人。担当付款人是由付款人为了支付方便,与出票人约定的,可由出票人在出票时记载,也可由付款人在承兑时记载。若汇票上有此记载,持票人应向担当付款人作付款提示,若远期汇票需作承兑,仍应向付款人提示。

(二) 预备付款人(Referee in Case of Need)

出票人在汇票上载明付款人后,还记载一付款地的第三人作为预备付款人。万一付款人拒付,持票人可向预备付款人提示(包括提示承兑和提示付款)。出票人作这种记载的目的是为了保障出票人自己的信用,免受持票人的追索。

(三) 免作拒绝证书(Protest Waived)

票据上记明免作拒绝证书的持票人在遭到拒付时无需作拒绝证书,从而追索时也无需出示拒绝证书。

(四) 付一不付二(Pay the First/Second Being Unpaid)

商业汇票往往一套 2 张,但只代表一笔债务,故而需在 2 张汇票上分别注明"付一不付二"[Pay the First (Second Being Unpaid)]或"付二不付一"[Pay the Second(First Being Unpaid)]。付款人只承兑其中 1 张,只对其中 1 张付款。

(五) 无追索权(Without Recourse)

出票人在票面写上"无追索权"字样,或在他自己签名上记载"无追权"或"对我们没有追索权"字样,就是免除对出票人的追索权。背书人也可在他签名之上作同样记载,就是免除对背书人的追索权。

> **范例**
>
> Without recourse to us
> For A Co. Ltd. , London
> Signature

实际上是免除出票人或背书人对于汇票应负的责任。持票人可以把加注"无追索权"的签名视为划掉这个签名,从而减少了对汇票的负责人。《日内瓦统一票据法》第九条有着不同的规定:出票人可以解除他的保证承兑责任,但是任何解除出票人的保证付款责任的规定,视为无记载。

第二节 票 据 行 为

票据行为是指票据流通过程中,确定权利义务或行使权利或履行义务的行为。确定权利和义务的票据行为包括:出票(Issue)、背书(Endorsement)、承兑(Acceptance)、保证(Guarantee/Aval);行使权利的票据行为包括:提示(Presentation)、追索(Recourse);履行义务的行为包括付款(Payment)以及出票人或背书人或保证人接受追索偿付票款等行为。其中出票是主票据行为,是其他票据行为得以发生的基础。

一、出票

发出汇票包括两个动作,一个是写成汇票并在汇票上签字(to draw a draft and to sign it);另一个是将汇票交付收款人(to deliver a draft to the payee),这样就创设了汇票的债权,使收款人持有汇票就拥有债权。

交付(Delivery)意指实际的或推定的所有权从一个人转移至另一个人的行为。汇票的出票、背书、承兑的票据行为在交付前都是不生效的和可以撤销的,只有将汇票交付给他人后,出票、背书、承兑行为才开始生效,并且是不可撤销的。

开出汇票时,出票人签名于上,就要对汇票付款承担责任,而付款人对于汇票并不承担责任。因为汇票不是"领款单",汇票是由出票人担保的"信用货币",收款人的债权完全依赖于出票人的信用。

二、背书

背书是指汇票背面的签字。只有持票人,即收款人或被背书人才能有权背书汇票。持票人要把票据权利转让给别人,必须在票据背面签字并经交付,汇票权利即由背书人转移至被背书人。

背书包括两个动作,一个是在汇票背面签字,另一个是交付给被背书人,只有经过交付,才算完成背书行为,使其背书有效和不可撤销。

背书有五种类型:

(一) 特别背书(Special Endorsement)

特别背书又称记名背书,需要记载"支付给被背书人名称的指定人",并经背书人签字。

范例

Pay to the order of
B Co. , London
Signature

被背书人B公司可用背书和交付方法继续转让汇票。从一系列的特别背书可以看出背书的连续性如下：

当事人名称 \ 顺序	第一	第二	第三	第四	第五	
被背书人	B	C	D	E	F	最后被背书人是持票人
背书人	A(Payee)	B	C	D	E	

(二) 空白背书(Blank Endorsement or Endorsement in Blank)

空白背书又称不记名背书,即不记载被背书人名称,只有背书人的签字。当汇票空白背后书后,交付转让给一个不记名的受让人,他与来人抬头汇票的来人相同,可以不需背书,仅凭交付再行转让。因为他没在汇票背面签字,对汇票就不承担责任。

已作空白背书的汇票,任何持票人可将空白背书转变为记名背书。只要在背书人名称签字上面写明"支付给×××(持票人自己的名称或第三者的名称)的指定人"即可。此后被背书人还可作成空白背书,将其恢复为空白背书的汇票。

我国《票据法》规定,汇票的转让必须使用记名背书,禁止使用空白背书。若背书人作空白背书,该背书行为无效,汇票转让不能成立。

国外票据法对汇票允许转让使用记名背书或空白背书,但在实务中,主要采用记名背书。

记名背书的汇票在转让时,必须由被背书人再行背书。若每一次转让都采用记名背书的方式,可使汇票的债权债务关系明确,所有的原债权人在转让债权的同时,变成了担保债权得以实现的债务人,而不仅仅是把债权一转了之。这样,汇票的使用将更为可靠、安全。

(三) 限制性背书(Restrictive Endorsement)

限制性背书是指"支付给被背书人"的指示带有限制性的词语。

> **范例**
>
> "仅付A银行"(Pay to A Bank only)。
> "支付给A银行不可流通"(Pay to A Bank not transferable)。
> "支付给A银行不得付给指定人"(Pay to A Bank not to order)。

作成上述限制性背书的汇票,禁止被背书人把汇票再行流通或转让,他只能凭票取款。

(四) 带有条件背书(Conditional Endorsement)

带有条件背书是指"支付给被背书人"的指示是带有条件的。

> **范例**
>
> Pay to the order of B Co.
> On delivery of B/L No. 125
> For A Co. , London
> Signature

开出汇票必须是无条件的支付命令,作成背书是可以带有条件的。附带条件仅对背书人和被背书人有着约束作用,它与付款人、出票人无关。

当汇票向付款人提示要求付款时,付款人不管条件是否履行,可以照常付款给持票人,汇票即被解除责任。带有条件背书实际是指背书行为中的交付,只有在条件完成时方可把汇票交给被背书人。

(五) 托收背书(Endorsement for Collection)

托收背书是要求被背书人按照委托代收票款的指示,处理汇票的背书。通常是在"Pay to the order of B Bank"的前面或后面写上"for collection"字样。有时还可写出其他指示。

范例

For collection pay to the order of B Bank

委托收款的被背书人,得到的是代理权而不是债权,当然也就不能以背书方式转让本不属于他的汇票权利了。但是,该被背书人为了行使被委托的汇票权利,有权再委托他人,所以仍可作委托收款背书。

同样理由,由于委托收款背书并非转让票据权利,所以即便是限制性抬头("不得转让")的汇票,收款人仍可作委托收款背书。

以背书转让的汇票,背书应当连续。所谓背书连续,是指票据转让中,转让汇票的背书人与受让汇票的被背书人在汇票上的签章依次前后衔接。

我国《票据法》规定,"以背书转让的汇票,后手应对其直接前手背书的真实性负责"。从背书的连续性来看,每一个背书人,都对自己前一个背书人的签字的真实性负责,没有间断,从形式上可以推定最后的持票人为合法的票据权利人。

《英国票据法》第二十四条规定,伪造背书的后手不能成为持票人。当汇票转让给一个受让人时,他必须确定背书的连续性和证实前手背书的真实性,才能接受汇票使自己成为持票人。最后持票人即汇票提示人多是一家代收行,当它将汇票提示给付款行(Drawee Bank)要求付款时应作空白背书,付款行需要证实最后背书的真实性才能付款。

三、提示

持票人将汇票提交付款人要求承兑或要求付款的行为叫做提示。票据是一种权利凭证,要实现权利,必须向付款人提示票据,以便要求实现票据权利。提示可以分为两种:远期汇票向付款人提示要求承兑;即期汇票或已承兑的远期汇票向付款人或承兑人提示要求付款。即期汇票只需一次提示,把承兑和付款一次完成。远期汇票需两次提示,承兑和付款先后完成。

提示必须在规定的时限或规定地点办理,若逾期未作提示,则出票人和全体背书人解除对持票人的责任。至于合理时间的具体长度,应视汇票的种类、提示目的而定,详见表3-1。

表3-1　各国票据法汇票提示的合理时间规定

期限	目的	《日内瓦统一票据法》	《中华人民共和国票据法》	《英国票据法》	美国《统一流通票据法》
即期	付款	出票日起一年	出票日起一月	合理时间	合理时间
远期	承兑	确定日期 出票后定期 }→到期日前 见票后定期→出票日起一年	确定日期 出票后定期 }→到期日前 见票后定期→出票日起一月	到期日前的合理时间	确定日期 出票后定期 }→到期日当天或以前 见票后定期→合理时间
	付款	到期日或其后二个营业日	到期日起10日	到期日	到期日

持票人应在汇票载明的付款地点向付款人提示。如果汇票没有载明付款点,则向付款人营业所提示。汇票上记载有担当付款人时,持票人应向担当付款人提示要求付款。由于票据上的付款人绝大多数是银行,还可以通过银行票据交换所提示票据。

四、承兑

承兑意指远期汇票的付款人,以其签名表示同意按照出票人命令而付款的票据行为。付款人承兑汇票后成为承兑人,他的签名表明他已承诺付款责任,愿意按照承兑文义保证付款,他不得以出票人的签字是伪造的、背书人无行为能力等理由否认汇票的效力。

承兑包括两个动作:第一,写明"已承兑"(ACCEPTED)字样和签字;第二,将已承兑汇票交付持票人。这样承兑就是有效的不可撤销的。国际银行业务习惯上是由承兑行发出承兑通知书给持票人,用来代替交付已承兑汇票给持票人。见票后若干天付款的汇票,承兑日就是见票日,由此推算到期日,待到期日承兑行主动付款记入持票人账户。

承兑汇票意味着承兑人对于汇票付款做了进一步保证。当付款行承兑汇票后,按照《英国票据法》第五十三条文义,该汇票可以当做持票人要求支取汇票金额的领款单或过户转让书,故一般银行愿意贴现买进银行承兑的远期汇票。承兑人是汇票主债务人,出票人退居从债务人位置。

付款人是否承兑需要有考虑时间。《英国票据法》规定考虑时间在提示的次一个营业日营业时间终了之前。《日内瓦统一票据法》规定考虑时间可从第一次提示后之次日至第二次提示日为止。承兑时盖上"承兑"戳记,写上承兑日期,不写到期日,经承兑人签字即可。为了方便起见,可在汇票右上角写上到期日,例如:Due 15th Nov.,2012。也可在"承兑"行为中写成:

```
ACCEPTED
(date)
to mature
(date)
For name of drawee
signature
```

汇票的承兑有两种,即普通承兑和限制承兑。

1. 普通承兑(General Acceptance)

普通承兑是承兑人对出票人的指示不加限制地同意确认,通常所称的承兑即普通承兑。

2. 限制承兑(Qualified Acceptance)

限制承兑是指承兑时,用明白的措词改变汇票承兑后的效果。常见的限制承兑有以下几种:

(1) 带有条件的承兑(Conditional Acceptance)。即承兑人的付款依赖于承兑时所提条件的完成。

范例

ACCEPTED

1st June, 2001

Payable on delivery of Bills of Lading

For A Bank Ltd. , London

signature

(2) 部分承兑(Partial Acceptance)。仅是承兑和支付票面的一部分。

范例

票面金额为 USD1000.00 的部分承兑

ACCEPTED

3rd June, 2001

Payable on amount of USD800.00 only

For A Bank Ltd. , London

signature

由于付款人拒绝就汇票全部金额作出承兑,持票人可将其视为拒绝承兑,并以此为由向前手追索全部票款,但持票人也可以接受部分承兑,然后就未承兑部分的金额向前手追索。承兑部分的金额在到期日由承兑人支付,若届时承兑人拒付,持票人仍可以向前手追索该部分金额。这种处理方法虽然比较麻烦,但比起简单地以全额退票处理的方法有其优点,即就承兑部分的金额而言,承兑人承担主要付款责任,出票人承担连带责任,因而至少有两个责任当事人,尤其是承兑人为主债务人,因此收款可靠性较大。若以全额退票处理,持票人拒绝接受部分承兑,付款人对持票人就不再承担责任,持票人只有向前手追索这一唯一的利益保全方法。如果未能追回票款,持票人无权再要求付款人支付,因而有可能面临全部损失。

（3）地方性承兑(Local Acceptance)，即承兑仅在某一特定地点支付，亦即用文字明白表示汇票仅在那里(and there only)而不在别处支付。

> **范例**
>
> ACCEPTED
> 5th June, 2001
> Payable at The Hambros Bank and there only
> For A Bank Ltd. ，London
> signature

如果承兑的支付是在承兑人的账户行，即写出承兑人的担当付款行。在它的后面没有 and the only 则是普通承兑。

（4）延长时间承兑(Qualified Acceptance as to Time)。

> **范例**
>
> 出票日后3个月付款的汇票，承兑时写明6个月付款。
> ACCEPTED
> 5th June, 2001
> Payable at 6 months after date
> For A Bank Ltd. ，London
> signature

五、付款

票据的最终目的是凭以付款。即期汇票提示日即为付款到期日，见票后若干天付款的远期汇票从承兑日推算到期日。持票人在到期日提示汇票，经付款人或承兑人正当地付款(Payment in Due Course)以后，汇票即被解除责任。所谓正当地付款是指满足以下条件：

（1）在汇票到期日或以后付款。若提前支付，付款人自担风险，自负责任。例如，贸易结算中常使用一式两份的成套汇票，其中一份被解除，全套汇票即告解除；若付款人对其中一份提前支付，而其余汇票未被解除，整套汇票仍然有效。

（2）由付款人或承兑人支付。可以由其本人支付，也可以由其代理人（如往来银行）授权支付。其他人所作付款只是广义付款。为能解除汇票的债权债务，只能转移债权。

（3）向持票人支付。持票人的认定，除必须占有汇票外，还必须以必要背书的连续来证明。按《日内瓦统一票据法》与我国《票据法》的规定，背书的连续是指形式上的连续，因此付款人或承兑人只需检验背书的表面连续性即可，对背书真伪性不负认定之责。英美票据法规定必要背书的连续是实质上的连续，若必要背书欠缺、伪造、未经受权，则此后不出现持票人,所以付款人或承兑人不仅要检验背书形式上的连续性,而且还要检验背书的真伪性。

(4)善意地支付。这是指付款人或承兑人对持票人可能存在的权利缺陷不知悉;同时,付款的作出是在营业时间内按照正常的业务规范进行的。

在通常情况下,付款人或承兑人履行正当付款是解除汇票的最主要方式。汇票一经解除,出票人、承兑人、背书人、保证人等全体票据债务人的责任即告消灭。

六、退票及退票通知

退票(Dishonor)是指持票人依票据法规定作有效提示时,遭付款人或承兑人拒绝付款或拒绝承兑的行为。退票行为可以是实际的,也可以是推定的。前者指持票人正式提示时,付款人或承兑人明确地拒绝付款或拒绝承兑,从而构成实际退票;后者指付款人纯属虚构,或虽经适当努力仍无法找到,或者付款人或承兑人已死亡,或宣告破产,或被依法停止营业,则构成推定退票。

退票通知(Notice of Dishonour)的目的是要汇票债务人及早知道拒付,以便做好被追索的准备。《英国票据法》规定:持票人若不作成退票通知,并及时发出,即丧失其追索权。《日内瓦统一票据法》认为,退票通知仅是后手对于前手的义务,不及时通知退票并不丧失追索权。但如因未及时通知,造成前手遭受损失时,应负赔偿之责,其赔偿金额不超过汇票金额。发出退票通知有两种方法,见图3-1。

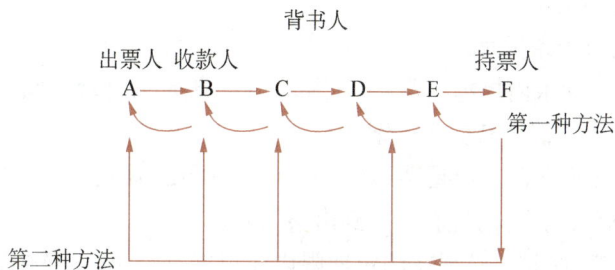

图3-1 发出退票通知的方法

发出退票通知的第一种方法是持票人应在退票后一个营业日内,将退票事实通知前手背书人,前手应于接到通知后一个营业日内再通知他的前手背书人,一直通知到出票人,接到退票通知的每个背书人都有向其前手进行追索的权利。如持票人或背书人未在规定时间内,将退票通知送达前手背书人或出票人,则该持票人或背书人即对接受通知的前手丧失追索权。但正当持票人的追索权不因遗漏通知而受到损害。

第二种发送方法是持票人将退票事实通知全体前手,如此则每个前手即无须继续向前手通知了。

七、拒绝证书

拒绝证书(Protest)是指由退票地公证机关或其他有权公证的机构或当事人出具的证

明退票事实的法律文件。

持票人请求公证人作成拒绝证书时,应将汇票交出,由公证人向付款人再作提示,仍遭拒付时,即由公证人按规定格式作成拒绝证书,连同汇票交还持票人,持票人凭拒绝证书及退回的汇票向前手背书人行使追索权。

如拒付地点没有法定公证人,拒绝证书可由当地知名人士(Famous Man)在两个见证人(Witness)面前作成。在我国可请公证处作成拒绝证书。

持票人要求公证人作成拒绝证书所付的公证费用,在追索票款时,一并向出票人收取。有时出票人为了免除此项费用,可在汇票上加注"免作拒绝证书"(Protest Waived)字样,则持票人不需作成拒绝证书,即可行使追索权。如果汇票有了此项记录,仍然作成拒绝证书,则该证书有效,但公证费用应由持票人自行负担。

八、追索权

追索权(Right of Recourse)是指汇票遭到拒付,持票人对其前手背书人或出票人有请求其偿还汇票金额及费用的权利。

行使追索权的对象是背书人、出票人、承兑人以及其他债务人,因为他们要对持票人负连带的偿付责任。持票人是票据上的唯一债权人,他可向对汇票负责之任何当事人取得偿付。被迫付款之出票人可以向承兑人取得偿付,被迫付款之背书人可以向承兑人或出票人或其前手背书人取得偿付。追索的票款应包括:汇票金额,利息,作成退票通知、拒绝证书和其他必要的费用。

行使追索权的三个条件是:

(1)必须在法定期限内提示汇票。《英国票据法》规定为合理时间内向付款人提示汇票,未经提示,持票人不能对其前手追索。

(2)必须在法定期限内发出退票通知。《英国票据法》规定为退票日后的次日,将退票事实通知前手,后者再通知其前手,直到出票人。

(3)外国汇票遭到退票,必须在法定期限内作成拒绝证书。《英国票据法》规定为退票后一个营业日内,由持票人请公证人作成拒绝证书。

只有办到这三条,才能保留和行使追索权,持票人或背书人必须在法定期限内行使追索权,否则即行丧失该权利。《英国票据法》规定,保留追索权的期限为6年。《日内瓦统一票据法》规定,持票人对前一背书人或出票人行使追索权的期限为1年,背书人对其前手背书人则为6个月。

持票人追索时,可不问债务顺序,自行选择追索对象,并可以同时向一个或一个以上对象进行追索。被追索人清偿债务后,可取得汇票和拒绝证书及持票人出具的收到利息和费用的收据,并享有持票人的权利进行再追索。

追索只能按债务顺序向前追索,即只能由后手向前手追索,而不能由前手向后手追索。在出现回头背书的情形中,如果背书转让的被背书人是出票人,或者是某一前手背书人,则其追索权受到限制。我国《票据法》规定,持票人为出票人的,对其前手无追索权,持票人为背书人的,对其后手无追索权。比如:出票人A签发一张汇票给收款人

B,B 背书转让给 C,C 再行转让……汇票又回头背书转让给 A 或 C,假定一个顺序如下：

$$A \to B \to C \to D \to E \to F \to A$$

如果 A 遭拒付,他实际上是最前顺序的债务人,所以不能向其形式上的前手追索。

假定另一个顺序如下：

$$A \to B \to C \to D \to E \to C$$

如果 C 遭拒付,C 实际上是第三顺序债务人,D 和 E 是其后手,所以 C 只能向 B 和 A 追索,而不能向其形式上的前手 D 和 E 追索。

出票人清偿后,还可以向承兑人追偿,直至向法院起诉。

九、参加承兑

参加承兑(Acceptance for Honour)是汇票遭到拒绝承兑而退票时,非汇票债务人在得到持票人同意的情况下,参加承兑已遭拒绝承兑的汇票的一种附属票据行为。其目的是为防止追索权的行使,维护出票人和背书人的信誉。参加承兑行为的人,称参加承兑人(Acceptor for Honour)。参加承兑人应在汇票上面记载参加承兑的意旨,被参加承兑人姓名,参加承兑日期并签字。参加承兑记载形式如下：

```
Accepted for honour
of _____
on _____
signed by _____
```

汇票到期时,如付款人不付款,持票人可向参加承兑人提示要求付款,通知他付款人因拒绝付款而退票,并已作成拒绝证书的事实。参加承兑人即应照付票款,从而成为参加付款人。

被参加承兑(The Person for Whose Honour Acceptance Has Been Given)是指被"参加承兑人"担保信誉的任意债务人。举例如图 3-2 所示。

一张汇票,出票人 A,付款人 B,收款人 C 将汇票背书转让给 D,D 再背书转让给 E,E 作为持票人向付款人 B 提示要求承兑,但遭拒绝(①),参加承兑人 F 参加承兑(②),并指定被参加承兑人,即参加承兑人 F 向持票人 E 担保 C 的信誉,汇票到期,付款人 B 拒不付款,而由参加承兑人 F 付款(③),则 F 即成为参加付款人,对被参加承兑人 C 及其前手 A 有请求偿还权(④),而被参加承兑人 C 的后手 D 被免除票据责任。

《日内瓦统一票据法》规定,凡参加承兑而没有记载被参加承兑人者,则应视出票人为被参加承兑人。

参加承兑人于参加承兑后两个营业日内,应将参加承兑事实通知被参加承兑人,如未

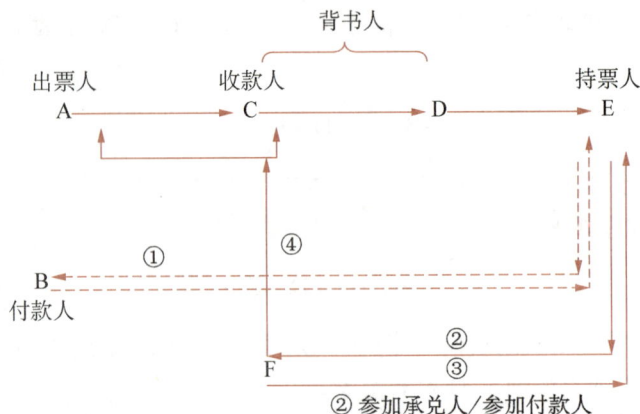

图3-2　参加承兑流程图

通知,致使被参加承兑人受到损失,则应由参加承兑人负赔偿责任。

持票人同意第三者参加承兑后,即不得于到期日以前向前手行使追索权。

见票后若干天付款的汇票被参加承兑时,其到期日从作成拒绝承兑证书之日起算,而不是从参加承兑日起算。持票人于到期日时须先向付款人提示要求付款,遭到拒付时,才得向参加承兑人要求付款,参加承兑人则应照付票款。

由于汇票遭到拒绝承兑以后,再找参加承兑人是不容易的,故参加承兑行为很少发生。

十、参加付款

在因拒绝付款而退票,并已作成拒绝付款证书的情况下,非票据债务人可以参加支付汇票票款。参加付款者要出具书面声明,表示愿意参加付款,说明被参加付款人的名称,并由公证人证明后,即成为参加付款人(Payer for Honour)。

参加付款(Payment for Honour)与参加承兑的作用,同为防止持票人行使追索权,维护出票人、背书人的信誉,而且两者都可能指定任意债务人作为被参加人,所不同的是参加付款人不需征得持票人的同意,任何人都可以作为参加付款人,而参加承兑须经持票人的同意;同时参加付款是在汇票拒绝付款时为之,而参加承兑则是在汇票遭拒绝承兑时为之。

参加付款后,参加付款人对于承兑人、被参加付款人及其前手取得持票人的权利,有向其请求偿还权。被参加付款人之后手,因参加付款而免除票据付款人。

参加付款人未记载被参加付款人者,则出票人应视为被参加付款人。

参加承兑人在参加付款时,应以被参加承兑人作为被参加付款人。

由第三者作为参加付款人时,应将参加付款的事实在两个营业日内通知被参加付款人,如未通知而发生损失时,应负赔偿之责。

参加付款的金额应包括票面金额、利息和拒绝证书费用,付款时,参加付款人收回汇票和拒绝证书,然后向被参加付款人及其前手请求偿还。

由于汇票遭到拒绝付款以后,再找参加付款人,事实上不容易,故参加付款行为极少发生。

十一、保证

汇票一般是以非汇票债务人作为保证人(Guarantor),出票人、背书人、承兑人、参加承兑人均可作为被保证人(The Person Guaranteed)。保证人与被保证人所负的责任完全相同,为承兑人保证时,应负付款之责;为出票人、背书人保证时,应负担保承兑及担保付款之责。一般情况下都是对汇票金额全部付款加以保证(Guarantee of Aval),等于是为承兑人保证。

保证行为可在汇票上作出,或在粘单上作出,保证形式并不统一,常见形式如下:

范例

GUARANTEED	PER AVAL	PAYMENT GUARANTED
For a/c of _____	Given for _____	Signed by _____
Guarantor _____	Signed by _____	Dated on _____
signature _____	Dated on _____	

仅在票面上签字,而签字人不是出票人和承兑人时,即构成保证行为。如未载明被保证人名称时,以付款人作为被保证人。按照银行实际做法,当付款人是被保证人时,保证人就直接承担汇票到期付款的责任。

作出保证行为时,保证人可向被保证人收取一定的押金或担保品,保证人在偿付票款后可以行使持票人的权利,即对承兑人、被保证人及其前手行使追索权。

票据被保证以后,增强了票据付款信誉,促使票据易于转让流通,所以保证常被用作票据融通资金的手段。

知识扩展

票据的涂销、更改、伪造

票据的涂销

票据涂销是指行为人以一定的方法,将票据上的自我签名或者自己记载的其他事项予以消除的行为。票据涂销通常为有相应权限的人所为,票据涂销仅限于对票据上记载内容的去除,不包括对票据上记载内容的增添。

票据的涂销可以分为两类,即法定涂销和任意涂销。

1. 法定涂销

法定涂销是指票据法明确规定了法律效力的涂销。在一般情况下,法定涂销不影响票据的效力,但依所涂销的具体内容不同,涂销本身可能发生不同的效力。

法定涂销主要有三类:

(1)票据背书的涂销。票据背书的涂销是指将票据上已进行记载的背书予以消除的行为。涂销人通常为背书人本人,也可以为其他票据权利人。

可能发生背书涂销的情况有：

● 持票人在将票据交付受让人之前,涂销自己先前拟背书转让的记载;

● 背书人在接受追索后取得票据,将自己的背书涂销;

● 贴现申请人向贴现银行买回贴现票据时,涂销自己先前的贴现背书;

● 涂销错误的背书;

● 背书人涂销后手的背书直接取得票据,以代替回头背书。

票据法通常规定,票据背书的涂销视为无记载,即该背书无效。但背书涂销不影响票据的效力,即票据上的其他记载仍然有效。

(2) 汇票承兑的涂销。汇票承兑的涂销,是指将汇票上已进行记载的承兑予以涂销的行为。其涂销人只能是接受持票人的承兑提示,并在票据上记载承兑文句的付款人或承兑人,涂销时间是在承兑记载之后,尚未将已经承兑的汇票交付提示人之前。

如果已经将承兑票据交付提示人,承兑人则不能再将其承兑涂销。

汇票承兑的涂销,具有将该承兑记载完全去除,从而表明付款人撤销承兑的效力,但承兑涂销并不影响其他记载的效力。

(3) 支票划线的涂销。支票划线的涂销是指将支票上已有的划线予以消除的行为。票据法不承认对划线支票的涂销,即使对划线支票进行了涂销,仍视为未涂销。也就是说,特别划线支票不能因涂销变成一般划线支票,一般划线支票不能因涂销变成普通支票。转账支票的涂销效果与此相同。

2. 任意涂销

任意涂销是指票据法未明确规定其法律效力,应依其他有关规定确定其效力的涂销。

(1) 保持票据效力的涂销。如果所涂销的是非必要记载事项,则票据的涂销不影响票据自身的效力,持票人可依涂销后的票据文义主张权利,如果涂销的是必要记载事项,只要持票人能证明这种涂销并非由有涂销权限的人故意所为及能证明被涂销部分的实际内容,即可要求票据权利。

(2) 丧失票据效力的涂销。如果涂销为票据权利人故意所为。所涂销部分的票据权利消灭;如果所涂销的部分为必要记载事项,则票据权利全部消灭。

票据的更改

更改是指有权限人对票据记载内容进行变更、订正的行为。更改不但包括涂销原记载内容,而且包括增加新的内容。由于票据是要式凭证有严格的形式要求,因此票据法对票据更改也有严格规定。根据更改后票据的效力不同,更改可分为两种:

1. 丧失票据效力的更改

对于票据上的实质性内容,票据法一般不允许更改,否则票据无效。

我国《票据法》规定:票据金额、日期、收款人名称不得更改,更改的票据无效。

2. 保持票据效力的更改

对于一些相对次要的内容,通常可以作更改。

我国《票据法》规定,除票据金额、日期、收款人以外的其他记载事项,原记载人可以更改。不过,更改时原记载人应签章证明。在这种情况下,不仅票据仍然有效,而且更改后的内容也有效。

票据的伪造

伪造是指假借他人名义而出票的行为。票据伪造的行为人称为伪造人,其票据伪造行为,可以采取模仿他人的手书签名、私刻他人印章、盗用他人印章等方法。被其假借名义的他人称为被伪造人,被伪造人通常是实际存在的人。

如果伪造票据仅是签名的伪造,在票据形式上是完备的。因此,属于形式上有效的票据。根据票据行为独立原则,签名的伪造并不影响真实签名人的票据行为效力。真实签名人不得以票据上存在伪造的签名,而主张免除自己的票据责任。

如果被伪造人对票据伪造一事无重大过失,伪造票据的持票人就不能对被伪造人主张任何票据上的权利,而只能对伪造人提出赔偿请求;如果被伪造人有重大过失,且持票人是善意取得票据的,那么持票人有权对被伪造人主张票据上的权利。

持票人负有证明票据签名为真实签名的责任,即证明该票据签名确为名义上的行为人自己的签名,或其印鉴确为名义上行为人自己的真实印鉴。

由于伪造票据的签名不是依被伪造人自己的意志而完成的票据行为。因而,对被伪造人而言,不应因此而承担任何票据责任。不过,被伪造人要能证明其印鉴是被盗用的。但被伪造人本身对票据伪造一事有重大过失的例外。

票据伪造人应该对其票据伪造行为负责。伪造人应对受害人承担损害赔偿的责任。此外,还要承担刑事责任。我国《票据法》规定,伪造票据或故意使用伪造票据都属于欺诈行为,要依法追究其行为人的民事责任和刑事责任。

(资料来源:1.《中华人民共和国票据法》(2004年修订)。2. 张东祥、高小红:《国际结算》(第3版),武汉大学出版社2004年版。)

第三节 汇票在融资中的运用

汇票在资金融通中的运用,主要有贴现、融通和承兑等几种方式。

一、汇票的贴现

贴现(Discount),是指持票人在票据到期前为获取现款向银行贴付一定的利息所作的票据转让。贴现业务中使用的票据,除汇票、本票以外,还有国库券、银行存单等需到期偿付的凭证。就汇票的贴现而言,通常应是银行承兑汇票,因为银行信用的可靠性通常较好,可以增强贴入汇票银行届时收款的安全性。由工商企业承兑的商业承兑汇票,除非承兑人享有一流的资信,否则很难进入贴现市场,即使办理贴现,其贴现率也会高于银行承兑汇票的贴现率。

持票人以贴现的方式转让票据给银行,并获得提前收款的融资。这样一种融资业务与普通银行贷款的区别主要是：(1)信用关系的当事人不同。银行贷款的当事人是贷款银行和借款人，有时还有保证人；贴现的当事人是贴入银行、贴现人以及票据各当事人。贴现票据不获偿付时，贴现人及票据各当事人均为债务人，因而对融资银行来说，贴现比贷款更安全。(2)信用期限不同。一般贷款的期限可以长达1年或数年，而贴现的期限绝大多数不超过6个月，因此融资银行的流动性在贴现业务中体现得更好些。(3)收付利息的时间不同。普通贷款的利息是在贷款期末一次性收付或在期内分期收付，但都是先贷后收息，而贴现业务中银行预扣贴现利息。如果两者的利率相同，考虑到货币的时间价值，贴现业务的盈利性要更高些。

二、汇票的融通

汇票的融通(Accommodation)是指一人为了帮助另一人获得资金融通，在没有从后者收取对价的情况下，以出票人、承兑人或背书人的身份在汇票上签字，从而使后者能以持票人身份将汇票转让而筹集资金。签字提供帮助之人称为融通人(Accommodation Party)，接受帮助的持票人称为被融通人(Accommodated Party)。融通人没有从被融通人处获得对价支付，其签字目的是为了将自己的良好资信出借给被融通人，帮助他获得融资，因此融通人对被融通人不承担责任。但是融通人作为汇票的签字当事人，必须对后手中的对价持票人及正当持票人承担票据责任，无论他们是否知悉融通事宜，都不得以融通中未收到对价为由提出抗辩；若融通人对上述持票人清偿了票据，可向被融通人及其前手行使票据权利。

汇票的融通做法，在英国较为典型，在英美票据法中有明文规定，在《日内瓦统一票据法》中却无相应规定。我国《票据法》则规定票据的签发与取得必须具有真实的交易关系和债权债务关系，必须给付对价(税收、继承、赠与除外)，因此禁止汇票的融通这种做法。这主要是因为我国的票据业务还处于初级阶段，实践经验尚不丰富，有必要从严管理以防止出现混乱。

根据英美法律的规定，汇票的融通可以出现于出票、承兑或背书等行为中，但只有融通人以承兑人身份签字的汇票才称为融通汇票(Accommodation Bill)，缩写为A/B，其特点是：

1. 融通人，即融通汇票的承兑人，通常是银行，尤其是专营此项业务的票据承兑所(Accepting House)或商人银行(Merchant Bank)。票据承兑所或商人银行以自身名义承兑汇票，赚取承兑手续费，但不垫付资金，汇票经其承兑后信用等级提高，可以在货币市场上贴现。

2. 被融通人，即融通汇票的出票人与收款人，在出票与承兑时并未支付对价给融通人，因此不能要求融通人对被融通人承担票据责任；相反，他必须在汇票到期前将足额票款交付给融通人以备到期支付。

3. 若被融通人未将足额资金提前交给融通人，后者将拒付汇票。届时贴入汇票的银行将向被融通人追索，在其清偿后汇票即告解除。若被融通人未能清偿票款，贴入汇票的银行可以强制融通人支付，因为后者是承兑人，必须按汇票文义承担责任。

融通人为了规避被融通人违约的风险,事先都与后者达成融通协议。该协议可能以跟单信用证的方式存在,即银行保证凭合格的货运单据对汇票作承兑,并取得押金及货运单据的物权保障。该协议也可以承兑信用额度(Line of Acceptance Credit)的形式存在,即规定额度有效期、承兑总金额、每张融通汇票的限额、担保品等条款。对于额度内的融通汇票银行将自动承兑。

范例

A 公司欲融通资金,得到了经营融通票据业务的 B 银行的承兑信用额度的承诺后,A 公司可以开出以 B 银行为付款人的远期汇票。A 公司作为该汇票的出票人,同时又是收款人,B 银行在汇票上承兑,成为该汇票的主债务人。利用 B 银行的信誉,A 公司得以在金融市场上将汇票贴现,获得所需资金,其金额为汇票的面值扣减至到期日的贴现息。然后,在汇票到期日之前,A 公司将足额票款交付 B 银行。受让汇票的贴现银行于汇票到期日向承兑人 B 银行提示,B 银行即偿付票款。

本例中 B 银行为融通人,A 公司为被融通人(即筹资者),所开立的汇票为无对价关系的融通票据。B 银行向 A 公司授信而无须提供资金,但可收取承兑手续费;A 公司利用 B 银行的信用筹措到所需资金,付出的代价是贴现息的授信(承兑)费用;而贴现银行所获得的利益是贴现息。

三、汇票的银行承兑

银行承兑汇票(Bankers' Acceptance,缩写为 B/A)是指出票人开立一张远期汇票,以银行作为受票人命令它在确定的将来日期,支付一定金额给收款人。这张汇票经受票行承兑后,承兑行就承担到期付款的责任。持票人凭着承兑行的承兑信用保证,可将汇票请求任何银行贴现,贴进汇票的银行,还可以立即把它出售到票据市场上,经过出票、承兑、贴现、重贴现,获得融资机会。

银行承兑汇票在美国较为典型。根据美国联邦储备法第 13 款的规定,流通于纽约市场的银行承兑汇票交易,需符合以下的要求:

1. 融资货物必须是现时的货运(Current Shipment),即指承兑日必须在提单装运日的 30 天以内,因此可以使用银行承兑汇票的货运有效期最长为提单日起 30 天。

2. 必须向承兑银行声明要求融资的货物没有获得其他的资助,以表示销售该货的钱可以用来偿还到期票款。

3. 银行承兑汇票应跟随单据,以示确有一笔货运交易。汇票如果没有跟随单据,则承兑银行在需要时有权索看货运单据副本,以证实此笔货运。

银行承兑汇票融资适用的范围如下:

1. 美国与外国,或美国以外国家之间的进出口货物(Importation-Exportation of Goods),包括信用证项下的银行承兑汇票,托收项下的银行承兑汇票,以及银行承兑光票(又称直接融资汇票)。

2. 美国境内的货物运输(Domestic Shipment of Goods)应将物权单据给承兑银行。

3. 美国境内仓储货物(Storage of Goods)应将仓库收据(Warehouse Receipt)交给承兑银行作为质押品,融通期限最长为 90 天。

4. 出口备货融资(Pre-export Financing)应将合同交来证实确有一笔出口交易,将在 180 天内装货出口,在出口前准备货物需要融资。

由于美国以外的国家间的进出口货物,可以使用银行承兑汇票融资,外国银行若提供进出口货运资料,也可开出银行承兑光票(Clean Acceptance),采用美国承兑银行直接资助(Direct Acceptance Finance)方法筹集资金,用作外国银行放款,以获取贴现利率与放款利率之间的利差。这样,外国银行可以先同美国承兑银行订立承兑信贷额度,将预先签字的空白汇票寄交美国承兑银行妥为保存,然后发电提供所需资料。

美国承兑银行接到电报或电传提供的资料,立即填制汇票,经承兑、贴现后,将净款贷记外国银行设在该行的账户,外国银行利用此项资金做放款业务。

美国银行以承兑汇票时收取承兑手续费,在贴现汇票时,收取贴现息,承兑贴现一起办理时就要收取这两种费用,把这两种费率合并成为一种综合利率(All-in-rate)当作 B/A 的价格报出。

范例

承兑手续费率 1%,市场贴现率 9% 年率,则报出综合利率是 10% 年率。倘若汇票金额为 1000 美元,汇票期限为 6 个月,综合费用是:

$$贴现息 = \frac{1000 \times 180 \times 10\%}{900} = 50(美元)$$

$$贴现净款 = 1000 - 50 = 950(美元)$$

这样,客户按年度 10% 预先付出综合费用 50 美元,得到融资 950 美元。如按贷款 950 美元,于到期日付出 50 美元的贷款利息计算,则:

$$实际利率 = \frac{50}{950} \div \frac{180}{360} \times 100\% = 10.53\%$$

所以,票据综合利率如与贷款利率比较,首先要将综合利率折成实际利率(Effective annual interest rate)方可进行比较。

$$实际利率 = \frac{R}{1 - \frac{t}{360} \times R} \times 100\%$$

$R = 综合利率\ \text{All-in-rate}$　　$t = 到期天数\ \text{Tenor in days}$

外国银行申请美国银行承兑、贴现汇票时,首先要求承兑银行报出综合利率,然后按上述公式折成实际利率,再与当天 LIBOR (London Interbank Offered Rate)利率比较。

如果低于 LIBOR,可以叙做 B/A,获得资金,用于银行同业拆放,或向贸易商放款。如果 B/A 综合利率折成实际利率略高于 LIBOR,就不能叙做 B/A,以免赔钱。一般情况下,美国 B/A 综合利率与英国 LIBOR 相比,平均约低 0.5%。

知识扩展

《日内瓦统一票据法》、《英国票据法》、《中华人民共和国票据法》关于汇票的不同规定

法律 / 项目	《中华人民共和国票据法》	《英国票据法》	《日内瓦统一票据法》之《汇票本票统一法公约》
汇票的定义	汇票是指由出票人签发的,委托付款人在见票或者在指定的日期无条件支付确定的金额给收款人或者持票人的票据。	由出票人向另一人签发的要求即期、定期或者是在可以确定的将来时间,向某人或其指定人或来人无条件支付的一定金额的书面命令。	《汇票本票统一法规定》(以下简称《汇》)并没有给出"汇票"的定义,只是直接规定了汇票的要项。
汇票必要记载项目	第二十二条规定:表明"汇票"的字样;无条件支付的委托;确定的金额;付款人名称;收款人名称;出票日期;出票人签章。	第三条(4)规定:汇票不因下述原因而无效:(a)无出票日;(b)未说明已付之价值,或过去已付之价值;(c)无出票地或付款地。	《汇》第一条规定:1. 票据主文中列有"汇票"一词,并以开立票据所使用的文字说明之;2. 无条件支付一定金额的命令;3. 付款人(受票人)的姓名;4. 付款日期的记载;5. 付款地的记载;6. 受款人或其指定人的姓名;7. 开立汇票的日期和地点的记载;8. 开立汇票的人(出票人)的签名。
票据名称	第二十二条规定:在汇票中要表明"票据"字样。	无明文规定。	《汇》第一条第二款规定:汇票应记载其为汇票的文句,否则汇票无效。
无条件支付的委托	无明文规定。	是指出票人要求付款人无条件支付一定金额的命令。	无明文规定。
确定的金额	中文大写加数字小写,二者必须保持一致,若出现错误,则票据无效;同时金额、日期,以及收款人名称不得更改,否则无效。	与《日内瓦统一票据法》的规定相同。	文字大写加数字小写同时记载,如有差错以文字大写为准。
载有利息条款	无明文规定。	如未注明利率汇票无效。	如未注明利率,不影响票据本身的有效性,以出票日开始计算,直到付款日。

法律 项目	《中华人民共和国票据法》	《英国票据法》	《日内瓦统一票据法》之 《汇票本票统一法公约》
载有分期付款条款	无明文规定。	允许分期付款。	不许分期付款。
付款人名称	《票据法》规定为必须记载项目；作为相对必要记载事项，规定未记载明的，以出票人为付款人（中国台湾省）。	付款人可以是出票人自己，如汇票的付款人是出票人本人或者付款人为虚构或者为无行为能力人，持票人可自行规定，可以视之为汇票或者是本票。	付款人名称作为必须记载项目加以记载。
来人抬头	不允许来人抬头。	允许来人抬头。	不允许来人抬头。
出票人签章	第七条规定：票据上的签章，为签名、盖章或者签名加盖章。法人和其他使用票据的单位在票据上的签章，为该法人或者该单位的盖章加其法定代表人或者其授权的代理人的签章。	无明文规定。	《汇》第一条规定：开立汇票人的签名。
付款日期	第二十五条规定：付款日期可以按照以下形式之一记载：见票即付；定日付款；出票后定期付款；见票后定期付款。	无定期付款的规定，却允许采用"某一将来必定发生事件后是期川款"的办法。	《汇》第三十三条规定：见票即付；见票后定期付款；出票后定期付款；定日付款；其他到期日的汇票或分期付款的汇票均属无效。
出票地点	第二十三条规定：汇票上未记出票地的，出票人的营业场所、住所或者经常居住地为出票地。	第三条(4)规定：汇票不因下述原因而无效：(a)无出票日；(b)未说明已付之价值，或过去已付之价值；(c)无出票地或付款地。	《汇》第二条规定：未载出票地的汇票，出票人姓名旁所载的地点视为出票地。
付款地点	第二十三条规定：汇票上未记载付款地的，付款人的营业场所、住所或者经常居住地为付款地。	第三条(4)规定：汇票不因下述原因而无效：(a)无出票日；(b)未说明已付之价值，或过去已付之价值；(c)无出票地或付款地。	《汇》第二条规定：如无特殊记载，受票人姓名旁记载的地点视为付款地；同时视为受票人的住所地。
免于追索	出票人或背书人不能免于追索。	出票人和背书人均可以用文句来免除当票据被拒绝承兑或者拒绝支付时受追索的责任。	出票人只能免除担保承兑的责任，不能免除担保付款的责任。

法律 项目	《中华人民共和国票据法》	《英国票据法》	《日内瓦统一票据法》之 《汇票本票统一法公约》
提示承兑	第三十九条规定:定日付款或者出票后定期付款的汇票,持票人应当在汇票到期日前向付款人提示承兑。 第四十条规定:见票后定期付款的汇票,持票人应当自出票日起一个月内向付款人提示承兑,见票即付的汇票无需提示承兑。	规定提示承兑必须在合理的时间内完成,只要不是故意拖延就是合理。	出票日后一年内允许出票人将该法定的提示期限予以缩短或者延长,背书人亦可对该法定的提示期予以缩短
付款人承兑	《票据法》规定是否承兑的考虑期为三天。	无明文规定。	《汇》规定持票人第一次提示时,付款人可以不做承兑,而要求持票人翌日做提示,但面对第二次提示,必须做出是否承兑的决定。
保留性承兑	《票据法》规定视保留性承兑为拒绝承兑。 经持票人同意视部分承兑为承兑(中国台湾省)。	第四十四条规定:保留承兑之责任。(1)汇票持票人得拒绝接受保留承兑,如未取得无保留之承兑,可视汇票为因拒绝承兑而退票。(2)如保留承兑被接受,而出票人和背书人未明示或默示授权持票人接受保留承兑,在其后又未予以同意,出票人及该背书人可解除汇票责任。本款之规定不适用于已对部分承兑发出通知之部分承兑。如对外国汇票作成部分承兑,其未承兑部分必须作成拒绝证书。(3)如汇票之出票人或背书人收到保留承兑之通知,而未在合理时间内向持票人表示不同意,应被视为同意保留承兑。	承认部分承兑而不加任何附加条件,持票人可对部分承兑作出拒绝,但承兑人仍就其部分承兑负责。

项目 \ 法律	《中华人民共和国票据法》	《英国票据法》	《日内瓦统一票据法》之《汇票本票统一法公约》
承兑票据外的第三人	无明文规定。	只有票据债务人以外的第三人才能够参加承兑。	《汇》第二十七条规定:如汇票出票人表明以付款人住所以外之地为付款地,但未表明在第三人的地址付款时,则付款人得在承兑时指定该第三人。如未指定,即视为承兑人承担在付款地内自己付款的责任。
参加承兑方式	《票据法》不承认参加承兑。	无明文规定。	《汇》第五十七条规定:参加承兑应在汇票上表明,由参加人签名,并应注明被参加人姓名,如无该项记载,应视出票人为被参加承兑人。
参加承兑的效力　参加承兑人	《票据法》不承认参加承兑。	向参加承兑人提示汇票。(1)如遭退票之汇票已被参加承兑,或有关于预备付款之记载,则必须在向参加承兑人或预备付款人提示付款之前,作成拒绝付款证书。(2)如参加承兑人的地点与拒绝付款证书作成地相同时,汇票必须在不迟于到期日的次日向参加承兑人提示;如参加承兑人的地点与拒绝付款证书作成地相异时,汇票必须在不迟于到期日的次日送出,以便向参加承兑人提示。(3)如对延迟提示付款或不作提示付款可予宽恕的情况发生于向参加承兑人延迟提示或不予提示时,同样可以宽恕,持票人对延迟提示或不作提示可予免责。(4)当汇票遭参加承兑人退票时,对参加承兑人必须作出拒绝付款证书。	参加承兑人在参加承兑后两个营业日内将参加承兑事告知被承兑人,使之做好到期偿还或做好向前手做好追索的准备。

续 表

项目＼法律		《中华人民共和国票据法》	《英国票据法》	《日内瓦统一票据法》之《汇票本票统一法公约》
参加承兑的效力	持票人	《票据法》不承认参加承兑。	《英国票据法》规定:持票人有权不接受参加承兑,如果同意则在到期前不得行使追索权。	第五十六条规定:凡持票人对可承兑的汇票在到期前的追索权者,在任何情况下均得参加承兑。如汇票表明已指定一人必要时在付款地承兑或付款,持票人在到期前不得对该在必要时的受托人或其后手签名人行使追索权,除其已向该在必要时的受托人提示汇票,并经后者拒绝,且已由拒绝证书证明者外。如在其他情况下参加承兑,持票人得拒绝接受参加承兑。但如同意接受,即丧失其在到期前对被参加承兑人及其后手签名人的追索权。
保证		《票据法》规定:只有票据债务人以外的第三人才能充当保证人。	无明文规定。	《汇》规定:允许任何人充当保证人,包括在汇票上签字的债务人。
付款中受提示人票据交换地		汇票通过票据交换系统提示付款的,视持票人提示付款。	《英国票据法》第四十五条(4)规定:汇票在下述地点提示者,即为在合适之地点提示:(a)如汇票上已指明付款地,汇票在该地提示;(b)汇票上未指明付款地,但有受票人或承兑人之地址,汇票在该地提示;(c)汇票上未指明付款地亦无受票人或承兑人之地址,在受票人或承兑人之营业处所提示,则该处所属已知者。如属不知,则在已知之彼等之惯常居所提示;(d)在任何其他情况下,如能找到付款人或承兑人,则向彼等提示,或在其最后为人所知的营业处所或居住地提示。	《汇》第三十八条规定:汇票通过票据交换系统提示付款的,视持票人提示付款。

续 表

法律 项目	《中华人民共和国票据法》	《英国票据法》	《日内瓦统一票据法》之 《汇票本票统一法公约》
远期付款的提示付款的时间和地点	《票据法》规定:自到期日起十日内提示。	《英国票据法》规定:必须在到期日提示。	《汇》规定:为到期日或其后的两个营业日之一。
拒绝证书	无明文规定。	必须在拒付日的第二天内完成。	《汇》规定:远期汇票拒绝承兑证书及即期汇票的拒绝付款证书必须在拒付日第二天终了前完成;远期汇票拒绝付款证书必须在到期日及以后两天内完成。
拒付通知	《票据法》规定:持票人或者背书人发出通知的时间均为三天。	如果前手在同地,持票人必须在拒绝证书做好的第二天内通知到;如果在异地,则在拒绝证书做好后的第二天发出通知。	持票人必须在拒绝证书做好后第四天内,背书人必须在收到通知书两天内通知前手。

(资料来源:百度文库:http://wenku.baidu.com/view/0c65cd225901020207409ca2.html.)

第四节 汇票的分类

汇票可以按不同标准,从不同角度进行分类。

一、根据汇票的付款时间,可以分为即期汇票与远期汇票

即期汇票(Sight Bill)是指要求见票即付的汇票,或者是没有规定付款期限的汇票,远期汇票(Time Bill 或 Usance Bill)是指约定在将来确定的或可确定的时间进行支付的汇票,这种汇票通常要先做承兑提示以明确当事人的责任。

二、根据出票人身份,可以分为银行汇票与商业汇票

银行汇票(Bank's Draft)是指由银行签发的汇票,其付款人亦为银行,通常用于资金转移(如汇款等)业务中。商业汇票(Trader's Draft)是指由非银行(通常是工商企业、个人)签发的汇票,其付款人可以是银行也可以是非银行,广泛用于各类经济交易中。

三、根据承兑人身份,可以分为银行承兑汇票与商业承兑汇票

银行承兑汇票(Bank's Acceptance Bill)是由银行承兑的汇票,以银行信用为基础,信用等级较高,可以进行贴现。商业承兑汇票(Trader's Acceptance Bill)是指由非银行的工

商企业或个人承兑的汇票,以承兑人的商业信用为基础,信用等级一般要低于银行承兑汇票,因此,通常较难办理贴现。

四、根据汇票支付使用的货币,可以分为本币汇票(Local Currency Bill)与外币汇票(Foreign Currency Bill)

本外币的区分,既可以站在出票人的角度,也可以站在付款人及收款人的角度,因此具有相对性。

五、根据汇票的流通地域,可以分为国内汇票与国际汇票

国内汇票(Inland Bill 或 Domestic Bill)是指出票地与付款地处于同一国家的汇票。国际汇票(International Bill),也称为外国汇票(Foreign Bill),是指出票地与付款地分处两国的汇票。这一区分的意义在于确定汇票遭退票时制作拒绝证书的必要性。

六、根据当事人的重复性,可以分为普通汇票与变式汇票

普通汇票的出票人、付款人、收款人各不相同,若有重复则为变式汇票。变式汇票有三类:出票人与付款人相同的已付汇票;出票人与收款人相同的已收汇票;收款人与付款人相同的付受汇票。

七、根据附属单据的情况,可以分为光票与跟单汇票

光票(Clean Bill)是指不附有货运单据的汇票,有时可附有发票或价格清单,但绝不会附有代表权的货运单据。因此,光票代表单纯的资金请求权,与物权相分离,它在市场上的流转完全依赖于当事人的信用,不能给持票人带来物权的保障。所以,光票很少用于国际贸易结算中,主要用于资金转移业务中。跟单汇票(Documentary Bill)是指附有货运单据的汇票,而且通常是商业汇票。跟单汇票代表资金请求权与物权的结合,持票人既受票据当事人的信用保证,又受所附货运单据代表的物权的保障。但持票人在资金与货物中只能两者得其一,即付款人付款时,持票人必须将汇票连同所附货运单据放弃给付款人,从而使后者得享物权。这一机制非常适合国际贸易结算的需要,因而跟单汇票成为进出口结算的主要票据。

┌─ **本章案例** ──■

利用伪造汇票诈骗案

某年 11 月,Z 省医药器具公司持一张从香港商人处得到的出口项下的即期汇票 Demand Draft 到某银行要求鉴别其真伪。该张汇票的出票人为美国新泽西州 FIRST FIDELITY BANK,付款人是哥斯达黎加的 AMERICAN CREDIT AND INVEST CORP,金额分别为

32 761.00 美元,付款期限为出票后 180 天。

从票面上看,该张汇票的出票人是银行,但付款人的名称记载是"美洲信托与投资公司",该名称分不清是公司或银行,因而汇票种类难以判定,疑为伪造汇票。

(1) 一般情况下,我方出口商通过香港中间商和国外进口商产生贸易,在资信情况不十分了解的情况下,通常不会采用汇票方式办理结算。

(2) 汇票在付款期限记载上自相矛盾。汇票显示"DEMAND DRAFT"表明这张汇票是即期汇票。即期汇票项下,收款人提示汇票当天即为汇票到期日,而该张汇票标明的到期日与出票日相差 180 天。若说这张汇票是远期汇票,那么汇票上应注明"见票后固定时期付款"或"出票后固定时期付款"(AT 180 DAYS AFTER SIGHT 或者 AT 180 DAYS AFTER DATE HEREOF,而该汇票在右上方的"DATE OF ISSUE"的下面直接标出一个"DATE OF MATURITY"而无"AT... DAYS AFTER SIGHT PAY TO..."或"AT ... DAYS AFTER DATE OF THIS FIRST EXCHANGE PAY TO..."的语句。付款日期的写法不符合汇票的要求。

(3) 该汇票的出票人在美国,用美元付款,而付款人却在哥斯达黎加。美元的清算中心在纽约,世界各国发生的美元收储最终都要到纽约清算。既然美元汇票是由美国开出的,付款人通常的、合理的地点也应在美国。两张汇票在这一点上极不正常。于是该行一边告诫公司不要急于向国外进口商发货,一边致电出票行查询。不久,美国新泽西州 FIRST FIDELITY BANK 回电证实,该行从未签发过上述汇票。

(资料来源:蒋琴儿、秦定:《国际结算》,清华大学出版社 2007 年版。)

关键词

汇票、出票、背书、承兑、提示、转让、出票人、付款人、收款人、承兑人、背书人、被背书人、持票人、正当持票人、保证人

思考题

1. 英国票据法对汇票的定义是什么？它与《日内瓦统一票据法》的定义有什么不同？
2. 汇票的当事人有哪些？其基本要项有哪些？
3. 汇票有哪些票据行为？
4. 汇票的融资功能有哪些？

第四章 本票与支票

★ **学习目标**

掌握本票的概念及要项；本票与支票的当事人及其责任、本票与支票行为及其具体表示；本票与支票使用中的风险，以及本票与支票的融资功能；了解本票、汇票、支票的异同及关系。

★ **本章概要**

本票是国际结算中应用非常广泛的金融票据。本票的基本当事人有三人：出票人、收款人和付款人。本票的记载内容包括必要记载项目和非必要记载项目。票据行为包括出票、背书、承兑、参加承兑、提示、付款等。本票与汇票有很多相似的地方，但也有很多区别。在国际结算中，常见的本票形式有商业本票、银行本票、国际小额本票、旅行支票流通存单等。

支票是汇票的一种，是一种银行作为付款人的短期汇票，支票有多种形式，在贸易结算中应用非常广泛，尤其是在国内结算中的应用比汇票更加普遍。

第一节　本　票

一、本票的定义及必要项目

《英国票据法》关于本票的定义是：A promissory note in an unconditional promise in writing made by one person to another signed by the maker engaging to pay on demand or at a fixed or determinable future time a sum certain in money on or to the order of a specified person or to bearer. 中文含义是：本票是一项书面的无条件的支付承诺，由一人制成，并交给另一人，经制票人签名承诺即期或定期或在可以确定的将来时间，支付一定数目的金钱给一个特定的人或其指定人或来人。

我国《票据法》对本票的定义是："本票是出票人签发的承诺自己在见票时无条件支付确定的金额给收款人或者持票人的票据。本法所称本票，是指银行本票。"

根据《日内瓦统一票据法》的规定，本票必须具备以下几项：(1)写明"本票"字样；(2)无条件支付承诺；(3)收款人或其指定人；(4)制票人签字；(5)出票日期和地点（未载明出票地点者，制票人名字旁的地点视为出票地）；(6)付款期限（未载明付款期限者，视为见票即付）；(7)一定金额（大写和小写）；(8)付款地点（未载明付款地点者，出票地视为付款地）。

兹将上列项目标明在附式 4－1 本票例样中。

附式 4－1

(1)　　　　　　　　　(7)	(5)
Promissory Note for GBP 800. 00	London, 8th Sept. , 2000

(6)　　　　　　　　　　(2)

At 60 days after date we promise to pay

(3)

　　　　Beijing Arts and Crafts Corp. or order the sum of

(7)

Eight hundred pounds

　　　　　　　　　　　　　　　　　　　　　(4)

　　　　　　　　　　　　　　　　　　　For Bank of Europe,

　　　　　　　　　　　　　　　　　　　　　London

Signature(4)

二、本票与汇票的异同

(一) 本票与汇票的相同点

1. 本票的收款人与汇票的收款人相同。

2. 本票的制票人相似于汇票的承兑人。

3. 本票的第一背书人相似于已承兑汇票的收款人，他与出票人是同一人。

（二）本票与汇票的不同点

1. 基本当事人不同。本票有两个基本当事人，即制票人和收款人；汇票有三个基本当事人，即出票人、付款人、收款人。一般常说"制成"本票（to make a promissory note），因此制成人（Make）就是制票人，我们还说"开出汇票"（to draw a bill of exchange），因此出票人就是 Drawer。

2. 付款方式不同。本票的制票人自己出票自己付款，所以制票人向收款人承诺自己付款，它是承诺式的票据。

汇票是出票人要求付款人无条件地支付给收款人的书面支付命令，付款人没有义务必须支付票款，除非他承兑了汇票。所以汇票是命令式或委托式的票据。

3. 名称的含义不同。本票（Promissory Note）英文直译为"承诺券"，它包含了一笔交易的结算。汇票（Bill of Exchange）英文直译为"汇兑票"，它包含着两笔交易的结算。

4. 承兑要项不同。本票不需：(1)提示要求承兑；(2)承兑；(3)参加承兑；(4)发出一套。而汇票必须要有(1)至(4)项。

因为本票没有承兑，所以《英国票据法》主张远期只有 after date，没有 after sight。但《日内瓦统一票据法》认为可有 after sight 本票，须持票人向制票人提示请他"签见"（visa），从签见日期起算，确定到期日，如制票人拒绝签见，从提示日起算。

5. 国际本票遭到退票，不需作成拒绝证书。国际汇票遭到退票，必须作成拒绝证书。

6. 主债务人。本票的主债务人是制票人，汇票的主债务人，承兑前是出票人，承兑后是承兑人。

7. 本票不允许制票人与收款人作成相同的一个当事人，汇票允许出票人与收款人作成相同的一个当事人。

三、本票的用途

本票在国际贸易结算中的使用比不上汇票，在国内贸易结算中的使用则比不上支票，因此支付手段并非本票的主要作用。本票最重要的作用是作为信用工具在融资市场上为筹集资金服务，因而比汇票与支票更具有投资工具的特性。正因为本票兼具投资工具的特性，所以它在贸易与融资相结合的进出口交易中，才成为一种常用的结算工具，并可进入资金或资本市场交易，发挥融资工具的作用。具体体现在以下几方面：

（一）商品交易中的远期付款，可先由买方签发一张以约定付款日为到期日的本票，交给卖方，卖方可凭本票如期收到货款，如果急需资金，可将本票贴现或转售他人。

（二）用作金钱的借贷凭证，由借款人签发本票交给贷款人收执。借款合同订有利率和担保人时，可将本票写上利息条款，注明利率和起算日，并请担保人在本票上作成"担保付款"的行为。

（三）企业向外筹集资金时，可以发行商业本票，通过金融机构予以保证后，销售于证券市场获取资金，并于本票到期日还本付息。

（四）客户提取存款时，银行本应付给现金。如果现金不多，可发给存款银行开立的即期本票交给客户，以代替支付现钞。

四、本票的常用形式

本票的制票人相当于汇票的出票人和付款人结合为一人。任何票据的出票和付款重叠在一个当事人身上,该票据就是本票形式或是带有本票性质的票据。

(一) 商业本票(Trader's Notes)

商业本票是以贸易公司作为制作人而发出的即期本票。由于制票人的支付信誉不甚卓著,所以商业本票的收款人不愿接受。现在签发即期商业本票作为支付工具已经几乎没有了。

美国较大的公司签发远期商业本票,在美国称为"商业票据"(Commercial Papers)。它是由美国工商企业或金融机构发行的,无抵押品保证的远期本票。发行单位承诺将于到期日支付票面金额给持票人,而不提供任何资产保证,只凭其现有的清偿能力、盈利能力保证到期日一定偿还票款。

(二) 银行本票(Banker's Notes)

本票广泛地应用于银行,由商业银行签发即期付给记名收款人的不定额的银行本票可以当作现金,交给提取存款的客户。商业银行还发行即期定额付给来人的银行本票,又称银行券,客户拿现钱购买后,便于携带,也可当作货币,互相支付。但是,如果各大商业银行竞相发行即期定额付给来人的银行本票,流通到市场上,容易造成货币投放量骤增,扰乱国家纸币发行制度。因此,各国不允许商业银行发行定额不记名(来人)的本票,而归中央银行垄断发行,商业银行可以发行不定额的记名银行本票。

(三) 国际小额本票(International Money Order)

国际小额本票是由设在货币清算中心的银行作为签票行,发行该货币的国际银行本票,交给购票的记名收款人持票,带到该货币所在国以外的世界各地旅游时,如需用钱,即将小本票提交当地任何一家愿意兑付的银行,经审查合格,即可款予以兑付。然后将国际小额本票寄经货币清算中心的代理行,给票据交换,收进票款归垫。兑付的代理行如有签票行账户,即可借记账户归垫。

国际小额本票是在货币清算中心签发中心本票,让持票人带到海外使用,然后流向中心付款。发行国际小额本票的银行不拨头寸,收取了购票人的资金,可以等国外寄来本票托收时,再把资金付出,这对签票行非常有利。

(四) 旅行支票(Traveller's Cheque)

旅行支票仅从付款人就是该票的签发人这一点来看,它是带有本票性质的票据。但旅行支票的发行,实际上是购票人在发票机构的无息存款,兑付旅行支票等于是支取此笔存款,故旅行支票又带有支票性质。

购买旅行支票时旅游者要当着出售银行职员的面,在票上初签,然后带到国外旅游。当需要兑付时,持票人要当着付款代理行的面,在票上复签,经代理行核对复签与初签相符,即予付款,但需要扣减贴息,支付净款。旅行支票发行时,签发行占用旅游者的资金,直到旅行支票寄回索款。每当兑付之际,付款代理行向旅游者扣收贴息,银行两头受益。因此这是银行乐于承做、有利可图的业务。

(五) 流通存单(Certificate of Deposit,简称 CD)

存单最早是由美国各大银行开发发行的,它是一种大额、固定金额、固定期限的存款单证。它的期限为 3 个月、6 个月或 1 年,最长为 5 年。存单带有利息,到期日发行银行支付本利和。存单金额最低为 2.5 万美元,一般为 10 万、20 万、30 万至 100 万美元,最高的 1000 万美元,并以 100 万美元的固定金额最受欢迎,可以享受优惠率。

第二节　支　票

一、支票的定义及必要项目

《英国票据法》关于支票的定义是:Briefly speaking, a cheque is a bill of exchange drawn on a bank payable on demand. Detailedly speaking, a cheque is an unconditional order in writing addressed by the customer to a bank signed by that customer authorizing the bank to pay on demand a sum certain in money to or to the order of a specified person or to bearer. 中文意思是:简单地说,支票是以银行作为付款人的即期汇票。详细地说,支票是银行存款客户向他开立账户的银行签发的,授权该银行即期支付一定金额给一个特定人,或其指定人,或来人的无条件书面支付命令。

实际上,支票是存款人用以向存款银行支取存款而开出的票据,首先交给收款人,再由收款人凭票提示取款,或由收款人转让给别人向银行提示取款。

根据《日内瓦统一票据法》的规定,支票必须具备以下几项:(1)写明其为"支票"字样;(2)无条件支付命令;(3)付款银行名称和地点;(4)出票人名称和签字;(5)出票日期和地点(未载明出票地点者,出票人名称旁的地点视为出票地);(6)写明"即期"字样,如未写明即期者,仍视为见票即付;(7)一定金额;(8)收款人或其指定人。

现将上列项目在附式 4-2 的支票例样中标出。

附式 4-2

31st Jan. , 2000	①　　　　　　⑤
Payee	Cheque　　　　London, 31st Jan. , 2000 No, 652156
Tianjin Economic	③
& Development	BANK OF EUROPE
Corp	LONDON
	②　⑥　⑧
	Pay to Tianjin Economic & Development Corp.
	or order the sum of Four hundred ｜ ⑦ £450.0
£450.0	and fifty pounds
	For Sino — British Trading Co. , London④
	signature
652156	652156　　60…2116　　02211125　　000045000
↑	↑　　　　↑　　　　↑　　　　↑
Counterfoil	支票编号　付款行代号　出票人在付款行的　根据支票面额 磁性编码　磁性编码　支票专户账号磁码　加编的磁码

二、支票的种类

(一) 按有无收款人姓名记载分为记名支票和不记名支票

收款人姓名是支票的相对应记载事项。

1. 记名支票

记名支票写明收款人姓名,这种支票在取款时必须由收款人签章,在流通时以背书方式转让。收款人姓名可以由出票人在出票时记载,也可以由出票人授权补记。

2. 不记名支票

不记名支票不记载收款人姓名或仅记载"付来人"(To Bearer),取款时仅凭支票,付款人即向持票人付款,转让时可仅凭交付也可凭背书转让。

我国《票据法》未把收款人作为支票必须记载事项,在法律上认可了不记名支票这一形式。

(二) 按附加的付款保障方式分为划线支票和保付支票

1. 划线支票

划线支票是指在支票正面划有两条平行线,支票经划线后,只能通过银行收款,不得由持票人直接提款,其目的是使不正当持票人转让支票或领取票款更为困难。划线支票有两种(见图4-1):一种是普通划线(General Crossing),即在支票上仅划两条平行线,这种划线支票收款人可以委托任何银行向付款行收取票款;如在划线中加列"不可流通"(Not Negotiable),则出票人只对收款人负责,收款人虽仍可转让该支票,但受让人的权利不等于收款人;如在划线中加列"记入收款人账户"(Account Payee),则收款行只能将收到的票款记入收款人账户而不得直接付现。另一种划线支票称特殊划线(Special Crossing),在平行线中记有收款银行的名字,有这种划线的支票只能通过该指定收款银行向付款行提示付款。

出票人和持票人均有权划线。

我国《票据法》中没有支票划线制度的规定,但有对现金支票和转账支票的规定。实务中,在支票左上角加两条平行斜线可作为转账支票使用。

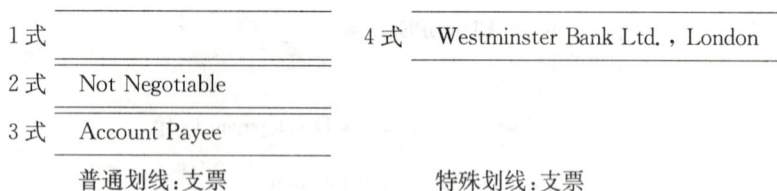

1式	＿＿＿＿＿＿	4式　Westminster Bank Ltd. , London
2式	Not Negotiable	
3式	Account Payee	
	普通划线:支票	特殊划线:支票

图4-1　支票划线类型

2. 保付支票

保付支票是指由付款银行在支票上加"保付"(Certified to Pay)字样并签章。银行在保付时,需查核出票人支票存款账户,并将相应金额转入保付支票账户名下。支票一经保付,即由银行承担付款责任,其他债务人一概免责;持票人可以不受付款提示期的限制,在支票过期后提示,银行仍要付款。

美国和日本有关于支票保付的规定,但日本的保付只限于在支票提示期限内有效。

我国《票据法》、《英国票据法》、《日内瓦统一票据法》均无支票保付的规定。

三、支票的止付与退票

支票是一种短期票据,是由出票人向收款人担保并向付款人授权(委托)的代替现金的支付工具,若出票人撤销其担保或授权,即为对支票的止付。

在支票实务中,如果支票遗失或毁坏,作为一种安全措施出票人可以止付支票。此外出票人认为收款人不愿或不能执行出票人为之签发支票的合同,出票人也可以止付支票。当出票人止付支票后,受票行兑付支票的一切责任和授权都告终止。但是支票止付,不能终止出票人或任何背书人对于正当持票人的责任。

撤销付款通知,如果先作口头的,以后必须有书面的通知,并以送达银行方为有效。银行接到止付通知后,应立即在客户分类账中记上止付详情,并将书面通知附此。如果该支票是来人支票,止付通知还应交持有目前生效的、兑付该客户的经常付款的所有分支行。如果客户止付通知被受票行收到在前,而受票行兑付在后,受票行就应承担由此产生的全部损失。

关于支票的止付,各国立法的规定不尽相同。

《日内瓦统一票据法》禁止在有效期内止付支票。这一规定类似于承兑后的汇票,承兑人作为主债务人必须承担付款责任。支票的主债务人亦为出票人,同样在有效期内(支付提示期)必须承担其保证付款的责任,以保障支票的流通和使用。过了有效期后,付款人有权决定是否对持票人的提示予以付款。英国法律规定,必须由出票人出具正式签字的书面止付通知并送达银行,才能有效地止付支付,因为支票是该出票人对银行的委托,亦只有该出票人才能撤销这项委托,而且付款银行应实际知悉这项止付才受其约束,推定知悉其不生效。美国与我国的《票据法》规定,失票人可以通知付款银行止付,也可以在法院提起诉讼或公示催告。

支票除因止付而遭退票外,还可能因下列原因被退票:

1. 空头支票。
2. 超过合理的提示期限,即支票是过期支票。
3. 背书欠缺或不连续。
4. 出票人签章不符合预留式样。
5. 破损支票,若损失支票要件(如出票人签字、支票金额等),银行当退票,但若要件完整不受破损影响,银行仍可通融支付。
6. 大小写金额不符。
7. 其他原因。

四、支票与汇票区别

支票是汇票的一种,所以支票与汇票有许多共性。但支票要发挥其支付作用,又具有许多不同于汇票的特殊性。

(一)支票是银行存款客户作为出票人,以他的开户行作为受票人签发的书面支付命令,授权它借记出票人账户,支付票款给收款人。因此出票人是银行客户,受票人是开户银行,支票是授权书。汇票的出票人、受票人是不受限定的任何人,汇票是委托书。

（二）支票支付工具,只有即期付款,没有承兑,也没有到期日的记载。汇票是支付和信用工具,它有即期、远期或板期几种期限,它有承兑行为,也可有到期日的记载。

（三）支票的主债务人是出票人,汇票的主债务人是承兑人。如在合理时间内未能正当提示要求付款,支票的背书人解除责任,但出票人不能解除责任。如遇延迟提示受到损失时,出票人只能解除受到损失的数额,而汇票的背书人和出票人均被解除责任。

（四）支票可以保证付款。为了避免出票人开出空头支票,保付支票提示时付款,《统一流通票据法》规定:受票行可应出票人或持票人的请求,在票面写上"证明"(CERTIFIED)字样并签字。这张支票就成了保付支票。保付银行的责任等于远期汇票受票行的承兑,它要将票款借记出票人账户,贷记在一个备付账户,准备用来付款,这时出票人和背书人的责任即告解除,完全由保付行承担付款责任,商业信用转为银行信用。汇票没有保付的做法,但有第三者保证。

（五）划线支票的受票行要对真正所有人负责付款,而即期汇票,或未划线支票的受票行要对持票人负责付款。

（六）支票可以止付,汇票承兑后即不可撤销。

（七）支票只能开出一张,汇票可以开出一套。

知识扩展

《中华人民共和国票据法》《英国票据法》《日内瓦统一票据法》中关于本票的不同规定

法律 项目	《中华人民共和国票据法》	《英国票据法》	《日内瓦统一票据法》之《日内瓦统一汇票本票法公约》
定义	本票是出票人签发的,承诺自己在见票时无条件支付确定的金额给收款人或者持票人的票据。	本票是一人向另一人签发的,保证即期或者定期或者在可以确定的将来时间,对某人或其指定人支付一定金额的无条件的书面承诺。	无明文规定。
本票的记载项目	《票据法》规定:本票必须记载事项:(一)表明"本票"的字样;(二)无条件支付的承诺;(三)确定的金额;(四)收款人名称;(五)出票日期;(六)出票人签章。	支付时间,支付金额,无条件支付。	《汇》第七十五条规定:本票应包含下列内容:1.票据主文中列有"本票"一词,并以开立票据所使用的文字表示之;2.无条件支付一定金额的承诺;3.付款日期的记载;4.付款地的记载;5.受款人或其指定人的姓名;6.签发本票的日期和地点的记载;7.签发本票的人的签名(签票人)。
持票人见票提示的有效提示期限	《票据法》规定:本票自出票日起一个月。自出票期起六个月(中国台湾省)。	无明文规定。	自出票日起一年。

《中华人民共和国票据法》《英国票据法》《日内瓦统一票据法》
有关支票的不同规定

项目 \ 法律	《中华人民共和国票据法》	《英国票据法》	《日内瓦统一票据法》之《支票统一法公约》
定义	第八十一条规定：支票是出票人签发的，委托办理支票存款业务的银行或者其他金融机构在见票时无条件支付确定的金额给收款人或者持票人的票据。	第七十三条规定：支票之定义。支票是以银行为付款人的凭票即付之汇票。除本节另有规定外，凡适用于凭票即付之汇票之本法条文也适用于支票。	无明文规定。
支票的记载项目	第八十四条规定：支票必须记载下列事项：(一)表明"支票"的字样；(二)无条件支付的委托；(三)确定的金额；(四)付款人名称；(五)出票日期；(六)出票人签章。	无明文规定。	《支票同意公约》(简称《支》)第一条规定：支票应包含下列内容：1.票据主文中列有"支票"一词，并以开立票据所使用的文字说明之；2.无条件支付一定金额的命令；3.付款人(受票人)的姓名；4.付款地的记载；5.开立支票的日期和地点的记载；6.开立支票的人(出票人)的签名。
提示付款的有效期	《票据法》第九十一条规定：支票的持票人应当自出票日起10天内提示付款。	第七十四条规定：在决定何为合理时间时，应考虑票据之性质、商业和银行惯例，以及具体案例的事实。	第二十九条规定：在出票国付款的支票，应于8日内作付款提示。 在付款国以外的国家签发的支票，应于20日或70日内作付款提示，该期限的长短，依签发地和付款地是否位于同一洲或不同洲而定。就本条而言，凡在一欧洲国家签发而在沿地中海的国家付款的支票，视为在同一洲签发及付款的支票。反之亦然。 上述期限，应依支票上所载的出票日期起算。
收款人	第八十六条规定：支票上未记载收款人名称的，经出票人授权，可以补记。出票人可以在支票上记载自己为收款人。	支票收款人的做法和本票汇票相同。	《支》规定：支票可以做成来人抬头。

续　表

法律 项目	《中华人民共和国票据法》	《英国票据法》	《日内瓦统一票据法》之 《支票统一法公约》
付款金额	第八十五条规定：支票上的金额可以由出票人授权补记，未补记前的支票，不得使用。 第八十七条规定：支票的出票人所签发的支票金额不得超过其付款时在付款人处实有的存款金额。出票人签发的支票金额超过其付款时在付款人处实有的存款金额的，为空头支票，禁止签发空头支票。	无明文规定。	利息记载无效。
与特别划线 有关的规定	无明文规定。	如持票人自己就是特别划线所指定银行，即可以自己提示付款，也可以在已有的划线中加一个委托银行代其提示付款。	《支》规定：一次划线只能有一个银行，而且一张支票最多有两个特别划线，其中一个必须是由另一个指定的银行所做的委托收款划线。
划线变更与 撤销	无明文规定。	第七十八条规定：划线是支票的重要部分。本法准许的划线是支票的重要部分。任何人涂抹划线，或除非为本法所准许加列或改变划线，都是非法的。	《支》第三十七条规定：普通划线得转换成特别划线，而特别划线则不得转换成普通划线。涂改划线或银行名称，应视为未涂改。
支票止付	无明文规定。	允许止付支票，但只能在收到由出票人签字的书面通知后才能够止付，如有确凿证据证明出票人已经死亡或者破产，付款人有权止付支票。	禁止在有效期内止付支票，即使出票人已经死亡或者破产。

(资料来源：百度文库，http://wenku.baidu.com/view/0c65cd225901020207409ca2.html)

知识扩展

美国史上最大的支票诈骗案

20 世纪 90 年代,美国联邦调查局经过绝密的调查,破获了该国历史上最大一起通过偷取大公司和大机构的支票进行诈骗的集团。该犯罪集团在近 4 年的时间里通过这一手段总共非法骗取了 4 亿多美元的资金,其每天的银行利息就将近 50 万美元。警方最后逮捕了 10 名作案人员,其中一些骨干分子是尼日利亚人。

据联邦调查局掌握的证据,该犯罪集团的总部设在美国洛杉矶,他们主要勾结联邦快递(FedEx)的邮递员和一些善于偷盗的个人,偷取一些大公司和大机构的转账支票或空白支票,然后把这些支票改头换面,将里面的钱取出存入该集团在美国、印度尼西亚、塞内加尔、德国、英国以及香港等地的银行账户。这些账户都由该集团的骨干分子掌握。一些世界著名的公司或机构,如加州大学、福克斯电视台、索尼图片社都曾遭到该集团的"毒手"。由于这些公司都是大公司,每天来往的支票很多,偶尔丢失一两张支票也不会引起注意,但等到他们发现自己的支票被人非法取走时,这些支票里的钱早已存入了别的银行账户,成了别人的钱。

美国联邦调查局早在案发的 4 年前就发现有这样一个非法集团在活动,并调集多名有经验的调查人员成立专案组,还将这种行动命名为"支票行动"。无奈该犯罪集团的组织实在过于严密,调查人员在费尽千辛万苦之后,才于 4 年后将这一案子破获。根据警方的调查显示,在该组织内"上级"和"下级"之间往往都是单线联系,这样即使是集团内部的人都不知道其他人在干什么。该组织的一些成员甚至不知道组织内总共有多少人,彼此互不认识。这些都给破案造成了很大困难。

负责此案的联邦调查局官员里克·韦德特别强调,这是美国历史上最重大的支票诈骗案。此案涉及的金额如此巨大,一时间成为国际媒体关注的焦点。事后,警方公布了两名犯罪嫌疑人的情况。其中一位被告名叫哈维·马歇尔,41 岁,曾经当过邮递员。他被控仅在 1996 年中的几天内就作案 3 次,所得非法收入分别为 1300 美元、2170 美元和 41 000 美元。另一位被告名叫詹姆斯·费尔,他被控仅在 1997 年 8 月和 9 月间共偷取价值 32.4 万美元的支票。

负责调查此案的联邦调查局官员韦德说,这个包括 6 名尼日利亚人在内的犯罪集团,是"美国历史上最大的支票诈骗集团。"他还说"与其他犯罪组织不同的是,他们都是十分专业和老练的罪犯。他们不同于从邮件偷窃社会保险支票的青少年,他们非常清楚自己的行动,预先有策划,并建立一个组织以执行盗窃计划。"

(资料来源:《人民日报海外版》,2000 年 07 月 29 日第三版。)

本章案例 ─■

利用本票的变造、伪造欺诈案

G省M外贸公司经介绍与Q工贸集团建立了外贸代理业务关系,签订了外贸代理协议。Q集团于某年7月将一笔五金工具出口业务的外商与供货厂家一并介绍给了M外贸公司。这笔贸易涉及100多万元港币,买方为香港P公司,供货厂家为Z省某市的五金工具企业。M外贸公司审核Q集团提供的资料后,决定承做此笔代理业务。

同年8月,经多方协商,由M外贸公司与香港P公司签订了100多万港币的外销合同。然后,由Q集团与五金工具厂签订采购合同。外销合同签订采用信用证结算。合同签订后,P公司认为信用证手续太麻烦,要求改为银行本票结算,并同意在装货港一手交票、一手交货,并经Q集团同意。8月下旬,P公司派人依约前来验货,M外贸公司催促P公司出示银行本票,P公司出示了一张本票影印件,内容不全,金额空缺,P公司的解释是因现在买票占压很多资金,故在取得出票行同意后买来这个号码,并称此种做法有担保性质。某银行G省分行当即提醒M外贸公司,这种说法纯属捏造。P公司在M外贸公司强烈要求下,于8月29日从香港邮来一张银行本票的传真件,内容、要式、签名齐备,金额为45万港币。某银行G省分行应M外贸公司要求,于8月30日和9月3日两次致电出票行,请其就该张本票加以确认。9月5日出票行回电称,从未开出过所查号码和金额的支票,提请M公司注意。

9月4日,P公司派人带一名专家前来验货,提出包装箱规格不一,牢度欠佳,要求更换包装,并改为空运。M外贸公司当时同意了,双方商定于9月15日最后交割。但9月7日,M外贸公司不慎将已查出本票有问题的信息泄漏给了P公司。次日P公司的代办人员借故全部离去。M外贸公司更换货物包装后准备空运,通知P公司前来验货。但P公司人员一直未来,只是指责M外贸公司定价太高,声称不能接受这笔生意。

某银行G省分行将本票传真至出票行后电话查询,出票行告知:本票号码、出票日期、签字及收款人全部无误,只是实际出票金额要比传真金额小得多。因规定限制,无法告诉具体开出额。

(资料来源:蒋琴儿、秦定:《国际结算》,清华大学出版社2007年版。)

关键词

本票、支票、商业本票、银行本票、旅行支票、普通支票、划线支票、特殊划线支票、记名支票、无记名支票、现金支票、转账支票、空白支票

思考题

1. 汇票与本票的主要异同有哪些?
2. 本票和支票分别有哪些种类?
3. 本票的必要记载事项有哪些?

第五章　托　收

★ **学习目标**

　　掌握托收的基本概念、托收的当事人、跟单托收的流程、跟单托收的交单方式及交单条件、跟单托收项下的融资方式及融资特点、托收的风险及其防范、托收的国际法律及惯例等。

★ **本章概要**

　　托收是一种传统的国际结算方式。由于跟单信用证结算方式的周期长、费用高、比较复杂，托收方式结算变得越来越流行。本章主要介绍托收的概念及流程、托收的当事人及其责任、托收的种类及特点、跟单托收的交单方式、托收项下的贸易融资、托收的风险及其防范等。

第一节 托收的定义

托收(Collection)是国际结算中常用的方式,它是指收款人或债权人为了取得因劳务、商品及其他交易引起的应收款项,将有关单据交与本地银行,委托该银行通过其国外代理行向付款人或债务人交单取款的业务。国际商会《托收统一规则》(URC522)对托收作了如下定义:

"(1)'托收'是指银行收到的指示,对下述(2)项中定义的单据进行处理,以求:

① 获得付款和/或承兑,或

② 凭付款和/或承兑交单,或

③ 凭其他条件交单。

(2) 单据是指金融单据和/或商业单据:

① '金融单据'是指汇票、本票、支票或其他用来获得现金付款的类似凭证;

② '商业单据'是指发票、运输单据、所有权单据或其他类似单据,或其他任何不附金融单据的单据。

(3)'光票托收'是指不附商业单据的金融单据的托收。

(4)'跟单托收'是指对下列单据的托收:

a. 附有商业单据的金融单据;

b. 不附金融单据的商业单据。"

根据上述定义可知,托收分成光票托收和跟单托收两种。光票托收中,债权人委托银行为金融单据获得付款或承兑。

跟单托收中,债权人委托银行凭债务人的付款或承兑或其他条件向其交单,债权人为得到债务人的付款或承兑或其他行为,所提交的单据是商业单据,可以有金融单据,也可以没有金融单据。

国际贸易结算中,大多是跟单托收,其基本做法是:出口方先行发货,然后备妥包括运输单据在内的有关商业单据,并开出汇票(或不开汇票),把全套单据交出口地银行,委托其通过进口地的分行或代理行,向进口方收取货款,凭进口方的付款或承兑向进口方交付全套单据。

第二节 托收的当事人及其责任

一、托收的当事人

托收业务涉及的基本当事人有四个:委托人、托收行、代收行和付款人,此处还可以有提示行和需要时的代理等两个当事人。

(一) 委托人(Principal)

又称"本人"是委托银行取得国外付款人的付款或承兑后向其交单的人,通常就是出口方、出票人及托运人。

（二）托收行（Remitting Bank）

它是委托人的代理人，为委托人转托国外分行或代理行办理托收的银行，通常为出口地银行。

（三）代收行（Collecting Bank）

它是托收行的代理人，接受托收行的指示，在取得国外付款人的付款或承兑后向其交单，并最终得到付款的银行，通常为进口地银行。

（四）付款人（Drawee）

它是按照托收指示作成提示的被提示人，通常为进口商。

（五）提示行（Presenting Bank）

它是向汇票付款人作成提示的代收行。如果托收行不指定一家特定提示行，多数情况下提示行就是代收行，但也有时提示行与代收行是分离的两家银行。

（六）需要时的代理（Representative in Case of Need）

这是委托人指定的在付款地的代理人，其作用是在付款人拒绝付款、拒收货物时，代表委托人接受单据并处理货物。例如为货物办理存仓、投保、转售及运回等事宜。需要时代理可以为委托人对汇票作参加承兑或参加付款以取得单据，但是除非委托人在托收申请书中明确记载需要时的代理的名称、地址及权限，否则有关银行不接受需要时的代理的任何指示。

托收当事人之间的关系见图 5-1

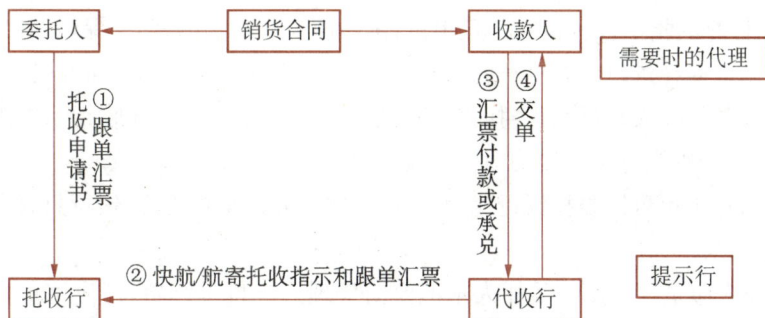

图 5-1 托收当事人之间的关系

二、托收当事人的责任

托收当事人的责任具体分析如下：

（一）委托人

跟单托收的委托人，即国际货物买卖合同的出口商，在委托银行办理托收时，需填写托收指示（也称托收申请书），如果银行接受委托，则该托收指示为委托人与托收行之间的契约。委托人有下列义务：

(1) 托收指示应表明该托收受《国际商会托收统一规则》(URC522)约束。

(2) 委托人填写的托收指示应按情况包含下列内容：

① 委托人的详情,包括名称、地址、电话、传真、电传号码。

② 付款人的详情,包括名称、地址、电话、传真、电传号码。

③ 发出托收的银行的详情,包括全称、邮政及电讯(SWIFT)地址、电话、传真号码和编号。

④ 提示行(如指定的话)的详情,包括名称、地址、电话、传真、电传号码。通常当委托人了解付款人的账户且该行资信良好的情况下,会指定其为提示行。

⑤ 托收的金额和币种。

⑥ 随附单据清单及其份数。

⑦ 交单的条件:凭付款和/或承兑;凭其他条件。

⑧ 托收的费用,表明可否放弃。一般情况下,进口商和出口商各自负担本国银行的费用,但委托人应对银行收取的服务费用承担责任,如果付款人不愿支付费用时,代收行可将应收取的费用从已收货款中扣除。若托收指示明确规定须由进口商负担的托收费不得放弃时,一旦进口商拒付费用,代收行将不交单,对因延误交单而引起的任何后果不负责任。

⑨ 所托收的利息(如进口方逾期付款),表明可否放弃。

⑩ 付款方式和付款通知的形式。代收行收妥货款后一般即划入托收行账户,账户行向托收行发出贷记通知书,托收行再向委托人付款。故委托人在托收指示中应规定用电汇不是用信汇方式划拨款项,目前一般都采用电汇方式。

⑪ 在拒付时的指示。进口商一旦拒付,出口商应对货物的存仓、保险、转售或运回作出安排。如出口商在进口地有可靠的代理人,则应在托收指示中指定需要时的代理,或在汇票上记载预备付款人,以代表委托人处理货物。但必须同时在托收指示中规定该预备付款人的权限,否则银行将不接受预备付款人的指示。

在托收指示中也可以委托银行代为处理,但银行并不承担责任,银行只就它自己同意的条件采取行动。

(3) 委托人应负担费用。委托人不但要向代理人支付手续费,还应该负担代理人在执行委托时支出的各项费用,如电讯费、代办费等。

(二) 托收行

1. 托收行应完全按照委托人的托收指示行事

托收行在向代收行寄单时必须附上和委托人指示严格一致的托收指示。

2. 托收行应按有关惯例的规定和常规行事

《国际商会托收统一规则》(URC522)规定,如委托人未指定代收行,委托行可以自行指定代收,万一托行收发出的指示未被执行,托收行不承担责任。它还规定,托收行以通常方式邮寄单据,对传递过程中的延误或灭失所引起的后果概不负责。

对于其他需要处理的业务,凡委托人在托收指示中未予规定的,托收行按惯例和常规办事,可不承担风险责任和费用。

3. 托收行应以善意和合理的谨慎行事

托收行应以专业的标准来衡量银行行为是否符合这一要求。比如将代理托收过程中发生的事情及时通知委托人，并及时向代收行发出指示等。如未及时发出，银行应承担过失责任。

4. 托收行对所收单据的免责

托收行对收到的单据，仅负责确定单据表面上系托收指示中列明的单据，即仅审核单据的种类和数目应和托收指示所列一致，如有遗漏或所列不符，应立即通知委托人。银行无须对单据进行审查，可按原样寄单，对交易所载的完整性和真实性及其法律效力不负责任。

5. 毫无延误的付款

收妥的款项（按情况扣除手续费、支出或费用）必须按托收指示的要求毫无延误地交由发出托收指示的一方支配。

（三）代收行

代收行作为代理人，其基本责任与托收行相同，即应严格遵照托收指示行事；按惯例和常规行事；以善意和合理的谨慎行事；代收行对收到的单据内容及其有效性不承担责任。代收行的其他责任为：

1. 保管好单据

跟单托收是通过银行凭单据取得付款人的承兑和付款。因此，当付款人未履行交单条件时，代收行不能把单据交给付款人，并有义务妥善保管好单据。

2. 托收情况的通知

代收行应按托收指示规定的方式毫不延迟地将付款通知、承兑通知或拒付通知送交托收行；付款通知中应详细列明收到的金额、已扣除的费用以及处理款项的方法；一旦发生拒付，代收行应尽力查明拒付原因。

托收行在收到拒付通知后，必须作出处理单据的相应指示，在发出拒付通知的60天内，代收行仍未接到相应指示的，可将单据退回托收行，代收行不再承担任何责任。

知识扩展

托收统一规则（URC522）

托收统一规则（URC522）全称是 Uniform Rules for Collections。是国际商会为统一托收业务的做法，同时为了减少托收业务各有关当事人可能产生的矛盾和纠纷，制定的协调国际贸易结算中托收业务的统一规则。它的前身是1958年国际商会草拟的《商业单据托收统一规则》。1978年国际商会对该规则进行了修订，改名为《托收统一规则》（The Uniform Rules for Collection，ICC Publication No. 322）。1995年再次修订，称为《托收统一规则》国际商会第522号出版物（简称《URC522》），1996年1月1日实施。需要注意的是，该规则本身不是法律，因而对一般当事人没有约束力。只有在有关当事人事先约定的条件下，才受该惯例的约束。

> 《托收统一规则》(URC522)共 7 部分,共 26 条包括总则及定义、托收的形式和结构,提示方式,义务与责任,付款,利息、手续费及其他费用,其他规定。根据《托收统一规则》规定托收意指银行根据所收的指示,处理金融单据或商业单据,目的在于取得付款和/或承兑,凭付款和/或承兑交单,或按其他条款及条件交单。上述定义中所涉及的金融单据是指汇票、本票、支票或其他用于付款或款项的类似凭证;商业单据是指发票、运输单据、物权单据或其他类似单据,或除金融单据之外的任何其他单据。
>
> (资料来源:国际商会,ICC。)

第三节　跟单托收的交单条件

跟单托收依据交单条件分为承兑交单、即期付款交单和远期付款交单三种。

一、承兑交单

承兑交单(Documents against Acceptance,缩写为 D/A)就是凭远期汇票的承兑而交出单据。单据凭承兑汇票交出,则代收行对单据就不承担进一步的责任。因为实现了托收行的指示,履行了自己的义务。D/A 程序见图 5-2。

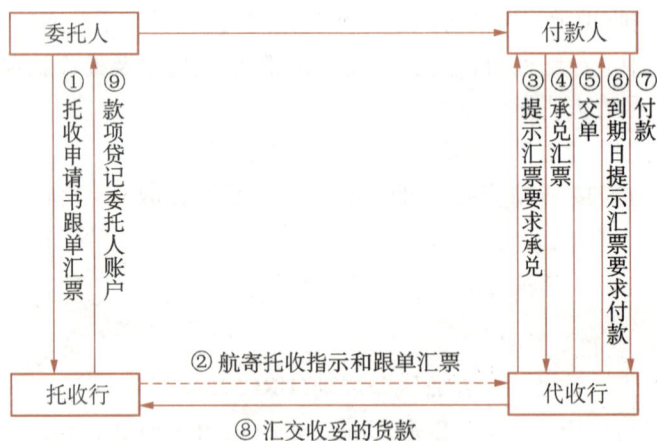

图 5-2　承兑交单程序

二、即期付款交单

即期付款交单(Documents against Payment,缩写为 D/P 或 D/P at Sight),就是凭即期汇票付款或简单地凭付款而交出单据。单据凭汇票付款或简单地付款而交出,代收行不承担进一步的责任。D/P 程序见图 5-3。

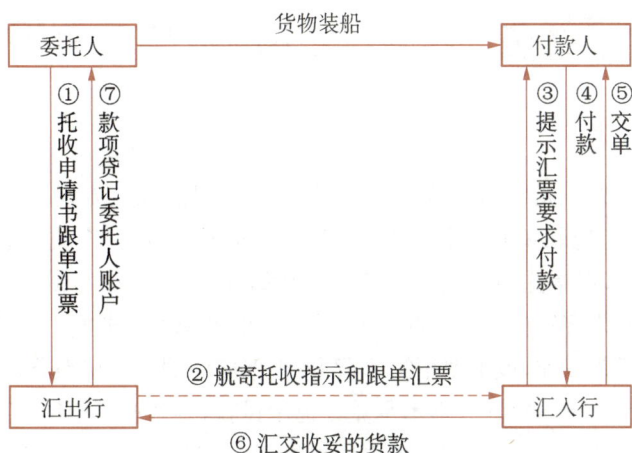

图5-3 即期付款交单程序

三、远期付款交单

远期付款交单(D/P at ×× Days After Sight),就是凭远期汇票付款而交出单据。远期付款交单的**缺点**是在"远期"的时间间隔之内,如果货物已经抵达目的港,而买方尚未付款,不能得到单据,无法提取货物,以致货物滞留港口码头,易遭受损失或罚款。由于代收行执行托收指示,不得不将单据延至付款以后交出,故 URC522 明确指出:"如果托收包含在将来日期付款的汇票,以及托收指示注明商业单据凭着付款而交出,则单据实际交出只能凭着这样的付款,代收行对产生于延迟交单的任何后果不负责任"。

委托人为了防止远期付款交单与承兑交单混淆。可在托收指示上写明"付款后才能交单"。对于汇票"远期"的时间掌握应该不得长于海上航行时间。远期付款交单程序见图5-4。

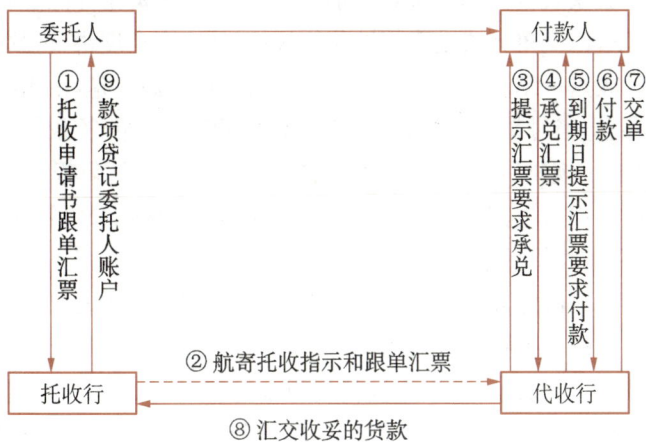

图5-4 远期付款交单程序

第四节 跟单托收中的汇票与单据

一、托收中的汇票

托收汇票的出票人是出口商或卖方,付款人是进口商或买方,收款有三种情况:1.受益人是收款人,当它把跟单托收汇票提交托收行时,受益人应作成托收背书交托收行。2.托收行是收款人,汇票注明托收出票条款,用以表明为了托收目的而作成汇票收款人,当它把跟单托收汇票寄给代收行之前,均应作成托收背书给代收行。3.代收行是收款人,代收行收到跟单汇票以前,该汇票不需要背书,汇票应注明托收出票条款。

跟单托收中代收行向付款人提示承兑或提示付款,倘若遭到拒绝,银行应尽力查明拒绝承兑或拒绝付款的原因,但没有义务去作拒绝证书。事实上也没有必要去作拒绝证书,因为银行作为持票人,是出票人的代理人,根本没有追索的对象。如果出口商为了诉讼而在托收指示中要求作拒绝证书,代收行应该照办,费用由委托人负担,但这种情况很少发生。

即期付款交单中,付款人在银行提示单据时即行付款,所以汇票的作用并不重要,完全可以由商业发票取代,所以即期付款交单方式,出口商可以开立即期汇票,也可以不开,但远期付款交单和承兑交单中,汇票是必不可少的。

二、托收中的运输单据

因运输方式的不同,运输单据可分为海运提单、航空运单、铁路运单、多式联运单据等。在托收中最常用的海运提单,因为海运提单具有货物所有权凭证的性质。跟单托收的本意,就是出口商将作为货物所有权凭证的商业单据向进口商提示,进口商只有付款或承兑后才能取得货物所有权凭证,凭此提取货物。托收的业务程序就是,建立在交付物权凭证的基础上。由于航空运输和铁路运输中,运输单据并不具有货物所有权凭证的性质,必须在运输单据上表明收货人的名称,货到目的地,由收货人凭身份证明有效证件提货。因此,在这种情况下,以交单方式是不能转移物权的,从这个角度讲,付款交单或承兑交单均没有意义。但托收这一结算方式还是可以使用的。具体做法是,由银行作为收货人,委托货运代理提货存仓,当付款人付款或承兑后,银行开出提货单,授权付款人提货。但是,按《国际商会托收统一规则》(URC522)的规定:"在没有事先征得银行同意时,货物不应该直接运交银行或以银行或其指定人为收货人"。所以,在使用非货物所有权凭证的商业单据作托收时,应在托收指示中明确说明在该项托收业务中代收行或其指定人为收货人。但必须特别注意的是,《国际商会托收统一规则》(URC522)中又规定:"即使有特别指示,银行也没有责任就与跟单据托收有关的货物采取行动,包括货物的仓储和保险,银行只就它自身同意的条件、时间和程度根据不同情况采取这样的行动"。在一般情况下,代理人应严格遵照委托人指示办事。如果银行决定不办理它收到的托收或任何有关指示,它必须立即通知委托人。但上述情况却是一个例外,即使委托人在托收指示中明确要求代收行代办提取货物事项,而代收行只能在有限度的条件下办理,代收行甚至可以不通知委托人。所以,以交货的方式取代交单方式办理托收,单据只作为履约证书,银行在付款人付款或承兑后,向其交货,委托人应特别注意选择合适的代收行(或委托托收行选择),以保证安全地处理货物。

三、其他托收单据

除了汇票和运输单据之外,跟单托收委托人还必须提交其他商业单据,其种类取决于合同条款,所提交的单据应能在表面上证明卖方已履行了所承担的合同义务。比如以CIF方式成交,卖方的义务是将货物装上船并办理运输保险,所以卖方提交的单据中应包括已装船提单和保险单;若以FOB方式成交,卖方并无办理保险的责任,当然就不必提交保险单;以FCA、CPT、CIP方式成交,卖方的交货责任是把货物交给承运人监管,则在海洋运输的贸易中,卖方可以提交备运提单而不必一定要提交已装船提单。发票是必要的单据,其他如装箱单、产地证明等,都应按合同要求制作。

以托收方式结算的贸易合同,除特殊单据外,一般不像信用证方式那样对商业单据作专门的规定。出口商根据合同义务,决定应提交的单据种类、份数以及单据的内容。托收行则核对单据的种类和份数是否与托收指示中所记载的一致,没有审核单据内容的义务。但如果托收单据的种类、份数和内容与合同不符,买方有权拒付。

综上所述,跟单托收是一种凭单付款的结算方式,故而单据在结算过程中十分重要。卖方必须严格按照合同内容、妥善制作单据,避免由于单据不能在表面上证明卖方已履行合同义务而遭到买方拒付。

第五节 托收风险与资金融通

一、托收中出口商的风险与防险措施

跟单托收方式是建立在商业信用基础上的,若进口商由于某种原因,不按合同履行付款义务,出口商就将蒙受损失。

出口商在跟单托收中,可能承担如下风险:

(1)发货后进口地的货价下跌,进口商不愿付款赎单或承兑取单,就借口货物规格不符,或包装不良等原因要求减价。

(2)因政治或经济原因,进口国家改变进口政策,进口商没有领到进口许可证,或是申请不到进口所需的外汇,以致货物抵达进口地而无法进口,或不能付款。

(3)进口商因破产或倒闭而无力支付货款等。

即使跟单托收方式给出口商带来许多风险,但因当前国际市场出口竞争日益剧烈,出口商在急于求售的情况下,或者是货物本身质量的关系,有时不得不接受这种方式,为了避免风险,出口商最好在国外有自己的机构,或事先在当地找好代理人,以便在出口货物遭到拒付时,由自己的国外机构或代理人代办货物的存仓、保险、转售或运回等手续。当

然在买卖成交之前应该做好调查工作,如进口商的资信情况、经营作风、进口地的市场销售情况、进口国的贸易和外汇管制法令、海关的规定,以及进口商是否已领到该批货物的进口许可证,或者是否已申请到外汇等等。此外,对于托收商品的成交贸易条件,应争取CIF贸易条件。出口商委托银行办理托收业务时最好能够提供进口商的账户行作为代收行,以利于进口商获取融资,按时付款。

二、银行在托收业务中的资金融通

在托收业务中,银行只作为代理人行事,不提供信用保障,但是在适当的条件下,银行也可以为进出口商提供融资便利,具体方式有以下几种:

(一) 托收押汇(Collection Bill Purchased,简称 B/P)

在通常情况下,出口商将全套单据交给托收行后,必须等到进口商付款且托收行收妥以后才能结汇,资金占用时间较长。如果托收行承做托收押汇,会在出口商委托时买入全套商业单据,提前支付绝大部分贷款给出口商,从而缓解其资金周转的困难。在进行托收押汇时,托收行按汇票或发票金额扣除从押汇日到估计收款日的利息及银行费用,将净额交付给出口商,托收行成为全套单据的正当持有人,因此押汇也叫作议付。

由于托收行凭押汇成为全套单据(包括汇票与物权单据)的正当持有人,因此有权要求付款人支付货款。在正常情况下,这是托收行收回押汇款项的主要渠道。如果付款人拒付,托收行可以向出口商追索,但如出口商破产倒闭,追索无望时,托收行可以寻求物权的保障,通过处理单据及货物来回笼资金,并且保留就不足部分对出口商索偿直至参与破产清理的权利。

但是,为了防止遭进口商拒付的风险,避免陷入追索出口商甚至被迫变卖货物的被动局面,托收行在叙做托收押汇时都比较慎重,托收行必须对出口商的资信充分信任,对其海外客户及交易的可靠性有足够了解。对进口商的正常付款有相当把握,而且托收行应事先与出口商签订质押书(Letter of Hypothecation)。只有这样,托收行才可能提供押汇融资,而且即便如此,押汇的利率也是比较高的,因此,这不是一种常用的融资方式。

(二) 托收预付款(Advance against Collection)

托收预付款实际上是部分押汇与部分托收的结合做法。托收行只对托收总金额的一定比例提供押汇融资,在扣除相应的利息及费用后,将净额预付给出口商,其余部分作托收处理。如果进口商支付货款,则托收部分款项就结汇给出口商,押汇部分由托收行回收。如果进口商拒付,则托收部分与银行无关,押汇部分银行可向出口商追索,如果追索不着根据托收行对单据及货物享有的质权,银行可以处理货物或单据回收押汇资金,若有结余则应归还出口商。

可见托收预付款中托收行承担的风险与押汇业务中承担的风险很相似,只是因为预付款是针对部分托收款项,而押汇针对全部托收款项,银行的风险头寸要小得多,而且通过质权弥补损失的可靠性更大些,因此托收预付款银行的风险要小一些。

(三) 承兑信用(Acceptance Credit)

这是指进口商或出口商签发以融资银行为付款人的融通汇票,由融资银行提供承兑信用,然后通过贴现以取得资金的融资方式。

出口商利用承兑信用融资时,会签发一份票面金额不超过托收金额、付款期限略长于托收期限的融通汇票。该汇票以托收行为付款人,连同其他托收单据交与托收行。托收行暂不承兑该汇票,而是等收到代收行传来的付款人承兑托收汇票的通知后才承兑融通汇票,然后可以直接在托收行办理贴现,也可以由出口商持汇票到其他银行贴现。届时付款人支付的货款就由托收行保留以弥补贴现支出,或待贴现行到期提示时支付票款。

进口商利用承兑信用而开出融通汇票,其目的是利用借来的资金付款赎单,然后及时地处理或转卖货物,利用回笼的资金在融通汇票到期前支付给承兑银行。如果一切顺利,进口商可以不动用自己的资金而完成交易并赢利。因此,融通汇票的面额应略大于托收金额,以便使扣除承兑费用和贴现利息后的净额正好能满足付款赎单的需要。但若银行对汇票金额有限制,例如,银行为获得物权的抵押而只愿承兑不超过货款70%的融通汇票,则进口商必须照办。

在承兑信用融资方式中,银行控制风险的主要手段是事先与出口商或进口商签订承兑信用额度协议,以及由抵押品或质押书确立的物权担保。

(四) 信托收据(Trust Receipt,简称 T/R)

在远期付款交单方式中,在承兑汇票之后、付款到期之前,是进口商寻求融资的时间。此时,信托收据就是一种很好的融资工具。所谓信托收据,是指进口商承认以信托的方式向代收行借出全套商业单据时出具的证明。进口商借得单据后,处理货物,回笼资金,在承兑汇票到期时支付足额货款,收回汇票,赎回信托收据,该项融资业务即告结束。

这种做法是 D/P 托收的变通,又称为见票后若干天付款交单,以开出信托收据换取单据(D/P at ××Days after Sight to Issue Trust Receipt in Exchange for Documents,简称 D/P,T/R),其业务程序见图 5-5,信托收据格式见附式 5-1。

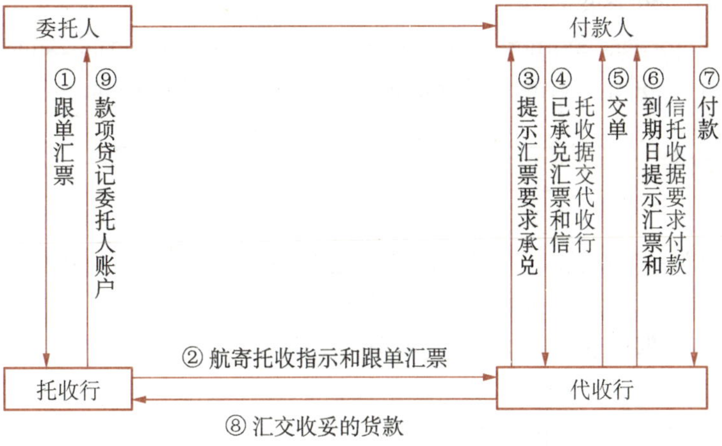

图 5-5 D/P,T/R程序

附式 5 - 1

信托收据格式
T R U S T R E C E I P T

TO：_____　　　　　　　　　　place _____ , Date _____

Received from the Said Bank（a full set of shipping documents evidencing）the merchandise having an invoice value of _____ say _____ as follows：

MARKS AND NUMBERS	QUANTITY	DESCRIPTION OF MERCHANDISE	STEAMER

　　And in consideration of such delivery in trust，the undersigned here by undertakes to land，pay customs duty and/or other charges or expenses，store，hold and sell deliver to purchaser the merchandise specified here in，and to receive the proceeds as Trustee for the said Bank，and the undersigned promises and agrees not to sell the said merchandise or any part there of on credit，but only for cash and for a total amount not less than the invoice value specified above unless otherwise authorised by the said Bank in writing.

　　The undersigned also undertakes to ··

　　The undersigned further acknowledges assents and agrees that in the event the whole or any part of the merchandise specified here in is sold or delivered to a purchaser or purchasers derived or to be derived from such sale or delivery shall be considered the property of the said Bank and the undersigned here by grants to the said Banks full authority to collect such proceeds directly from purchaser or purchasers without reference to the undersigned.

　　The guarantor，as another undersigned，guarantees to the said Bank the faith and proper fulfillment of the terms and conditions of this Trust Receipt.

Guaranteed by：_____　　Signed by：_____

　　　　　　　_____　　　　　　　　_____

　　凭信托收据提取的货物其产权仍属银行，进口商处于代为保管货物的地位，称为被信托人(Trustee)或代保管人(Bailee)。他的义务是：

　　(1) 将信托收据项下货物和其他货物分开保管。

　　(2) 售得的货款应交付银行，或暂代银行保管，但在账目上须与自有资金分别开立。

　　(3) 不得把该项下的货物抵押给他人。

　　代收银行则是信托人(Truster)，他的权利是：

　　(1) 可以随时取消信托，收回借出的商品。

（2）如商品已被出售，可随时向进口商收回货款。

（3）如进口商倒闭清理，对该项下的货物或货款有优先债权。

利用信托收据融资时，受托人（进口商）有可能违反信托规定，不愿或无力退还货物或货款，这是一个潜在的风险。发生这种情况时，如果该项融资得到过委托人的同意或授权，则风险由委托人自负；如果未经委托人同意，而是由代收行主动提供这项融资，则风险由代收行承担，届时代收行必须对托收行支付票款，就好像是进口商已经支付一样。因为此时代收行已经无法退回全套单据了。

（五）担保提货（Shipping Guarantee）

在有些特殊情况下，托收项下的货物可能早于商业单据抵达进口地港口。由于没有正本提单，进口商无法提货，而延期提货会使进口商增加额外开支，或者承受进口商品行情下跌、市价回落的风险。因此进口商会向代收行申请银行担保，凭担保在没有正本提单的情况下提货，银行保证向承运人赔偿因为不凭正本提单交货而遭受的损失。进口商应向代收行保证付款赎单，并且保证在收到正本提单后退还银行担保。为了防止进口商凭担保骗取货物，银行应对进口商作审查，确信其为该批货物的收货人，并且可以要求进口商对代收行提供担保，以备不测。

本章案例

承兑交单(O/A)顶下产生的拖欠

1999年春季广东交易会，广东某进出口公司（以下称广东公司）与埃及 HUSSEIN 公司建立了业务关系，HUSSEIN 公司向广东公司订购了近3万美元的货物，双方同意以信用证方式结算。初次合作较为愉快，广东公司及时地收回货款。之后，BUSSEIN 公司继续向广东订购货物，货物总值达26万美元。这次，HUSSEIN 公司提出了 D/A 60天的付款方式，要求广东接受。广东公司急于开发市场，接受了 HUSSEIN 公司的付款要求。货物发出后，广东公司及时议付单据，HUSSEIN 公司承兑了汇票并接受了货物。可是汇票到期之日，该公司拒绝付款。广东公司自行催收一年后，HUSSEIN 公司以货物质量问题，不符合当地市场需求，货物仍未售出等为由，坚决拒付货款。

广东公司在货权完全丧失的情况下，委托东方国际保理中心（以下简称东方中心）向埃及 HUSSEIN 公司追讨。开始，该公司的态度极为强硬。坚持说货物尚未卖出，不能付款。为了把损失降到最低点，东方中心向他们提出退单、退货的要求。在强大的追讨压力下，该公司承认，他们早已售完广东公司的货物，并把货款用到了其他生意上。由于该笔生意的失败，加上公司的经营及管理不善，导致该公司亏损严重，已近关门倒闭的边缘，根本无法偿还广东公司的欠款。经过进一步的调查，东方中心发现这家公司还有一些库存商品可以变卖。最后，广东公司追回了4万美元。

即期付款交单情况下的托收风险

某年某月，某服装贸易公司与美国一家公司签订了一笔10万美元的服装出口合同，价格条件为 FOB 上海,支付条件为 DIP AT SIGHT,出口货代公司为买方指定的 ABC 公司。由于在此之前公司与该客户曾采用 HC 支付方式通过该货代公司做过两笔订单,所以没有对该货代公司进行详细了解。该服装贸易公司将货物发出后,将包括三份正本货代提单在内的全套货运单据通过中国银行转交对方指定的代收行收款,但在规定的时间内没有收到。在此后的一个多月内,对方一会儿说没见着单据,一会儿说正在和银行商量赎单,一会儿又传来一份真假难辨的银行付款底单。在忍无可忍的情况下,公司只好指示代收行将全套单据转让给公司在美国的分公司,让其先代收此货然后再与买方交涉,以避免港口滞港费的损失。当美国分公司拿着正本提单去提货时,发现货已被买方提走。公司与买方交涉,但对方既不回传真,也不接电话,随即公司派法律顾问带人赶往上海,准备对 ABC 公司采取行动。赶到上海时,ABC 公司早已人去楼空,再到工商部门一调查,才发现该公司根本没有货代资质,仅为一家运输咨询公司。在万般无奈的情况下,该出口公司只好采取委托授权的方式,通过美国分公司请美国律师起诉进口方。但得知该客户已申请了破产保护。按美国的法律,该出口商只能参加破产清算,经计算,如参加清算,其所得可能还不够支付律师费用,公司只好撤诉。

(资料来源:蒋琴儿,秦定:《国际结算》,清华大学出版社 2007 年版。)

关键词

跟单托收、光票托收、D/P、D/A、T/R、URC522

思考题

1. 什么是托收?托收的当事人有哪些?
2. 跟单托收中的交单方式有哪几种?各有什么特点?
3. 托收项下的贸易融资方式有哪些?
4. 托收方式下的风险有哪些?如何防范?

第六章　信用证

★ **学习目标**

　　掌握信用证的概念、特点、种类,了解信用证业务的基本程序,明晰信用证业务带来的风险及如何防范这些风险。

★ **本章概要**

　　在中国的进出口贸易实践中,大约 60% 的进出口企业选择通过信用证的方式来结算货款,因此,信用证业务是重要的贸易结算方式之一。本章首先介绍了信用证业务的定义、性质特点,并在此基础上以国际商会制定的《跟单信用证统一惯例》为依据,对信用证业务中涉及的重要概念、信用证种类以及基本的业务流程进行了详细讲述,同时对该业务中可能面临的风险及其防范进行了归纳和介绍,最后用实例来分析和演示信用证的具体应用。

第一节 信用证概述

一、信用证的定义

信用证(Letter of Credit,简称 L/C)是银行出具的一种有条件的付款保证。《跟单信用证统一惯例》对信用证的定义如下:

"'跟单信用证'和'备用信用证'(以下统称'信用证')意指一项约定,不论其如何命名或描述,系指一家银行('开证行')应客户('申请人')的要求和指示或以其自身的名义,在与信用证条款相符的条件下凭规定的单据:

(1)向第三者('受益人')或其指定人付款,或承兑并支付受益人出具的汇票,或

(2)授权另一家银行付款,或承兑并支付该汇票,或

(3)授权另一银行议付。"

在国际贸易中,上述信用证定义中的申请人是进口方,开证行是进口地银行,受益人是出口商。于是可以对信用证作这样的理解:

(1)信用证是开证行应进口方的请求向出口方开立的在一定条件下保证付款的凭证。

(2)付款的条件是出口方(受益人)向银行提交符合信用证要求的单据。

(3)在满足上述条件的情况下,由银行向出口方付款,或对出口方出具的汇票承兑并付款。

(4)付款人可以是开证行,也可以是开证行指定的银行。收款人可以是受益人,或者是它指定的人。

从以上分析可知,信用证业务中存在着三角契约安排如图 6-1 所示。

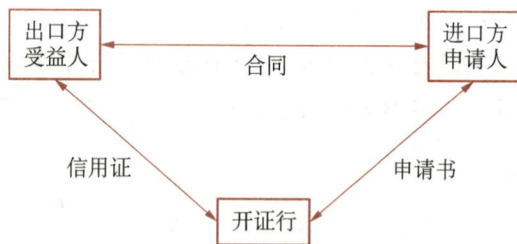

图 6-1 跟单信用证业务中的三角契约安排

第一,进出口商之间的销售合同。

第二,开证申请人和开证行之间的申请书,还包括担保协议或偿付协议。

第三,开证行与受益人之间的跟单信用证。若跟单信用证被另一家银行保兑,则保兑行与受益人之间同样存在着跟单信用证的契约安排。

申请人因与开证行之间或与受益人之间的关系而产生索偿或抗辩不得影响银行的付款承诺。受益人不得利用银行与银行之间,或申请人与开证行之间的现存契约关系。故每一项契约都是独立的并控制当事人之间的各自关系。

二、信用证的性质

1. 开证行承担第一性付款责任

信用证是开证行对受益人有条件的付款保证,但是就银行的责任而言,信用证与普通的保证不同。在普通的保证中,银行作为保证人虽与被保证人承担相同的责任,但银行的责任是第二性的连带责任。被保证人是主债务人,应首先清偿债务,只有被保证人违约,受益人(即债权人)才能凭保证要求银行清偿。因此受益人首先仍面临债务人违约的风险,而且因为银行的清偿顺序排在被保证人之后,受益人获得清偿的程序也比较麻烦。相比之下,信用证对受益人作出的是银行首先作直接付款的保证,简化了从银行取款的手续,而且因为银行信用一般比较可靠,受益人获得支付的可靠性也有明显改善。因为开证行承担第一性付款责任,所以只要受益人提供合格单据,银行必须首先安排付款,然后再与开证申请人清算,即使申请人已破产或明显不能支付信用证款项,开证行也不能解除其对受益人的付款责任。正因为这一特点,信用证才成为一种比较安全的结算方式。

2. 信用证是一份独立、自足的文件,不依赖于贸易合同

信用证虽然是针对贸易合同的支付所达成的合同,却具有不依赖于贸易合同的独立性,一经有关当事人接受,就与贸易合同无关。有关当事人必须按信用证指示办理有关事项,才能获得信用证项下的应有权益。信用证交易已与贸易合同交易相分离,成为一项独立的关于银行支付的交易,这就是信用证的独立性。

3. 信用证业务只处理单据,不涉及商品及/或劳务

银行承担信用证项下付款责任的唯一先决条件是受益人提供符合信用证要求的全套合格单据,目的是督促出口商合格地交货并取得相应的合格单据,但银行对于出口商的实际交货状况是无法控制的,而且银行也绝不愿意卷入进出口双方关于贸易合同的争议或纠纷,因此银行绝不过问商品及/或劳务的实际情况。银行唯一的责任,就是根据信用证的条款,按照所收单据的表面状况进行审查,只要单据表面上符合"单证一致、单单一致"的要求,银行就应承担付款责任,如果表面上不符合上列八字要求,银行就有权拒付。

三、信用证的作用

1. 进口商开证资金占用小

对进口商来说,采用信用证方式付款,在申请开证时不用交付开证金额,只需交付一定比例的保证金;也可以凭开证行授予的授信额度开证,这样可以避免流动资金大量积压。通过信用证条款控制出口商的装货日期,使货物的销售能适合时令。通过适当的检验条款,保证货物在装船前的质量、数量,使进口商所收到的货物,在一定程度上能符合合同规定。如果开证行在履行付款义务后,进口商在筹措资金上有困难,他还可以使用信托收据等方式,要求开证行先交单据,然后再付货款。进口商付款以后,可以立即取得货物的单据。

2. 出口商收款有保证

对出口商来说,他只要收到资信较好银行的有效信用证以后,就可向他的往来银行申

请打包放款,或其他装船前贷款。在货物出运以后,只要将符合信用证条款规定的货运单据交到出口地与他有往来的银行,或信用证内指定的银行,即可由该行议付单据,取得货款,一般不必直接向国外付款银行交单取款。

3. 开证行贷出信用不占用资金

对开证行来说,它开出的信用证是贷给进口商的信用,而不是资金。不仅不占用其自身资金,而且还有开证手续费收入,贷出的信用是有保证金或担保的,不是无条件的。当开证行履行付款后,还有出口商交来的货运单据作为保证。如果进口商不付款,开证行可以处理货物,以抵补欠款;如果出售的货款不足以抵偿,仍有权利向进口商追偿其不足部分,所以风险较小。

4. 出口地银行可以进行议付业务

对出口地银行来说,只要出口商交来的单据符合信用证条款的规定,即可垫款做押汇,收取手续费和贴息,然后再向开证行或指定的偿付行索偿。

四、信用证的当事人

信用证的基本当事人有 3 个:开证申请人、开证行和受益人。其他关系人有通知行、保兑行、议付行、偿付行、承兑行等。

1. 开证申请人

开证申请人,(Applicant/Opener/Buyer/Importer)。根据 UCP 600 第一条"申请人指要求开立信用证的一方",开证申请人是指向开证银行申请开立信用证的人,即进口商。开证申请人在信用证中的主要权利和义务如下:

(1) 对信用证承担最终责任

申请人作为信用证业务的委托人,对信用证承担最终的责任。即如果有关当事人在信用证名下确立的债务债权关系不能得到清偿,则应由申请人负责偿付。例如,开证行不履行向受益人付款或受益人未按信用证规定支付银行费用等,均应由申请人承担偿付责任。

(2) 及时付款赎单

申请人在接到开证行赎单通知时,应立即向开证行偿还垫款。如果申请人发现单据与信用证规定不符,则有权拒绝赎单,开证银行将承担因不可追索的付款而造成的一切后果。

2. 开证银行

开证行,(Originating Bank, Opening Bank, Issuing Bank),又被称为经办银行(Dealing Bank, Credit Writing Bank)。UCP 600 第二条表明,开证行指应申请人要求或者代表自己开出信用证的银行。承担开证的银行遵循开证申请人的要求和委托,开立信用证,并按信用证规定的条款承担付款责任。开证银行通常是在进口商所在地的银行,银行可代表自己开立备用信用证,旨在融资。信用证作为支付方式是否能顺利进行,开证银行的信用证至关重要,故选择信用好、业务经验丰富而手续简便的银行,作为开证银行为妥。

开证行在信用证中的主要权利和义务如下：

（1）根据开证申请人的指示开证

开证申请书是申请人对开证行的委托指示。开证行作为代理人，应按通常代理人所遵循的三条原则行事，即按委托人指示行事、按常规行事、以从事专业所应有的谨慎原则行事。其中按常规行事，应理解为开证行有义务向信用证有关当事人提供一切服务，如答复通知行咨询、向申请人提出有利于信用证业务的建议和提供咨询等；按谨慎原则行事则应理解为银行必须对自己工作中的过失负责。

（2）应按照《跟单信用证统一惯例》（UCP 600）的要求开立信用证

开证行在开立信用证时，除了应严格按照申请人的指示拟定信用证的内容外，还应按上述惯例来制作信用证。《跟单信用证统一惯例》（UCP 600）规定："如果信用证含有某些条件而未列明需提交与之相符的单据，银行将认为未列如此条件，且对此不予理会。"因此，开证行在开立信用证时，必须把申请人在开证申请书上所提出的条件，都加以"单据化"，使受益人通过提交单据来证明已履行了合同的义务。开证行在开立信用证时，不得违反上述惯例中的有关规定；否则，将导致不能有效地进行支付业务，甚至使信用本身无效。

（3）承担独立的、首先的付款责任

开证行在信用证中向受益人承诺，只要受益人提交与信用证规定相符的单据，开证行即向受益人或其指定的银行付款。尽管开证行是接受申请人的委托而作出了付款承诺，但这一承诺不受申请人和开证行之间关系变化的影响，所以即使申请人破产倒闭，开证行仍必须履行其在信用证中所作出的保证付款的承诺。一旦付款，即无追索权。

（4）开证行的拒付

信用证是一种有条件的支付承诺，因而，当提交的单据不符合信用证规定时，开证行有权拒付。按《跟单信用证统一惯例》（UCP 600）规定："开证行及/或保兑行（如有的话）或代理它们的指定银行在收到单据时，必须仅以单据来确定它们是否表面上符合信用证条款。如果单据表面上不符合信用证条款，银行可拒绝接受单据。"如果银行拒绝接受单据，即拒绝付款，则"必须毫不迟延地以电讯方式就此发出通知，如不可能，就以其他方式发出通知，但不得迟于收到单据次日起的第七个工作日，这种通知必须发给从它收到单据的银行。或者，如从受益人处直接收到单据，则发给受益人"。该通知必须列明关于银行拒受单据的所有不符点，还需说明它是否保留单据听候交单人处理或退回交单人。如果银行未按上述规定行事，则银行将无权称单据与信用证条款不符，不得行使拒付的权力。

（5）取得质押的权利

开证行在接受申请人开证申请时，为了避免风险，有权要求申请人支付押金及在开证申请书中列明质押文句，即保证申请人在无力支付时，货物作为质押品，可由开证行自行处理。

由于银行通常不愿承担货物所带来的麻烦，所以开证行主要是通过收取押金的方式来控制申请人。对于风险较大的业务，开证行会增加押金，甚至收取相当于信用证金额百分之百的押金。在实务中，许多银行对于资信良好的客户，在授信额度之内，免予收取押金，作为一种提供优惠服务以承揽国际结算业务的营销手段。

(6) 开证行对其受托银行的责任

在信用证中,有时开证行会委托其他银行作为保兑行、议付行、付款行、偿付行或其他代理银行办理有关业务。如果受托银行接受委托为开证行垫付了资金,开证行应及时偿还。这些受托银行在其代理权限内行事,由开证行承担可能发生的风险责任,并按费率表向各银行支付有关费用。如果信用证中规定银行费用由受益人承担,则各银行应向受益人收取。

3. 受益人

受益人,(Beneficiary/Seller/Exporter/Shipper/Drawer/Addressee)(抬头人)等,根据 UCP 600 第二条——受益人指接受信用证并享受其利益的一方,因此受益人是在信用证中载明有权使用信用证,并可依照信用证所列条款签发汇票或提示单据收取信用证所列金额者。

在国际贸易中,受益人为货物销售合同的卖方;在信用证业务中,受益人接受信用证意味着受益人即得到了开证行的付款保证,也确认了开证行在信用证中所提出的付款条件。受益人由信用证规定的权利和义务如下:

(1) 受益人所提交的单据,必须做到单单一致、单证一致。《跟单信用证统一惯例》(UCP 600)规定,银行只"凭表面上符合信用证条款的单据付款,承担延期付款责任、承兑汇票或议付……"又规定,"单据之间出现的表面上彼此不一致,将被视为单据表面上与信用证条款不符"。因此,在信用证业务中,受益人要得到开证行付款,必须做到"单单一致"和"单证一致"。只要受益人所提交的单据表面上符合上述两个一致,开证行应履行其付款承诺。

(2) 受益人所提交的单据必须符合《跟单信用证统一惯例》(UCP 600)的规定。信用证中对单据的规定,具体体现了相应的货物销售合同对卖方的要求,这些被要求提交的单据实际上是卖方的履约证明书。但是《跟单信用证统一惯例》(UCP 600)对于单据提出了普遍必须遵守的规则。例如海运提单上规定"承运人或船长的任何签署或证实,必须视情况可识别其为承运人或船长……"等等。受益人所提交的单据如果不符合《跟单信用证统一惯例》(UCP 600)的规定,将不被银行接受。

(3) 受益人有要求改证的权利。作为一种有条件的支付承诺,信用证中单据化的条件必须与货物销售合同中卖方所承担的义务相一致。如果不一致,受益人将无法以递交单据作为履约证明的方式实现其请求付款的权利。因而信用证的内容与合同不一致,受益人有权要求申请人指示开证行修改信用证。

4. 通知银行

通知银行,(Advising Bank/Notifying Bank/Transmitting Bank),根据 UCP 600 第二条——通知银行指应开证行的要求通知信用证的银行,因此通知银行是指受开证银行的委托,将信用证转交给受益人的银行。通知银行通常是在出口商的所在地。通知银行只负责通知、传递信用证,不承担义务。通知行在信用证中的主要权利和义务如下:

(1) 验明信用证的真实性。如果开证行将信用证直接送交受益人,受益人无法确认其真实性,故而在信用证业务中,要求开证行将信用证先行寄送受益人当地的代理行,即信用证的通知行,由其鉴定信用证上的签字、印鉴或密押,确定其真实无误后,以通知行的身份签发通知书将信用证转交受益人。受益人从当地银行直接得到信用证真实性的保证,有效地避免了对方伪造信用证的风险。

如果通知行无法鉴别信用证的表面真实性,应毫不迟延地通知开证行说它无法鉴别。如果通知行仍决定通知受益人,则必须告知受益人它未能鉴别该证的真实性。

(2)通知行的审证责任。通知行除了审核信用证的真实性之外,还在道义上承担审核信用证有关内容的责任,以力求向客户提供良好的服务。审证内容通常包括开证银行的资信、偿付路线是否合理以及信用证文句是否存在疏漏错误等。

5. 议付银行

议付银行(Negotiating Bank)又称购票银行、押汇银行或贴现银行(Discount Bank)。在信用证的各种偿付方式中,议付是最常见的一种。议付行即是买入受益人所交汇票和单据的银行,开证行可在信用证中指定一家议付银行。如果开证行在开出议付信用证时未指定议付行,则接受受益人交单并议付的任何一家银行被视为议付行。议付行在信用证中的主要权利和义务如下:

(1)议付行在单证相符的前提下才能议付

议付行之所以议付,是因为开证银行的付款承诺,相信开证行的信用。开证行的付款承诺是有条件的,所以议付行进行议付也应满足同样的条件,即单证一致和单单一致,这样才能在垫付货款后,从开证行处收回垫款。

(2)议付行有追索权和取得质押的权利

议付是可以追索的,议付行在议付后,如果不能从开证行处得到付款,议付行有权向受益人追索已垫付的货款。此外,银行为了避免风险,除了在受益人交单议付时明确追索权外,还往往要求受益人出具质押书,声明一旦发生意外时,议付行有权处理单据及其所代表的货物。

(3)议付行收取贴息及手续费

对即期汇票,计息天数为议付行向开证行的寄单邮程、开证行审单日程和汇款日程;如果为远期汇票,则在上述天数外,还需加上汇票上所规定的见票后定期付款的天数。

(4)背批信用证

议付行在议付单据后,应把议付金额、日期、受益人发票号码等有关内容记录在信用证背面,这种记录称为背批。背批用来说明使用信用证的情况,以防止超额或重复使用信用证。

6. 保兑行

保兑行,(Confirming Bank),根据 UCP 600 第二条"保兑行指根据开证行的授权和要求对信用证加具保兑的银行"。因此,应开证行的请求,在信用证上加具保兑的银行称为保兑行。保兑行和开证行一样,对信用证承担付款责任。保兑行对受益人的承诺,也是独立的、第一性的,受益人或议付行可以在开证行和保兑行之间任择一家交单,保兑行收到符合信用证条款的单据,必须按信用证的规定予以付款或延期付款或承兑后到期付款。保兑行的付款同样是不可追索的。保兑行付款后,向开证行索偿,由开证行偿还其垫付的货款。

在国际贸易中有时因开证银行规模较小、信誉不明或开证银行所处的国家的经济情况不佳等原因而需受益人所熟悉的另一家银行加以保兑,保兑银行通常是出口商所在地的通知银行或其他信誉良好的银行,此担保银行称保兑银行。

7. 付款行

付款银行,(Paying Bank),开证行在信用证中指定一家银行为信用证项下汇票的付款人或是不需要开立汇票的付款信用证的执行付款的银行,称为付款行。付款银行的责任是根据提交的符合信用证要求的单据向受益人履行付款责任,故称付款银行。按汇票付款,不管汇票的持有人是谁,只要汇票符合信用证规定的条件,银行应予以付款,故亦称受票银行(Drawee Bank),付款银行通常是由开证银行来承担。如果是另一家银行,通常为出口地银行,目的在于简化汇兑手续。

8. 偿付行

偿付行,(Reimbursing Bank),亦称清算银行(Clearing Bank)。若信用证规定受益人应签发以开证银行或进口商为付款人的汇票,同时又载明议付银行于议付之后可向另一家银行求偿,该另一家银行称偿付银行。开证行之所以指定偿付行是为了便于调拨资金,所以偿付行总是开证行在国外的账户银行,并且双方订有代理业务的协议。开证行在信用证中指定偿付行的同时,应给予偿付行适当指示。出口地银行在议付或付款后,一面把单据寄给开证行,一面向偿付行发出索偿通知书,偿付行在开证行授权范围内予以清偿。

9. 其他当事人

(1)指定银行(Nominated Bank)指信用证可在其处兑用的银行,如信用证可在任一银行兑用,则任何银行均为指定银行。

(2)承兑行在承兑信用证中,开证行可以在信用证中规定由自己或指定的另一家银行作为汇票的付款人,承兑受益人出具的远期汇票,并到期向受益人付款。该指定银行即为承兑行。

(3)转交银行(Processing Bank)若信用证载明限定议付银行,而限定议付银行非受益人的往来银行,或受益人因某种原因不愿向指定银行请求议付,则受益人可通过其往来银行转交有关单据请求议付,此往来银行称转交银行。

(4)再议付银行(Re-Negotiation Bank),亦称再押汇银行。若在信用证中载明限定议付字样,而限定议付银行并非受益人之往来银行,受益人可直接向往来银行请求议付,由议付银行再向信用证指定的议付银行办理议付,此指定银行亦再议付银行。

第二节 跟单信用证统一惯例主要内容及其演变

一、跟单信用证统一惯例演变背景

信用证在国际贸易中的使用已有数百年历史了,早在 18 世纪,英国法院就已有了关于跟单信用证的判例。进入 20 世纪后,信用证(尤其是跟单信用证)业务更有了长足的进步。随着运输方式与通讯技术的迅速发展,信用证业务的运作方式也在不断变化。此外,各国、各地区贸易发展的不平衡也导致了业务实践上的差异。为了协调各国、各地区在信用证业务方面的做法以及适应新技术、新方法，国际商会制定并数度修改关于跟单信用证业务的统一惯例。最早制定的是 1930 年的《商业跟单信用证统一规则》，编号为国际商会第 74 号出版物。由于这一规则以法国银行实践为主，仅得到了法国与比利时银行界的承认，影响并不大。此后于 1933 年、1951 年分别出版了两个名为《商业跟单信用证统一惯例》的修订本，编号分别为第 82 号、第 151 号。自 1963 年实施的第 3 个修订本（编号第 222 号）起，更名为《跟单信用证统一惯例》(Uniform Customsand Practicer Documentary Credits，简称 UCP)；1974 年第 4 次修订，于 1975 年 10 月 1 日实施，编号第 290 号；1983 年第 5 次修订，于 1984 年 10 月 1 日实施，编号第 400 号；1993 年第 6 次修订，于 1994 年 1 月 1 日实施，编号第 500 号；2006 年第 7 次修订，编号第 600 号，于 2007 年 7 月 1 日实施。

二、UCP 600 与 UCP 500 相比的主要修改

目前《跟单信用证统一惯例》（以下称 UCP 600）经国际商会银行委员会通过，并于 2007 年 7 月 1 日正式生效，这无疑对我国进出口企业、银行、法律、司法、船运以及保险界都将产生重大的影响。而以前的 UCP 500，不论是其条款的全面性、实务的针对性，还是其内容与如今现实发展不同步性，乃至近年来有关跟单信用证的诉讼案激增，均导致了其惯例已经不能适应这个时代发展的需求。国际商会(ICC)的 UCP 600 对 UCP 500 的修改过程中，全面地回顾 UCP 500 实施以来 ICC 发布的各类出版物、意见及决定，吸收了其中的合理条款；全面地反映近年来国际银行业、运输业和保险业出现的变化，并体现了一定的前瞻性；在结构上借鉴了 ISP98 的模式，改变了 UCP 500 分类不科学，次序排列不足，语言繁杂欠精练等；UCP 600 比之 UCP 500，从整体结构到具体条款都出现了显著变化。UCP 600 与 UCP 500 相比的修改主要体现在以下几个方面：

1. 条款结构和措辞上变化

UCP 600 对 UCP 500 的 49 个条款进行了大幅度的调整及增删，在全文结构上的变化是按照业务环节对条款进行了归结。简而言之，就是把通知、修改、审单、偿付、拒付等环节涉及的条款在原来 UCP 500 的基础上分别集中，使得对某一问题的规定更加明确和系统化，极大地方便了使用者查找相关条款。

UCP 600 在第一条作出了"除非信用证明确修改或排除"(unless expressly modified or excluded in the credit)总括性规定，替代了 UCP 500 中出现 30 多次的"除非信用证另有规定"；如 UCP 600 第二十条对原 UCP 500 第二十四条只使用了一半的文字进行修改，显现出更加简洁。UCP 600 中拒付通知的格式及内容增加"a single"弥补原 UCP 500 的漏洞，显现出条款更加严格。关于 5% 溢短的变化，UCP 600 将修订为"not to exceed 5%"，既消除了误解，又与关于 about 的规定相统一。UCP 600 中措辞"and/or"修订"or"，单、复数同义，UCP 600 仅在需要的地方保留了三处"and/or"，其余均修订为"or"，大大让惯例的行文更加清晰；UCP 600 增加了对银行因遭受恐怖袭击(Acts of Terrorism)导致银行停业所造成后果免责的规定，是由于近年来恐怖活动激增，成为影响国际贸易的潜在因素，这一条款增加，显示出 UCP 与时俱进的先进性。

此外，UCP 600 从条款文字措辞上显现了通俗易懂、简约化，改变了 UCP 500 难懂的语句，取消了易造成误解，如"合理时间"（Reasonable Time）条款的删除、从根本上消除 UCP 500 规定的不确定性，同时也消除司法部门以"不合理"为由干涉正常银行业务的隐患；"在其表面"（on Its Face）仅保留一处（UCP 500 中出现 28 次），以此表明银行仅为负责单据表面一致性没有改变；对表达不确切、内容过时以及与国际贸易实务相脱节的条款进行修改或删除，如"可撤消信用证"在实务中已经不存在，应予以删除；对"运输行单据"条款的删除并未改变 UCP"不接受运输行仅以运输行身份签发运输单据"的做法；对"风帆动力批注"的删除，显然对不符合现代航运要求的必然；对"运输单据之额外费用"的删除，因为此类费用不论在运输行业还是信用证操作中，均是被接受的正常费用，不宜限制范畴。UCP 600 在措辞上更为简洁、严格、统一、清晰。

2. UCP 600 删除 UCP 500 信用证"可撤销"的概念

UCP 600 对信用证"可撤销"概念进行了删除，这对明确信用证的特征，促进信用证的发展具有重要意义。众所周知，信用证是一项提供银行独立信用支持和明确的支付承诺的专门业务，它通过有别于银行资金的银行信用的方式来满足买卖双方之间的支付需求，与赊销和托收相比，能够为买方提供资金融通，在开立信用证时并不需要支付 100％的现金，并可使买方取得相对较长的支付期；而对于卖方来说，信用证即等于是开证银行的确定的付款保证，卖方不再完全需要依赖买方的付款意愿和能力，从而减少或消除了商业风险，外汇和政治风险。另一方面，信用证受到了众多法律法规的支持和保护，而 ICC 的跟单信用证统一惯例自 1933 年开始生效以来，一直是一套普遍公认的跟单信用证运作的法规。然而，以上所提及的有关信用证的特性，都建立在一个前提上，那就是该信用证必须是不可撤销的信用证。

按照 UCP 500 第六条和第八条，信用证分为可撤销和不可撤销两种。可撤销信用证是应开证申请人的指示开给受益人并给予买方最大限度的灵活性的信用证，因为它可以不经受益人同意，甚至直到开证行所委托的相应银行付款时都不需预先通知受益人，在任何时候都可以修改撤回或取消。可撤销信用证可根据申请人要求规定到期日，也可以不规定。如不规定到期日，从银行通知受益人那天算起，有效期为 6 个月。而且进口商对出口方所交货物或交货日期等任何地方不满意时，都可以对信用证加以修改或撤销，这种行为受到惯例 500 的保护。可撤销信用证对受益人有很大的风险。因为跟单信用证在货物运输中及单据提示前，或者虽然单据已提示却在付款前，或者在延期付款跟单信用证的情况下，单据未被接收以前，都可能被修改或取消。在此情况下，信用证成了一纸空文，卖方无奈只能直接要求买方付款。可见，可撤销信用证对受益人没有提供任何保障，因此不能为受益人提供货物服务和行为的公平交易。

为什么 UCP 500 要承认可撤销信用证呢？事实上这种信用证的比例并不大，因为其一贸易本身要受到贸易合同的约束，单方不履约的行为会被罚款并影响商业信誉。其二出口商对某些滞销货物才使用这种信用证。一般是有库存现货，接到信用证马上发货交单，或在信用证开出之前就已发货制单。正因如此，UCP 500 才规定早于信用证开出之日出具的单据银行应予接受。其三开这种信用证一般为美洲一些国家的习惯。当地贸易市场较为成熟和规范，当买卖双方长期友好往来，而且开证行资信又较好时，开证行可以允许申请人不必存入过多的开证保证金,对开证申请人是一种资金上的融通。有时用于有附属关系的当事人之间或分支机构之间,还用于一些特殊交易,或者用来代替付款承诺或付款通知。

在国际贸易实务中,可撤销信用证却往往被一些不法进口商打着"受惯例保护"的旗号进行利用,使出口商的利益受到威胁。可撤销信用证的开证行对于受益人的交单,并不构成"确定的"付款"承诺",即开证行对受益人的义务处于不稳定状态,因而也是不充分的,因此和其他形式的付款方式没有任何区别:信用证的"银行"信用沦为"商业"信用。可撤销信用证因早期的实务需要而得以在惯例的历次版本中保留,但受益人明显缺乏保护,信用证的性质也容易受到置疑,因此不利于信用证业务的存在和发展。只有不可撤销信用证才能给予受益人以更大的付款保证。这也就是 UCP 600 删除信用证"可撤销"内容的根本原因。这对于顺应国际贸易实务的发展,将信用证业务发扬光大有着重要意义。如果实务中确有开立可撤销信用证的需要,按照 UCP 600 起草小组的评述,必须在信用证中列明具体条款以反映信用证的可撤销特性。

3. UCP 600 还增加了对信用证、通知行、保兑行、议付和交单等关键词语的解释,提高了文本的清晰度。

例如引入了第二通知行的概念,即收到经第一通知行通知的信用证。在申请人方面则提出了 party 的概念,the party on whose request the credit is issued,即要求开立信用证的一方,明确银行工作日仅指受理单据业务的工作日,并不是按照储蓄经营时间来计算等等;同时 UCP 600 简化了银行审单的时间限制,将银行审单时间锁定在 5 个工作日内完成;缩减了单据的种类,删除了 UCP 500 第三十条货运代理签发的运输单据等。上述内容修改的目的就是使信用证规则更加清晰,容易操作。

三、UCP 600 中与"付款"相关的基本概念

付款是信用证操作中非常重要的一环,而关于付款,国内出版物就有承付、兑付、议付、偿付、代付五个概念。下面,将结合 UCP 600 的规定对这些概念加以分析、比较。

1. 承付、兑付或付款(Honour)

承付、兑付实为同一含义,它们对应的都是 UCP 600 中第二条"定义"中的"Honour",只是由于翻译的不同,各学者采取了不同的叫法,甚至在同一本书中前后叫法也有所不同[①]。"Honour"为 UCP 600 在定义中新增的一个概念。那么,根据 UCP 600,承付(兑付)意为:

a. 对于即期付款信用证即期付款。

b. 对于延期付款信用证发出延期付款承诺并到期付款。

c. 对于承兑信用证承兑由受益人出具的汇票并到期付款。

在这一定义中,UCP 600 将三种付款行为统一到一个概念下,对即期付款信用证、延期

---

① 例如,陈国武主编《〈跟单信用证统一惯例(2007 年修订本)〉第 600 号出版物》第 5 页,用"承付"一词,第 7 页用"付款";李金泽主编《UCP 600 适用与信用证法律风险防控》第 18 页,"引入 Honour(兑付)的概念"用的是"兑付",第 28 页"与银行付款有关的定义"用的是"承付",第 30 页"各种与付款有关的概念辨析"用的是"承付"。

付款信用证和承兑信用证下银行的责任进行了统一的界定,即"承付(兑付)责任"。结合UCP的其他条文可知,开证行对受益人的付款行为均称为承付(兑付),而其他银行,包括保兑行、指定银行的行为可能是承付(兑付)或议付,要根据信用证规定的兑用方式具体确定①。

2. 议付(Negotiation)

"议付",即 UCP 中的"Negotiation",在信用证业务中一直是一个富有争议的词。ICC 银行技术与惯例委员(the ICC's Commission of Banking Technique and Practice)在UCP 500 及后续解释中给出的"支付对价"、"承担付款责任"等说明模糊的用词令各种充满歧义的解释充斥在大量的纠纷中。UCP 600 则是对议付一词给出了明确的说明和界定,具体体现在以下几个方面:

(1) 议付的含义 UCP 600 修改了 UCP 500 关于"议付"的定义。根据 UCP 600 第二条关于议付(Negotiation)的表述,"议付"是开证行授权的被指定银行(Nominated Bank)采取的一项有效行为。"议付是经开证行授权的,可以是保兑行,也可以是其他被指定银行。议付有自由议付和限定议付之分。在自由议付的情况下,被授权的指定银行可以是任何一家银行。同时"议付"也是一种购买行为,而购买的对象有两种,一种是汇票,一种是单据。议付项下银行的行为也有两种,一种是预付(Advancing Funds),一种是同意预付(Agreeing to Advance Funds)(即做出预付承诺)。由指定银行在审单无误后,按票面金额扣减议付日到开证行偿付日这段时间的议付行的垫款利息及议付费、单证邮寄费等后,将净款付给受益人。对受益人而言,在信用证项下办理议付,意味着付款到期日前,只要提交与信用证条款相符的单据,就能通过贴现得到货款。

(2) UCP 600 对"议付"的修改　根据 UCP 500 第十条,信用证分为即期付款信用证、延期付款信用证、承兑信用证和议付信用证四种。该条 b 款第 II 项将议付定义为"被授权议付的银行对汇票或单据付出对价(Giving the Value)",并强调"仅审核单据而未付出对价并不构成议付";UCP 600 第二条定义中对议付定义的规定更加详细,并且承认了远期议付信用证的存在(即同意预付,Agreeing to Advance Funds)。此外,UCP 600 关于议付的一个重大改变就是,第二条定义将信用证分成:即期付款信用证、延期付款信用证和承兑信用证三种形式,删去了议付信用证。

3. 偿付(Reimbursement)

偿付(Reimbursement),主要出现在 UCP 600 第七条 c 款、第八条 c 款和第十三条。与其相关的内容如下:第七条 c 款(开证行的承诺)——开证行保证向对于相符提示已经予以兑付或者议付并将单据寄往开证行的被指定银行进行偿付。无论被指定银行是否于到期日前已经对相符提示予以预付或者购买,对于承兑或延期付款信用证项下相符提示

---

① 在我国香港地区,部分银行开立的中文或中英文对照的信用证中,大多把 honour 译为"付款"。因而,有的学者并未将 honour 译为"兑付"或"承兑",而是"付款"。其理由就是 UCP 600 第二条定义中对"honour"所作的三点解释。如将"honour"翻译为"兑付",似乎更容易理解为是将"承兑"和"付款"合为一个词。而实际上,在上述三大类信用证(即期、延期(迟期)和承兑信用证)中,需要办理承兑手续的,只有一种,即承兑信用证。此外,无论何种信用证,最后都有"付款"这个环节,所以将"honour"广译为"付款"更妥当。当然,将"honour"译为付款,与将"payment"译为"付款"是有区别的。前者的含义更加广泛,它不仅体现最后的"付款"环节,还包括"付款"前的环节,诸如"提示"、"付款承诺"及"承兑"等。

的金额的偿付都于到期日进行。开证行偿付被指定银行的承诺独立于开证行对于受益人的承诺。第八条 c 款(保兑行的承诺)——由另一家被指定银行延期付款而该被指定银行未承担其延期付款承诺,或者虽已承担延期付款承诺但到期未予付款。第十三条(银行间的偿付约定)——a. 如果信用证规定被指定银行("索偿行")须通过向另一方银行("偿付行")索偿获得偿付,则信用证中必须声明是否按照信用证开立日正在生效的国际商会《银行间偿付规则》办理。b. 如果信用证中未声明是否按照国际商会《银行间偿付规则》办理,则适用于下列条款……

从这些条款内容可知,"偿付"是银行之间进行款项索要时使用的一个概念,该概念专指银行之间的付款行为,不能使用在其他场合。

4. 代付

信用证代付(Reimbursement Refinance)是指进口商申请开证行联系外资银行或海外分行代为付款,在融资到期日再偿还信用证款项、融资利息和银行费用的融资业务。它包括两种情况,一是进口商在开立信用证前与开证申请人签订《进口信用证项下代付协议》,付款时由开证行联系外资银行或海外分支机构代为付款,融资到期进口商再偿还本息;二是进口商在信用证付款到期日之前如有融资需求,在开证行资金紧张或资金成本较高的情况下,开证行联系外资银行或海外分支机构代为付款,进口商在融资到期日再偿还本息。

信用证代付业务在 UCP 600 及以前版本中均未有规定,也没有专门规范此业务的法律或惯例。信用证代付是近期在实践中发展起来的一项业务,与近年来经济背景是分不开的。由于受人民币升值的影响,企业普遍减少外汇资产存量,银行外汇存量也较以前减少。与此同时,在海外金融市场上,融资成本较低,筹资渠道较多,海外银行资金相对充足。因此,国内银行利用海外银行的资金成为破解这一难题的金钥匙,信用证代付业务便应运而生。目前,工农中建四大国有银行都开办了信用证代付业务,通过其海外分支机构融资。海外分支较少或没有海外分支的股份制商业银行或地方银行就通过在华的外资银行或是其他中资银行的海外分支机构进行融资,办理代付业务。代付业务可以在进口商资金紧张的情况下为其办理融资,同时又不占用开证行资金,因而近几年发展迅速。

5. 付款(Honour)与议付(Negotiation)的区别

"付款"(承付、兑付)(Honour)与议付(Negotiation)是信用证在银行实务中两个不同的侧面。付款是义务人履行义务或其他银行受付款义务人委托代付款义务人履行义务的行为。而议付侧重的是当受益人在提示议付行议付时,议付行买入受益人的汇票或单据,其性质是议付行对受益人的一种融资。这两种行为在对汇票的要求、受益人取得款项的途径等很多方面是不同的。具体说来,二者有以下不同:

(1) 付款可以不要求开立汇票,而议付则要求开立汇票。付款的三种方式中(即期、延期和承兑)只有承兑要求必须开立汇票,其他两种方式是没有此种要求的。而对于议付,受益人通过议付行购买汇票和单据得到兑现,汇票是重要的支付工具,因此必须开立汇票。而且该汇票必须是可以转让的,汇票的收款人应做成指示式抬头(Pay to the Order of ×××)。

(2) 在付款情况下,受益人从付款行取得的货款是不受追索的;而在议付情况下,受益人从议付行取得的货款是有可能受追索的。这是付款和议付最大的不同。

(3) 在付款情况下,受益人可从付款行取得足额的发票或汇票金额。而在议付情下,受益人从议付行取得的款项是打过折扣的。议付行在议付时,通常要扣除垫款期间(即寄单索偿与得到付款期间)的利息、手续费等项费用及外汇利差,因此,受益人从议付行不能取得足额的发票或汇票金额。

(4) 在付款中,付款行承担审单风险,但不承担信贷风险;而议付情况下议付行不承担审单风险,但承担信贷风险。付款行有责任谨慎地审核单据,查找不符之处。一旦付款行凭不符单据付款,开证行是不负偿付义务的,而付款行对受益人的付款又是不能追索的,因此,付款行有审单风险。在接到开证行付款委托时,付款行可以用开证行提供款项完成付款,也可以拒绝接受委托,付款行是没有信贷风险的。而在议付情况下,议付行在开证行以单证不符为由拒绝付款时,可以向受益人追偿,在此意义上,议付行不承担审单风险。由于议付行是以自有资金垫付的,若开证行拒付,它可能向受益人追不回货款而承担信贷风险。

此外,完成"付款"与完成"议付"的银行也不完全一样。开证行只能称为"付款"行为,而不能称为"议付";议付行只能称为"议付",不能称为"付款";被指定银行(Nominated Bank)或保兑行既可以称为"付款",也可以称为"议付"。

6. 代付与偿付的比较

代付与偿付最大不同在于银行地位不同。偿付行是代开证行向付款银行付款,而代付行是为受益人提供融资的银行。从代付业务的偿付环节看,代付行扮演了类似信用证下偿付行的角色,二者也有一定的相似性。两者的不同在于,开证行在开立偿付信用证时就能确定偿付行,并在信用证中注明,以使受益人知晓;而在代付业务中,开证行可能在付款之前才确定代付行,受益人一般不知晓代付行的存在。

第三节 信用证的一般业务程序

国际贸易结算中使用的跟单信用证有不同的类型,其业务程序也各有特点,但都要经过申请开证、开证、通知、交单、付款、赎单这几个环节。信用证的一般业务程序如图6-2所示。

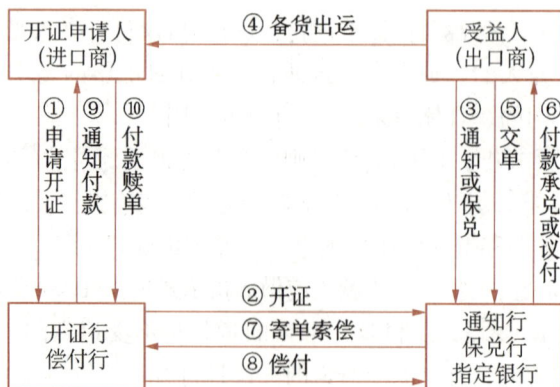

图 6-2 跟单信用证业务程序

一、进口商提出开证申请

如果进出口双方在销售合同中规定采用跟单信用证作为结算方式，那么进口商就必须在合同规定的装运期以前及时地向银行提出开证申请。进口商必须提交一份详细的开证申请书，其格式由开证行提供。此外，如果进口国外贸、外汇管理当局有特定要求，进口商还需提供其他文件，如进口许可证、外汇额度证明以及合同文本等。就信用证业务本身而言，最重要的文件是开证申请书。

二、开证行开出信用证

银行在收到进口商的开证申请后，首先要作出审查。一是审查申请人的资信，是否为本银行客户，有无授信额度等，从而确定开证的风险以便确定应收取押金的比例。二是审查该进口交易是否符合国家关于外贸、外汇管制的规定，是否获得了有效的进口许可证、外汇额度批文等文件。三是审查开证申请书的内容，这是最主要的审查项目。主要审查开证批示是否完整、明确、简洁，是否带有非单据化条款，内容是否有自相矛盾之处等等。

银行将根据开证申请书的规定正式开出信用证。若采用信开证方式，则通常缮制正本一份，副本若干，其中正副本各一份，寄通知行转交受益人，开证行与申请人各得副本存档。若采用电开方式，则需注意以电报、电传以及 SWIFT 系统开立信用证总是可以被各方当事人接受；而以传真方式开立却可以被其他当事人拒绝，因为传真方式可能不太安全。

三、信用证的通知、转递、保兑及修改

1. 信用证的通知

如果信用证以电讯方式开立，开证行总是将电讯文件直接发送给通知行，由通知行核对密押无误后以信用证通知书的形式转告受益人。如果信用证以信件方式开立，开证行一般将信用证直接寄给通知行（转递行），由其核对授权签字无误后转递给受益人，但有时亦会将信用证直接寄给受益人。由于受益人无法核对授权签字的真伪性，他还会将信用证交其往来银行或其他同开证行有代理关系的银行，以检验签字的有效性。因此，这种以受益人为收件人直接寄送信用证的情况比较少见，开证行一般通过通知行（包括转递行）向受益人转交信用证。

2. 信用证的转递

被要求通知或转递信用证的银行没有义务一定要执行开证行的指示，但必须将拒绝通知或转递的情况及时通报开证行。如果通知行决定照办开证的指示，首先必须将信用证的真伪性鉴定准确。过去有些银行（尤其是东南亚一带的银行）认为通知行的责任只是原样传递信用证，不需核对其签字或密押。其实这一观点有极大的潜在的危险。因为受益人无法检验信用证真伪性，而且他相信通知行传递给他的信用证应该是真实无误的，所以通知行不说明信用证的真伪性就是默认其真实性，如果恰好碰到伪造的信用证，受益人就会面临巨大损失。为了强化对受益人的保障《跟单信用证统一惯例》（UCP 500）规定，

除非银行不准备通知信用证，否则必须检验其真伪性。

3. 信用证的保兑

关于信用证的保兑，可能是因受益人对开证行资信不满意而引起，也可能是因开证行主动要求而引起，但无论在何种情况下，都只有开证行才有权指示另一银行对信用证加具保兑。收到保兑邀请的银行应根据开证行的资信、与本银行的关系等因素决定是否保兑。一旦作出保兑，就要对受益人承担与开证行完全一样的首要付款责任，而且不带有追索权。如果保兑行无法从开证行获得偿付，就会处于非常被动、不利的局面。因为保兑行与开证申请人并无合同关系，无法强制申请人付款赎单，因此保兑行只能处理单据及货物，或者作为开证行的债权人对其提出清偿要求。所以，银行一般只对与自己有良好业务关系的联行或代理行开立的信用证提供保兑。

4. 信用证的修改

受益人如对信用证条款不满意，可以通过申请人向开证行提出修改要求，申请人本人也可以主动提出修改要求。但不管由谁提议，在目前普遍使用不可撤销信用证情况下，每一项修改都需得到开证行、受益人以及保兑行（如有的话）的一致同意。如果开证行不同意修改信用证，就会拒绝发出修改书，但一经同意并发出修改书后，则受其约束。由于此时尚不清楚受益人是否会接受，开证行必须做好两种准备：若受益人接受，按修改后的信用证条款审单；若受益人拒绝，则按信用证原来条款审单。另外，开证行还必须通过原通知行通知信用证的修改，否则应对由此产生的后果负责。

四、出口商按信用证要求办理货物的出运

出口商在收到以他为受益人的信用证后，首先应对其进行审核。审核的目的：一是要判定开证行的资信状况，并决定是否要求信用证得到其他银行的保兑；二是要判定信用证条款是否与合同一致，是否带有无法办到的要求，是否存在着软条款，并决定是否提请申请人要求修改信用证。受益人必须注意，在没有收到合格的信用证以前，或在没有将信用证修改至令人满意的情况以前，受益人绝不能发货，否则就会丧失主动权。如果因延迟发货而遭受损失，可以凭合同向进口商提出索赔。

另外，对于不可撤销信用证项下的修改，受益人拥有最后的接受权或否决权。对于修改书，受益人同样应予以仔细审核，并决定是否接受。受益人可以明确地向通知行表示接受或拒绝，也可以通过默认的方法表明态度。即当受益人交单时，如果单据包括了修改书的内容，则表明接受了该修改；如果单据仅符合修改以前的信用证条款，则表明拒绝该修改。但是受益人对于同一份修改书中的多项修改应全部接受或全部拒绝，不能部分接受，部分拒绝。

五、受益人交单

为确保安全收汇，受益人应努力使单据符合信用证的规定，因此单据的种类、名称、份数、内容、出单时间、出单人身份等都应与信用证条款相吻合。如果单据内容有修改，应在修改处加盖修正章并由出章人签字或简签。

受益人交单应在合理时间内进行。这一合理时间的截止期限应是信用证到期日与最迟交单两者中先到的日期。但若由此确定的交单截止日期恰逢银行正常的非营业日,则可顺延至下一个营业日,接受单据提示的银行应证明这一顺延。

受益人交单还需在指定地点进行。除非信用证明确规定仅在开证行办理付款,否则交单的指定地点必定是信用证规定的指定银行。当然,受益人向开证行或保兑行(如有的话)直接交单总是允许的,但开证行或保兑行应采取措施防止第二套相同单据向指定银行提示,防止重复承兑或议付。另外,受益人交单时还应交出正本信用证及所有修改书,以便银行审查核对。

六、指定银行付款、承兑或议付

指定银行或保兑行在收到受益人或其委托银行交来的单据后,应及时地以合理谨慎的态度审核信用证所要求的单据。如果有信用证未作要求的单据,银行无义务审核,可以退还受益人或寄单行,也可以原样寄交开证行而不承担任何责任。

银行审单应仅仅根据信用证及其修改书,不应涉及任何其他文件或事实。银行应遵守《跟单信用证统一惯例》所规定的国际标准,对单据的表面状况作审核,以判断单据是否在表面上与信用证要求相符合。如果单据符合"单证一致、单单一致"的标准就是合格单据,银行应接受单据,并根据信用证规定作出即期付款、延期付款、承兑或议付;如果单据不合格,则有权拒收单据,拒绝安排付款。

七、指定银行向开证行寄单索偿

指定银行在对受益人办理付款等事项后,应按信用证规定向开证行寄单。如果信用证规定一次性寄单,则一次性寄出全套单据。如果信用证规定分两次寄单,则需按信用证注明的每批单据种类及份数分两次寄出。指定银行的索偿批示应向开证行发出。如果信用证中另行规定了偿付行,则应首先向偿付行索偿。索偿方法应符合信用证规定,并写明偿付行应向哪家银行的哪个账户划出资金头寸。如果偿付行未能提供偿付,则可以立即向开证行索偿,并要求追加因延迟偿付而产生的利息。

八、开证行或偿付行提供偿付

开证行在收到指定银行或保兑行或受益人寄来的单据后,应在 7 个银行工作日内完成审单工作,并在第 7 个工作日结束之前作出是否支付信用证款项的决定。如果单据合格,则开证行应对受益人作出付款安排,或向寄单行安排偿付。如果信用证规定由另定的偿付行对寄单行作偿付,则开证行应事先向该偿付行发出偿付指示或授权说明信用证号码、开证日期以及信用证金额,并说明偿付行费用由开证行支付还是向索偿行收取。若规定费用向索偿行收取,但偿付行未能收到这笔费用,则开证行仍有责任作补偿;若偿付行未能在索偿行第一次索偿时可立即进行偿付,开证行仍需对索偿行连本带息地进行偿付,除非此时开证行提出单据有不符点而决定拒付。

第四节　信用证的类型、风险以及防范

一、常见的信用证类型

1. 光票信用证与跟单信用证

（1）光票信用证

光票信用证是指不需要商业单据，尤其是不需要与物权有关的运输与保险单据，而仅凭金融单据（通常是受益人开立的汇票），或者再加上诸如发票、垫款清单、受益人声明等文件而进行付款的信用证。银行虽然也是凭合格单据承担付款责任，但因为得不到关于物权的单据，所以得不到物权的保障。如果光票信用证用于常规的贷款结算，银行的风险就会很大，而且因为对受益人的单据要求很简单，受益人伪造单据欺诈的可能性也增大了。

（2）跟单信用证

跟单信用证是指凭附有货运单据的跟单汇票或仅凭货运单据进行付款的信用证。跟单信用证的关键是要有代表物权或证明货物已经装运的商业单据，汇票则是可有可无的。出于避免为流通票据缴纳印花税的考虑，跟单信用证不要求有汇票的情况已相当普遍。跟单信用证给银行带来的好处就是可以为其垫款提供物权保障，增加银行收回资金的安全性，特别适合进出口贸易结算中凭单据作"象征性交货"的特点，因此被广泛地用于贸易结算中。本节所提及的信用证，若无特别说明，即指跟单信用证。

2. 可撤销信用证与不可撤销信用证

（1）可撤销信用证

可撤销信用证是指开证行可以不经过受益人同意先通知受益人，在付款、承兑或议付以前，随时修改信用证内容或撤销信用证。在可撤销信用证上，一般开证行应写明"Revocable"字样，以资识别。有些银行往往在信用证上加注表示开证行有权随时撤销的文句。

可撤销信用证的开立，给予买方最大的灵活性，因为它可以随时修改、撤回或注销，不经受益人同意，甚至不必事先通知受益人，直到它被开证行指定可使用信用证的银行付款时为止。可撤销跟单信用证包含对受益人的风险，因为信用证可以修改或注销，当货物在运输中和交单前或单据虽已交来，却在付款以前，或者如为延期付款信用证，在接受单据承担延期付款责任以前，该证已经修改注销，卖方将面临向买方索取付款的问题。可撤销信用证平时极少使用，偶尔用于子公司之间或特殊贸易，或作为支付承诺的代替物。

（2）不可撤销信用证

不可撤销信用证未经开证行、保兑行（如有）和受益人的明确同意，该证既不能修改，也不能撤销，这就是不可撤销信用证的本质，即信用证的不可撤性。

不可撤销信用证如需修改（或撤销）必须获得开证行、保兑行（如有）和受益人的明确同意，修改书才能生效。由于不可撤销信用证代表了开证行的确定付款承诺，因此，对受

益人来说无疑要比可撤销信用证安全得多。尤其是当开证行在申请人的授意下发出不利于受益人的修改时,受益人完全可以坚持采用原信用证条款,并通过合格单据迫使开证行承担责任。因为未经受益人同意的,任何修改都是没有效力的,不能对受益人构成约束。同样,如果保兑行同意修改,并将其保兑责任扩展到修改书上,但受益人不同意修改,则受益人仍有权凭提示符合原信用证规定的单据要求保兑行承担责任;反之,若保兑行拒绝修改,而受益人接受,则受益人只能向开证行或其指定银行提示符合修改后的信用证规定的单据,若向保兑行提示则会因单证不符而遭拒付。在这种情况下,保兑行的责任实际上已被解除了,因为受益人不能再提交满足保兑行要求(即原信用证要求)的单据了。

3. 保兑信用证与不保兑信用证

(1) 保兑信用证

根据开证行的授权或要求,另一家银行(保兑行)对不可撤销信用证加以保兑,只要信用证规定的单据在到期日那天或以前提交至保兑行或指定银行,并与信用证条款和条件相符,则保兑行付款、承兑汇票,或议付。

不可撤销保兑的信用证给予受益人双重的付款承诺。因为信用证规定的单据交到保兑行或其他指定银行,且符合信用证条款,构成在开证行确定付款承诺以外的保兑行的确定付款承诺。这种承诺,在程度上和文义上(除议付信用证项下构成保兑行无追索权的"议付"承诺代替开证行的"付款"承诺外)与开证行的承诺完全不同。

(2) 不保兑信用证

开证行的不可撤销跟单信用证被一家通知行予以通知,信用证下面的通知行作为开证行的代理人,除了合理谨慎地核验所通知信用证的表面真实性外,对受益人不承担任何责任,这就是不可撤销不保兑的信用证。

4. 即期付款、延期付款、承兑及议付信用证

根据受益人交单结算的方式,信用证可分为即期付款信用证、延期付款信用证、承兑信用证、议付信用证。具体分类如图6-3所示。

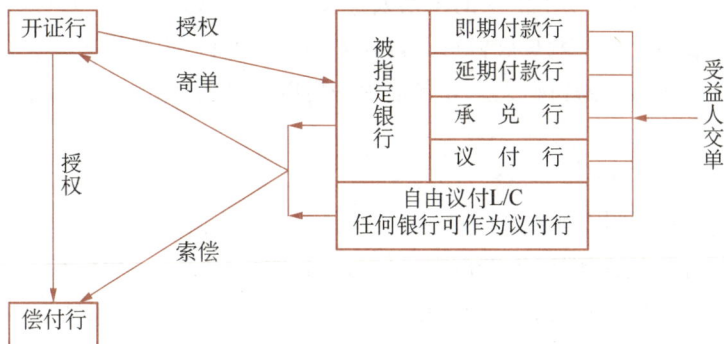

图6-3 即期付款、延期付款、承兑及议付信用证

(1) 即期付款信用证

即期付款信用证指开证行或指定的付款行一收到与信用证条款相符合的单据即予以付款的信用证。即期付款信用证有以下特点:

首先,一般不需要汇票,只凭商业单据付款;也可以开立以指定付款行为付款人的即期汇票。

其次,信用证在付款行所在地到期。典型的即期付款信用证,开证行往往指定出口地银行(比如通知行)为付款行,受益人只要向当地的付款行交单,即可得到无追索权的付款,且可以不被扣除议付程序中需扣除的利息。这是一种对受益人很有利的信用证。

某些即期付款信用证的付款行可以不在出口地,而在进口地的开证行或指定货币清算中心的一家银行,则受益人必须在信用证有效期内将单据寄交异地付款行,且对因邮寄延误承担责任。受益人可以自己直接寄单,也可以通过当地中介银行寄单。由于开证行并未在信用证中对议付作出承诺,故该中介银行只是寄单行,至于是否愿意做出口押汇,是中介银行与出口方之间的问题,与开证行无关。

(2)延期付款信用证

延期付款信用证指受益人不开具汇票,仅向开证行或其指定付款银行提交规定单据,付款行在未来某一特定日期付款的信用证。例如信用证上写明"在提交单据后××天付款"或"在提单出单日期后××天付款"等。《跟单信用证统一惯例》(UCP 600)规定:对于延期付款信用证,开证行和保兑行(如果有)应按信用证规定中所确定的日期付款。这种信用证由于无须开立汇票,因此无法进行贴现业务。

(3)承兑信用证

这种信用证要求受益人开立以指定银行(承兑行)为付款人的远期汇票,连同规定单据向承兑行作承兑交单,承兑行收下单据后将已承兑的汇票(或以承兑通知书方式)交还受益人(或受益人的委托银行),并到期付款。承兑信用证的汇票付款人是指定银行,包括开证行自己使用和另一受票银行被指定使用信用证。

(4)议付信用证

议付又称"押汇",按《跟单信用证统一惯例》(UCP 600)的定义,是指被授权进行议付的银行给付对价购买受益人提交的汇票及/或单据的行为,按议付方式使用的信用证即为议付信用证。议付信用证项下汇票的出票人是受益人,收款人是受益人自己,再由他背书转让给议付行,或者收款人就是议付行。付款人多是开证行,也可以是议付行以外的其他银行,但不得以申请人作为付款人。如果信用证仍以申请人作为付款人,银行将视此汇票为附加单据。

(5)自由议付信用证

自由议付信用证不限制某银行议付,可由受益人选择向任何愿意议付的银行提交汇票、单据进行议付,该银行就成为被指定议付行。自由议付信用证可以规定在一个城市或在一个国家的任何银行自由议付,但不宜规定全世界的任何银行自由议付,因为那将带给开证行很大的风险。

二、几种特殊类型信用证

由于各种特殊安排或特殊条款的存在,出现了许多处理程序不同于常规信用证的特殊信用证,主要有以下几种。

1. 可转让信用证

可转让信用证是指开证行允许被指定的转让行在受益人(第一受益人)要求下,将信用证部分或全部转让给一个或数个第二受益人使用的信用证。

所谓转让行就是信用证中指定的承担即期付款、延期付款、承兑和议付的指定银行,如果系自由议付信用证,则为由开证行特别授权办理信用证转让的银行。由于《跟单信用证统一惯例》(UCP 600)并未规定只能由一家银行担任转让行所以在经过第一受益人、申请人、保兑行(如有的话)的同意后,开证行可以指定一家以上的银行担任转让行,供受益人从中选择,但这种做法并不多见。被指定的转让行并无义务一定要接受第一受益人转让信用证的要求,除非该银行同意转让的范围和方式并照此办理。此外,转让行的各项开支费用应由第一受益人支付,但另有约定者除外。如果转让行同意办理转让,在上述费用未付清之前,转让行没有义务转让该信用证。

可转让信用证只能转让一次。如果信用证允许分批装运,第一受益人可以将原信用证分成若干部分,分别转让给两个或多个第二受益人,只要转让的总金额不超过原信用证金额,则仍看成是一次转让。任何第二受益人都无权再将自己得到的部分转让给第三受益人,但若出于各种原因,将部分转回给第一受益人则是允许的,此时第一受益人可以将转回的部分在原信用证有效期内再转给另一第二受益人。可转让信用证之所以只允许转让一次,是为了避免重复多次转让对申请人的利益造成不利影响,因为申请人只信任第一受益人及其选定的第二受益人,但不能信任由第二受益人选定的第三受益人等。更何况多次转让容易造成混乱,令有关银行的业务处理变得极为麻烦,所以可转让信用证只能转让一次。

通过可转让信用证所转让的权利,是受益人凭信用证发货、交单及取款的权利。此类信用证的第一受益人通常是中间商,本身无货或只有部分货物,必须按信用证要求向供货人采购,于是将信用证转让给供货人,使其成为第二受益人,直接按信用证要求发货,并以第二受益人自身的名义交单取款。但是即使信用证禁止转让,受益人仍可以将款项让渡给第三者,只是该第三者不能以自身名义发货交单,因而不能获得信用证所授予的权利,只能要求受益人代为行使有关权利。

可转让信用证的业务程序如图 6-4 所示。

2. 背对背信用证

普通信用证的受益人不能把信用证转让出去,可转让信用证不能满足受益人的商业要求,作为中间商的受益人自己不能供货,需要从供货人那里购买货物,他将国外开来受益于他的原始信用证,又称主要信用证作为担保品,请求银行依据原始信用证条款,开出以供货人为受益人(第二受益人)的信用证,称为背对背信用证,又称第二信用证,或补助信用证,凭此信用证由第二受益人发货、制单、索款。

背对背信用证的运作程序如图 6-5 所示。

背对背信用证与原始信用证相比较,有如下几个特点:

① 不可撤销跟单信用证(原始第一信用证)的益处在于第三方可以使用它,即当第一受益人用此信用证为抵押品或担保品去获得另一跟单信用证(背对背信用证)时,受益于实际供货人。

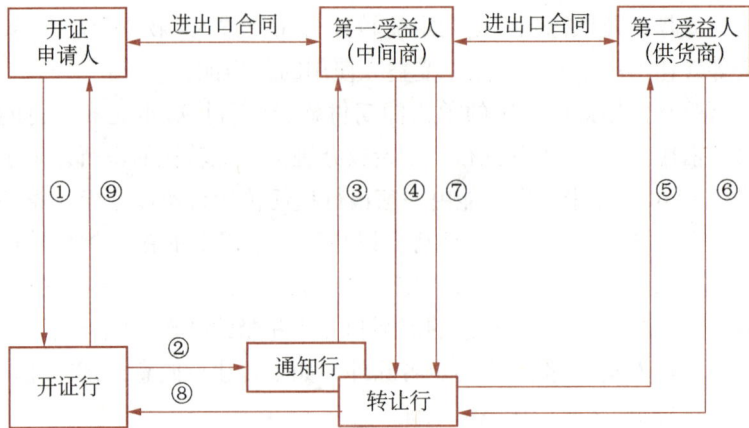

图6-4　可转让信用证业务程序

图例说明：
① ——进口商向银行申请开立可转让信用证。
② ——开证行开出可转让信用证并发送给通知行。
③ ——通知行向第一受益人通知可转让信用证。
④ ——第一受益人向信用证指定的转让行(可能就是通知行)发出转让指示。
⑤ ——转让行向第二受益人转让信用证。
⑥ ——第二受益人交单领款。
⑦ ——转让行通知第一受益人更换单据。
⑧ ——转让行将第一受益人提供的发票(和汇票)和第二受益人准备的其他单据寄往开证行索偿。
⑨ ——开证行审单无误后对转让行作偿付，并通知申请人办理付款赎单。

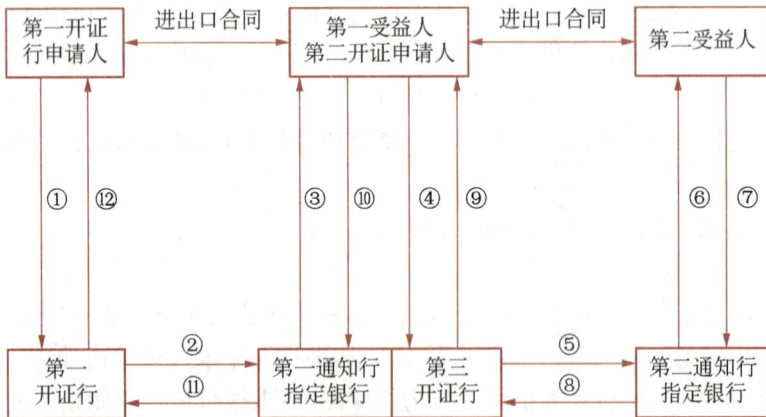

图6-5　背对背信用证运作程序

图例说明：
① ——申请证。　　　　　② ——开立第一证。
③ ——通知第一证。　　　④ ——申请开立第二证。
⑤ ——开立第二证。　　　⑥ ——通知第二证。
⑦ ——交单取款。　　　　⑧ ——寄单索偿。
⑨ ——付款赎单。　　　　⑩ ——交单取款。
⑪ ——寄单索偿。　　　　⑫ ——付款赎单。

② 原始信用证受益于第一受益人；背对背信用证从第一受益人账户付款，受益于供货的第二受益人。原始信用证的第一受益人成为背对背信用证的申请人，在此安排下供货的第二受益人获得比款项让渡还要大些的保证。

③ 背对背信用证必须按照原始信用证的措辞开立，以便在原始信用证要求的期限内，按照原信用证的规定制作单据（发票除外），使第一受益人能在该证期限内交单索款。

背对背信用证与可转让信用证的比较如表 6-1 所示。

表 6-1　背对背信用证与可转让信用证比较

背对背信用证	可转让信用证
1. 背对背信用证的开立，并非原始信用证申请和开证行的意旨，而是受益人的意旨，申请人和开证行与背对背信用证无关	1. 可转让信用证的开立是申请人的意旨，开证行同意，并在信用证上加列"transferable"字样
2. 凭着原始信用证开立背对背信用证，两证同时存在	2. 可转让信用证的全部或部分权利转让出去，该证就失去那部分金额
3. 背对背信用证的第二受益人得不到原始信用证开证行的付款保证	3. 可转让信用证的第一受益人可以得到开证行的付款保证
4. 开立背对背信用证的银行就是该证的开证行	4. 转让行按照第一受益人的指示开立变更条款的新的可转让信用证，通知第二受益人，该转让行地位不变，仍是转让行

3. 对开信用证

在易货贸易、补偿贸易及来料加工等业务中，为了平衡贸易，防止只出不进或只进不出的单向交易，贸易双方会相互向对方开立信用证，而且经手的银行也相同，此类信用证就是对开信用证。

对开信用证业务包含两份信用证：当一方当事人开立以另一方为受益人的信用证后，原受益人向原通知行申请开立第二信用证，俗称回头证，经原开证行通知给原开证申请人，从而将两笔相向交易联系起来。为了防止第一证开出后对方不开立回头证的风险，第一证可以规定受益人在交单时应附带一份担保书，保证在规定时间内开立合格的第二证。第一证也可以规定本证暂不生效，待受益人开出合格的回头证，由申请人接受后通知对方银行两证同时生效。对开信用证的运作程序如图 6-6 所示。

4. 预支信用证

开证行在申请人的授权下，在信用证中向受益人承诺，在受益人装运交单前，可签发光票向开证行或指定银行（比如是受益人选定的议付行）支取部分货款，以帮助受益人备货装运。如果到期受益人未能装运，则由开证行负责向预支行偿还本息，由申请人对开证行负责。这是进口方利用开证行信用帮助受益人融资的一种方式，由进口方承担最终融资的风险。预支信用证中预支条款内容包括：其一，预支的最高额度，分全部预支或部分预支两种；其二，开证行向预支行的担保声明；其三，受益人应向预支行按时交单，预支行在议付或付款时扣除预支款和利息。

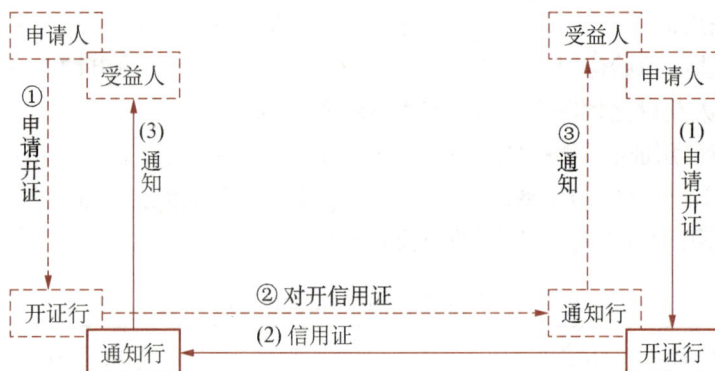

图6-6   对开信用证运作程序

（1）全部预支信用证。全部预支信用证的进口商意欲向出口商融资，在其申请开证时就将全部预支款项足额交给开证行，开证行在信用证上加列预支条款，授权指定银行凭受益人交来光票(或收据)以及承诺书(承诺在信用证有效期内，装运货物，提交信用证要求的单据)予以议付购买，而将全部信用证金额扣减利息预先垫付给受益人，并收存受益人交来的正本信用证，背书议付金额，妥为保管，以备将来议付货运单据之用。对于预支垫款将从以后议付货运单据款项扣还，然后按照正常办法向开证行寄单索偿。

（2）红条款信用证。红条款信用证属于部分预支信用证的一种，最早使用是在澳洲购买羊毛时需要预付部分货款，于是对澳洲开出信用证加列预支条款。为了醒目，起初用红墨水书写，由此得名为红条款信用证。由于垫款是融资，有时指定银行可以同受益人签订"预支条款信用证垫付放款合同"，证明以议付款项偿还垫款本息。垫款金额一般是信用证金额的一部分，以备将来议付金额足够偿还垫款本息。倘若信用证到期日以前出口商不能办理议付，则垫款本息应由开证行负责偿还，然后由它向申请人追索此款。

5. 循环信用证

循环信用证带有条款和条件，使其金额可以更新或复活，不需修改信用证。循环信用证可以是可撤销的，也可以是不可撤销的和按时间或按金额循环的。在进出口双方订立长期合同、分批交货，而且货物比较大宗单一的情况下，进口方为了节省开证手续和费用，即可开立循环信用证。

循环信用证分为两种：一种是按时间循环使用的信用证；另一种是按金额循环使用的信用证。不论是按时间循环或者是按金额循环，凡是上次未用完的信用证余额，可以移到下一次一并使用的称为积累循环信用证；凡是上次未用完的信用证金额不能移到下一次一并使用的称为非积累循环信用证。

按时间循环的信用证是指受益人在一定的时间内(如1个月)可议付信用证规定的一定金额议付后，在以后一定时间内(如下1个月)余额又恢复至原金额仍可议付使用，在若干个月内循环使用，直至该证规定的总金额用完为止的一种信用证。

按金额循环的信用证是指受益人按照该证规定的一定金额进行议付后，该证仍恢复到原金额，可供再议付使用，直至该证规定的总金额用完为止的一种信用证。其特点有：(1)自动恢复循环。每期金额用完不必等待开证行通知，即可自动恢复到原金额使用。

(2)非自动恢复循环。每期金额用完必须等待开证行通知到达后信用证才能恢复到原金额使用。(3)半自动恢复循环。每次议付后一定时期内开证行未发出停止循环使用的通知,则在下期开始起,就可自动恢复到原金额使用。

三、信用证方式下的风险与防范

1. 标准信用证下的风险与防范

一般来说,标准信用证因当事人资信不良、操作失当或某一方蓄意欺诈等原因也会带来结算风险。主要风险类型是:

(1)开证行资信欠佳。全球银行有数万家,但并非所有银行都具备开立信用证的资格。对于一些资信度较低的银行(大多为那些实力较弱的小银行,或是外汇短缺国家的银行)来说,它们开立的信用证一旦被受益人接受,往往意味着收汇困难。尽管国际商会提倡开证行不要以非实质性的不符点作拒付依据,在结算时这种银行还会违背国际惯例,千方百计在受益人提交的合格单据中挑毛病,拒付货款,或者是开证行破产倒闭。其结果受益人往往是货款两空。

(2)结算人员工作疏漏。在信用证结算工作中,常常发生因结算工作人员对国际结算的有关国际惯例不熟悉、缺乏实践经验,或工作责任心不强、明知故犯、违规操作等各种原因,忽视了关键环节的审核,产生了程度不同的疏漏,造成单证不符、单单不符,遭到开证行拒付,或使蓄意欺诈者有机可乘。

(3)外商伪造单据。信用证结算的主要特征之一是单纯的单据交易,与基础贸易相分离。在科学技术发达的今天,不法外商往往运用先进技术,并收买串通船方、商检机构、开证行或其他有关机构,伪造各种单据,如假提单、假汇票、假支票、假商检证书、假保险单等,进行诈骗,并屡屡得手。这些假单据往往冠以知名度较高的出具机构名称,数额巨大,仿真度极高,而信用证又是真实的,结果使付款方难辨真伪,遭受巨大损失。

在标准信用证风险防范方面,要注意以下几点:

第一,重视对国外开证行资信审查。国内出口商可以委托国内通知银行审核开证行资信。如果发现国外开证行资信有疑问,应要求国外客户调换资情较好的银行作为开证行,或由资信度高的或欧美大银行加具保兑。也可要求由偿付行确认偿付,或在信用证规定可分批情况下,分批出运以分散风险。

第二,提高结算人员素质和结算工作质量。对结算工作人员加强国际经贸知识尤其是结算知识的系统培训,提高他们的责任感和风险意识。对关键岗位,如审单、制单,要配备富有经验的业务人员,举办专题培训班,使他们充分认识结算风险的危害及其特点与规律,高度理解并严格遵守有关规章制度的必要性,从而在工作中做到仔细审核和制作每一张凭证、每一个印鉴、每一份证明书、每一个条款,及时发现隐藏的蛛丝马迹,防止风险发生。

2. 可转让信用证、假信用证下的风险与防范

(1)可转让信用证下的风险与防范

可转让信用证一般用于第一受益人为中间商,第二受益人则是实际供货商的情况。

中间商通过转让信用证,把开证行所给予的有条件的付款保证转让给实际供货商,后者得以凭单据向银行要求付款。

可转让信用证在发生纠纷时,如果第二受益人的议付行和开证行没有授权议付的关系,特别是开证申请人和开证行相互勾结时,由于转让信用证的转让行一般对转让受益人不负任何责任,此时第二受益人的权益较难保障,比付款交单好不到哪里。因此在以可转让信用证结算时,首先,第二受益人一定要选择资信好的客户作为中间商;其次,对于交单期和有效期在国外,交单期期限很短的来证要拒绝接受,因为有效期在国外,国内方面较难控制有效期并容易造成逾期。此外,对于付款条件是转让行收到原有开证行付款后,再付款给国内公司这样的信用证,受益人也不能接受,因为如果原开证行或进口商资信差,则国内出口商收款风险极大。

(2) 假冒信用证下的风险与防范

伪造的或假冒的信用证其风险是不言而喻的,因为国外不法商人伪造或假冒信用证总是出于欺诈目的。伪造假冒信用证主要有两种:无密押电开信用证和假印鉴信用证。它们的具体表现形式如下:

- 电开信用证无密押。
- 电开信用证声称使用第三家银行的密押,而所谓第三家银行的确认电报又没有加押,实际上"第三家银行"纯属虚构。
- 电开信用证的签字无从核对。
- 电开信用证随附印鉴样式系假冒。
- 开证行名称、地址不清。
- 单据要求寄往的第三家收单行不存在。
- 信用证金额大而有效期特短。

对付这类假信用证的办法主要是通知行应加强核对密押或印鉴,特别是出口商收到直接由进口商寄来的信用证(一般不予接受),一定要经银行核对印鉴,必要时可按信用证上开证行地址直接查询或请开证行当地专业机构协助查核,此时假信用证的身份往往会原形毕露。

3. "软条款"信用证下的风险与防范

从目前国际结算实务来看,"软条款"信用证所带来的风险来势较猛。人们过去总是对可转让信用证慎之又慎,对其所隐含的风险格外重视。但是一份带有"软条款"的信用证,其性质无异于一种欺诈,与转让信用证的风险程度相比,有过之而无不及。所谓"软条款"信用证,目前学术上和法律上并无统一的严格定义,一般是指信用证表面上要式完备,但是规定了一些难以遵从的限制性条款,或者规定了一些含糊不清、责任不明的条款。这种信用证可随时因开证行或开证申请人单方面的行为而解除,成为一种可撤销的"陷阱"信用证,或者说是一种名义上不可撤销、实际上可撤销的信用证。

"软条款"信用证中的"软条款"常见的有以下几种:

(1) 规定开证行另行指示或通知之后方能生效。此类信用证中,待开证申请人通知的项目有装船期、船名及装载数量、样品检验认可等。实际中一旦行情发生不利变化,开证人往往不发通知。即使有时开证行在信用证有效期内作出指示,也常因为有效期临近,导致延迟装运或其他不符点产生,给开证行拒付提供了把柄。

（2）规定必须在货物抵达目的地后经买方检验后方予付款。这项规定,使信用证项下银行的付款保证已无从谈起,实质上把信用证结算变成了托收业务中的远期承兑交单,出口风险陡增。

（3）规定某些单据必须由指定人签署方能议付。例如,规定由指定人(常由开证申请人指定)签发商检单。这样,实际上把不可撤销信用证变成了可撤销信用证,且在实际上即使开证申请人出具了商检单,仍随时可以商检单签章与留底不符为由拒付贷款。

（4）无明确的保证付款条款,或明确表示开证行付款以进口商承兑出口商汇票为前提。这样,实际上已经将信用证业务中银行信用转变为商业信用。

（5）要求提供不易获得的单据。例如,违反运输常规,要求提供装在舱内的集装箱提单等。

（6）设置表面上不难办到而实际上很难办到甚至根本办不到的条款。这样,出口商难以取得合格单据,从而开证行保留随时可拒付的权利。例如,在海运提单中规定将内陆城市确立为装运港。

据不完全统计,我国企业每年因"软条款"信用证造成数千万元人民币的巨额损失。国外不法商人的行骗对象往往是一些外贸业务不熟、缺乏国际贸易经验的出口单位。对于"软条款"信用证,不少人都知道其危害,却常常热衷于使用,其中既有国内也有国外的原因。近几年国内供货市场较混乱,外贸体制的改革和经济的发展,推动了出口迅猛增长,但由于国内各外贸公司业务交叉、多头对外,迅速形成一股畸形买方市场趋势,供大于求导致出口公司竞相采取不正当手段拉拢客户,容忍和接受买方的不正当条件,使"软条款"信用证得以实施。而国外某些开证行之所以频频开出这种信用证,在于这种信用证对其切身利益并无多大危害,更无损失。何况这其中还有银行自己客户的需要,以及国外银行激烈竞争因素的影响。

当然,也有某些"软条款"信用证被侥幸执行的情况。但是,一旦发生纠纷,受益人风险特别大。目前国际商会有关信用证的文件对"软条款"信用证并无特别的说明和限制,受益人接受了这种信用证后,其利益难有保障。从当前来看,"软条款"信用证大多是被不法商人和资信差的银行作为欺诈手段,所以为防范这种风险,应做到:

首先,严格审证,拒绝"软条款"信用证。在收到买方来证后,应认真仔细地审查信用证条款,注意发现其中的"陷阱"条款,并坚决要求对方按合同要求修改信用证上的此类条款。审证中,不能把所有似是而非的条款统统看成是软条款。即使软条款是圈套,也有大圈套、小圈套之分,有的则根本上就是自相矛盾的条款,或者是开证行的失误。仔细审证,把它们挑出来,要求对方澄清和修改,可以避免风险。

其次,即使货物出运时才发现信用证含有软条款,也要冷静对付,寻求突破。有些"软条款"信用证本身就存在漏洞和矛盾冲突之处。实践表明,在有些情况下,只要出口方受益人和银行严格把关,制作高质量的单据,坚持《跟单信用证统一惯例》的结算原则,指出对方开证行的违规之处,据理力争,有理有据、有礼有节,从而可以最大限度地避免损失。

本章案例 ■

跟单信用证应用实例

1994 年 4 月 11 日,某公司(以下称为 JS 公司)与 GT 公司达成一份出口合同:合同号 No. 94JS-GT102, 4950dz of 45x45/110x70 T/C yarn-dyed shirt with long sleeve(涤棉长袖衬衫), 5% more or less are allowed, 单价 USD28.20/dz CFR Hongkong, 总数 USD139,590.00,1994 年 8 月底以前装运,付款方式为 by 100% irrevocable L/C to be available by 30 days after date of B/L。

JS 公司于 5 月底收到由意大利贸易银行那不勒斯分行(Banca Commercial Italy, Naples Branch)开来的编号为 6753/80210 的远期信用证,信用证的开证申请人为意大利的 CIBM SRL,并将目的港改为意大利的那不勒斯港,最迟装运期为 1994 年 8 月 30 日,同时指定承运人为 Marvelous International Container Lines(以下略称 MICL 公司),信用证有效期为 9 月 15 日,在中国议付有效。

JS 公司收到信用证后,没有对信用证提出异议,并当即组织生产。因为生产衬衫的色织面料约定由 GT 公司指定的北京 GH 色织厂提供,而此后北京 GH 色织厂未能按照 JS 公司的要求及时供应生产所需面料,并且数量也欠缺,导致 JS 公司没有赶上信用证的 8 月 30 日的最迟装运期限。为此 GT 公司出具了一份保函给 JS 公司,保证买方在收到单据后会及时付款赎单。JS 公司凭此保函于 9 月 12 日经由信用证指定的 MICL 公司装运了 4700 打衬衫(总货款为 USD132,540.00),并取得编号为 GM/NAP-11773 的海运提单,提单日期为 1994 年 9 月 12 日。

9 月 14 日,JS 公司备齐信用证所要求的成套单据当面送交议付行。但却收到意大利贸易银行那不勒斯分行的拒付信,理由是单证不符:1. 数量欠缺;2. 提单日跨越了信用证的最迟装运期。此后 JS 公司多次与 GT 公司和意大利的 CIBM SRL 联系,但二者都毫无音讯。

10 月 19 日,开证行来函要求撤消信用证,JS 公司当即表示不同意撤证。

11 月 1 日,JS 公司收到 CIBM SRL 的传真,声称货物质量有问题,要求降价 20%。JS 公司据此揣度 CIBM SRL 已经提货,接着便从 MICL 海运公司处获得证实。并且据 MICL 称 CIBM SRL 是凭正本提单提出货物。因此 JS 公司当即经由议付行要求意大利贸易银行那不勒斯分行退单。此后还多次去电敦促退单事宜。

11 月 15 日,意大利贸易银行那不勒斯分行声称其早已将信用证号 6753/80210 项下的成套正本和副本单据寄给了 JS 公司的议付行,但议付行仅收到了一套副本单据。

JS 公司意识到意大利贸易银行在上海开设了服务处,并当即与该服务处的人员交涉,严正指出作为在国际银行界有一定地位的意大利贸易银行,私自放单给买方是一种严重违背 UCP 500 及国际惯例的行为,但愿意大利贸易银行尽快处置这一事务,不然 JS 公司将会采取进一步的法律步骤,以维护自身的合法权益。

12 月 2 日,意大利 CIBM SRL 公司的总司理 L. Calabrese 主动要求来华与 JS 公司协商解决这一贸易纠纷。12 月 5 日,JS 公司组成 3 人谈判小组赴上海与 L. Calabrese 谈判。在确认了 CIBM SRL 是从银行取得正本提单并提货后,谈判中虽然 CIBM SRL 以短量和货物质量为由要求降价,但 JS 公司未予答理。12 月 10 日,JS 公司收到 CIBM SRL 公司汇来的全部货款。

关键词

UCP 600、UCP 500、跟单信用证、保兑信用证、议付信用证、可转让信用证循环信用证、背对背信用证、预支信用证、议付、付款、偿付、代付

思考题

1. 信用证的定义及特点是什么?

2. 作图描述议付信用证业务的基本流程。

3. 付款与议付、偿付与代付的区别是什么?

4. 案例分析:

(1) 我公司对欧盟出口两批商品,价值 10 万欧元。国外来证装运条款如下:"Shipment of possible either on a Japanese or European ship or a Chinese ship but transshipment in Hongkong compulsory on a Japanese ship CFR Marseilles. "我方安排国轮直运马赛港,单寄开证行遭拒绝,结果我方延迟两个月收款,蒙受了一定的利息损失。请写出分析意见。

(2) 我公司与外商按 CIF 条件签订一笔大宗商品出口合同。合同规定的装运期为 8 月份,未规定具体的开证日期。我公司从 7 月末开始连续多次电催外商开证。8 月 8 日,收到开证的简电通知,为不耽误装运期,我公司于 8 月 20 日办理了装运。8 月 25 日收到信用证,证中对应交单据作了与合同不符的要求。公司发货后持全套货运单据交银行议付,银行议付后将单据寄交开证行,但开证行以单据不符为由拒收单据,拒付货款。试分析我公司应从此业务中吸取哪些教训?

第七章　银行保函与备用信用证

★ **学习目标**

　　了解银行保函的定义、当事人和种类；了解备用信用证的定义和特点；掌握银行保函、备用信用证和跟单信用证三者的异同。

★ **本章概要**

　　本章阐述了银行保函的定义、当事人和种类，着重介绍了见索即付银行保函的特征及直接担保和间接担保的区别。备用信用证可以成为具有信用证性质的银行保函。备用信用证具有担保或融资的性质，它是单据化的业务。本章阐述了定义和特点，区分了银行保函、备用信用证和跟单信用证三者的异同，并通过案例分析让同学们了解银行保函、备用信用证使用时的注意事项。

第一节　银 行 保 函

一、银行保函的定义

在国际经济交往中,如果一方未能履约,就会使对方蒙受较大损失。为使双方能放心大胆地达成交易,常常需要由一个第三者作为担保人,向一方提供另一方一定履约的保证,由担保人以自己的资信向受益人保证对委托人履行交易合同项下的责任义务,或偿还债务,承担责任。银行因为有雄厚的资金和较强的经营能力,常应客户要求,担当这种担保人,这成为银行的经常性业务。

银行保函(Bank's Letter of Guarantee,L/G)指银行应其客户的要求而开立的书面承诺,保证在委托人违约时在规定货币金额范围内对受益人进行支付。它也可理解为,当合同的当事人不履行义务时,银行将担当付款义务,且这项义务是不可撤销的。

担保人由于委托人未尽其义务或违约、过失应承担的付款(或赔款)责任,有时是第一性偿付责任,有时是第二性偿付责任。第一性偿付责任或称独立性的付款承诺,即担保人的偿付责任独立于委托人在交易合同项下的责任义务。只要担保文件规定的偿付条件已经具备,担保人便应偿付受益人的索偿。至于委托人是否确实未履行合同项下的责任义务,是否已被合法地解除了该项责任义务,担保行不负责任。第二性偿付责任或称从属的偿付责任,即担保人的偿付责任从属于或依附于委托人在交易合同项下的责任义务。如果委托人业已履行合同项下的责任义务,或委托人根据交易合同条款,经权力机构裁决,业已被解除了交易合同项下的责任义务,则担保人也随之免除了对受益人的偿付责任。目前,国际上通行担保人负第一性偿付责任的银行保函,很少使用第二性偿付责任的银行保函。

二、银行保函的当事人

(一) 委托人(Principal)

委托人是指向银行提出申请,委托银行开立保函的当事人。委托人是合同当事人,通过银行保函的方式来向对方提供履约保障。例如,在投标保函中,委托人是投标人,在进口付款保函中,委托人是进口方等等。如果委托人违约,在银行替他付款后,他必须向银行赔偿。

(二) 受益人(Beneficiary)

受益人是保函的开立使其受益的当事人。他有权按照保函规定向担保银行提出索赔。例如,投标保函的受益人是招标人,进口付款保函的受益人是出口方。在保函见索即付的交易性质下,受益人不承担委托人不履行义务的风险。即使委托人不履行义务,他仍可获得一定金额的货币赔偿。

(三) 担保人(Guarantee)

担保人是开立保函的银行或者金融机构承诺在委托人违约时,凭规定的见索即付的书面文件和其他文件,赔款给受益人。担保人不需要判断受益人和委托人是否履行了基础交易中的义务,这与他无关。

(四) 指示人(Instructing Party)

指示人是开立反担保的银行或金融机构,或其他实体和个人,其根据委托人的要求,开立以受益人所在国的银行或金融机构为受益人的反担保,并要求后者以委托人的名义开立保函,以反担保内指明的某一特定的人为受益人。

三、银行保函的种类

为了种种目的,银行开立保函的种类很多,主要有投标保函、进口付款保函及履约保函。但在实际操作中,还有补偿贸易保函和来料加工、来件装配保函等。

(一) 投标保函(Tender Guarantee)

投标保函是银行应投标人的要求开立的,以海外招标人为受益人的一种担保。担保人在保函中承诺如果委托人不履行由于递呈标书而产生的各项义务,则支付受益人一定金额的货币。如果保函的受益人通知担保人:投标人在到期之前撤销投标;投标人不接受所签订的合同;投标人在合同签订之后没有以履约保函替换投标保函,则担保人在受益人第一次索偿时必须支付保函内规定的全部金额。银行的责任全凭保函内的明确措辞。在投标保函中,受益人是招标人,如果投标人没有履行它由于递呈标书而产生的各项义务,招标人有权获得赔偿。委托人是招标人,他将履行由银行保证的由于递呈标书而产生的各项义务。担保人是银行,他必须按保函条款履行其承诺,但不会卷入受益人与委托人之间。由于投标交易可能发生纠纷,保函金额通常是投标金额的1%—5%。有效期一般是合约签订或履约保证书开立前的3—6个月。

知识扩展

投 标 保 函
TENDER GUARANTEE

TO: ＿＿＿ (BENEFICIARY)　　ISSUING DATE: ＿＿＿

GUARANTEE NO. ＿＿＿

WE HAVE BEEN INFORMED THAT RESPONDING TO THE TENDER NOTIFICATION NO. ＿＿＿ (BID NO.) BY ＿＿＿ (HEREINAFTER CALLED "THE PRINCIPAL") WILL APPLY TO YOU FOR THE TENDER'S QUALIFICATION.

FURTHER MORE, WE UNDERSTAND THAT, ACCORDING TO YOUR REQUIREMENT, FOR OVERSEA APPLICANT APPLYING FOR THE TENDER'S QUALIFICATION, A TENDER GUARANTEE MUST BE PRESENTED.

AT THE REQUEST OF THE PRINCIPAL, WE (NAME OF BANK) _____
HAVING OUR REGISTERED OFFICE AT (ADDRESS OF BANK) _____ ,
HEREBY IRREVOCABLY UNDERTAKE TO PAY YOU ANY SUM OR SUMS
NOT EXCEEDING IN TOTAL OF _____ (AMOUNT IN WORD) UPON
RECEIPT BY US OF YOUR FIRST DEMAND IN WRITING AND YOUR
WRITTEN STATEMENT STATING THE OCCURRENCE OF ONE OR MORE
OF THE FOLLOWING CONDITIONS ONLY, WITHOUT STATING ANY
REASON OF SUCH DEMAND.

1. THE PRINCIPAL WITHDRAWS HIS OFFER BETWEEN THE DATE OF
PRESENTATION OF HIS OFFER AND YOUR ANNOUNCEMENT OF THE
BIDDING RESULT WITHOUT YOUR PRIOR AGREEMENT;

2. ON THE DATE THAT THE PRINCIPAL HAVING BEEN NOTIFIED BY
YOU TO BE THE SUCCESSFUL BIDDER, FAILS OR REFUSES TO SIGN THE
DEAL CONFIRMATION WITH YOU;

3. ON THE DATE THAT THE PRINCIPAL HAVING SIGNED THE
CONTRACT WITH YOU, THE PRINCIPAL FAILS OR REFUSES TO EFFECT
PAYMENT TO YOU FOR THE FIRST INSTALLMENT OF _____ .

THIS GUARANTEE WILL EXPIRE ON _____ AT THE LATEST. ANY
DEMAND FOR PAYMENT IN RESPECT THEREOF MUST BE SENT TO US
(ADDRESS: _____) ON OR BEFORE THAT DATE.

ALL BANKING CHARGES UNDER THE GUARANTEE ARE FOR ACCOUNT
OF THE PRINCIPAL.

ISSUING BANK: _____
SIGNED BY: _____
OFFICIAL SEAL: _____

（资料来源：豆丁网. http://www. docin. com/）

(二) 付款保函 (Payment Guarantee)

进口付款保函是应进口商要求开立,担保进口商按有关合同支付货款。它主要是应用于货到付款的一种支付方式。如果在合同规定的时间内,进口商没有付款,担保行承诺支付未付的出口商所提交货物的款项,并加上利息。例如,买卖双方签订了一份 12 个月的合同,交易消费品和劳务。以货到付款的方式支付货款,买方每月在收到发票的 10 天后付款。如果买方没有按照合同中规定的按月支付货款,卖方可以根据银行保函向担保人索偿。

（三）履约保函（Performance Guarantee）

履约保函是指银行（担保人）应货物或劳务供应商或承包商（委托人）的要求，向买方或雇主（受益人）提供的一种保证。在保函中担保人承诺在供应商或承包商没有正当履行与受益人签订的合约条款时，向受益人支付一定金额的货币。在履约保函中，受益人是签订合约的当事人，如果供应商或其他承包商不履行合约，他有权获得赔偿。委托人是接受合约的当事人，银行担保他会按合约条款履行义务。担保人是保证委托人按合约条款履行义务的银行。保函的金额一般是合约金额的 10％。保函对全部金额有效，直到合约完全履行。有效期可以是 1 年、2 年或更长。

（四）补偿贸易保函（Compensation Guarantee）

补偿贸易是设备进口方以引进设备所生产的产品支付进口设备价款的贸易方式。补偿贸易保函是银行应进口商的要求，向出口方提供的保证。如果进口方没能按照合同要求以所引进设备所生产的产品支付设备价款，则担保行承诺向出口方支付设备价款及利息。

（五）来料加工、来件装配保函（Processing Assembly Guarantee）

来料加工、来件装配保函是银行（担保人）应基础合同受托人（委托人）的要求，向基础合同委托人（受益人）提供的保证。银行承诺，如果受托人在收到与基础合同相符的原料或零部件后，没有按合同规定向委托人提供成品，则银行向受益人支付一定金额的货币。

四、见索即付银行保函

见索即付银行保函是指银行、保险公司或其他组织或个人（即担保人）以书面形式出具并凭提交与保函条款的索赔书或保函所规定的其他单据付款的保函、担保或其他付款承诺。

（一）见索即付银行保函的特征

1. 保函必须以付款为目的

保函向受益人担保委托人将履行其义务，如果委托人不能够履行，则由担保人来履行义务，但委托人必须赔偿担保人。付款始终是委托人的责任，而不是担保人的。

2. 付款的唯一条件是单据

保函的付款条件是，对方提交保函中所规定的一种或几种文件，且保函只在委托人对于基础交易违约时才生效。基础交易中的违约事实及违约的实际情况与担保人是无关的，担保人只与文件发生关系。当被提交的文件与保函的条款不符，或者被提交的文件互相之间不相符，则担保人应该拒绝付款。保函中所规定需提交的文件在不同情况下有很大的不同，最简单的，只需要提交一份书面的见索即付要求的文件，连委托人违约的证明都不需要。最严格的，则需要法院的判决书或仲裁书。

3. 保函的独立性是相对的

尽管保函中有对该合同或投标条件的任何引用，但担保人与该合同或投标条件仍然毫不相关，也不受其约束。《见索即付保函统一规则》（国际商会出版物第 458 号）规定，担保人或保函开立人的付款责任在于，保函中规定的见索即付文件和其他文件被提交，而不是以委托人在基础交易中的违约为条件。在新规则中,保函是独立文件,担保人的责任与基础合同不相关。

(二) 直接担保和间接担保

银行保函有直接担保和间接担保两种,当受益人居住国外时,往往采取间接担保的方式。直接担保是客户授权银行直接开立保函给受益人,其业务流程如图7-1所示。

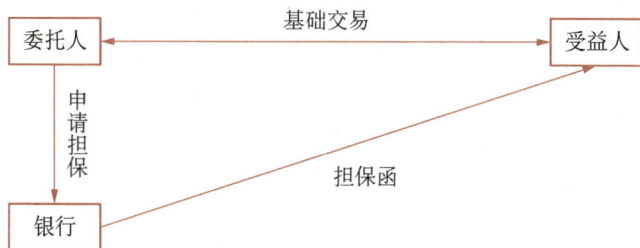

图7-1　直接担保业务程序

间接担保是有第二家银行介入的保函。这家银行(通常是受益人所在国外国银行)应开证行的要求,凭后者的反担保开立保函。这样开证行就能保护银行免遭由于受益人在外国银行保证书项下提出索偿而带来损失的风险。开证银行必须正式作出保证,一经担保银行要求立即支付受益人根据保函索偿的那些金额。间接担保的业务流程如图7-2所示。

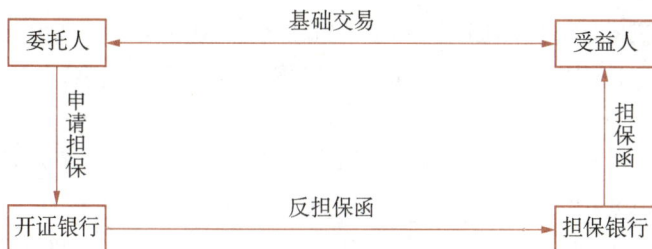

图7-2　间接担保业务程序

第二节　备 用 信 用 证

一、备用信用证的定义和特点

备用信用证(Standby Letter of Credit)是一种信用证,即由银行应申请人的请求或以自身名义向受益人出具的、保证凭规定的单据向受益人支付一定数额款项的书面凭证。但备用信用证又不同于一般的跟单信用证。开立备用信用证的目的,不是由开证行向受益人承担首先支付货款的责任(这正是跟单信用证的目的),而是由开证行向受益人承担一项义务:保证申请人履行有关合同义务;若申请人未能履约,则由银行负责向受益人赔偿经济损失。因此,备用信用证要求受益人提交的单据也和跟单信用证不同,不是代表物权或证明卖方履约的商业货运单据,而是受益人出具的关于申请人违约的声明或证明文件。倘若申请人按合同履行了有关义务,受益人就无须向开证行递交此类违约申明,以要求赔偿经济损失。这样,已开立的备用信用证也就是"备而不用"了。

因此,备用信用证既具有信用证的特点,也具有保函的特点。可以说备用信用证是一种具有保函性质的信用证。它有三个特点:备用信用证是一个独立的文件;开证行承担第一性付款责任;受益人提交的单据如符合该证的条款和条件,应付款给受益人。

知识扩展

备用信用证样本

TO：_____BANK
FROM：_____
DATE：_____

STANDBY LETTER OF CREDIT

WITH REFERENCE TO THE LOAN AGREEMENT NO. _____ (HEREINAFTER REFERRED TO AS "THE AGREEMENT") SIGNED BETWEEN BANK OF COMMUNICATIONS, _____ BRANCH (HEREINAFTER REFERRED TO AS "THE LENDER") AND _____ (HEREINAFTER REFERRED TO AS "THE BORROWER")FOR A PRINCIPAL AMOUNT OF RMB _____ (IN WORDS), WE HEREBY ISSUE OUR IRREVOCABLE STANDBY LETTER OF CREDIT NO. _____ IN THE LENDER'S FAVOR FOR AMOUNT OF THE _____ WHICH HAS ITS REGISTERED OFFICE AT _____ FOR AN AMOUNT UP TO UNITED STATES DOLLARS _____. (USD _____) WHICH COVERS THE PRINCIPAL AMOUNT OF THE AGREEMENT PLUS INTEREST ACCRUED FROM AFORESAID PRINCIPAL AMOUNT AND OTHER CHARGES ALL OF WHICH THE BORROWER HAS UNDERTAKEN TO PAY THE LENDER. THE EXCHANGE RATE WILL BE THE BUYING RATE OF USD/RMB QUOTED BY BANK OF COMMUNICATIONS ON THE DATE OF OUR PAYMENT. IN THE CASE THAT THE GUARANTEED AMOUNT IS NOT SUFFICIENT TO SATISFY YOUR CLAIM DUE TO THE EXCHANGE RATE FLUCTUATION BETWEEN USD AND RMB WE HEREBY AGREE TO INCREASE THE AMOUNT OF THIS STANDBY L/C ACCORDINGLY.

PARTIAL DRAWING AND MULTIPLE DRAWING ARE ALLOWED UNDER THIS STANDBY L/C.

THIS STANDBY LETTER OF CREDIT IS AVAILABLE BY SIGHT PAYMENT.
WE ENGAGE WITH YOU THAT UPON RECEIPT OF YOUR DRAFT(S) AND
YOUR SIGNED STATEMENT OR TESTED TELEX STATEMENT OR SWIFT
STATING THAT THE AMOUNT IN USD REPRESENTS THE UNPAID
BALANCE OF INDEBTEDNESS DUE TO YOU BY THE BORROWER，WE
WILL PAY YOU WITHIN 7 BANKING DAYS THE AMOUNT SPECIFIED IN
YOUR STATEMENT OR SWIFT. ALL DRAFTS DRAWN HEREUNDER MUST
BE MARKED DRAWN UNDER BANK _____ STANDBY LETTER OF
CREDIT NO. _____ DATED _____.

THIS STANDBY LETTER OF CREDIT WILL COME INTO EFFECT ON
_____ AND EXPIRE ON _____ AT THE COUNTER OF BANK OF _____.

THIS STANDBY LETTER OF CREDIT IS SUBJECT TO UNIFORM CUSTOMS
AND PRACTICE FOR DOCUMENT CREDITS INTERNATIONAL CHAMBER
OF COMMERCE PUBLICATION NO. 500.

（资料来源：豆丁网．http：//www. docin. com/）

二、备用信用证与银行保函的异同

（1）备用信用证与见索即付保函从法律观点来看，它们属于两种规则，即跟单信用证统一惯例和见索即付保函统一规则。它们之间的不同并不是在法律上，而是在实务与业务专用术语上。

（2）备用信用证已发展成比一般的见索即付保函使用范围更广泛的一种通用的金融支持工具。因此，备用信用证用于支持委托人履行金融上与非金融上的义务，并对主要的金融担保起信用增强的作用。

备用信用证与银行保函的异同见表7-1。

表7-1　备用信用证与银行保函的异同

异同	备用信用证	银行保函
相同点	① 从定义上看，法律当事人基本相同。 ② 从应用上看，都可以提供担保。 ③ 从性质上看，都具有第一性、独立性、单据化等特点。	
不同点	① 独立性、自足性、单据化，与基础合约无关。 ② 有统一的国际惯例，而且国际惯例有深远的影响，当事人在执行过程中受国际惯例的制约。	① 保函应具有从属性保函与独立保函之分，传统保函是从属性的，属于第二性的付款责任，属单据化业务，与基础无关。 ② 各国对保函的法律规范各不相同，没有统一的保函国际惯例，而且现有国际惯例影响较小，比较难执行。

三、银行保函与跟单信用证的异同

从根本上说,银行保函与跟单信用证有许多相似之处,但两者也有明显的区别。

(1)跟单信用证只能用于凭单付款的货物贸易项下,向出口方提供付款保证。银行保函可用于任何类型经济交易的合同。银行承诺当委托人违约时,向受益人付款。

(2)跟单信用证项下开证行承诺的是,只要提交的单据与信用证条款相符,开证行一定付款、承兑与支付汇票,或议付汇票或单据,或者履行信用证项下其他义务。而银行保函只有在委托人不履行其职责时才得以有效使用。两者的目的不同。

(3)跟单信用证项下付款所要求提供的单据是包括运输单据在内的商业单据。银行保函要求提供的则是证明委托人违约的文件。

(4)跟单信用证有保兑行、议付行、付款行、偿付行、承兑行和开证行。银行保函只有提供担保的开证行一家银行。

(5)跟单信用证不仅有开证行的承诺,还有保兑行的承诺。单据可向开证行提交也可以向保兑行提交。银行保函的受益人只能向担保行交单。

(6)《跟单信用证统一惯例》(UCP 600)没有规定管辖法律和裁决权。如果信用证项下发生任何纠纷,要在何处解决此争端是一个复杂问题。在保函项下,国际商会出版物第458号和第325号都明确规定管辖法律和裁决权,即管辖法律应在保证人或指示人业务所在地。如果业务所在地有一个以上,则应在开立保证书或反担保的所在地。

(7)跟单信用证常用于国际贸易融资。银行保函的受益人则不能通过保函获得融资。

四、备用信用证与跟单信用证的异同

开立备用信用证是支持一项基于贷款或合约或预付款到期、履约或违约后的支付义务,或其他不确定的事件发生或不发生所产生的支付义务的履行。开立跟单信用证是支持基于运交货物或提供服务而产生的支付义务的履行。备用信用证和跟单信用证都是在不同情况下订立的独立承诺。

备用信用证可被认为是具有信用形式的银行保函。与跟单信用证相比,备用信用证的适用范围更广。备用信用证有违约预付款型和直接付款型之分,而跟单信用证无此种分类。

本章案例 ▪

一、与银行保函相关的案例

我国玩具生产企业 A 公司,参与欧洲某企业 B 公司(保函受益人)的委托玩具招标后,收到了中标通知书。于是 A 公司向我国某银行(担保银行)申请开立履约保函。担保行审核中标通知书及有关资料后,建议保函的申请人(A 公司)联系受益人(B 公司)进行以下修改:

(1) 原标书规定的保函合同金额的 20%,比例过高,建议降到 10% 以下。

(2) 原标书、合同规定允许分批装运,建议在保函中允许加列保函金额随申请人履约情况按比例予以递减。

(3) 原标书规定中标方接到中标通知书以后就出具银行保函,同时与买方签订合同。买方根据合同开立延期付款信用证。担保行建议 A 公司与招标方商议,先把合同签订下来,并在买方开来信用证后,再按照买方要求开立履约保函。

买方(保函受益人)先于保函的开立和买卖合同的签订,开来了两笔信用证。我国 A 公司也申请对外开立了履约银行保函。

接下来,A 公司按照合同正常出货。然后,向担保银行提出撤销保函,担保银行致电对方银行,要求确认保函失效并解除担保行的责任。但是没过几天,收到对方银行的来电,申明保函受益人已经递交正式文件,申明保函申请人违约,要求赔付全部保函金额,并要求申请担保行偿付。经了解得知,因 A 公司的第二批货晚到港两天,为对方提供了索赔的理由。为了保存信誉,担保行不得不对外赔付,并最终向 A 公司追索。

二、与备用信用证相关的案例

2005 年 8 月 26 日,某省 C 银行通过电传接到由其总行转发的,据称是美国 D 银行开来的、金额为 500 万美元,期限自 2005 年 8 月 21 日至 2006 年 8 月 21 日、申请人为该省 F 市 H 公司、受益人是该省 C 银行辖属的 F 市分行的一份备用信用证,该证格式规范、条款清晰,主要用于 H 公司向 F 银行申请外汇担保项下的人民币贷款之用。

但由于改证没有密押,C 银行无法确认该备用信用证的表面真实性,因此于当天下午以 MT799 格式,通过 SWIFT 系统向美国 D 银行发出查询书,要求其通过 SWIFT 系统对该证进行确认。

8 月 27 日,C 银行又通过电传接收到据称从美国 M 银行发来的、金额为 500 万美元的加押电传,经 C 银行核实,密押相符,但电传报文内容不完整、措辞含糊,且未直接回答某省 C 银行提出的查询内容。

为了对受益人(贷款银行)负责,C 银行又于当天中午第二次通过 SWIFT 系统以 MT999 格式要求美国 D 银行再一次确认该备用信用证的真伪并要求一定通过 SWIFT 格式回复。

经过两天的等待,8 月 30 日早上 I 银行收到美国 D 银行通过 SWIFT 系统以 MT999 格式的回复。该回复声称该证不是美国 D 银行所开,系伪造的备用信用证,而且美国 D 银行多引用的备用信用证参考号和受益人有误。

为了对申请人(借款人)负责,C 银行又于当天继续通过 SWIFT 系统以 MT999 格式向美国 D 银行发出第三次查询,以进一步明确该备用信用证的真伪以及美国 M 银行的回复中参考号和受益人引用是否有误。

经过近一个星期的等待,未见美国 D 银行的答复,C 银行又于 9 月 7 日通过 SWIFT 系统以 MT999 格式第四次发出查询,要求美国 M 银行尽快答复。

9 月 10 日,C 银行收到美国 D 银行通过 SWIFT 系统以 MT999 格式发来的查询回复,明确答复该备用信用证系伪造的。至此,C 银行成功地堵截了一起伪造备用信用证的行动,并及时制止了一起拟以伪造的备用信用证申请人民币贷款的金融诈骗活动。

(资料来源:蒋琴儿、秦定:《国际结算理论·实务·案例》,清华大学出版社 2007 年版。)

关键词

银行保函、见索即付银行保函、直接担保、间接担保、投标保函、付款保函、履约保函、补偿贸易保函、备用信用证

思考题

1. 银行保函的基本种类有哪些？
2. 银行保函业务中有哪些当事人？
3. 试述银行保函与备用信用证的区别。
4. 试述备用信用证与银行保函的区别。

第八章 跟单汇票与发票

★ **学习目标**

了解信用证结算业务中常见单据的种类、特点及作用,并根据相关国际惯例的规定来制作汇票等相关单据。

★ **本章概要**

在"象征性交货"的贸易及结算方式中,当事各方处理的重点是各种"单据",因此了解和掌握相关的单据知识便十分必要。本章介绍了其中两种重要单据——跟单汇票和发票的当事人、主要内容及国际惯例对这两类单据的相关规定,并要求能够依据信用证的要求来制作相关汇票。

商业单据可以分为两大类:第一类是基本单据(Basic Documents),即指交易中必不可少的单据,主要指发票和运输单据,在 CIF(运保费付至价)、CIP(成本加运保费价)贸易条件下,还需要提交保险单据;第二类是附属单据(Auxiliary Documents),即指进口商根据进口当局的规定,或其他需要特别提交的单据,如海关发票、领事发票、检验证书、产地证、包装单、尺码单等。本章重点讨论跟单汇票及发票。

第一节　跟　单　汇　票

一、跟单托收中的汇票

跟单托收中的汇票是由出口方签发的一种商业汇票。卖方为了向买方证实已经发货，常把货运单据随附于汇票，所以这种商业汇票是跟单汇票，所附单据用以支付卖方的付款请求。

跟单托收中的汇票出票人是出口方，付款人为进口方，收款人通常就是出口方，称之为已收汇票。当出口方委托银行代收货款时，就在汇票背面作委托收款背书，被背书人是托收行，作为出口方的代理人行使付款请求权。

实务中跟单托收汇票的收款人也有写作托收行，然后托收行做成记名背书给代收行。如果托收行对出口商所交单据进行出口押汇，则说明托收行支付了对价，成为汇票的债权人，所以把托收行作为收款人是合理的。但如果托收行未做押汇，与出票人（出口方）之间并无对价关系，在这种情况下，把托收行作为收款人，在票据所代表的债权债务关系上是不真实的。我国《票据法》规定："不得签发无对价的汇票用以骗取银行或其他票据当事人的资金。"上述无对价的汇票并非用于欺骗，故这种汇票并不被认为是违反我国《票据法》的。

相比之下，以出口方为收款人，然后以委托收款背书交付托收行的方式，更符合托收当事人之间的法律关系。

跟单托收分为付款交单和承兑交单。付款交单又分为即期付款交单和远期付款交单。即期付款交单，可使用见票即付的即期汇票，也可以不使用汇票，而使用发票表明所托收的款项，远期付款交单和承兑交单使用远期汇票，付款期限按合同规定可以是见票后定期或出票后定期或定日付款。

汇票金额与币种应和发票一致，如果货价中含佣金，汇票金额就可能小于发票金额，因为进口方付款时把佣金代扣给进口方的购买代理人了。

二、信用证汇票

信用证项下汇票是由出口商开给银行的书面的无条件命令，即发出命令的出口商签名，要求接受命令的银行，立即或定期或在可以确定的将来时间把一定金额的货币支付给自己或其指定之人。

汇票作为支取信用证金额的凭证，附在汇票下面的是全套单据，也称为跟单汇票。它不是单据，而单据却是汇票的附件，银行需要审核汇票，就像审核其他单据一样，必须符合信用证的规定。因此，有时也可将汇票视作信用证所要求的单据之一。信用证项下汇票式样见附式 8 - 1。

附式 8-1

Exchange for USD 100 000. 00　　　　　　　　Tampa，May 27th，2005

　　　At sight of the bill of exchange pay to the order of

　　　　　　Ourselves　　　　　　　the sum of

One hundred thousand U. S. dollars

Drawn under The French Issuing Bank，Paris，France Documentary Credit No. 12345 dated April 10th，2005

Value received and charge same to account of

To The French Issuing Bank,　　　　　　　The American Exporter

　　　　38 rue Fuancois ler　　　　　　　Co. Inc.，Tampa

　　　　75008，Paris，France　　　　　　　signature

使用跟单信用证,除即期付款信用证可以不要汇票和延期付款信用证不使用汇票外,议付信用证和承兑信用证均要求收益人开具汇票。

跟单信用证汇票,除按所适用的票据法规定做到要式齐全外,还应符合《跟单信用证统一惯例》(《UCP 600》)的要求和信用证规定,具体掌握的规定如下:

(一) 汇票当事人

汇票的出票人只能是受益人,一般印在汇票的右下角。

收款人可以是受益人,也可是议付行,一般为后者。实务中,议付行常常就是通知行。

汇票的付款人,一般印在汇票的左下角。付款人名称须填全称,应为信用证中指定的银行,可以是开证行、保兑行或指定的付款行。若信用证没有规定,则付款人应为开证行。《跟单信用证统一惯例》(UCP 600)规定:"开立信用证时,不应以申请人为付款人,如信用证仍规定汇票付款人为申请人,银行将视此汇票为附加单据。"这一规定目的在于把信用证所承诺的银行责任和汇票当事人的责任统一起来。

(二) 汇票金额

汇票的金额和币种,必须和信用证规定相符无误。金额不得模棱两可,信用证中规定:"按全部发票金额开立"或"按95%发票金额开立"等。由于信用证并未直接规定汇票的具体金额,那么开立汇票必须注意金额允许范围。例如,信用证规定汇票金额为发票金额的98%,而发票金额为 USD10 000. 00,则汇票金额为 USD9800. 00。又例如,信用证规定金额为 USD1000,且不允许分批装运,则汇票金额不能超过信用证金额,也不能低于该金额的95%以下,即应在 USD950~1000 之间。若信用证在规定金额前加有"大约"(About Approximate)字样时,则汇票金额可在该金额上下 10%的范围内开立。比如 About USD1000,汇票金额可在 USD900~1000 之间开立。

货币符号必须使用国际货币标准符号。数字要清楚,不能涂改。汇票金额可以使用小写,也可以大小写并用,但大小写必须一致。我国企业开立的汇票必须大小写并用,而且两者必须一致,大写金额应以"ONLY"结尾。

(三) 出票地点和出票日期

出票地点一般应是议付地点,通常位于汇票右上方,和出票日期相连。出票日期一般填议付日期,该日期不能早于跟单单据的签发日。例如不能早于发票的制单日或运输单据的签发日。另外,汇票和全套单据应在信用证的有效期和交单期之前提交,所以汇票的出票日期不得迟于信用证规定的交单期限或出运日起 21 天,且无论如何,最晚不得迟于信用证的有效期。

(四) 出票条款

跟单信用证名下的汇票必须写有出票条款(Drawn under Clause),亦称出票文句。出票条款包含三个内容:开证行完整名称、信用证编号和开证日期,内容应完整、准确并和信用证一致。信用证中往往并不规定出票条款的要求,《跟单信用证统一惯例》(UCP 600)也无此规定,但在实务中,出票条款已被认为单证相符的一个常规要求,汇票上必须列明。无证托收的汇票则无上述要求。

(五) 汇票编号

由出票人自行编号填入,一般都以相应的发票号兼并汇票编号,以便于查考。

(六) 付款期限

该项目重要,应当清楚、明确地予以记载。按不同付款期限,可采用下列方式制作:

1. 即期付款。汇票上一般印有期限字样,如:"AT _____ SIGHT"。如即期付款,应在空白处打上" * ",如"AT ＊ ＊ SIGHT "。

2. 见票(后)若干天付款。提示汇票给付款人见票承兑和确定到期日,俟到期日付款。信用证中,常将"after"一字省略。确定单据相符之日就是见票日。

3. 出票日后若干天付款。提示汇票须经付款人承兑,表示他负责在确定到期日付款。

4. 装运日或提单日后若干天付款。

(1) 要求汇票是在装运日以后 30 天付款。若装运日期是 03 July 2005,可开出汇票日期就是装运日期即 03 July 2005,汇票期限写明"At 30 days date"的方法来满足上述要求(见附式 8 - 2)。

(2) 要求汇票是在提单日期以后 30 天付款,可将实际提单日期(如 15/06/2005)写在后面,即"At thirty days after bill of lading date 15/06/2005 pay to ..."(见附式 9 - 2)。此方法很适用。

5. 在固定的将来时间付款(at a fixed future time)。例如,固定在 2006 年 8 月 3 日支付给_____的指定人("On 3 August, 2006 fixed pay to the order of _____")。提示汇票须经付款人承兑,表示他负责到期日付款。

附式 8 - 2

```
Exchange for USD 100 000. 00                          03, July, 2005
        ① At thirty days date pay this first bill of exchange
or      ② At thirty days after bill of lading date 15/6/05 pay this first bill of exchange (second
        unpaid) to the order of ourselves the sum of USD one hundred thousand
        Drawn under...
To Mellon Bank International,
        New York

                                                     For seller / exporter
                                                     Hong Kong
```

第二节　商 业 发 票

一、商业发票的主要作用

商业发票(Commercial Invoice)简称发票，又称发货单(Delivery List)，是出口商对进口商开立的发货价目清单。其主要作用有：

（一）交易证明

由于商业发展中详细记载了成交货物的品名、种类、数量、包装、价格、金额、支付方式、运输细节以及其他项目，因此能对整个交易作充分完整的反映，是交易的证明文件。进口商可以凭发票的描述核对所列货物及其他事项是否符合信用证或合同的要求。

（二）核心单据

由于商业发票能较全面地证明交易事项，它也成了出口商制作整套货运单据的核心。其他单据，例如运输单据、保险单据、商检单据等只能反映交易某一方面的细节，不能反映交易的全貌。因此，这些单据在制作时应以发票为中心，在货物名称、内容描述等方面应参照发票记载，如果不使用完全一致的表述，也至少应使用不与发票相矛盾的概括性描述。只有这样才能保证全套单据互相联系、协调一致。

（三）记账凭证

由于商业发票中载明了货物的单价、数量及金额，有些发票中还详细列明了价格构成，例如离岸价、运保费、佣金、折扣等，因此可以为进出口双方的会计工作提供详细的信息，属于会计处理中的原始凭证。

（四）报关依据

由于商业发票中列明了货物种类、金额、产地等项目，在出口地或进口地报关、清关时可以作为计算税额的依据。

（五）代替汇票

在许多即期交易(例如即期信用证，D/P托收等)中，当事人为了避免因使用汇票而增加印花税负担，往往不签发汇票，而直接以发票作为索款清单及收据，则此类商业发票上往往载有款项收讫的文句。

除上述五项作用外，商业发票还常用于投保、商检、托运、理赔、签证等环节，因而用途广泛，需要的发票总份数较大。

二、商业发票的主要内容

商业发票的格式由出口商自行拟订，并无一定的规格，记载事项也依交易内容而定。下面只对商业发票上常见的一些主要项目作出说明。

（一）"发票"字样

必须标明"Invoice"字样，或者写明"Commercial Invoice"以便同其他单据相区别。

（二）卖方名称与地址

卖方名称与地址应与出口合同订约人的名称地址完全一致。在信用证交易中，发票应由受益人(卖方)开立,但若允许转让,也可以由第二受益人(供货人)开立并作为卖方的发票。有些交易中买方为了便于转售进口的商品,可能要求发票中不出现卖方的名称地址,而是以指定人员的名称地址或干脆空白不填,这就构成了中性发票,属于中性单据的一种。在这种情况下,卖方如缮打发票就须使用白纸制作,不能使用印有本公司名称地址的固定发票格式。

(三) 买方名称地址

买方名称地址同样应与销售合同中的有关记载相一致,在信用证交易中通常就是开证申请人,除非信用证或合同明确要求以不同于买方的第三者名称作为发票的抬头人。

(四) 发票编号与开立日期

发票编号由出口商编制,当其他单据的某些内容需参照发票的相应规定时,可以用发票号码来代替。发票的开立日期不应迟于装运日,但若早于信用证的开立日,也可以接受。因为许多出口商的习惯做法是在签订合同后即备货制作发票,而此时信用证可能尚未开立,因此信用证惯例允许银行接受开立日早于信用证的发票。

(五) 定单号、合同号或信用证号码

商业发票必须写明所起源的交易的编号,即国外买方的定单号码或进出口合同号码。如交易采用信用证结算,则在信用证项下支付货款而开立的发票常常还应注明信用证号码、开立日期及开证行名称。

(六) 装卸港口、运输工具、航次

此项内容应与运输单据的有关描述相一致。

(七) 运输标志与号码

运输标志(Shipping Marks)又称唛头,是刷制在货物运输包装上供承运人识别货物用的记号,应与运输单据上载明的标志相一致。若货物有标志则必须列出,若无标志则可以空白不填或填入"N/M"(即"No Marks")。

(八) 货物的描述

货物的描述可以包括品名、规格、标准、货号、包装、数量、重量、价格条件等要素,具体依货物情况或信用证要求而定。在信用证对货物描述作出说明时,发票上应一字不差地原样照录,否则就可能因不是严格相符而被银行拒付。如果货物有两种不同的名称,虽然业内人士都清楚这两种不同的名称指的是同一种商品,但不能指望银行也熟悉这一特定行业的规矩。因此,若信用证也使用了一种名称,则发票中绝对不能使用另一种名称。例如,"Raisin"和"Dried Grapes"都是指葡萄干,"Coromandel Peanut"就是"Machine Shelled Peanut"(机剥花生仁),但若信用证使用了一种表述,发票就不能使用另一表述,否则就是单证不符。

出运货物的数量及/或重量应符合信用证规定,如信用证规定的数量及/或重量前有诸如"About"、"Circa"之类表示估计的修饰语,则可以理解为允许有不超过±10%的溢短装,但若信用证金额为一确定数值,则即使溢装也不能多收货款。如果信用证规定的数量及/或重量为一确定数值,但货物并非按包装或个体计数(主要是指散装货),那么只要不突破信用证总金额,即使不允许分批装运,实际出运量也可以有不超过±5%的伸缩。

（九）单价与总金额

单价应按合同规定开列。如采用信用证结算,则应与信用证的规定相一致。如信用证关于单价的规定带有"About"或类似词语,则允许在±10%范围内伸缩,这一伸缩同样适用于金额前带有此类修饰的情况。很显然,发票金额不能突破信用证允许支用的最高金额,否则有可能银行拒付。但是,如果信用证的指定银行接受了超额发票,只要发票其他内容以及其他单据合格,而且该指定银行仅按信用证金额给予付款、承兑或议付,那么按惯例的规定,此项付款、承兑或议付仍属有效,对开证行及申请人同样构成约束。在禁止分批装运的信用证项下,如货物一次性装足,而且单价未违反信用证规定,则发票额低于信用证金额不超过±5%时仍为有效。

（十）出口商签字

传统的做法是在正本发票上由出口商签字,副本发票不用签字。但现在的《跟单信用证统一惯例》规定除非信用证要求提示经过签字的商业发票(Signed Commercial Invoice),否则商业发票无论正本副本都无须签字。这一规定免除了受益人在大量发票上重复签字的麻烦。

（十一）其他条款

其他条款一般根据买卖双方的协议或信用证要求而注明,或者是出口商在发票中印就的固定的说明性文句。常见的条款有:①产地条款。但是,如果信用证规定有产地证书,则不能以此代替,必须单独制作。②收款方式条款。例如注明60%凭信用证支付,40%凭托收支付等。③有错当查条款。有错当查原文是"错误与遗漏不在此限"(Errors and Omission Excepted,简称E&OE),是为了对错误与遗漏便于更正而作的预告声明。但发票内容应该是准确无误的,有些信用证还要求发票上加注证实内容无误的声明,则此项条款显然有违于这一基本要求,因此应取消。

知识扩展

电 子 单 据

电子单据甚至在低端领域也正成为记账客户的一种可行方法。从实用账单如电话单和用电单,到经电子零售商务的账单,都趋向不打印,而是提供电子邮件账单并加以说明。许多服务商如Sprint和AT&T都推出各种电子账单的优惠措施,比如,对申明接受电子账单的消费者提供一定的折扣。大多数会计系统让用户的电脑或传真机能够接收来自他们电脑或传真机上的电子账单或传真账单。最务实的单位意识到无纸化办公所带来的成本节约,纷纷加紧进行无纸化办公过渡。

第三节　其 他 发 票

一、海关发票(Customs Invoice)

海关发票是出口商按照进口商海关的特定格式填制的发票,供进口商在货物进口报关时使用。这种发票是进口国执行差别待遇政策和排挤别国商品的一种工具。目前主要是一些原英国属地或殖民地国家要求使用海关发票,例如加拿大、新西兰、新加坡、马来西亚等。海关发票的主要内容与商业发票相似,但它特别要求注明出运商品的国内市场价格以及产地,并要求出口商就此作出正式申明。因此,海关发票有 3 项主要作用:①便于进口国海关核定货物的原产地,从而按照不同国家的判别税率征收关税。此处所指的关税是特别关税以外一般关税,按其税率由低到高可分为双边优惠关税、普遍优惠制关税、最惠国关税及普通关税,其平均水平可低至零,亦可高达 40%。②便于进口国海关核定货物在出口国的国内市场价格,防止倾销(Dumping),并根据实际倾销幅度征收反倾销特别关税,或者防止出口商故意虚报价格以帮助进口商逃避关税的现象。③可以为进口国海关及有关当局提供关于进口额的统计资料。由于不同贸易条件下价格构成不同,因此通常以 FOB(装运港船上交货)价为统计对象,运费、保费等另项统计,列入非贸易(劳务)支出项目。鉴于海关发票的前两项主要作用,海关发票也可称为价值与产地联合证明书(Combined Certificate of Value and Origin)。

二、形式发票 (Proforma Invoice)

形式发票也称为预开发票,是出口商对外发盘(Offer)时使用的一种固定书面形式,上面印有"形式发票"字样,其他内容与正式的商业发票基本相似,通常载明买方名称、地址,商品的名称、规格、货号、包装、数量、单价、总值、交付期、支付方式等。但是,形式发票与商业发票有本质上的区别。商业发票是在买卖双方成交之后签发的发票,是对已有交易的说明,因而也称为正式发票;而形式发票只是一种发盘,供买方确认成交或办理成交前的必要手续(例如申请进口许可证或外汇额度等),该发票签发时交易尚未正式达成,发票中记载的内容也可变更,因此称为非正式发票。形式发票往往应进口或外汇管制较严国家的买方要求而签发,作为发盘内容是相当完整明确的,但卖方有权最后确认,因此形式发票上常印有如下条款:"This invoice is supplied to enable you to apply for the necessary Import Licence. Actual orders shall be subject to our final confirmation"(本发票供你方申请必要的进口许可证之用。实际定单须经我方最后确认)。

三、领事发票 (Consular Invoice)

领事发票也称为法定发票(Legalized Invoice)或签证发票(Visaed Invoice),是指经进口国在出口国或邻近地区的领事签证的发票。领事发票的制作和格式各国不一,有的规定了领事发票的固定格式,出口商必须照规定格式制作;有的则规定由领事在普通商业发票上签证即可;也有的规定不仅要对发票签证,还要对其他单据甚至全部商业单据签证。签证费用的算收,有的按固定金额收取,有的则按发票金额的一定比例收取。领事发票的主要作用有:①代替产地证明书,由领事核定货物的原产地,便于进口国海关采取不同税率的差别待遇政策。②代替进口许可证,作为限制或禁止进口的措施。因为领事发票是装运单据的一部分,是进口报关的必要单据之一,若无领事发票则禁止进口或课以最高税率。③作为进口国海关和贸易主管部门的统计资料。

四、证实发票(Certified Invoice)和宣誓发票（Sworn Invoice）

证实发票也称为确证发票(Confirmed Invoice)，与宣誓发票的区别仅在于名称不同，其内容与作用完全一致。此类发票除了同商业发票一样列明当事人名称、地址、商品名称、规格、货号、单价、总金额、运输标志等常见项目外，还特别地加注有关证明文句。证明的内容视进口商要求而定，常见的证明事项包括发票内容真实无误；货物原产地为某某国；商品品质与合同规定相符；本发票内容与某某号形式发票的内容相同无更改；价格正确；本发票为唯一的发票，等等。

证实发票或宣誓发票的主要作用是：①证明发票价格中未含有佣金成分，因此进口商可以此为凭要求出口商作价以补偿。②证明出口商未向进口商开立与本发票内容不同的第二张发票，以便使进口国海关相信出口商未虚报价格以帮助进口商逃税。③有些情况下可以代替海关发票用于报关或申请优惠关税。

五、制造商发票(Manufacturer's Invoice)

制造商发票也称为厂商发票，是由出口货物的制造厂商出具，以本国货币表示出厂价格的发票。制造商发票的作用与海关发票类似，可提供进口地海关作估价、核税之用。但应注意以本币表示的出厂价格折算成外币后应不超过 FOB 价格，否则就有压价销售的嫌疑，有可能被进口地海关征收反倾销税。

六、银行发票(Banker's Invoice)

有些情况下信用证规定的发票内容要比合同要求简略得多，若出口商按合同要求制作详尽的发票，可能被银行拒收，因为银行不愿意承担审核超过信用证要求的条款的责任。为了满足银行只按信用证条款审核发票的要求，出口商就按信用证规定制作内容简略的发票，作为信用证项下发票供银行审查，此类发票就是银行发票。出口商另行制作详尽发票，径直寄给进口商，以便后者办理接货报关等有关手续。

知识扩展

无纸化贸易

无纸贸易(即通常我们指的 EDI)是一种在公司之间传输订单、发票等作业文件的电子化手段。它通过计算机通信网络将贸易、运输、保险、银行和海关等行业信息，用一种国际公认的标准格式，实现各有关部门或公司与企业之间的数据交换与处理，并完成以贸易为中心的全部过程，它是 80 年代发展起来的一种新颖的电子化贸易工具，是计算机、通信和现代管理技术相结合的产物。由于使用 EDI 可以减少甚至消除贸易过程中的纸面文件，因此 EDI 又被人们通俗地称为"无纸贸易"。EDI 是英文 Electronic Data Interchange 的缩写，中文可译为"电子数据互换"，港、澳及海外华人地区称作"电子资料联通"。它是一种在公司之间传输订单、发票等作业文件的电子化手段。

　　它通过计算机通信网络将贸易、运输、保险、银行和海关等行业信息,用一种国际公认的标准格式,实现各有关部门或公司与企业之间的数据交换与处理,并完成以贸易为中心的全部过程,它是 80 年代发展起来的一种新颖的电子化贸易工具,是计算机、通信和现代管理技术相结合的产物。国际标准化组织(ISO)将 EDI 描述成"将贸易(商业)或行政事务处理按照一个公认的标准变成结构化的事务处理或信息数据格式,从计算机到计算机的电子传输"。而 ITU—T(原 CCITT)将 EDI 定义为"从计算机到计算机之间的结构化的事务数据互换"。又由于使用 EDI 可以减少甚至消除贸易过程中的纸面文件,因此 EDI 又被人们通俗地称为"无纸贸易"。

　　与传统贸易相比:

　　无纸贸易可以大量减少甚至消除在传统贸易过程中的各种纸面文件和单据,避免数据的重复输入,简化工作程序,它不仅能够加快信息的反馈速度、减少差错、降低成本、提高效益,还可以及时得到更多的商业信息,获得更多的贸易机会和条件。其中,最重要的是提高贸易效率。

　　贸易效率在贸易,尤其是国际贸易中极为重要。由于国际贸易涉及到众多参与方,而且是一项复杂的跨越时间与空间的贸易行为,其贸易流程、规则、惯例、法律、政策等因素都会影响贸易。其中,以流程,也就是执行程序影响最为显著。据调查,在国际贸易执行程序的全球平均费用占到国际贸易总值的 7%—10%,而孕育国际贸易单据文件的处理费用则占国际贸易总成本的 30%。

　　经济体共同合作促进发展,最大限度地整合无纸贸易人力资源、技术、标准、认证、法律法规等资源是取得无纸贸易最佳效果的前提。为此,加强经济体之间标准化和内部无纸贸易参与方的协调与资源整合力度,是推进无纸贸易的最有效的可靠保证。与此同时,经济体相互交流合作平台,开展各项服务,不但能够满足企业的客观需求,对整个亚太地区贸易无纸化进程将起到巨大的推动作用。APEC 电子商务工商联盟积极致力于推动电子商务的发展,大力推动贸易过程的无纸化,从而为亚太地区电子商务应用向更深层次、更广泛领域扩展提供了便利的交流与合作服务。

┌ 本章案例 ──■

票据权益纠纷案

案件简述:

　　2004 年 7 月 6 日,我国 B 公司向我国 A 行提交一份《托收款项申请书》和一张金额为 35 150 美元的支票委托其办理托收款项。该支票显示签发日期为 2004 年 6 月 22 日,付款人为美国 H,付款行为美国 T 行。《托收款项申请书》托收人承诺"右列托收款项收妥后,如将来发生退票、追索等情,本人愿负责偿还全部票款及费用。"我国 A 行于 2004 年 7 月 6 日向美国 C 行办理托收,7 月 26 日,A 行收到 C 行的付款通知,C 行对上述支票托收金额 35 150 美元扣除电报费用 10 美元后,将 35 140 美元贷记原告账户。7 月 27 日,A 行将 35 140 美元扣除手续费

56.33 美元后结汇人民币 289 941.97 元转让 B 在 A 行的结算账户。8 月 30 日，A 行收到 C 行电报，称上述支票为伪造票据，C 行贷记 A 行账户 35 162 美元（含退票手续费 12 美元）。A 行在收到上述电报后立即通知 B，要求其立即退还票款、利息和费用，并与 9 月 8 日正式向被告发函，要求被告履行退还全部票款和费用的责任。B 拒不付款，故 A 行将 B 上诉。

判决过程：

根据《中华人民共和国票据法》，本案应识别为涉外票据纠纷，并在 B 所在地的拥有涉外商事管辖权的法院行使管辖权，同时，鉴于我国票据法对涉外票据的托收规则没有规定，我国亦没有参加相关的国际条约，故本案可适用主要调整托收法律关系的国际惯例《国际商会托收统一规则》(ICC Uniform Rules for Collections ICC Publication No. 522)。

根据《统一规则》，托收是指银行依据所收到的指示处理金融单据或商业单据以便于取得付款或承兑，或凭以付款或承兑交单，或按照其他条款和条件交单。其中，不附有商业单据的金融单据项下的托收是光票托收。本案中可认定 A 行和 B 公司建立了光票托收法律关系。在托收法律关系中，委托人是委托银行办理托收的有关人，寄单行是委托人委托办理托收的银行，代收行即除寄单行以外的任何参与处理托收业务的任何银行，付款人即根据托收指示向其提示单据的人。在本案中：B 公司为委托人，A 行为寄单行，C 行为代收行，T 行为付款人。

无论采取何种托收方式，寄单行仅需对委托人托收的票据进行表面审查，而无须对该票据的有效性负责。同时，寄单行的最终义务是把收妥的款项扣除相关手续费用后支付给委托人，本身不负有代垫款项的义务。本案中，A 行为寄单行，也办理相关的票据托收手续向付款人提示付款，并把付款人承兑支票的款项扣除手续费后所得款项支付给被告。至于托收的支票最后被付款行认定为变造票据而被追索票款，其主要审查义务在于付款行，原告对该票据的真实有效性并不负有审查义务。可见，在票据托收的过程中，原告已履行相应义务，本身不存在任何过错。故此，被告以原告不严格依照托收规则进行托收导致票款被追索，从而丧失了追索权为抗辩理由，与事实不符，本院不予采纳。关于原告是否有权向被告追索票款的问题，《统一规则》对此没有规定，应从原、被告约定的原则处理。被告在《托收款项申请书》中承诺："右列托收款项收妥后，如将来发生退票、追索等情况，本人愿负责偿还全部票款及费用"。对于该申请书左侧印有的此项委托人承诺，原告无异议，但被告认为这是原告提供的免除其责任的格式条款，在填写申请书时原告未提醒被告注意，属于原告的重大过失，且因该过失造成了被告的财产损失，被告主张依据《中华人民共和国合同法》的规定认定该免责条款无效。本院认为，托收款项申请书作为银行结算凭证，其格式是由金融监管部门规定的，申请书上的承诺条款印在申请书的显著位置，被告作为办理银行结算业务的公司客户，对结算凭证应有所了解，不可能没有注意到该承诺条款的存在，原告在提请被告注意问题上并无重大过失。鉴于申请书上盖有被告真实的财务专用章和法定代表人印章，申请书上的承诺条款应认定具有法律效力，对双方均有约束力。

判决结果：

B 公司向 A 行偿还 35 162 美元以及该款从 2004 年 8 月 30 日起至清偿日止按中国人民银行规定的同期美元存款利率计算的利息。同时，案件受理费由 B 公司支付。

关键词

　　跟单汇票、托收汇票、信用证汇票、商业发票、海关发票、领事发票、形式发票、证实发票、制造商发票、银行发票

思考题

　　1. 跟单托收、跟单信用证中的汇票与普通的汇票有什么区别?

　　2. 商业发票的作用是什么?

第九章　运输单据

★ 学习目标

　　了解海运提单、空运单据、铁路运单、多式联运单据的作用、内容、种类以及这些单据使用中的注意事项。

★ 本章概要

　　本章阐述了海运提单的定义、作用和种类,并详细介绍了海运提单的内容;介绍了国际航空运输的特点及使用的单据和相关国际公约;介绍了国际铁路联运单的特点;介绍了多式联运单据的特点和内容。

第一节　海运提单

一、海运提单的定义及作用

海运提单(Ocean Bill of Lading or Marine Bill of Lading),常简称提单(Bill of Lading,B/L),是货物承运人或其代理人(轮船公司)签发给托运人,证明托运的货物已经收到,或装运到船上,约定将该项货物运往目的地交予提单持有人的物权凭证。国际上约束海运提单的《汉堡规则》对提单的定义是:"提单是指证明海上运输合同和货物由承运人接管或装载以及承运人保证凭以交付货物的单据。单据中关于货物应按记名人的指示或不记名人的指示交付或交付给提单持有人的规定,即是这一保证。"

从上述海运提单的概念中和国际海运的实践中可知,它具有如下三方面的重要作用:

(一) 作为承运人收到托运货物的书面收据(Receipt for the Goods)

海运提单是海运承运人签发给托运人,确认已按提单上所记载的有关货物的标志、数量以及货物的表面状况等内容收到或接管货物的证明。

作为货物收据,一般认为,承运人签发的提单是"推定证据"或"初步证据",只要承运人有相反证据,就可以否定提单的证据效力。但是按照国际惯例,如果提单被托运人转让出去,承运人一定要负责向收货人交付提单上所描述的货物,不得对善意受让人提出抗辩。

(二) 作为运输合同的证明(Evidence of the Contract of Carriage)

提单是承运人与托运人处理双方在运输中的权利和义务问题的主要依据。如果承运人与托运人之间除提单外另外订有运输合同,则在把提单转给第三方之前,提单条款内容只能被认为是原订合同的补充,如果提单条款与原订合同有冲突,应以原订合同为准。若承运人与托运人之间没有其他约定时,提单往往被视作双方之间的运输合同。

(三) 作为货物所有权证书(Documents of Title)

提单代表货物所有权。收货人或提单合法持有人,有权凭提单向承运人提取货物。通过提单的转让可以实现货物所有权的转让。按西方法律,承运人可以不凭提单发货,但若提货人并非真实货主,承运人须负责任;相反,若承运人凭提单善意交货,即使收货人不是真实货主,承运人也无责任。由于提单是物权凭证,所以在国际市场上,提单可以在载货船舶抵目的港之前办理转让或凭以向银行办理抵押贷款,即提单具有可转让性,交付提单与交付货物所有权具有同等效力。

此外,提单还可作为收取运费的证明,以及在运输过程中起到办理货物的装卸、托运和交付等方面的作用。若货物运输途中遇险,货主向船公司或保险公司索赔时,提单还是索赔的依据之一。

二、海运提单的当事人

海运提单涉及的基本当事人,一是承运人,二是托运人。承运人是负责承运货物的货物运输公司(船方)。托运人一般是出口方,是将货物委托给承运人发送到指定目的港的当事人(货方)。由于提单有时出现交接、背书、转让等情况,还会出现收货人、被通知人、受让人、持单人等关系人。

三、海运提单的内容

海运提单是由各航运公司自行设计的具有法律效力的单据,但它们具有一致的基本格式与基本内容。

《跟单信用证统一惯例》第 600 号(UCP 600)特别强调了海运提单的下列特性:

其一,应是已装船(已装运)提单,单据须标明货物"Shipped"或"On Board";

其二,单据表面须有已装上船的具体船名,而不是不确定的船名;

其三,海运提单又称港至港提单(Port to Port B/L),应载明信用证规定的装运港和目的港,这是对《海牙规则》钩至钩原则的保留。

完整的提单内容一般包括正面内容和背面内容。

(一) 提单的正面内容

1. 当事人名称和地址

在提单的当事人中,承运人与托运人的名称地址必须明确写出,收货人与被通知人只需填列一项即可。如果是记名收货人,则名称地址都应写明,而被通知人可空白不填;如果是指定人作收货人,则被通知人名称地址必须写明。

2. 货物的描述

货物的描述应包括以下四个方面:

(1) 货物的品名、规格、性质等。托运人必须如实反映这些信息,承运人对此不负责任。但是,如果托运人故意隐瞒或描述错误,并因此而使承运人受到损失或产生费用,则托运人应负赔偿之责。

(2) 运输标志与号码。托运人应负责在货物外包装上印制清晰、准确、易于识别的标志与号码,尤其是目的港应以不小于 5 厘米的标出,并且在运输过程中不模糊。

(3) 货物的数量、重量及体积。数量应与标志中的件数相吻合,重量应标明毛重、皮重、净重等。这些信息一般由托运人提供,但承运人可以自由决定是否进行核实。

(4) 货物的包装及表面状况。承运人可以对此作出检查,如果不符合良好标准,则应作出相应的批注。

3. 船名、航次及开航日期

这是提单上不可缺少的一项重要内容,其意义不只是提供船名、航次等表面信息,更重要的是为托运人或收货人进一步了解承运船舶的具体状况提供极有用的线索。在一般情况下,托运人并不了解承运船只的具体情况,例如船龄、船级、载重吨位等,也不知道承运人指定的船舶是否真的适合承运所托运的货物,甚至根本不知道该记名船舶的存在与否。对于 CFR(成本加运费价)或 CIF 价格条件下的买方来说,也有必要了解承运船只的状况以避免风险。事实上,国际海运界经常发生船东利用"方便旗船"或"鬼船"进行欺诈的情况。鉴于此类欺诈事件的严重危害性,托运人与收货人都应谨慎核查船舶的实际情况,确保记名船舶进行承运并在指定时间内装货。这方面的信息可以通过著名的船级社的资料查得,例如劳氏船级社每星期出两期劳氏船舶动态资料(Lloyd's Shipping Index),公布各国船舶的船级、载重量、船龄、船期、现处位置,便于货方确认与租用有关船舶。

4. 有关港口的名称

提单必须明确写清装货港(Port of Loading)与卸货港(Port of Discharge)的名称,如果允许转运,并已安排了转运,则需表明转运港(Port of Transshipment)名称。有时为了方便托运人转售或接货,可能写明不止一个卸货港,供货方选择。在此情况下,托运人必须早于船舶抵达某一卸货港之前48小时向承运人发出通知,告知最终确定的卸货港,否则承运人有权选择其中的任一港口卸货,并对由此可能造成的收货人无法及时提货的后果不负责任。此外,在采用集装箱运输时,承运人可能在不同于装货港的地点收到货物,则应注明接受监管地,如果另有不同于卸货港的最终目的地(Final Destination),则同样应标明。

5. 签发日期

一般情况下提单是在托运的货物全部装上承载船舶后签发,因此若无相反的批注或注明,提单的签发日应视为装船完毕之日,这对于事先标明或印就"已装船"("On Board")这样的提单更是如此。但是,有些提单是在承运人收到货物时签发的,而货物尚未装船,只是收妥待运,则该提单的签发日期只是承运人对货物接受监管的日期,真正的装船日期需另外批注说明。装船批注(on Board Notation)应包括装船日期、船名,以及承运人或其代理人签字或简签和盖章。有些提单已写出了船名、装船日期、装货港及卸货港,但注明"预期(Intended)"字样,这表明这些事项只是承运人的计划安排而非实际情况,随时可能出现变更,不是明确的。因此,在装船批注中应把船名、装船日期、港口名称等内容作明确记载,即使同原先的预期完全一样,也必须照样列出。否则的话,由于预期的内容不是确定有效的内容,提单上就会缺乏相应项目的明确记载。

6. 运费

提单上一般不会写明运费的具体金额,而是只标明其支付情况。在FOB价格条件下,应由进口商负责租船订舱,则运费可能是"预付"("Prepaid")或"已付"("Paid"),也有可能是"到付"("To Collect")或"应付"("Payable")。如果出口商受进口商委托代办托运,则运费通常是到付。在CFR或CIF价格条件下,托运事宜应由出口商负责,并已将运费计入货价,则运费应由托运人支付,故提单应标明运费预付。在租船情况下,往往只注明"按约定"("As Arranged"),而不写明运费金额或支付情况。

7. 提单号码与签发地点

提单号码由承运人编制,以便于核查与通知。提单签发地点应是装货地或承运人接受监管地。

8. 正本提单份数

正本提单可以仅有一份,也可以一式多份。在有多份正本提单的情况下,提单应标明正本的份数,此时完整的物权由全套正本提单代表,因此转让时受让人务必核对正本份数。但是,每一份正本都可以提货,承运人一份正本交货就算是履行了运输合同规定的交货责任。

9. 其他预先印就的条款

提单上除载有前述各项在签发时才填写的内容外,还有一些预先印就的条款,如无相反的批注,则以印刷条款为准。常见的预印条款有:(1)承运人已收到表面状况完好的货物,并已装上指定船舶。(2)承运人对托运货物详细的内在情况不知悉、不负责,这些细节均由托运人提供,承运人不作核对。(3)托运人、收货人及其他持单人都同意提单正、反面所列的内容与条款。(4)正本提单一式若干份,其中一份提货期于均告失效。

10. 签字

在《跟单信用证统一惯例》(UCP)第 400 号中,只规定提单可由承运人或其代理人签字,但随着运输业务提单实践的发展,最新的 UCP 600 已允许四种当事人签署提单,即承运人、承运人的代理人、船长及船长的代理人。四种当事人签发提单对其签字的形式要求各不相同。因此,相对应的就有以下四种签字形式:

(1)承运人签字。(2)承运人的代理人签字。(3)船长签字。(4)船长的代理人签字。

(二) 提单反面的内容

提单反面的运输条款常因承运人、提单种类及运输方式而异,但基本内容大体相似,主要有以下条款:

1. 定义条款(Definition)

该条款对"Shipper"作出定义,泛指托运人、收货人、持单人以及货主,因而是货方的统称。

2. 司法权条款(Jurisdiction)

该条款规定,解决提单或由提单引起的争议的适用法律与有权管辖的法院,应为承运人国籍的法律及法院。

3. 首要条款(Paramount Clause)

该条款规定提单适用于哪一种国际公约,例如《海牙规则》、《维斯比规则》以及《汉堡规则》。这些规则对承运人、托运人的权利义务有明确规定,因此适用某一公约就意味着对当事人的权责作了规定。

4. 运费条款(Freight)

5. 留置权条款(Lien)

该条款规定,在运费与其他费用以及共同海损分摊额未付清之前,承运人对货物及有关单据享有留置权。如果货方未能支付这些费用,则承运人可以不经事先通知,以公开拍卖和私下成交的方式出售货物,假如所有款项仍不足以支付上述费用及销售或拍卖费用,则承运人仍有权要求货方赔偿差额。

6. 赔偿条款(Compensation)

7. 包装与唛头条款(Packing and Marks)

8. 转运条款(Transhipment)

9. 特殊货物条款(Special Cargo)

(1)舱面货、植物和鲜活货(Deck Cargo, Plants and Live Animals)。

(2)冷藏货(Refrigerated Cargo)。

（3）危险品和违禁品(Dangerous Goods and Contraband)。

10. 战争、检疫、冰冻等条款(War, Quarantine, Ice, etc.)

11. 其他条款(Others)

知识扩展

海 运 提 单

Shipper YUANYUAN TRADE CORPORATION 222 ZHONGSHAN ROAD SHANGHAI CHINA		B/L NO. HJSHBI 142939 *ORIGINAL* 中 国 对 外 贸 易 运 输 总 公 司 CHINA NATIONAL FOREIGN TRADE TRANSPORT CORPORATION 直 运 或 转 船 提 单 BILL OF LADING DIRECT OR WITH TRANSHIPMENT
Consignee or order TO ORDER OF SHIPPER		SHIPPED on board in apparent good order and condition（unless otherwise indicated）the goods or packages specified herein and to be discharged or the mentioned port of discharge of as near there as the vessel may safely get and be always afloat.
Notify address TKAMRA CORPORATION 6 - 7 KAWARA MACH OSAKA JAPAN		THE WEIGHT, measure, marks and numbers quality, contents and value, being particulars furnished by the Shipper, are not checked by the Carrier on loading.
Pre-carriage by	Port of loading SHANGHAI	THE SHIPPER, Consignee and the Holder of this Bill of Lading hereby expressly accept and agree to all printed, written or stamped provisions, exceptions and conditions of this Bill of Loading, including those on the back hereof.
Vessel PUDONG V. 503	Port of transshipment	IN WITNESS where of the number of original Bill of Loading stated below have been signed, one of which being accomplished, the other(s) to be void.
Port of discharge OSAKA	Frail destination	

Container Seal No. or marks and Nos.	Number and kind of packages Designation of goods	Gross weight（kgs.）	Measurement（m³）
GATU0506118 T. C TXT264 OSAKA C/NO. 1 - 300	100% COTTON COLOURL WEAVE T-SHIRT SAY THREE HUNDRED（300） CARTONS ONLY TOTAL ONE 40' CONTAINER CY TO CY FREIGHT PREPAID	3300KGS	66CBM

REGARDING TRANSHIPMENT INFORMATION PLEASE CONTACT		Freight and charge FREIGHT PREPAID	
Ex. rate	Prepaid at	Fright payable at SHANGHAI	Place and date of issue SHANGHAI JUN. 18, 2006
	Total Prepaid	Number of original Bs/L THREE	Signed for or on behalf of the Master as Agent

四、海运提单的种类

海运提单可以从不同的角度进行分类。

(一) 已装船提单和备运提单

已装船提单(Shipped 或 on Board B/L)指在提单上注明货已装上船的提单,应该是货物装船后由承运人、船长或他们的代理人所签发的提单。

备运提单(Received for Shipment B/L),又称收货提单,是指船公司已收到货物,备装船只时所签发的提单。

(二) 直达提单、转船提单和联运提单

直达提单(Direct B/L),又称直运提单,是指货物运输途中不转船,直接从起运港运抵目的港的提单。

转船提单(Transhipment B/L)指从起运港载货的船舶不直接到达目的港,须在中途其他港口换船转运时签发的提单。

联运提单(Through B/L)指需经两种或两种以上运输方式的海陆、海空和海海的联合运输,由第一承运人签发的、包括全程的、在目的地可以凭以提货的提单。

(三) 清洁提单与不清洁提单

清洁提单(Clean B/L)亦称洁净提单,一般指不载有明确宣称货物或包装有缺陷的条款或批注的提单,提单一般在正面印就的契约文句中都注有货物"表面状况良好"字样。

不清洁提单(Unclean B/L)指承运人在提单上加注货物外表状况不良或包装不当如"破裂、污染、潮损"等批注的提单。

(四) 班轮提单与租船提单

班轮提单(Liner B/L Rregular 或 Liner B/L)中的班轮是指公布船期、按规定航线行驶、沿途停靠固定港口、在目的港有预定泊位、向公众揽货的船舶。货物由班轮承运而签发的提单称班轮提单,银行接受班轮提单。

租船提单(Charter Party B/L),又称租船契约提单。在大宗商品交易时,货主为节省运费通常包租不定期船(Tramp),整船运输,货方与船方签订租船契约。货物装上所租船只后,船方出具的就是租船提单。

(五) 记名提单、不记名提单或指示提单

记名提单(Named Consignee B/L),也称直交式提单(Straight B/L)或收货人抬头提单,是指在提单收货人一栏中只写指定收货人名称。

不记名提单(Open B/L),即空白提单(Blank B/L, Bearer B/L),又称货交来人提单,是指在提单收货人一栏不填写具体收货人或指示人的提单,提单收货人一栏留空白,或填写"To Bearer"。

指示提单(Order B/L)是在提单收货人栏内填写"To Order"凭指示或"To Order of"凭某某人指示的提单。

五、管辖海运提单的国际公约

由于各国关于提单的立法不同,对承运人及托运人的责任、权利、免责的规定不尽相

同,导致了许多提单纠纷的出现。此外,由于承运人往往实力雄厚,可以影响有关立法的制定,从而使提单条款过度偏袒承运人利益,对托运人保护不周,这也多次触发船方与货方的争议。鉴于提单立法方面各自为政的局面,国际上曾先后制定了三项关于提单的公约,以协调各国提单立法,给予承运人与托运人尽可能平等的保护。

(一)《海牙规则》(Hague Rules)

《海牙规则》全称为《统一提单若干法律规则的国际公约》(International Convention for the Unification of Certain Rules of Law Relating to Bill of Lading),1921 年在海牙制定,1931 年 6 月生效。该规则制定了承运人的最低责任和免责范围、托运人的责任、承运人的赔偿责任、诉讼时效等事项,适用于缔约国签发的提单。

(二)《维斯比规则》(Visby Rules)

该规则是《海牙规则》的修改和补充,全称为《1968 年布鲁塞尔议定书》(The 1968 Brussels Protocol)。20 世纪 60 年代初,在国际海事协会上,提出修改 1924 年《海牙规则》的方案,并在 1968 年 2 月 23 日在布鲁塞尔通过。因修改工作是在瑞典的维斯比讨论的,故称《维斯比规则》。

(三)《汉堡规则》(Hamburg Rules)

《海牙规则》实施 30 多年后,各国鉴于其规定的发货人与承运人的权、责过于偏向承运人的利益而提出异议,特别是发展中国家积极主动对该规则进行全面修改。同时,由于近年来海洋运输技术的迅速发展及集装箱运输的广泛应用,《海牙规则》某些规定已不合时宜。因此联合国于 1978 年 3 月在汉堡召开了 78 个国家参加的会议,通过了《1978 年联合国海上货物运输公约》(U. N. Convention on the Carriage of Goods by Sea,1978),即《汉堡规则》,它把承运人的责任扩大为对驾驶与管理船舶的过失也负责的"完全过失责任制"。

第二节 空 运 单 据

一、国际航空运输的特点和方式

航空运输(Air Freighting)是指使用飞机将国际贸易货物从一国的始发机场运至另一国目的机场的运输方式,是国际货物运输的主要方式之一。航空运输的主要特点是运送速度快,航空路线不受地形条件的限制,具有较高的灵活性。但是航空运输易受恶劣气候的影响,运送量较小,运输成本及运费较高。过去航空运输主要运送鲜活易腐商品、季节性商品或市场急需的商品,但现已扩大到电讯器材、机械零件及高精尖的小件商品等。凡是需要迅速、安全、准点运送的商品,都可以采用空运。国际航空运输的方式主要有:

(一)班机运输(Scheduled Airline)

它是指定期开航的定航线、定始发站、途经站与目的站的飞机运输,一般是客货混载,故载货量有限。一些大航空公司货源较多,在一些航线上辟有全货机运输货物。

(二)包机运输(Chartered Carrier)

包机运输分为整架包机和部分包机两种。整架包机运输是航空公司与包机代理公司,按事先与租机人约定的条件,将整架飞机租给包租人进行国际货物运输。部分包机运输是由包机公司把一架飞机的舱位分别卖给几家航空货运代理公司,或是后者联合包租整架飞机。

(三) 集中托运(Consolidation)

指由航空货运代理公司将若干单独发运的货物集中起来的向航空公司托运,填写一份总运单发送至同一目的站,由航空货运代理公司委托目的站的代理人收货、报关并分拨给各实际收货人的托运方法。航空货运代理公司对每一委托人另发一份由代理公司签发的运单,以便委托人转给收货人凭以提货或收取货物价款。这种托运方式因运价较低,在国际航空运输中使用很普遍。

(四) 急件传送(Air Express Service)

即由空运基建传送公司办理的"desk to desk"运输(桌至桌运输),是国际航空运输中最快捷的运输方式,主要用于急需药物、医疗器械、图纸资料、货样、单证和书报等小件货的运送。

(五) 联合运输(Combined Transport)

这是包括空运在内的两种以上运输方式的紧密结合运输,如陆空陆联运(火车—飞机—卡车,简称 TAT)、陆空联运(卡车—飞机或火车—飞机,简称 TA)等。

二、空运单据的作用

航空运输中使用的空运单据(Air Transport Document)主要有以下两个作用:第一,作为空运合同的证明。该空运合同须由承运人和托运人或他们各自的代理人签字后方能生效。有时承运人和托运人的代理人是同一机构(例如运输行,英文为 Forwarder),则该代理人应分别代表承运人和托运人签署两次,空运单据的正面记载此次空运业务的细节内容,反面则列明空运合同的一般条款,因而能充当空运合同之证明。第二,作为货物收据,表明承运人已按单据中记载的内容收妥该批货物。由于托运货物的细节由托运人或其代理人提价或填写,因此托运人或其代理人应确保申报内容的准确性,若有差错,并使承运人及其他人因此而受损失,托运人必须赔偿。

三、空运单据的主要内容

正面内容主要包括:承运人、托运人、收货人以及承运人之代理人的名称地址;运单号;开立日期与地点;起运机场与目的地机场;航班号及飞机日期;运费及其他费用的金额与支付情况;托运货物的品名、件数、重量、体积等;有关当事人签字;正本份数及编号;等等。根据《跟单信用证统一惯例》第 600 号(UCP 600)对空运单据的规定,下列事项需要作特别说明:

(1) 发运日期(Date of Dispatch)

(2) 承运人或其代理人签字(Signature of Carrier or Agent)

(3) 起飞机场和目的地机场

(4) 全套正本(Full Set of Originals)

(5) 注明货物已收妥待运

（6）承运条款和条件

四、管辖航空运单的国际公约

1929 年在波兰华沙制定了《统一国际航空运输某些规则的公约》〔(Convention for the Unification of Certain Rules Relating to International Carriage by Air，1929)，简称《华沙公约》(Warsaw Convention)〕，并于 1933 年 2 月生效。《华沙公约》对航空货运单的内容与性质以及承运人和托运人的权利义务均作了详细规定。1955 年在海牙对《华沙公约》作了修订，制定了《海牙议定书》(Hague Protocal)，并于 1963 年 8 月生效。该议定书对《华沙公约》做了 20 多处修改，例如将航空货运单改名为航空运单（AWB)，并简化了许多项目，删除了一些承运人免责条款，等等。

第三节　铁路运单

一、国际铁路运输的特点与方式

铁路运输已有很长的历史，和其他运输方式相比，它具有运量大、速度快、运输准确性和连续性强、受气候自然条件影响小、安全可靠、运输成本相对低廉等优点，在国际货运中地位仅次于海运。

二、国际铁路联运单

国际铁路联运是指由铁路负责办理两个或两个以上国家铁路全程运送的货物运输。其特征是在由一国铁路向另一国铁路移交货物时无须发货人和收货人参加，其运单是使用一份统一的国际联运单据。

国际铁路联运业务集中在欧亚大陆，由两大片共同组成。一片是由《国际货协》(全称为《国际铁路货物联运协定》)参加国组成的，成员国有：前苏联、波兰、匈牙利、保加利亚、捷克、罗马尼亚、蒙古、朝鲜、中国等国。另一片是《国际货约》(全称为《国际铁路货物运送公约》)参加国所组成，成员国有：法国、德国、比利时、卢森堡、荷兰、瑞士、奥地利、南斯拉夫、土耳其等国。《国际货协》和《国际货约》都规定片内可办理同一运单的联运，即把货物发往片内任何一个车站，只需在发货站办理一次手续。由于不同片的接壤国家之间双边协定的订立，所以可以办理跨片联运，但在货物出片时需要再办理一次手续。

三、承运货物收据

承运货物收据(Cargo Receipt，简称 C/R)是以运输行身份签发的运输单据，它既是承运人的货物收据，又是承运人与托运人的运输契约。中国内地对港澳地区陆运出口的货物，由中国对外贸易运输公司承运，并签发承运货物收据给托运人，供结汇用。承运货物收据性质上相当于海运提单或国际联运运单副本，代表货权，是收货人提货凭证，属有价证券。签发单位要对货物全程运输负责。

承运货物收据一般出具一份正本,主要内容有:编号、托运人、收货人、被通知人、车号、运单号、装车日期、起运地、目的地、货物名称、件数、毛重、标记、运费支付声明、签发日期、承运人印章等。如信用证要求出具正本两份,应照办。

承运货物收据的签发日一定要和铁路运单上的发车日一致,且一定要在实际发运以后或同日签发。车号和运单号和铁路运单上的记载一致。

第四节 多式运输单据

国际多式联运(International Multimodal Transport),旧称国际联合运输(International Combined Transport),美国称为 International Transport,是在集装箱运输的基础上产生和发展起来的一种综合性的连贯运输方式。它一般以集装箱为媒介,把各种运输方式有机结合起来,组成一种国际性连贯运输。在这种运输方式下,产生了多式运输单据。

一、多式运输方式及其特点

根据 1980 年联合国制定的《联合国国际货物多式联运公约》的定义,国际多式联运是按照多式联运合同,以至少两种不同的运输方式,由多式联运经营人将货物从一国接受地运至另一国境内指定交货地的一种运输方式。

多式联运的特点是:不论路途多远,运程中手续如何复杂,货主只办理一次托运,支付一笔运费,取得一张联运单据。多式联运经营人对全程运输负总责。

知识扩展

《联合国国际货物多式联运公约》

第二部分 单 据

第五条 多式联运单据的签发

(1)多式联运经营人接管货物时,应签发一项多式联运单据,该单据应依发货人的选择,或为可转让单据或为不可转让单据。

(2)多式联运单据应由多式联运经营人或经他授权的人签字。

(3)多式联运单据上的签字,如不违背签发多式联运单据所在国的法律,可以是手签、手签笔迹的复印、打透花字、盖章、符号、或用任何其他机械或电子仪器打出。

(4)经发货人同意,可以用任何机械或其他保存第八条所规定的多式联运单据应列明的事项的方式,签发不可转让的多式联运单据。在这种情况下,多式联运经营人在接管货物后,应交给发货人一份可以阅读的单据,载有用此种方式记录的所有事项,就本公约而言,这份单据应视为多式联运单据。

第六条 可转让的多式联运单据

(1)多式联运单据以可转让的方式签发时:

① 应列明按指示或向持票人交付；

② 如列明按指示交付，须经背书后转让；

③ 如列明向持票人交付，无须背书即可转让；

④ 如签发一套一份以上的正本，应注明正本份数；

⑤ 如签发任何副本，每份副本均应注明"不可转让副本"字样。

(2) 只有交出可转让多式联运单据，并在必要时经正式背书，才能向多式联运经营人或其代表提取货物。

(3) 如签发一套一份以上的可转让多式联运单据正本，而多式联运经营人或其代表已正当地按照其中一份正本交货，该多式联运经营人便已履行其交货责任。

第七条　不可转让的多式联运单据

(1) 多式联运单据以不可转让的方式签发时，应指明记名的收货人。

(2) 多式联运经营人将货物交给此种不可转让的多式联运单据所指明的记名收货人或经收货人通常以书面正式指定的其他人后，该多式联运经营人即已履行其交货责任。

第八条　多式联运单据的内容

(1) 多式联运单据应当载明下列事项：

① 货物品类、识别货物所必需的主要标志、如属危险货物，其危险特性的明确声明、包数或件数、货物的毛重或其他方式表示的数量等，所有这些事项均由发货人提供；

② 货物外表状况；

③ 多式联运经营人的名称和主要营业所；

④ 发货人名称；

⑤ 如经发货人指定收货人，收货人的名称；

⑥ 多式联运经营人接管货物的地点和日期；

⑦ 交货地点；

⑧ 如经双方明确协议，在交付地点交货的日期或期间；

⑨ 表示该多式联运单据为可转让或不可转让的声明；

⑩ 多式联运单据的签发地点和日期；

⑪ 多式联运经营人或经其授权的人的签字；

⑫ 如经双方明确协议，每种运输方式的运费；或者应由收货人支付的运费，包括用以支付的货币；或者关于运费出收货人支付的其他说明；

⑬ 如在签发多式联运单据时已经确知，预期经过的路线、运输方式和转运地点；

⑭ 第二十八条第(3)款所指的声明；

⑮ 如不违背签发多式联运单据所在国的法律，双方同意列入多式联运单据的任何其他事项。

(2) 多式联运单据缺少本条第(1)款所指事项中的一项或数项，并不影响该单据作为多式联运单据的法律性质，但该单据必须符合第一条第(4)款所规定的要求。

第九条　多式联运单据中的保留

(1) 如果多式联运经营人或其代表知道，或有合理的根据怀疑多式联运单据所列货物的品类、主要标志、包数或件数、重量或数量等事项没有准确地表明实际接管货物的状况，或无适当方法进行核对，则该多式联运经营人或其代表应在多式联运单据上作出保留，注明不符之处、怀疑的根据、或无适当核对方法。

(2) 如果多式联运经营人或其代表未在多式联运单据上对货物的外表状况加以批注，则应视为他已在多式联运单据上注明货物的外表状况良好。

第十条　多式联运单据的证据效力

如果已对第九条准允保留的事项作出保留，则除其保留的部分之外：

① 多式联运单据应是该单据所载明的货物由多式联运经营人接管的初步证据；

② 如果多式联运单据以可转让方式签发，而且已转让给正当地信赖该单据所载明的货物状况的、包括收货人在内的第三方，则多式联运经营人提出的反证不予接受。

第十一条　有意谎报或漏报的赔偿责任

如果多式联运经营人意图诈骗，在多式联运单据上列入有关货物的不实资料，或漏列第八条第(1)款①项或②项或第九条规定应载明的任何资料，则该联运人不得享有本公约规定的赔偿责任限制，而须负责赔偿包括收货人在内的第三方因信赖该多式联运单据所载明的货物状况行事而遭受的任何损失、损坏或费用。

第十二条　发货人的保证

(1) 多式联运经营人接管货物时，发货人应视为已向多式联运经营人保证，他在多式联运单据中所提供的货物品类、标志、件数、重量和数量，如属危险货物，其危险性等事项，概属准确无误。

(2) 发货人必须赔偿多式联运经营人因本条第(1)款所指各事项的不准确或不当而造成的损失。即使发货人已将多式联运单据转让，仍须负赔偿责任。多式联运经营人取得这种赔偿的权利，并不限制他按照多式联运合同对发货人以外的其他任何人应负的赔偿责任。

第十三条　其他单据

多式联运单据的签发，并不排除于必要时按照适用的国际公约或国家法律签发同国际多式联运所涉及的运输或其他服务有关的其他单据。但签发此种其他单据不得影响多式联运单据的法律性质。

(资料来源：新华网。)

二、多式联运单据的特点及内容

多式联运单据(Multimodal Transport Document，简称 MTD)是一种概称，由于大多数情况下包括海运，所以很多多式联运单据名称仍使用 Combined Transport B/L(联合运输提单)，《跟单信用证统一惯例》(UCP 600)对此并不强求统一。国际商会 298 号出版物

《联合运输单据统一惯例》(Uniform Rules for a Combined Transport Document,简称CTD)认为,CTD是指证明以联合运输方式或将安排以联合运输运送货物的合同文件。《联合国国际货物多式联运公约》对CTD的定义是:"联合运输单据是一种证明联合运输及证明联合运输商已经收到货物并保证按合同规定交付的文件。"因此,CTD至少具有货物收据和运输合同证明这两个作用。在单据作不记名抬头或指示抬头时就是物权凭证。

因此,多式联运单据的特点与内容是:

(1)表示至少有两种不同运输方式的运输,即至少包含海运、空运、铁路、公路、内河运输方式中的两种。但同一运输方式、不同运输工具的联结不视作多式联运。

(2)多式联运承运人的责任是从接受货物起至交付货物止,因此多式联运单据正面有货物已经收妥待运的表述,因此是备运提单。如加上"装船批注",则可转化为装运或已装船提单。

(3)多式联运单据的运输事项记载一般有6个栏目,即:①收货地至装运港所使用的运输工具。②承运人收货地。③海运段的装货港。④船名。⑤卸货港。⑥内陆交货地。其中①、②、⑥这三项为多式联运所特有。

(4)多式联运单据中的船名、装货港或卸货港如果有预期或类似修饰词,银行可予接受。因为多式运输是起运地至目的地的全程运输,只要起运地和交货地符合信用证规定,船名和装卸港即使不确定(如信用证无特别规定),银行可不予过问。

本章案例 ■

海 运 提 单

2000年1月份天津橡胶进出口公司和印度客商签订合同,出口17吨化工产品到印度,价格条件是:CIF MUMBAI(孟买到岸)。但客户开证过来后,橡胶公司发现卸货港注明:AHMEDABAD VIA MUMBAI PORT INDIA.此时货物已收妥备运,"AHMEDABAD"是印度的一个内陆城市,印度客商的进口许可证规定他只能在此报关提货,所以提单要显示最终目的地为"AHMEDABAD",而且信用证声明由孟买港至此内陆点的运费由买方(提货人)负担。但此批货物承运人拒绝承运货物至此内陆点,因其在此内陆点城市没有设立代理和分支机构。由于时间紧迫,橡胶公司几次催促客户修改信用证均遭拒绝,一时又找不到可以承运此内陆点的船公司,所以只能按预定航次发运。承运人出具提单卸货港只显示为"MUMBAI PORT INDIA",议付银行拒绝接受此提单,认为和信用证要求不符。最后经多方努力由一家船运代理公司(运输行)出具了符合要求的提单,注明从孟买至内陆点的运费和承运责任由提货人承担。此笔交易因此耽误了收汇时间,由于找代理出单,给发货人和收货人都带来了不必要的费用。

(资料来源:圣才学习网。)

关键词

海运提单、国际多式联运

思考题

1. 海运提单在国际结算中有什么重要作用?
2. 海运提单的种类有哪些?
3. 国际航空运输的主要方式有哪些?

第十章 福费廷与国际保理

★ **学习目标**

理解福费廷和国际保理的定义；掌握福费廷和国际保理的操作流程；了解国际保理和福费廷业务的异同。

★ **本章概要**

本章主要介绍国际结算中的融资业务福费廷和国际保理，主要介绍国际保理的定义、操作流程以及与福费廷业务的异同。

福费廷是一种新型的贸易融资工具，它是指包买商从出口商处无追索权地购买由进口商承诺支付并经进口地银行担保的远期承兑汇票或本票。本章主要介绍福费廷的定义、特点、当事人、福费廷业务的操作流程和注意事项等。

国际保理是由保理商向出口商提供服务，包括调查进口商的资信、买方信用担保、代收应用账款等。本章主要介绍国际保理的定义、操作流程以及它与福费廷业务的异同。

第一节　福费廷

一、福费廷的定义

福费廷（Forfaiting）一词源自法语"à forfait"，意指将权利放弃给他人，这正反映出福费廷业务的精髓。福费廷是指包买商（通常为银行或其附属机构）从出口商处无追索权地购买由进口商承诺支付并经进口地银行担保的远期承兑汇票或本票，故又称包买票据。

福费廷是一种新型的贸易融资工具，融资比例通常为100％，还款来源为出口项下的收汇款，出口方受益人承担的费用一般由利息、手续费和承诺费三部分构成。有的银行从同业竞争的需要出发，不收取手续费，而承诺费在客户违约时收取，仅仅收取利息。

福费廷业务的利息计算方法与出口押汇相同。

福费廷利息＝本金×利率（根据具体情况而定并高于押汇利率）×天数（融资日至到期日天数＋5个工作日）/360

出口方实际入账金额＝本金（汇票或发票金额）－利息－手续费－承诺费－出口议付应承担的费用（议付费、邮寄费、电报费）－国外预扣款（通常为300美元，在收汇后多退少补）

二、福费廷业务的特点

福费廷业务具有以下三个特点：

第一，这种远期票据应产生于销售资本货物，或提供技术服务的正当贸易中。在大多数情况下，票据的开立是以国际贸易分期付款交易为背景，有时还有少数国内贸易分期付款交易也开立远期票据。

第二，叙做包买票据业务后，出口商必须放弃对所出售债权凭证的一切权益，而包买商也必须放弃对出口商的追索权。

第三，出口商在背书转让作为债权凭证的票据时，均加注"无追索权"字样，从而将收取债款的权利、风险和责任转嫁给包买商。

出口商通过做福费廷业务，将远期应收账款变成了现金销售收入，有效地解决了应收账款资金占压问题。因为包买银行承担了收取债款的一切责任和风险，所以出口商原先面临的商业信用风险、国家风险、汇价风险、利率风险、资金转移风险等有效地得到了消除。只要出口商出售的是有效的、合格的，并有银行担保的债权凭证，他就不再承担上述一切风险了。

三、福费廷业务的当事人

福费廷业务涉及的当事人主要有四个：

（1）出口商，即提供商品或劳务并将应收票据出售的当事人。

（2）进口商，即福费廷业务中的债务人，承担到期支付票据款项的主要责任。

（3）包买商(Forfeiter)，即提供福费廷融资的商业银行或金融机构。如果业务金额庞大，单个包买商无力或不愿承担，可以联合数个包买商构成包买辛迪加，共同承做福费廷业务。

（4）担保人，即为进口商的按期支付提供担保的当事人，通常是进口地的银行。此外，如果存在二级福费廷市场，则会出现二级包买商，而直接从出口商处购买票据者称为初级包买商。当市场利率下跌，福费廷业务中购入的票据的市场价格就会上涨，初级包买商可以转卖这些票据以盈利。如果初级包买商希望回笼资金，或者希望减少风险金额，也可以在二级市场上转让购入的票据。

四、福费廷业务中包买票据的类型

（1）出口人出具的并已被进口人承兑的汇票；

（2）进口人出具的以出口人为收款人的本票；

（3）由进口人往来银行开出的远期信用证项下的已承兑的汇票；

（4）由包买商可接受的担保人出具的独立保函所保付的以进口人为付款人的汇票或进口人自己出具的本票；

（5）由包买商可接受的第三方加注了保付签字的汇票或本票。

五、有关福费廷业务的技术问题

(一) 债务工具

出口商所出售的进口商的债务可以用几种形式表示：汇票、本票、应收账款及信用证项下延期付款凭证。但是，由于后两种形式的交易往往很复杂，有关当事人必须了解债务人所在国家有关法律和商业惯例，而且这两类债务形式往往以一份文件体现，在转让方面也有诸多限制和不便，因此作为福费廷业务的债务工具缺乏吸引力。

绝大部分的福费廷业务使用汇票或本票作为债务工具。汇票应由出口商签发并以自身为收款人，由进口商作付款人并承兑；本票则直接由进口商签发，并承诺支付给出口商，为了适应分期付款及包买商再融资时资金与期限的搭配需要，一般将合同金额（已将延期付款利息与费用考虑在内）均分成若干期支付款，以一系列相隔固定时间（通常为6个月）到期的汇票或本票作为债务工具。汇票与本票之所以能在福费廷业务中占据绝对优势，一是因为它们在经济交易中长期使用，各方当事人对其都非常熟悉；二是因为汇票与本票所具有的内在流通性与无因性，使它们作为独立的可转让债权凭证而易于交易。

但是汇票与本票仍有差别。当出口商将这些票据无追索权地出售给包买商时，必定会在背书中注明"免受追索"字样，以达到彻底转移风险的目的。如果出口商使用的是本票则没有问题，作为背书人可以凭此项背书免除对票据（从而对持票人）的责任。但若出口商使用的是他自己签发并收款的汇票，按照《日内瓦统一票据法》的规定，他不能凭此项背书解除对汇票的责任。事实上出票人总要对汇票承担责任，不管他是否作了解除追索的背书。在这种情况下，出口商必须要求包买商明确承诺不行使追索权。虽然包买商出于资信不会对出口商作追索，但仅就票据而言，出口商总是承担票据责任。因此为了避免潜在的法律问题,出口商更倾向于使用本票,这也正是本票能用于资本货物交易的一个重要原因。

(二) 银行担保

由于福费廷业务的无追索权性质,包买商承受了来自债务人或其国家的一切风险,如果届时进口商无力或无法支付到期票据款项,包买商就不能从出口商处获得任何补偿,因此,除非包买商对债务人的一流资信绝对信任而放弃对担保的要求,包买商必定会要求债务人提供可接受的银行担保。如果能获得信誉,不仅风险可以有效地获得规避,而且在需要时能较容易地将票据在二级市场上进行转让。银行担保的形式有两种,即银行保函与背书保证。

(三) 无追索权条款

无追索权条款是福费廷业务的显著特色,是出口商转移风险的关键,也是包买商收取较高融资费用的依据,因为这里面包含了风险溢价的成分。但是,如果出口商想要寻求无追索权条款的保障,必须保证满足正当交易、有效票据以及有效担保 3 个条件。

所谓正当交易是指产生福费廷业务的基础合同交易是合法正当的交易,而且符合有关国家的规定,得到有关当局的批准。因此,出口商应向包买商诚实地说明交易内容,出示进出口国家的许可文件以及进口国允许对外支付外汇的批文等,以证明交易的正当性。所谓有效票据是指出口商签发的汇票或进口商签发的本票应各自符合本国票据法的规定,都属于合格有效的票据,而且出(签)票人以及承兑人的签字都是真实或经授权的。所谓有效担保是指符合担保人所在国的担保法和外汇管理的规定、担保人签字有效且不存在越权行为的担保。出口商只有同时满足这三个条件,才能享受免追索的待遇,如果欠缺任一条件,仍有可能遭到包买商的追索。

但是在大多数情况下,出口商只能负责他本人提供的汇票及本国有关部门提供的交易准许文件的有效性与真实性。对于进口商提供的本票、担保及其他所需文件,往往无法确定其真实性及有效性,因此大多委托包买商审核。如果包买商审核时未发现问题,因而提供了福费廷融资,届时却因票据或担保无效或其他事由而不获偿时,则包买商能否对出口商行使追索权,就成了一个棘手的法律问题,必须根据具体情况进行判断。

在通常情况下,出口商能够满足正当交易、有效票据法以及有效担保的条件,因而能得到充分的保障。即使因债务人或担保人破产倒闭等信用风险、进口国政府干预或外汇管制等国家风险而使包买商无法到期收款,也与出口商无关。

(四) 贴现计算

福费廷业务的计算与贴现业务的计算采用同一种方法,即使用一个固定的贴现率,分别计算并扣除各期票据的贴现利息,将贴现净值总额支付给出口商,但由于使用福费廷的基础交易一般金额较大,期限较长,因此各期票据的票面金额应反映货款及延付货款所产生的利息。确定各期票据金额的方法有多种,如先将货款等值分成若干期,再将各期票据支付时未清偿货款余额所产生的利息加入相应各期以确定相应各期金额,或者先将货款等值分成若干期,再将各份金额按复利方法计算至支付日的利息加入相应各期以确定其票款,也可以采用年金的计算方法确定各期的等额支付票款。

六、福费廷业务的操作程序

福费廷业务的程序如图 10-1 所示。

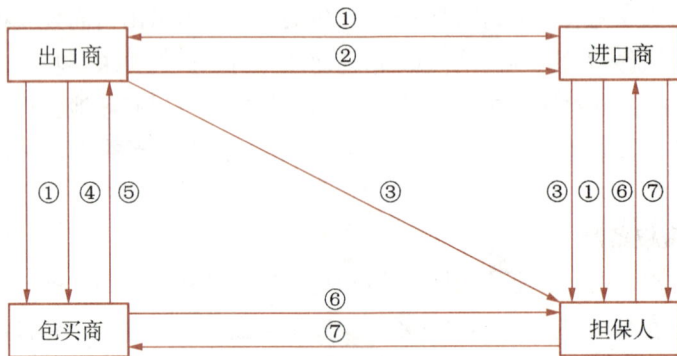

图 10-1 福费廷业务一般程序

图例说明：

① 进出口合同与福费廷协定的签订及银行担保的申请。

如果进出口双方同意采用福费廷方式融资，则出口商应在合同协商早期就与包买商接触，要求后者提供承办福费廷融资的报价，包括贴现率、承担费率、对票据金额与期限的要求以及对银行担保的要求，同时应向包买商介绍交易的有关内容供后者在决定报价时参考。出口商在收到报价后，应在选择期(Option Period)内回复包买商是否接受。因此出口商应尽快与进口商就货款(包括延付利息与融资成本在内)、支付方式、支付时间等达成协议。通常选择期的头 48 小时是不收费的，但若出口商迟于该免费期限后回复，无论接受报价与否，都需支付选择费。选择期短则几天，长则 1 个月，但在汇率、利率剧烈波动时期，包买商为避免过大风险往往不给予选择期。

如果买卖双方同意报价，则买方应及时向担保银行申请开立保函或提供票据保证，并将担保行情况通知出口商转告包买商。如果银行同意担保，且包买商亦认可该担保行，则进出口双方正式签订贸易合同，出口商与包买商签订福费廷协议。

② 出口商发货，并将货运单据(和汇票)寄给进口商。

如果合同规定买方预付定金，或者买方有权留置部分合同尾款，则这两项金额不能叙做福费廷业务。因为定金由卖方收到，无需融资，而留置金的支付取决于卖方交货质量，包买商不能对此获得无条件的、不受争议的债权，故不能对其融资。扣除这两项金额后的净额才可以叙做福费廷。出口商按合同规定发货后，将全套货运单据寄给进口商，如果采用汇票作为债务工具，则出口商签发一系列不同到期日的汇票，一并寄进口商要求承兑。

③ 进口商将承兑汇票或本票交担保人，获得担保后由担保人直接寄给出口商。

这一程序有两种做法：一种做法是进口商收到货运单据后审查合格，即承兑汇票，或按合同规定签发以出口商为收款人的本票，交给担保人。担保人可单独开出保函，也可以在每张票据上作背书保证,然后寄给出口商。另一种做法是出口商在签约后即开立汇票由买方承兑,或由买方开出本票,交担保人背书保证或随附保函后寄往出口地某银行暂存代管。出口商发货后凭有效货运单据要求代管行代填汇票的承兑日期或本票的出票日期,然后连同保函交给出口商。

④ 出口商将合格的票据(和保函)作“免除追索”背书后交包买商贴现。

照理,出口商应核查买方及担保人的签字的真实性与有效性,以确保票据和担保均有效,但很多情况下出口商都将这些工作委托给包买商办理。当出口商在选择期内回复包买商的报价时,选择期即告结束。若报价被接受并确认,则自确认日起开始承担期(Commitment Period)。如果出口商违约,未交来合格票据及其他必要文件,或者要求中止福费廷交易,就必须赔偿包买商因安排融资和抵补风险而引起的一切损失与费用。当然,如果出口商按约交来合格票据等文件,包买商仍可以收取承担费以弥补融资和风险抵补费用。如果包买商无法提供福费廷融资或要求中止交易,就必须赔偿出口商另外安排融资所产生的费用,如果新的融资安排成本更高(通常都是如此),则包买商还需补偿利息损失。

⑤ 包买商贴现票据。

包买商收到出口商交来的票据及其他文件(例如保函、许可证、外汇管理批件等)之后,必须准确审核其真实性与有效性。如果包买商无法审核某些签字,往往要求出口商或进口商的开户银行证实,待证实之后才无追索权地买入票据。

⑥ 包买商将到期票据经担保人向进口商提示。

⑦ 进口商经担保人支付票款。

每付一期款项,该期票据即被进口商收回注销。如果保函单独开立,则保函金额相应扣减,待全部票款付清后,保函金额亦扣减为零,自动失效。如果进口商拒付任一期票据,包买商应立即作成有效的拒绝证书,并要求担保人付款。如果遇担保人违约或破产包买商收款无着时,可以凭票据及担保向进口商或担保人起诉。如果系不正当交易、无效票据、不合格担保等原因造成退票,则包买商仍可向出口商追索。

七、福费廷业务的主要优势

对于出口商,福费廷与出口信用证项下的贴现融资条件相仿,而其承担的风险大大降低。福费廷业务越来越为广大出口商所接受,并正在成为新的主要票据融资工具。对于出口商来说,该业务的主要优势如下:

(1)可获得无追索权的中短期贸易融资,能将远期应收账款变成现金销售收入,有效地解决了应收账款的资金占用问题,改善了出口商的财务报告。

(2)有效地避免了因远期收款而带来的可能产生的利率风险,汇率风险,进口国家的政治和经济风险、外汇管制风险和付款人的信用风险。

(3)出口商不必再负担应收账款管理和催收工作及费用。

(4)手续简单、方便快捷。银行是否同意办理该业务,很大程度取决于担保人的资信状况,只要担保人的资信较好,在银行有授信额度,银行会在几小时甚至几分钟内就可办妥该业务。

（5）在得到票据贴现款的同时，即可获得可供出口收汇核销使用的进账单或结汇水单，加快了企业的收汇和核销，能帮助企业提前办理出口退税。

另外，福费廷对银行(包买商)也是有益处的。由于其承担的风险相对比信用证项下的押汇风险大，因此按"高风险、高收益"的原则，在同等条件下，其收款的利率通常较出口押汇高，从而能获得相对较高的收益。

八、福费廷业务实例分析

卖方：伦敦出口商人公司。

买方：法兰克福德意志进口商人公司。

包买人：伦敦包买银行。

货物：工业干燥设备。

金额：立即支付现金的销售金额 740 000 美元。

装期：20_____年 6 月 30 日。

第 1 步：伦敦出口商人公司于 4 月 1 日向包买商询价。

第 2 步：包买商报价贴现率 9.875%，可以支付净款740 000 美元。

出口商公司向包买商索取一张贴现率折合融资率的换算表，查出贴现率 9.875%，换算为相等的融资率 12.384%，按此计算 10 张本票应加融资利息金额。计算如表 10 - 1 所示。

表 10 - 1　本票贴现率与融资率换算表

到期日 1	未付总额 (P) 2	计息天数 (t) 3	按 12.38% 计算的利息 (Y) 4	每一期本金 5	本期票面金额 (FV) 6	贴现天数 (T) 7	贴现系数 8
02.01	740 000	186	47 348.16	74 000	121 348.16	188①	228 134.54
02.07	666 000	182	41 696.93	74 000	115 696.93	370	428 078.64
31.12	592 000	182	37 063.93	74 000	111 063.93	552	613 072.89
01.07	518 000	182	32 430.94	74 000	106 430.94	734	781 203.09
31.12	444 000	183	27 950.69	74 000	101 950.69	917	934 887.82
30.06	370 000	181	23 037.68	74 000	97 037.68	1098	1 065 473.73
	296 000	184	18 735.62	74 000	92 735.62	1282	1 188 870.65
30.06	222 000	181	13 822.61	74 000	87 822.61	1463	1 284 844.78
31.12	148 000	184	9367.81	74 000	83 367.81	1647	1 373 067.83
30.06	740 000	182	4632.99	74 000	78 632.99	1829	1 438 197.39
①加 2 天宽限日		1827	256 087.36	740 000	996 087.36		9 335 831.36

第 4 栏融资利息的计算，第 1 行即第 1 张本票利息：

$$I = \frac{P \times t \times r}{360 \times 100} = \frac{740\,000 \times 186 \times 12.384}{360 \times 100} = 47\,348.16(美元)$$

第 6 栏本票票面金额的计算是每一期的利息加上这期本金。例如,第 1 行即第 1 张本票票面金额 = 47 348.16 + 74 000 = 121 348.16（美元）,10 张票面金额总数是 996 087.36 美元。

为了证明融资率的正确,以及证明第 4 栏融资利息总额应该等于贴现息（只允许有小于 1 的误差）,所以增加第 7、第 8 栏。

$$第 8 栏的贴现系数 = FV \times T/100$$

以第 1 行即第 1 张本票为例:

$$贴现系数 = \frac{121\,348.16 \times 188}{100} = 228\,134.54(美元)$$

若贴现率为 9.875,则:

$$贴现息 = \frac{贴现总系数 \times 贴现率}{360} = \frac{9\,335\,831.36 \times 9.875}{360} = 256\,087.04(美元)$$

贴现息等于利息总额（误差小于 1）,证明利息率是正确的。

$$净款 = 996\,087.36 - 256\,087.04 = 740\,000.32(美元)$$

第 3 步:出口商人公司向进口商人公司报出销售金额为 996 087.36 美元,开出 10 张远期本票,每半年 1 期,分期支付票款,并提供法兰克福德意志银行担保。

第 4 步:包买商负责任地报出贴现价格仍为 9.875%,给予 2 天宽限期和年率 1% 的承担费,承担期从 4 月 1 日至 7 月 29 日。

第 5 步:出口商人公司接受报价,达成包买交易。

第 6 步:包买商发出承担书出口商人公司。

第 7 步:出口商人公司发运货物。

第 8 步:出口商人公司将全套单据交托收行。

第 9 步:托收行寄单给代收行。

第 10 步:代收行收到单据,通知进口商人公司签发本票,换取单据。

第 11 步:提交本票给德意志银行要求担保。

第 12 步:已担保本票交给进口商人公司。

第 13 步:进口商人公司将 10 张本票交给代收行,代收行将全套单据交给进口商人公司。

第 14 步:代收行寄送本票给托收行。

第 15 步:托收行将 10 张本票交给出口商人公司。

第 16 步:出口商人公司在本票上作成无追索权背书。

出口商人公司于 6 月 30 日提交 10 张本票,要求贴现,同时出口商人公司要负担从 4 月 1 日至 6 月 30 日的承担费,按照承担费率 1% 计算:

$$承担费 = \frac{996\,087.36 \times 90 \times 1}{360 \times 100} = 2490.22(美元)$$

此项承担费需支付给包买商。

第 17 步:包买商支付净款 740 000 美元给出口商人公司。

第 18 步:10 张本票的每一张本票到期日包买商提示给担保银行要求付款,担保银行借记进口商人公司账户,付款给包买商人,直至 10 张本票付完,债务全部结清。

知识扩展

承 担 书

致:伦敦出口商人公司　　　　　　　　　　　　伦敦,20　年 4 月 1 日

包买交易第 123789 号

无追索权地购买 10 张本票

在你公司提供资料和即将交来的票据,我公司确认你公司出售、我公司无追索权地购买下列本票:

金额:USD996087.36。

签票人:法兰克福德意志进口商人公司。

担保人:法兰克福德意志银行。

到期日:每半年 1 期的 10 次分期付款的 10 张本票。

第 1 张到期日 20　年 1 月 2 日金额为 USD121 348.16。

第 10 张到期日 20　年 6 月 30 日金额为 USD78 632.99。

付款地点:担保银行——德意志银行。

贴现条件:按 1 年 360 天加 2 天宽限日,贴现率为 9.875% 年率计算。

承担费:从今天(4 月 1 日)至交来票据日为止,按 1% 年率计算,每月预付 1 次。

特别条件:本票贴有德国印花税票,制票人的签字需经他的银行证实。

交来票据截止日:20　年 7 月 29 日。

我公司确认放弃对你公司作为收款人的追索权,并对以后将从我公司购买此项票据的人也同样承诺放弃追索权。

你公司已告我公司此笔包买交易的下列情况:

(1) 开出本票的国际贸易交易是从美国出口工业干燥设备至德国。

(2) 此笔交易所有进出口许可证已经获得。

(3) 到期日进口商应付款项外汇调拨已获批准。

(4) 支付本票票面金额不得有任何税款征收的扣减。

　　　　　　　　　　　　　　　　　　伦敦包买银行　　　签字

我公司接受上述条款和条件　　　伦敦出口商人公司　　　签字

(资料来源:岳华、杨来科:《国际结算双语教程》,立信会计出版社 2007 年版。)

第二节 国际保理

一、国际保理的定义

国际保理（Factoring）又称保付代理或承购应收账款业务。由保理商向出口商提供保理服务，包括调查进口商的资信，并为相应的信用额度提供付款保证、无追索权的资金融通以及代办托收和财务管理等。

当出口商想用赊销方式推动销售时，为了避免或减少风险，并获得资金融通，可以采用国际保理服务。出口商将准备签订合同内容和进口方的名称、地址告知保理商，在得到保理商对进口方资信的认可后，就可以赊销的方式与进口方达成交易，如进口方到期不能支付货款，保理商将承担付款责任。应出口方的请求，保理商还可为其贴现货运单据，提供短期融资。

国际保理业务起源于英国和北美，随着国际贸易的迅速发展，出现了全球性的国际保理组织，其中规模最大的是由 100 多家银行所属的保理公司于 1968 年组成的"国际保理商联合会（Factors Chain International，简称 FCI）"，总部设在荷兰的阿姆斯特丹。我国的国际保理业务开始于 1992 年，中国银行于 1993 年 2 月正式加入了"国际保理商联合会"，进一步推动了我国国际保理业务的开展。

保理机构是专门从事保理业务的商行，由商业银行出资或资助下建立，具有独立的法人资格。通过"国际保理商联合会"，各保理机构之间互换进口商的资信材料，掌握其付款能力。保理商之间互相委托代理业务，从而开展全球贸易的保理业务。

二、国际保理服务项目

（一）出口贸易融资

出口保理商为出口商装运的商品融通资金，可以根据有关应收账款作出预付款项，或立即付款购买应收账款，使出口商能够及时获得所需要的营运资金。保理商受让一笔应收账款，对有关的债权或物权拥有充分权利，故融资风险小、时间短，对于保理商是很有利的。

（二）买方信用担保

保理商要对进口商的债务逐一核定，预先评估信用额度。在执行保理合同的过程中，保理商要根据每一进口商的资信变化情况、收款考核实绩和出口商的业务需要，定期或经常为每个进口商核准或调整信用额度。凡在信用额度内的销售债权，称为已核准应收账款，超过信用额度的销售债权称为未核准应收账款。保理商只对已核准应收账款提供买方信用担保的服务。对因进口商无力支付而导致的坏账，保理商在已核准应收账款的范围内承担赔偿责任。

知识扩展

出口保理买方信用额度评估申请书

致：中国银行　　　　　　　　　　　行

　　我公司申请办理出口双保理业务，现申请买方信用额度。

(一)出口商资料和交易信息
1. 公司中文名称：＿＿＿＿＿＿＿＿ 　　公司英文名称(须与合同、订单、发票中相应信息一致)：＿＿＿＿＿ 2. 公司中文地址：＿＿＿＿＿＿＿ 　　公司英文地址(须与合同、订单、发票中相应信息一致)：＿＿＿＿＿ 3. 开户银行：＿＿＿＿＿＿　　　账号(a/c)：＿＿＿＿＿＿ 4. 出口产品或服务英文名称(请填统称，忌过于细分)：＿＿＿＿＿＿ 5. 付款条件(请与合同或订单相应信息一致)： 　　O/A＿天，起算日为[　]海运提单日，[　]发票日；其他：＿＿＿＿＿ 　　宽限期(如有)(宽限期指付款到期日后，出口商允许进口商推迟付款的期限)：＿＿＿＿＿ 6. 发票币种(须与合同、订单、发票中相应信息一致)：＿＿＿＿＿＿ 7. 预计买方所在国的买方总数：＿＿＿＿＿＿ 8. 预计对该国的发票总数量：＿＿＿＿＿ 9. 预计对该进口商的赊销出口总额：＿＿＿＿＿ 10. 服务需求：[　]无追索权，需要融资[　]仅作托收处理
(二)买方信息和拟申请买方信用额度
1. 买方英文名称(须与合同、订单、发票中相应信息一致)：＿＿＿＿＿ 2. 买方英文地址(须与合同、订单、发票中相应信息一致)：＿＿＿＿＿ 　　城市：＿＿＿＿＿省/州：＿＿＿＿＿邮编：＿＿＿＿＿国家：＿＿＿＿＿ 3. 进口商联系信息 　　联络人：＿＿＿＿＿　　　　　电话：＿＿＿＿＿ 　　传真：＿＿＿＿＿　　　　Email：＿＿＿＿＿ 4. 拟申请的买方信用额度：＿＿＿＿＿
公司联系人：　　　电话：　　　传真：　　　电邮：
说明：蓝色为非必填项
银行要求　填妥后请交正本和电子版(或发送至：(1)　　(2)　　　　@　　　)

公司签章

　　(资料来源：www. sdb. com. cn/aspapp/applycenter/corp_ck)

（三）应收账款的代收和偿付

　　在信用额度内赊销交易项下的应收账款，可委托保理商代收。保理商在合同规定期内收妥货款，扣除手续费和费用后，交付出口商，也可按事先推算出来的平均结算天数，确定给出口商的付款日期。如果进口商因财务上无偿付能力而不能在到期日付款，则保理商承担偿付责任。所以，这种方式使出口商能按期从保理商那里取得全部有保证的款项。

必须注意的是：保理商代收应收账款中所提供的担保仅仅针对财务风险，进口商不能付款的原因必须是财务方面无力偿还债务，包括进口商财力状况不佳或企业倒闭、破产而导致不能履行合同规定的付款义务。如果是由于货物品质低劣、数量短缺等原因引起争议，则应由买卖双方自己解决，保理商不予担保。

（四）承办应收账款的会计工作

保理商在出口商的要求下，可承办出口商应收账款的会计工作，还包括递交清单给买方和必要的查询工作。此外，保理商收到出口商提交的销售发票后，在电脑中设立有关分户账，并输入必要信息和数据，实行电脑化自动处理，承担账务管理工作，诸如记账、催收、清算、计息、收费、统计报以及打印账单等。

根据国际保理公约规定，保理商的职责是要履行上述四项中的至少两项。

知识扩展

中国银行保理业务的具体办理

浙江一家服装出口商预计对美国进口商年销售额为 200 万美元，支付条件（PAYMENT TERMS）为：赊销（O/A）30 DAYS，向中国银行申请做保理业务。

操作流程分析

1. 额度申请与核准

（1）出口商寻找有合作前途的进口商；

（2）出口商向出口保理商提出做保理的要求并要求进口商核准信用额度；

（3）出口保理商要求进口保理商对进口商进行信用评估；

（4）如进口商信用良好，进口保理商将为其核准信用额度。

2. 申请信用额度的计算

3. 出单与融资

（1）如果进口商同意购买出口商的商品，出口商开始供货，并将附有转让条款的发票寄送进口商；

（2）出口商将发票副本交出口保理商；

（3）出口保理商通知进口保理商有关发票详情；

（4）如出口商有融资需求，出口保理商付给出口商不超过发票金额 80% 的融资款。

4. 催款与结算

（1）进口保理商于发票到期日前若干天开始向进口商催收；

（2）进口商于发票到期日前向进口保理商付款；

（3）进口保理商将款项付出口保理商；

（4）如果进口商在发票到期日 90 天后仍未付款，进口保理商做担保付款；

（5）出口保理商扣除融资本息及费用，将余额付出口商。

（资料来源：蒋琴儿、秦定：《国际结算理论·实务·案例》，清华大学出版社 2007 年版。）

三、国际保理业务的分类

(一) 单保理模式

单保理模式下的出口地银行不是出口保理商,它与出口商之间没有订立保理合同,所以它不是保理业务的当事人,而是"中间媒介",故单保理有三个当事人:出口商、进口保理商、进口商。

出口商要与进口保理商签署保理分协议,再由出口商所在地的一家银行与进口保理商签署保理总协议,它只起到传递函电及划拨款项的功能,所以单保理存在以下缺点:

(1) 出口商与进口保理商处于不同国家,他在当地找不到一个能为其担当保理者的机构,出现业务问题时交涉比较困难。

(2) 出口商所在地银行只能办理传递函电的工作,不承担保理业务的责任和风险,因此对于开拓业务没有积极性。

(3) 进口保理商直接对出口商负责,缺乏出口国金融机构的帮助,难以准确地掌握出口商的履约能力,以进行全面的业务风险评估,随时了解有关贸易进展情况,以及时提供对出口商的有力帮助,不利于保证高质量的保理服务。

(4) 对于出口商的应收账款,一般由出口保理提供融资,单保理业务没有出口保理商,故出口商不能获得融资便利。

(二) 双保理模式

在双保理模式下,由出口商与出口国所在地的保理商签署协议,另外出口保理商与进口保理商双方签署协议,相互委托代理业务,并由出口保理商根据出口商的需要,提供融资服务。双保理业务有四个当事人:出口商、出口保理商、进口保理商及进口商。现在的国际保理就是指双保理模式,其主要优点有:

(1) 出口商与出口保理商签订协议后,一切有关问题均可与出口保理商交涉,而不必与国外的进口保理商联系。

(2) 出口商可向出口保理商提出融通资金的要求,并可得到有关应收账款管理等保理商提供的系列服务。

(3) 出口保理商与进口保理商之间签订代理合约,其业务往来将遵循《国际保理惯例》规则(International Factoring Customs,简称 IFC),使双方的权利、义务、责任清楚,遇到争议,有所遵循,便于解决。

(4) 有了进出口两个保理商,才能使出口商的债权得到保障,督促进口商清偿债务。

四、国际保理业务的操作流程

以双保理业务为例介绍保理业务的操作流程,如图 10-2。

图例说明:

① 出口保理商与进口保理商之间的关系是属于委托代理关系和应收账款转让关系,这种关系需经双方签订保理商代理合约加以确定。

② 出口商与出口保理商订立出口业务协议。

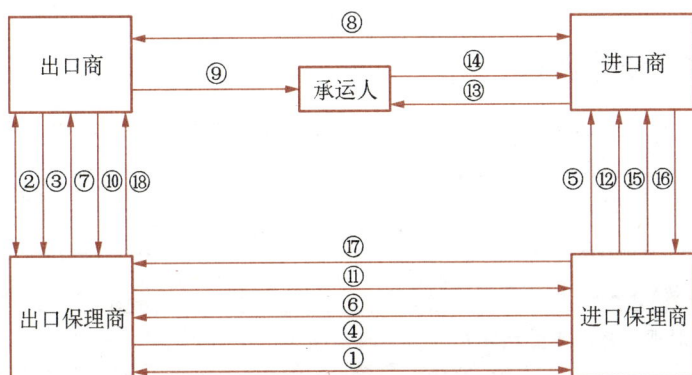

图 10-2 双保理业务操作程序

③ 出口商申请与他交易的进口商信用额度。填写"信用额度申请表",交给出口保理商。

④ 出口保理商将"信用额度申请表"传递给进口保理商。

⑤ 进口保理商对进口商进行信用评估,从而确定或批准进口商的信用。

⑥ 进口保理商将它对进口商核准的信用额度或拒绝核准信用额度通知出口保理商。

⑦ 出口保理商将进口保理商核准进口商的信用额度或拒绝核准信用额度通知出口商。

⑧ 出口商与进口商签订贸易合同,订明支付方式是 O/A 或 D/A 或类似方式。

⑨ 出口商按照合同装运日期发运货物。

⑩ 出口商填制"应收账款转让通知书"一式五联,并在应签字之处加上出口商签字,送交出口保理商。

倘若申请的信用额度全部遭到进口保理商的拒绝,则此出口属无信用额度担保的出口,进口保理商对于应收账款到期是否付款不承担责任。

⑪ 出口保理商签署应收账款转让通知书,并在发票盖上"再让渡"印戳,表示出口保理商将该笔应收账款再转让给进口保理商。

⑫ 进口保理商将单据传送给进口商。

⑬ 进口商把提单交给进口地的承运代理人,要求提货。

⑭ 进口地承运代理人交付货物。

⑮ 进口保理商于付款到期日向进口商索要应收账款。如果进口商无力付款,按照国际保理规则规定,进口保理商应于到期日后 90 天对出口保理商支付应收账款(担保下面的付款)加上迟付利息,其中利息部分还需加倍支付。

⑯ 在向进口商索取应收款时,进口商照付,如果建立 EDI 信息传输制度,进口保理商用 EDI 发出支付信息。

⑰ 进口保理商通过银行将应收账款汇交出口保理商。如果建立 EDI 信息传输制度,进口保理商用 EDI 发出付款信息。

⑱ 出口保理商将款贷记在出口商账户,办理结汇手续。如果出口商获得融资,则应扣还预付本息,将余款贷记出口商账户。

五、国际保理业务的优点

国际保理业务能为进出口双方在增加营业额、风险保障、节约成本、简化手续、扩大利润等方面带来好处,具体如表10-2所示。

表10-2   国际保理业务的优点

优点	对出口人而言	对进口人而言
增加营业额	对现有客户或潜在客户提供更具竞争力的O/A、D/A付款条件,便于拓展海外市场,增加营业额	利用O/A、D/A优惠付款条件,以有限的资金购进更多的货物,加快资金流动,扩大营业额
风险保障	进口商的信用风险转由保理商承担,出口方可以得到100%的收汇保障	以公司的信誉和良好的财务表现而获得卖方的信贷,无须抵押
节约成本	资信调查、财务管理和欠款催收由保理商负责,减轻业务负担,节约管理成本	省去了开立信用证和处理繁杂文件的费用
简化手续	免除了一般信用证交易的繁琐手续	在批准信用额度后,购买手续简化,进货快捷
扩大利润	由于出口额扩大,降低了管理成本,排除了信用风险和坏账损失,利润随之增加	由于加快了资金和货物流动,生意更加发达,从而能增加利润

六、国际保理业务与福费廷业务的异同

国际保理与福费廷都是属于贸易融资业务,即出口商都可在基础合同规定的收款期之前获得占货款面值大部分的预付款,从而能减少资金占用,加速资金周转,改善财务状况。另外,出口商获得的这些融资一般都是无追索权的,只要出口商提供的债权(无论是应收账款还是应收票据)是由正当交易引起的、没有争议的,而且符合包买商或保理商的其他规定,那么即使因进口商违约或破产而产生信用风险,或因进口国政策法令变化而产生国家风险,出口商都可以不受其影响,包买商或保理商自负收不回债款的风险。

但是,这两种融资方式也有明显的区别,见表10-3。

表10-3   福费廷与保理业务的区别

不同点	福费廷	保理
适用的基础交易不同	主要针对资本货物的进出口交易,金额巨大,债款回收期长达数年,而且都是一次性交易。	主要适用于日用消费品或劳务的交易,每笔交易金额相对较小,但一般是经常性持续进行的。
融资期限不同	融资期限取决于票据的付款期限,一般从半年直到五六年,甚至可以达到七年,因此平均融资期限多在三四年左右,属于中期融资业务。	融资期限取决于赊销期限,一般都在发货后一个月至六个月,个别可以长至九个月,但绝不超过一年,因此保理业务属于短期融资业务。

续　表

不同点	福费廷	保理
对担保的需求不同	福费廷业务的金额巨大、期限较长,而包买商对出口商又无追索权,因此风险较大,必须要有第三者(例如银行)担保进口商的到期支付。	保理业务因金额小,期限短,保理商承担的风险较小,因此多以设定赊销额度的方式控制风险,不需要买方提供第三者担保。
计息方法不同	福费廷业务的计息是按贴现方式进行,即融资额是预扣贴现利息后的净额,因此有效利率远高于名义贴现率。	保理业务的计算是以预付款为本金计算自预付日到预计收款日的利息,然后在收到债款后向出口商支付余额时扣除,因此是期末付息,而不是像贴现(以及福费廷)那样是期初付息,故有效利率等同于名义利率。
对出口商的利率与汇率风险不同	出口商一次出售全套应收票据,并收取按票据面值计算的贴现净值。因此从贴现日到票据到期日之间的利率或汇率变动与出口商无关,出口商完全不承受汇率或利率风险。	出口商一般只能收到不足 80% 的预付款,这部分预付款可免受利率与汇率风险,但尚有部分余额需在赊账到期日支付,因此受到利率或汇率变动的风险。如果保理形式为到期保理,则全部应收账款将承受利率与汇率风险。所以保理业务不能完全解除出口商承受的利率风险与汇率风险,甚至完全不解除此类风险。

本章案例

　　上海某出口 A 公司 2009 年 6 月初向日本 B 进口商出口女式全棉勾针衣。因为对债务人知之甚少,5 月 20 日,A 公司申请保理业务,发货前日本银行答复中国银行上海分行此债务人资信不佳,不能批准信用额度,也劝告出口商不要与之交易。

　　但因听信日商花言巧语,且货已备好,A 公司在 6 月初发货 50 万美元,付款方式 T/T 收货后 15 天。结果债务人到期不付货款,反而提出货物质量有问题,但货物却被提走,当时正在出售。现出口方正在委托收账,净损失将至少为货款的 20%。

关键词

　　福费廷、包买商、无追索权、国际保理、单保理、双保理、到期保理、预期保理

思考题

　　1. 福费廷业务中包买票据的类型有哪些?

　　2. 福费廷业务的操作流程是怎样的?

　　3. 以双保理业务为例,说明保理业务的操作流程。

　　4. 比较保理与福费廷业务的异同。

第十一章 其他融资与结算方式

★ **学习目标**

掌握提货担保、信托收据、进口押汇等进口贸易融资方式和打包贷款、票据贴现等出口贸易融资方式的操作；了解信用卡、旅行信用证和旅行支票的办理手续。

★ **本章概要**

在结算业务中,银行往往向有资格的客户提供融资服务,这类服务与国际结算过程密切相关,从而称为国际结算融资。根据银行提供融资对象的不同,国际结算融资分为进口贸易融资和出口贸易融资。本章介绍了提货担保、信托收据、进口押汇等进口贸易融资方式和打包贷款、票据贴现等出口贸易融资方式的概念和业务流程,并简单介绍了信用卡、旅行信用证和旅行支票的办理手续。

第一节　进口贸易融资

一、提货担保

（一）提货担保的概念与作用

提货担保（Shipment Guarantee，S/G）是指在跟单信用证或是跟单托收项下，货物运抵目的地后，包括提单在内的单据尚未寄到，而延期提货会使进口商增加额外开支，或者进口商品行情下跌、市价回落。进口商为了报关的需要，事先可以向开证行或代收行签具"申请提货担保书"连同进口商自己的担保函（又称联合凭证），以求通过银行的担保，及时通关提货。

通常情况下，收货人应凭正本提单向船公司办理提货。由于近海航行航程过短，货物常常先于单据到达。如果收货人急于提货，可以采用提货担保方式，请开证行出具书面担保后，请船公司先行放货，保证日后及时补交正式提单并负责交付船公司的各项费用及赔付由此可能遭受的损失。货物到港后，收货人便可凭提货担保及时提货，而不必等运输单据到达后提货，节省了收货人因等货运单据而可能产生的滞港费用和额外费用，避免了可能产生的损失。

（二）办理提货担保的业务流程

（1）在货物先于提单到达港口的情况下，开证申请人向开证行提出办理提货担保的申请。申请人应提供与本次提货担保申请有关的副本发票、副本提单和货物到港通知单，并填写提货担保申请书。提货担保申请书表明提货担保的一切后果均由开证申请人负责，决不使开证行蒙受损失，并同意一旦正式提单寄到，即将上述保证书换回，交回开证行注销，或由开证行直接将提单交给船公司换回上述提货担保书，以便解除开证行的担保责任。同时，开证申请人授权开证行无条件支付上列货物价款和（或）解除有关领取上列款项所提供的保证书。另外，进口商应按提货担保申请书格式内容填列准确、完整的资料。

（2）开证行根据实际情况，有条件地办理提货担保书，开证行要将申请书和担保书上填写的各项内容与信用证分户账页核对，以证实是该笔信用证项下的货物。银行应对进口商进行审查，确信其为该批货物的收货人，以防进口商借担保骗取货物，同时可以要求进口商提供担保或交纳保证金或抵押金，以维护银行的权益。

（3）开证申请人收到运输单据后立即向船公司换取提货担保。

（三）办理提货担保应注意的问题

提货担保有两个当事人：出具赔偿担保的银行（负第一性责任）和运输公司（被担保人）。

1. 船公司要求提货担保具备的要件

船公司要求的提货担保内容包含三个方面：(1)形式以船公司/承运人或银行抬头预先印制，并且表明它是提货担保以及承诺"不出示提单的交货"。(2)申请人和开证行二者都可以签署赔偿担保。如果提货担保直接由银行出具，只包含银行签名，应承诺：①担保应要求交付货物的任何性质的责任、损失或损害一律向船公司/承运人赔偿并保证它们不受损失;②对任何针对船公司/承运人的诉讼而进行的抗辩提供资金;③对由于货物产生的任何运费和(或)共同的海损(或费用)索要时立即支付。(3)一经收到正式提单马上提交,担保书不能带有限制责任赔偿和不能列有到期日。出具人承担不可撤销的赔偿责任。

2. 申请人应注意的事项

(1)进口商凭提货担保书提取货物,就丧失了拒付的权利,即使单据审核后发现不符点,但因正式提单已经交给船公司,无法退回提单,只能放弃拒付。进口商非万不得已最好不要办理银行担保先行提货。如果货物先到,进口商可以去码头看看货物情况,确有需要才采取办理提货担保。

(2)本保付仅限于开证行自身开立的信用证项下的商品进口,运输方式为海运,并在规定提交全套海运提单的条件下方可办理。

(3)提货担保属于银行的授信业务。进口商收到有关单据后,应立即用正式提单向船公司换回提货担保书并退回开证行。

(4)因出具提货担保而使开证行遭受的任何损失,开证申请人负赔偿之责。

3. 开证行应注意的事项

(1)银行为了便利进口商及时提货而有提货担保的做法,这是银行的服务项目,《UCP 600》未对提货担保作出规定。

(2)在办理提货担保书时,对于航程较远的进口货运,一般是单据先到开证行,货物后到目的港,不需要银行提供提货担保书。如进口商在这种情况下申请提货担保,显然系反常情况。开证行应调查情况,谨慎从事。

(3)开证行收到银行寄来的一套正式提单,最好自己交给船公司换回提货担保书,可以先交一份正本提单给船公司,自己保留其他两份。若船公司拖延退回提货担保书,日后又要求开证行履行保证责任时,可以再拿出另一份正式提单,凭以解除保证责任。

(4)申请提货担保书是由进口商提出的,开证行应该考虑进口商的信用是否可靠,必要时可以收取押金或货款,也可要求其他银行或贸易商在申请书上会签,防止上当受骗。

(5)提货担保只能限于正常的寄送正式提单晚到时银行予以提货担保,如果第一次寄来的是副本提单或其他情况时,银行不能做提货担保。

二、信托收据

信托收据(Trust Receipt,T/R)是指进口商以信托的方式向银行借出全套商业单据时出具的一种保证书。银行是信托人,代表委托人掌握物权;进口商是被信托人或受托人,代表信托人处理单据。进口商以银行受托人的身份代办提货、报关、存仓、保险等手续,物权仍归银行所有。如果货物出售,则货款存入银行。进口商在汇票到期后向银行偿付票款,收回汇票,赎回信托收据。

理论上,信托收据是进口人与开证行或代收行之间关于物权处理的一种契约,是将货物抵押给银行的确认书,银行可以凭此办理融资业务。

三、进口押汇

(一) 进口押汇的概念和作用

进口押汇(Inward Bill)是指信用证开证行在收到出口商或押汇寄来的相符单据后先行垫付货款,待进口商得到单据,凭单提货后再收回该货款的融资活动,它是开证行对申请人(进口商)的一种短期资金融通。其发生的主要原因是申请人因资金周转问题无法在开证行付款前赎单。

实务中,开证行收到单据后,如交单相符,或有不符点但申请人同意接受,开证行应立即偿付。进口商以信用证项下代表货权的单据为抵押,并同时向开证行提供必要的抵押、质押或其他担保,由开证行先行代付,这就产生了进口押汇的要求。

(二) 进口押汇利息的计算

进口押汇的融资比例为发票/汇票金额的100%。采用"后收利息法",在押汇到期后,银行从企业账户扣收押汇本金及利息。进口押汇一般使用信用证及单据使用的货币直接对外付款,不可兑换成本币使用(如本币与信用证使用的货币不一致)。开证行办理进口押汇通常不收取押汇手续费,其利息计算公式为:

$$押汇利息 = 本金 \times 融资年利率 \times 押汇天数 /360$$

进口押汇的天数一般以30天、60天计算,但最长不超过90天。

进口押汇与普通商业贷款相比,具有手续简便、融资速度快捷的特点。

(三) 进口押汇的步骤

(1) 单据到达开证行后,申请人向开证行提出进口押汇申请并签订有关协议。开证行审查进口押汇申请书内容。

(2) 开证行办理进口押汇并对外付款。

(3) 开证行凭信托收据向进口商交付单据,申请人将自己货物所有权转让给银行。

(4) 进口商凭单据提货及销售货物。

(5) 进口商归还押汇款本息,换回信托收据。

(四) 进口押汇应注意的问题

1. 申请人应注意的事项

(1) 进口押汇款项专款专用,不能结成人民币使用,只能用于履行信用证项下的对外付款。

(2) 进口押汇是短期融资,期限一般不超过90天。

(3) 进口押汇需要逐笔申请,逐笔使用,一般不设额度。

(4) 押汇比例及期限等根据实际情况与开证行协商解决。

2. 开证行应注意的事项

(1) 了解开证申请人的资信情况和经营能力。

(2) 了解进口货物的市场行情。

(3) 适当开立,增加其他安全措施,因为进口押汇还款来源单一,风险较大。在需要时,可以要求申请人增加第三方担保、房产抵押、有价证券抵押等,以增加申请人的谨慎程度,并使押汇的损失降到最低。

(4) 注意押汇后的管理,必要时监控申请人的进口货物资金回笼情况,并采取适当措施,减少损失。

知识扩展

中国贸易融资发展状况

中国商业银行融资业务操作管理较粗放,还没有完全建立各种融资业务的严格标准和规范的业务操作流程,开展的国际贸易融资业务以减免保证金开证、出口打包放款、进出口押汇等基本形式为主,而像国际保理等较复杂的业务所占比重较少,国际贸易融资业务量与市场提供的空间相比很不协调。因此,必须借鉴国际贸易融资的经验教训,结合中国实际,分析融资风险的成因。

(一) 对贸易融资业务的重要性和风险认识不够

首先,商业银行的高级管理人员和相关部门对国际贸易融资业务缺乏了解,也无经验,对国际贸易融资业务的风险性普遍认识较为肤浅,表现为两种倾向:一是错误地认为国际贸易融资不需要动用实际资金,只需出借单据或开出信用证就可以从客户那里赚取手续费和融资利息,是零风险业务,这直接导致 20 世纪 90 年代中期由于大量信用证垫款形成的银行不良资产;二是当出现问题后,又认为国际贸易融资风险很大,采取的措施又导致国际贸易融资授信比一般贷款难,审批时间长,制约了该业务的发展。

其次,商业银行的传统业务是本币业务,国际业务的比重相对较少,在机构、人才、客户方面均不占优势,以致大部分人以为与其花费大量人力、物力和财力去发展国际贸易融资,还不如集中精力抓好本币业务。另外,对国际贸易融资业务在提高银行的盈利能力,优化信贷资产质量等方面的作用认识不足、认为贸易融资业务在整个信贷资产中的数量少,作用不大。

(二) 银行内部缺乏有效的防范管理体系,风险控制手段落后

国际贸易融资业务所涉及的风险有客户风险、国家风险、国外代理风险、国际市场风险和内部操作风险。这些风险的管理需要先进的技术手段将银行相关部门之间、分支行之间高效有机地联系在一起。而国内银行在外汇业务的处理程序方面较为落后,不同的分支行之间、不同的部门之间业务相互独立运行,缺少网络资源共享,缺乏统一的协调管理,以致无法达到共享资源、监控风险、相互制约的目的。如融资业务由国际业务部一个部门来承担信贷风险控制、业务操作风险控制和业务拓展。风险控制既显得乏力,又缺乏银行内部相互制约和风险专业控制,面对中国进出口企业普遍经营亏损,拥有大量不良银行债务的客观现实,银行的贸易融资潜伏着巨大的风险。

(三) 融资业务无序竞争破坏风险管理标准

中国开展国际贸易融资业务时间相对国外较短,市场尚不成熟,各种约束机制还不健全,随着商业银行国际结算业务竞争的日益激烈,各家银行业务形式又较为单一,为争取更大的市场份额,竞相以优惠的条件吸引客户,对企业客户的资信审查和要求

也越来越低,放松了对贸易融资风险的控制,例如有的银行降低了开证保证金的收取比例;有的甚至采取授信开证,免收保证金;有的在保证金不足且担保或抵押手续不全的情况下对外开立远期信用证等等,这些做法破坏了风险管理的标准,加剧了银行贸易融资业务的风险。

(四)营销队伍薄弱,缺乏复合型的高素质业务人员

国际结算业务专业性强,对业务人员的素质要求较高,但中国商业银行在国际贸易融资方面人才匮乏,有限的人才资源也高度集中在管理层,同时,人才的知识结构单一。由于各家银行都是把国际业务当作独立的业务品种来经营,在机构设置上由国际业务部门负责国际结算和连带的贸易融资业务。这就造成相关从业人员只熟悉国际结算而缺乏财务核算和信贷管理等方面的业务知识,无法从财务资料和经营作风准确判断和掌握客户资信,对国际贸易融资的全过程的每一个环节没有充分的把握,降低了国际业务的产品功能和市场效果,对其风险也就缺乏了强有力的控制力度。

(五)国际贸易融资业务的法律环境不完善

国际贸易融资业务涉及到国际金融票据、货权、货物的抵押、质押、担保、信托等行为,要求法律上对各种行为的权利和责任有具体的法律界定,但是中国的金融立法明显滞后于业务的发展。有些国际贸易融资的常用术语和做法在中国的法律上还没有相应的规范。例如,押汇业务中银行对货物的单据与货物的权利如何,银行与客户之间的债券关系如何,进口押汇中常用的信托收据是否有效,远期信用证业务中银行已经承兑的汇票是否可以由法院支付等。因此,这种不完善的法律环境,使中国的贸易融资业务的风险进一步增大。

(资料来源:http://wenku.baidu.com/view/e4aa423510661ed9ad51f38d.html)

第二节　出口贸易融资

一、打包贷款

(一)打包贷款的概念和作用

打包贷款(Packing Loan)是信用证(L/C)下的贸易融资方式,出口商在提供货运单据前,以供货合同和从国外收到的、以自己为受益人的信用证向当地银行抵押,从而取得生产或采购出口货物所需的周转资金的一种装船前融资。

打包贷款的金额通常是信用证金额的70%—80%,一般不超过90%。贷款期限一般是自信用证的抵押之日到收到开证行支付货款之日为止,一般不超过该银行向开证行寄单收款之日,提供贷款的银行承担了议付义务,收到开证行支付的货款后即扣除贷款本息,然后将余额付给出口商。一般来说,企业办理外汇打包贷款的利息负担远远低于人民币的打包贷款利息。银行办理打包贷款通常不收取手续费,利息计算公式为:

打包贷款利息 = 信用证金额×打包折扣(70%—90%)×融资年利率×打包天数 /360

打包天数的计算为办理打包日至信用证最迟装运日的天数加 30 天。

(二) 打包贷款的业务流程

(1) 出口企业将信用证正本交银行,向银行提出打包贷款申请,并同时提供以下文件:①如企业第一次在该银行办理贷款等授信业务,办理打包贷款时必须提供企业的营业执照副本、税务登记证等基础资料;②填写并提交银行提供的《打包贷款申请书》;③交纳保证金、落实担保单位、抵押、质押等;④签订贷款合同;⑤签订其他需要的协议。

(2) 银行审核信用证和一切出口商提供的资料后,办理打包贷款。

(3) 出口企业收到国外货款后归还打包贷款本金及利息。

(三) 打包贷款应注意到的问题

1. 提供打包贷款银行应注意的问题

(1) 以正本信用证作抵押,但银行不能仅凭国外信用证就给受益人贷款,银行应仔细审核信用证的满足条件和要求。

(2) 银行应根据客户的资信情况和清偿能力为其核定相应的打包贷款额度,供其循环使用。

(3) 为保证安全、及时地收回打包资金,在贷款期间银行应与客户保持密切联系,了解、掌握业务的进展和有关合同的执行情况,督促客户及时发货交单。

2. 申请打包贷款的企业应注意的问题

(1) 向银行提交所要求的有关资料。

(2) 自身信誉良好,在该行没有不良记录。

(3) 关注信用证条款。

(4) 若企业为可转让信用证的第二受益人,也不能轻易地从银行取得打包贷款。

二、票据贴现

票据贴现(Discounting)是指票据持有人在票据到期前为获取现款而向银行贴附一定利息的票据转让。票据贴现必须是已承兑的远期汇票,承兑人一般是进口商、开证行或其他付款人,票据持有者一般是出口商。这类票据流动性强,可靠性高。

在办理该业务时,银行要与出口商签订质权书,确定双方的权利和义务。银行根据贴现费率扣减贴现利息和手续费后买下票据,票据到期收回票款,偿还垫款,余下的部分为贴现收益。如果到期收不回,银行有权向出口商进行追索。银行一般应对票据的付款人和承兑人的资信进行调查,确认符合条件后予以贴现。

办理票据贴现应注意的问题:

(1) 票据的信誉。银行承兑汇票信誉高于商业银行承兑汇票。

(2) 票据的风险。L/C 的远期汇票风险低于 D/A 和 D/P 项下的远期汇票。

(3) 要注意各国票据法的不同之处,如持票人享有的权利方面的差异。

(4) 票据本身的质量。加保兑的票据最可靠,如票据为不可流通或限制流通,则不容易被再贴现,影响票据的流通性。

知识扩展

中国贸易融资发展对策

1. 提高对发展国际贸易融资业务的认识

随着中国的进一步开放,国际贸易往来日益频繁,进出口总额将大幅提高,这必将为发展外汇业务尤其是贸易融资业务提供极大的市场空间。各级商业银行要更新观念,提高对发展外汇业务尤其是国际贸易融资业务的认识。应从入世后面临的严峻挑战出发,以贸易融资业务为工具积极发展国际结算业务,要调整经营策略和工作思路,密切注重外资银行的动向。因此,商业银行要加强市场信息搜索,采取有利于推进国际结算业务发展的各种政策措施。

2. 调整机构设置实行审贷分离原则

为满足业务发展的需要,银行有必要对内部机构进行调整,重新设计国际贸易融资业务的运作模式,将审贷模式进行剥离,实行授信额度管理,达到既有效控制风险又积极服务客户的目的。(1)应明确贸易融资属于信贷业务,必须纳入全行信贷管理。由信贷部对贸易融资客户进行资信评估,据此初步确立客户信誉额度。通过建立审贷分离制度,将信贷风险和国际结算风险由信贷部、信贷审批委员会和国际业务部负责,最终达到在统一综合授信管理体系下的审贷分离,风险专项控制,从而采取不同的措施,控制物权,达到防范和控制风险的目的。(2)授信额度应把握以下几点:一是授信额度要控制远期信用证的比例,期限越长,风险越大;二是控制信用证全额免保比例,通过交纳一定的保证金来加强对客户业务的约束和控制;三是建立考核期;四是实行总授信额度下的分向授信额度的管理;五是建立健全内部控制制度,跟踪基本客户的进出口授信额度,加强部门内部的协调和配合。

3. 建立科学的融资贸易风险管理体系

制定符合国际贸易融资特点的客户评价标准,选择从事国际贸易时间较长、信用好的客户。成立信用审批中心和贸易融资业务部门,影响国际贸易融资的风险因素相对很多,因此防范风险要求商业银行人员具有信贷业务的知识以分析评价客户的信用。从而利用人才优势事前防范和事后化解各种业务风险。

4. 完善制度实施全过程的风险监管

(1)做好融资前的贷前准备,建立贷前风险分析制度,严格审查和核定融资授信额度,控制操作风险,通过对信用风险、市场风险,自然风险和社会风险、国家宏观经济政策风险、汇率风险等进行分析以及对申请企业、开证人和开证行的资信等方面情况进行严格审查,及时发现不利因素,采取防范措施。

(2)严格信用证业务管理。信用证在国际贸易中一直被认为是一种比较可靠的结算方式。审核信用证是银行和进出口企业的首要责任。首先,必须认真审核信用证的真实性、有效性、确定信用证的种类、用途、性质、流通方式和是否可以执行;其次,审查开证行的资信、资本机构、资本实力、经营作风并了解真实的授信额度;再次是要及时了解产品价格、交货的运输方式、航运单证等情况,从而对开证申请人的业务运作情况有一个综合评价,对其预期还款能力及是否有欺诈目的有客观的判断;最后是要认真审核可转让信用证,严格审查开证行和转让行的资信,并对信用证条款进行审核。

(3)尽快建立完善的法律保障机制,严格依法行事。应该加强对现有的相关立法进行研究,结合实际工作和未来发展的趋势,找出不相适应的地方,通过有关途径呼吁尽快完善相关立法。利用法律武器最大限度地保障银行利益,减少风险。

5. 加强和国外银行的合作

在众多国外投资者看好中国市场、对外贸易发展良好的形势下,国有商业银行应该抓住这一有利时机,基于共同的利益和兴趣,与国外有关银行联手开拓和占领中国的外汇业务市场,共同争取一些在中国落户的、利用外资的大项目,多方面、多层次地拓展中国商业银行的贸易融资业务。

6. 防范融资风险的意识和能力

国际贸易融资是一项知识面较广、技术性强、操作复杂的业务,对相关从业人员的业务素质要求很高。中国开展这项业务时间短,急需既懂国际惯例、懂操作技术又精通信贷业务的复合型专业人才。商业银行国际结算业务的竞争,实质上是银行经营管理水平和人员素质的竞争。因此,提高贸易融资管理人员的素质,增强防范风险的意识和能力已成为当务之急,应尽快培养出一批熟悉国际金融、国际贸易、法律等知识的人才。首先,要引进高水平和高素质的人才,可充分利用代理行技术先进的特点,选择相关课题邀请代理行的专家作专题讲座,有条件的还可派员工到国外商业银行学习。其次,在平时工作中,要注意案例的总结分析,及时积累经验,并有意识地加强国际贸易知识和运输保险业务的学习,密切关注国际贸易市场动态,了解掌握商品的行情变化,培养对国际贸易市场的洞察力,增强识别潜在风险的能力,以不断提高自身业务水平。三是抓好岗位培训,不断提高员工的服务质量和道德修养。四是强化风险意识,不断提高员工识伪、防伪能力,努力防范和化解国际贸易融资风险。

(资料来源:http://wenku. baidu. com/view/e4aa423510661ed9ad51f38d. html)

第三节　信　用　卡

一、信用卡的定义与类型

信用卡是银行或专业机构发给其经过调研、资信较为可靠的客户购买商品和接受服务的一种短期消费信贷的凭证。信用卡持有人可以在指定的特约商店购物、餐厅用膳、旅店住宿,也可以向银行支取一定限额的现金。信用卡对发卡银行或专业机构来说,是开拓义务领域、扩大金融渗透面、发展结算功能的重要工具。

按照不同的标准,可以将信用卡分为不同的类型:

(1)根据发卡机构不同,可分为银行卡和非银行卡。如万事达卡、维萨卡属于银行卡,而运通卡、大来卡属于非银行卡。

(2)根据清偿方式不同,可分为贷记卡和借记卡。前者的清偿方式是"先消费,后还款";后者的清偿方式是"先存款,后消费"。

(3) 根据发卡对象不同,可分为公司卡和个人卡。

(4) 根据持卡人信誉、地位等资信情况不同,可分为普通卡和金卡。

(5) 根据流通范围可分为国内结算卡和国际结算卡。国内结算卡使用本国货币,如长城卡、牡丹卡,持卡人可以在国内旅游点的特约商店凭卡购物或向指定代付行取现。国际卡是在国际间可以流通使用的信用卡,为旅游者到各国旅行提供方便。

二、信用卡业务的基本流程

信用卡业务基本流程是指从发卡、建立特约商户、交易与授权、清算、信用控制、客户服务和业务管理的全过程。这一过程主要围绕发行、持卡人和特约商户三个基本当事人之间债权债务的发生与清偿关系进行的。

(一) 申请信用卡的条件

1. 公司卡申请条件

国内机关、团体、部队、企事业单位、三资企业等具有法人资格的单位,在华常驻机构均可申请中国境内各金融机构发行的信用卡。

2. 个人卡的申请条件

凡年满 20 周岁,有固定职业、稳定收入、信誉良好的国内公民或在中国境内有居留权并持有国籍所在国正式护照和中国公安部门签发的 1 年以上居住证,在国内有固定职业和稳定收入的港澳台同胞及外国人均可申请人民币个人信用卡。

(二) 信用卡的担保与保证金

1. 信用卡的担保

申请个人信用卡均需要担保,担保的个人应为本市常住户口的当地国家机关、企事业单位的正式职工,并且与持卡人无配偶或直系亲属关系。担保人必须承诺担保条款,并在申请表上签字。持卡人与担保人不得相互担保,不能连环担保,也不能一人担保多人。

2. 信用卡保证金

申请公司信用卡,应按注册资金、固定资产、企业性质缴纳一定数额的保证金。申请个人信用卡,保证金缴纳数额多少,需视申请人的经济实力、收入多少、所在工作单位的性质而定。

(三) 信用卡的审核制度

1. 初审

初审工作由信用卡部门的资信调查人员负责。审核内容为:所填申请表内容是否完整清楚,持卡人所提供的有关证件是否齐全;以公函、电话和上门调查等方式,对申请者提供的资料证件进行查证和落实;初步确定申请人需要缴存保证金的数额;核实担保情况,明确担保人;根据审查情况,负责初审的人员在申请表上签字。

2. 复审

复审工作一般由发卡行信用卡部门的负责人负责。复审的内容有:对申请人和担保人的全部资料及初审人员签署的意见进行复核,并对合格的申请表及时审批。经复审后的信用卡申请表交发卡部门输机、存档,并据此编制打卡清单。

(四) 打卡与发卡

发卡行经两级审核批准后,应缮制表外科目付出传票交管卡人领取空白卡,按申请人姓名及汉语拼音、性别、有效期打卡。发卡时首先确认领卡人,检验其身份证件,并要求领卡人当面在信用卡背面签字栏签字。

(五) 建立特约商户

为了扩展信用卡业务,方便持卡人、发卡人与愿意受理信用卡业务的商场、饭店、宾馆、机场等通过协商签定协议,由发卡行对该商户的有关财务人员进行培训。在具备一定条件的情况下,发卡银行可以为特约商户安装"终端机"或"电子清算机",实现授权终端和清算一体化,避免透支风险,同时提高了清算的效率。

(六) 交易与授权

持卡人以信用卡作为支付手段,在商户那里进行消费或在发卡行指定的机构取现、转账,标志着信用卡交易的开始,同时也是发卡行授权活动的开始。授权的实质是发卡行对特约商户、代办行每一笔交易的批准过程,也是发卡行对持卡人交易活动进行控制的重要环节,授权中心提供 24 小时授权服务,负责辖内各发卡行的授权服务。

(七) 信用卡的清算

信用卡的清算业务是以银行为中心处理持卡人、特约商户及银行之间相互支付的过程。基本上分为直接清算和间接清算两种形式。

1. 直接清算

直接清算的程序如图 11-1 所示。

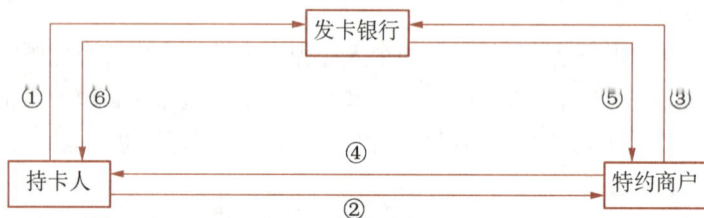

图 11-1　直接清算程序

图例说明:
① 持卡人向发卡银行存款。　② 持卡人持卡消费。
③ 特约商户向发卡行交单。　④ 特约商户为持卡人提供消费。
⑤ 发卡行付款给特约商户。　⑥ 发卡行向持卡人发对账单。

2. 间接清算

间接清算的程序如图 11-2 所示。

(八) 信用控制

信用控制是发卡银行对持卡人的交易活动资信变化情况和特约商户是否遵守协议及规定等实施监督,并及时采取措施,以防范各种风险的发生,确保发卡银行资金安全,维护银行、商户、持卡人的合法权益。信用控制是信用卡业务的重要组成部分,是促进信用卡业务健康发展的重要保障,发卡银行必须指定专人做好这项工作。

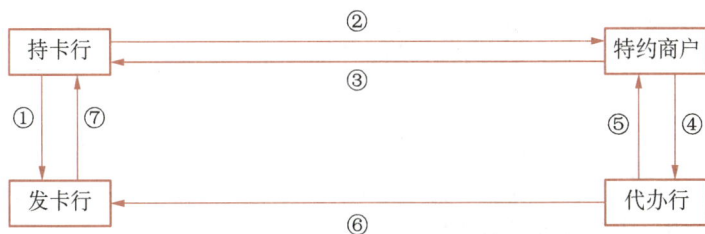

图 11-2　间接清算程序

图例说明：

① 持卡人向发卡银行存款。　　　　② 持卡人持卡消费。

③ 特约商户向持卡人提供消费。　　④ 特约商户向代办行提交签购单。

⑤ 代办行向特约商户付款。　　　　⑥ 代办行向发卡行提示，划拨收回所列金额。

⑦ 发卡行向持卡人发对账单。

知识扩展

信用卡的起源

信用卡于 1915 年起源于美国。最早发行信用卡的机构并不是银行，而是一些百货商店、饮食业、娱乐业和汽油公司。美国的一些商店、饮食店为招徕顾客，推销商品，扩大营业额，有选择地在一定范围内发给顾客一种类似金属徽章的信用筹码，后来演变成为用塑料制成的卡片，作为客户购货消费的凭证，开展了凭信用筹码在本商号或公司或汽油站购货的赊销服务业务，顾客可以在这些发行筹码的商店及其分号赊购商品，约期付款。这就是信用卡的雏形。

据说有一天，美国商人弗兰克·麦克纳马拉在纽约一家饭店招待客人用餐，就餐后发现他的钱包忘记带在身边，因而深感难堪，不得不打电话叫妻子带现金来饭店结账。于是麦克纳马拉产生了创建信用卡公司的想法。1950 年春，麦克纳马拉与他的好友施奈德合作投资一万美元，在纽约创立了"大来俱乐部"(Diners Club)，即大来信用卡公司的前身。大来俱乐部为会员们提供一种能够证明身份和支付能力的卡片，会员凭卡片可以记账消费。这种无须银行办理的信用卡的性质仍属于商业信用卡。

1952 年，美国加利福尼亚州的富兰克林国民银行作为金融机构首先发行了银行信用卡。

1959 年，美国的美洲银行在加利福尼亚州发行了美洲银行卡。此后，许多银行加入了发卡银行的行列。到了 20 世纪 60 年代，银行信用卡很快受到社会各界的普遍欢迎，并得到迅速发展，信用卡不仅在美国，而且在英国、日本、加拿大以及欧洲各国也盛行起来。从 20 世纪 70 年代开始，香港、台湾、新加坡、马来西亚等发展中国家和地区，也开始发行信用卡业务。

"信用卡"一词，本意是专指这个帖子里介绍的这种金融产品，可是由于以前国内准信用卡，甚至没有任何信用卡功能的储蓄卡大行其道，所以真正的信用卡，反而只能冠以"贷记卡"这种不伦不类的称呼。真正的信用卡，具有以下特点：不鼓励预存现金，先消费后还款，享有免息缴款期，可自主分期还款（有最低还款额），加入 VISA、MASTER 等国际信用卡组织以便全球通用。

（资料来源：http://wenku.baidu.com/view/547fd0d7195f312b3169a561.html）

第四节 旅行信用证

旅行信用证是为方便旅游者出国旅行时使用而开出的信用证。旅行信用证的申请人和受益人是同一人,即汇款人和收款人是同一人。旅行信用证准许在一定金额及有效期内,在该证指定的分支行或代理行支取款项。

一、兑付旅行信用证的手续

(1)旅行信用证的受益人到指定的银行取款,需将旅行信用证正本交指定兑付行审查。兑付行审查时应注意本行是否是被指定的兑付行,开证行在信用证上的签字是否与该行签字样本相符,信用证是否在有效期内,并有足够余额。

(2)要求受益人提供身份证件,如护照或身份证等,并在柜台当面重新签发收据或汇票。收据必须列明信用证号码、开证行名和日期,收据签名必须同"印鉴核对卡"或护照上的签名相符。支取金额必须在信用证金额之内,兑付行将支款日期、金额、行名背书于信用证之后加盖银行行章,将信用证连同应付外汇折成等值人民币,连同信用证交给受益人。然后将收据寄至开证行索汇,由开证行偿付归垫。

(3)信用证金额用完后,在信用证上加盖"用完"或"注销"戳记,不退受益人,将其连同收据一并寄开证行索偿和注销原证。

(4)因兑付行自己垫款可以扣收贴息,并向开证行收取手续费,也可根据约定不收费用。

二、旅行信用证程序

旅行信用证程序如图 11-3 所示。

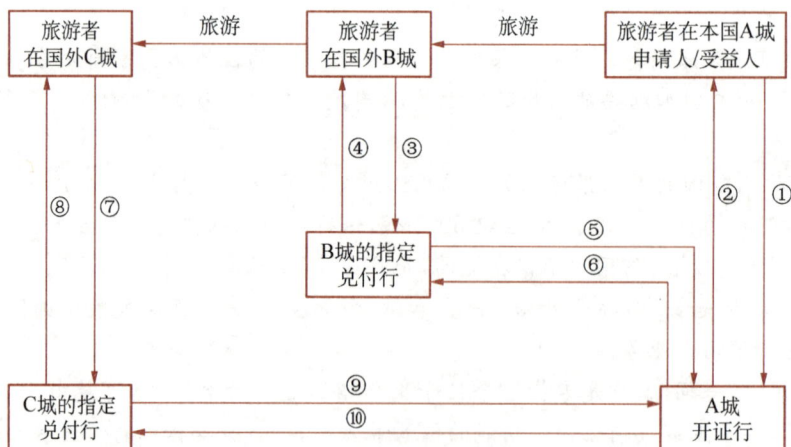

图 11-3 旅行信用证程序

图例说明:
① 申请开证。
② 开出旅行信用证。
③ 在兑付行柜台填写收据连同信用证。
④ 审查各项相符付款和背书信用证。
⑤ 寄出收据凭以索汇。
⑥ 偿付。
⑦ 在兑付行柜台填写最后一张收据连同信用证。
⑧ 审核各项相符后付款。
⑨ 寄出最后一张收据凭以索汇。
⑩ 偿付。

三、旅行信用证与汇款、外钞、旅行支票的比较

（1）汇款是汇出行将一定金额汇至另外一个地点的汇入行，一次性地解付给付款行；而旅行信用证则是开证行保证支付一定金额，可在数处指定的兑付行一次或分次支取，其未用完的余额自动退还给开证行。

（2）外钞指外币现款，而旅行信用证是银行保证支付的信用凭证。外钞遗失、被窃即告损失；旅行信用证只有受益人本人才可领取，他人拾到很难冒领。

（3）旅行支票可以转让他人，也可以支付旅游费用；旅行信用证只有受益人一人使用，不能转让。旅行支票是定额面值，一次支完；旅行信用证零整支取皆可。

总的说来，若从安全角度分析，汇款最优，旅行信用证第二，旅行支票第三，最后是外钞；若从使用的方便灵活角度分析，则外钞最优，旅行支票第二，旅行信用证第三，汇款第四。可见它们各具特点，各有长处和不足之处。

第五节　旅 行 支 票

旅行支票是由金融机构发行的一种特别印制的支票，发行人负责按面额支付给任何受款人，并承诺如支票在兑现前遗失或被偷则偿还给购票人。

一、旅行支票的关系人

旅行支票一般由发行机构签发，由其自己付款，并经旅行支票购买者重签的一种特殊支付凭证。因此，旅行支票有三个基本关系人：出票人、售票人和购票人。

（一）出票人

旅行支票正面印有发行机构的名称和地址。由于旅行支票通常是发行机构负责付款的，所以出票人也就是付款人。出票人即旅行支票发行机构负责人的签名，在印刷时一并印妥，而不像其他有些票据那样临时加签。

（二）售票人

如果出票人自己售出旅行支票，则出票人、付款人、售票人三者合而为一。如发行机构以外的代理行售出旅行支票，售出者就是代售行，代售行只是代发机构推销其旅行支票，付款责任仍由发行机构承担。

（三）购票人（或持票人）

购票人是从发行人或售票人处购买旅行支票者。在购买支票时，他必须在支票上签名，从而成为支票的持有人。

二、旅行支票的兑付程序

（1）首先要识别旅行支票的真伪，遇到有疑问时，应征得客户同意后通过银行办理托收。发现假票，立即扣留。

　　(2) 请客户出示护照并在旅行支票上当面复签,核对无误后即可兑付。如果签字走样,可请其在支票背面再签一次。

　　(3) 对已有复签的旅行支票,需请持票人在支票背面当着兑付人的面再签一次。如果与正面初签相符,并验对护照后将号码记录在支票背面,可予兑付。对空白和转让的旅行支票一般不予兑付,只能办理托收。

　　(4) 审查币别和旅行支票的金额。

　　(5) 缮制兑换传票,抬头栏上姓名要按照护照上的全名写清楚,并注明护照号码。

　　(6) 按照不同的支取方式提取现金。

　　(7) 索偿。兑付后的旅行支票应在票面加盖兑付行名的特别划线章,并在背面作成兑付行的背书,迅速寄给国外发行银行索偿票款,归还兑付行垫款。

三、旅行支票的特点

　　(1) 旅行支票比外钞和硬币安全。支票丢失或被偷后,如还未被兑现,发行人将会很快置换支票。

　　(2) 旅行支票具有全世界普遍接受性,能较容易地在银行、旅馆、火车站、飞机场和许多海外商店兑现。

　　(3) 旅行支票的各种不同面额便于旅游者在旅行期间使用以满足不同需要。

　　(4) 旅行支票的流通没有规定时间限制,一般在支票上没有规定到期日。

▬ 本章案例 ▬■

D/P、T/R 的风险

　　我国出口商 A 与德国进口商 E 达成一项出口合同,付款条件为付款交单,见票后 60 天付款,当汇票及所附单据通过托收行寄抵进口地代收行后,E 在汇票上履行了承兑手续并出具信托收据向代收行借得单据,先行提货转售。汇票到期时,E 因经营不善,失去偿付能力。代收行以汇票付款人拒付为由通知托收行,并建议我出口商 A 向 E 收取货款。对此,你认为我国出口商 A 应该如何处理? 为什么?

关键词

　　提货担保、信托收据、进口押汇、打包贷款、票据贴现、信用卡、旅行信用证、旅行支票

思考题

　　1. 简述打包贷款的业务流程。

　　2. 列出非贸易结算的类型。

　　3. 简述旅行信用证的业务程序。

参 考 文 献

1. 李金泽. UCP 600 适用与信用证法律风险防控[M]. 北京:法律出版社,2007.
2. 刘伟奇,丁辉君. 国际商务单证实务[M]. 上海:同济大学出版社,2007.
3. 蒋琴儿,秦定. 国际结算[M]. 北京:清华大学出版社,2007.
4. 吴开祺,郭秀芬. 现代国际结算学[M]. 上海:立信会计出版社,1997.
5. 应诚敏,刁德霖. 国际结算[M]. 北京:高等教育出版社,2000.
6. 周继忠. 国际贸易结算[M]. 上海:上海财经大学出版社,1997.
7. 苏宗祥,景乃权,张林森. 国际结算[M]. 北京:中国金融出版社,2003.
8. 贺瑛,漆腊应. 国际结算[M]. 北京:中国金融出版社,1998.
9. 张红. 国际结算[M]. 南京:南京大学出版社,1997.
10. 汤庆洪. 国际结算原理研究[M]. 广州:暨南大学出版社,1997.
11. 戚世忠. 国际贸易结算[M]. 杭州:浙江大学出版社,1989.
12. 冯大同. 国际商法[M]. 北京:中国人民大学出版社,1994.
13. [德]查尔斯·韦勒,马特·鲍姆佳特. 国际结算与国际贸易融资实务[M]. 李锴,等,译. 北京:经济管理出版社,1996.
14. 沈锦昶,等. 国际支付与结算[M]. 上海:上海外语教育出版社,1989.
15. 陈国武. 跟单信用证统一惯例(2007 年修订本)国际商会第 600 号出版物[M]. 北京:法律出版社,2007.
16. 秦定,高蓉蓉. 国际结算[M]. 北京:清华大学出版社,2010.
17. 岳华,杨来科. 国际结算双语教程[M]. 上海:立信会计出版社,2007.
18. Edward G. Hinkelman. International Payments. Shanghai Foreign Language Education Press,2000.
19. John S. Gordon Export & Import Letters of Credit and International Payment Methods:Making Payments in International Trade.[M]. 2009.

网络资源:

http://www.icc.org

http://www.swift.com

http://wenku.baidu.com/view/547fd0d7195f312b3169a561.html

http://wenku.baidu.com/view/e4aa423510661ed9ad51f38d.html

http://www.100xuexi.com/

http://www.sdb.com.cn/aspapp/applycenter/corp_ck

http://www.docin.com/

英文部分

CHAPTER 1　INTRODUCTION

Learning Objectives

- To understand the concepts of international payment and settlement
- To understand the history and evolution of international payment and settlement
- To learn the traditional methods for international payment
- To compare the risks and advantages of different payment methods

1.1 Concepts of International Payment[①]

International payments are financial transactions conducted among different countries/regions in which payments are effected or funds are transferred from one to another in order to settle accounts, debts, claims, etc. emerged in the political, economic or cultural activities among them. International payment consists of trade payment and non-trade payment. To be more precise, international payments may arise from:

a) Commercial settlements, that is, trade payment. In international trade, importers in one country must make payment to exporters in another country for their imported goods.

b) Payments for the services rendered. Services rendered by individuals or enterprises in one country to those in another country must also be paid, for example, insurance premium, freight, postage, cable charges, bank commission, etc.

c) Payments between governments. The government of one country may make payments to that of another country for political, military, or economic reasons, such as extending loans, giving aids and grants, providing disaster relief, etc.

d) Transfer of funds among countries. Following the general trend of capital internationalization in the world, capital is usually exported or imported among developed countries, among developed countries and developing countries, or even among developing countries by way of making investments, issuing loans, etc.

e) Others. Other international payments such as overseas remittances, educational expenses, inheritance, etc. should also be settled among countries.

Since most of the international payments originate from transactions in trade, in this book we will mostly lay emphasis on dealing with commercial payments.

1.2 The Evolution of International Settlement

1.2.1 From cash settlement to non-cash settlement

Before 600 B.C, goods were exchanged between traders in different countries on a barter basis. The cash settlement was emerged in 500 B.C, since then precious metals were used as a medium of exchange. Hence precious metals in the forms of coins, bars, or bullions

---

① International Payment does not fully reflect the content of this textbook and the Chinese equivalent "Guojijiesuan", sometimes it is also translated into "International settlement", or "International Payment and Settlement", the content scope in this book and the related course actually includes "International Payment Instruments and Methods", "Documents in International payment" and "International Trade financing".

were shipped among the trading countries, but this method was risky and expensive.

From 13th century, bills of exchange were created, thus non-cash settlement appeared. By the end of the 18th century, banks had begun to engage in foreign exchange transactions, and international payments could be settled by transferring funds through accounts maintained with these banks. This kind of settlement through transferring drafts was much safer than cash settlement. It is these original drafts that have gradually evolved into modern drafts frequently used in today's transaction.

1.2.2 From direct payment to indirect payment

Direct payment is based on barter or cash basis, i. e., a buyer makes payment directly to a seller without using any intermediaries. It was the main method of settling debts in the earlier years of international trade. With the growth of cross border trade and transactions, banks become more specialized in international settlement. With their capability of understanding the conditions of trade and foreign exchange controls in different countries, banks began to serve as intermediaries for international settlement between exporters and importers. Gradually, international payment also evolved from direct payment between traders into indirect payment via banks.

1.2.3 From simple price terms to complex price terms

Originally, international trade payments were settled under simple price terms, such as cash on delivery, cash on shipment, cash with orders, cash before shipment, etc. Over the centuries, it has developed into quite complex price terms. In the latest version of Incoterms 2000 (*International Rules for the Interpretation of Trade Terms 2000*), the price terms are using in todays' international trade includes:

EXW: Ex Works
FCA: Free Carrier
FAS: Free Alongside Ship
FOB: Free on Board
CFR: Cost and Freight
CIF: Cost, Insurance and Freight
CPT: Carriage Paid to
CIP: Carriage and Insurance paid to
DAF: Delivered at Frontier
DES: Delivered Ex Ship
DEQ: Delivered Ex Quay
DDU: Delivered Duty Unpaid
DDP: Delivered Duty Paid

1. 2. 4   From paper documents to electronic documents

In the past, documents related to international settlement were all physical ones. Banks had to reserve vaults of ready cash in order to settle debts. Today, however, documents and funds tend to be intangible items, and credits and debts are by large kept only in electronic version. There are a few payment systems mostly used in today's international payment: the Society for Worldwide Inter-bank Financial Telecommunication (SWIFT), the Clearing House Inter-bank Payment System (CHIPS), the Clearing House Automated Payment System (CHAPS), the Federal Reserve Wire Network (FEDWIRE), the Trans-European Automated Real-time Gross Settlement Express Transfer System (TARGET).

Box 1. 1

SWIFT

The Society for Worldwide Interbank Financial Telecommunication ("SWIFT") is a member-owned cooperative through which the financial world conducts its business operations with speed, certainty and confidence. More than 9,700 banking organizations, securities institutions and corporate customers in 209 countries trust it every day to exchange millions of standardised financial messages.

Its role is two-fold. It provides the proprietary communications platform, products and services that allow its customers to connect and exchange financial information securely and reliably. It also acts as the catalyst that brings the financial community together to work collaboratively to shape market practice, define standards and consider solutions to issues of mutual interest.

SWIFT enables its customers to automate and standardise financial transactions, thereby lowering costs, reducing operational risks and eliminating inefficiencies from their operations. By using SWIFT customers can also create new business opportunities and revenue streams.

SWIFT actually means several things in the financial world:

1. a secure network for transmitting messages between financial institutions;

2. a set of syntax standards for financial messages (for transmission over SWIFT Net or any other network);

3. a set of connection software and services, allowing financial institutions to transmit messages over SWIFT network.

SWIFT has its headquarters in Belgium and has offices in the world's major financial centres and developing markets. SWIFT provides additional products and associated services through Arkelis N. V. , a wholly owned subsidiary of SWIFT, the assets of which were acquired from Sun Gard in 2010.

SWIFT does not hold funds nor does it manage accounts on behalf of customers, nor does it store financial information on an on-going basis. This activity involves the secure exchange of proprietary data while ensuring its confidentiality and integrity.

Source: www. swift. com.

Box 1.2

International Chamber of Commerce

The **International Chamber of Commerce** (**ICC**) is the largest, most representative business organization in the world.

It is the voice of world business championing the global economy as a force for economic growth, job creation and prosperity.

Because national economies are now so closely interwoven, government decisions have far stronger international repercussions than in the past.

ICC - the world's only truly global business organization responds by being more assertive in expressing business views.

ICC activities cover a broad spectrum, from arbitration and dispute resolution to making the case for open trade and the market economy system, business self-regulation, fighting corruption or combating commercial crime.

ICC has direct access to national governments all over the world through its national committees. The organization's Paris-based international secretariat feeds business views into intergovernmental organizations on issues that directly affect business operations.

Setting rules and standards

- Arbitration under the rules of the ICC International Court of Arbitration is on the increase. Since 1999, the Court has received new cases at a rate of more than 500 a year.
- ICC's Uniform Customs and Practice for Documentary Credits (UCP 600) are the rules that banks apply to finance billions of dollars worth of world trade every year.
- ICC Incoterms are standard international trade definitions used every day in countless thousands of contracts. ICC model contracts make life easier for small companies that cannot afford big legal departments.
- ICC is a pioneer in business self-regulation of e-commerce. ICC codes on advertising and marketing are frequently reflected in national legislation and the codes of professional associations.

Promoting growth and prosperity

- ICC supports government efforts to make a success of the Doha trade round. ICC provides world business recommendations to the World Trade Organization.
- ICC speaks for world business when governments take up such issues as intellectual property rights, transport policy, trade law or the environment.
- Signed articles by ICC leaders in major newspapers and radio and TV interviews reinforce the ICC stance on trade, investment and other business topics.
- Every year, the ICC Presidency meets with the leader of the G8 host country to provide business input to the summit.
- ICC is the main business partner of the United Nations and its agencies.

Spreading business expertise

- At UN summits on sustainable development, financing for development and the information society, ICC spearheads the business contribution.
- Together with the United Nations Conference on Trade and Development (UNCTAD), ICC helps some of the world's poorest countries to attract foreign direct investment.
- In partnership with UNCTAD, ICC has set up an Investment Advisory Council for the least-developed countries.
- ICC mobilizes business support for the New Partnership for Africa's Development. At ICC World Congresses every two years, business executives tackle the most urgent international economic issues.
- The World Chambers Congress, also biennial, provides a global forum for chambers of commerce.
- Regular ICC regional conferences focus on the concerns of business in Africa, Asia, the Arab World and Latin America.

Advocate for international business

ICC speaks for world business whenever governments make decisions that crucially affect corporate strategies and the bottom line.

ICC's advocacy has never been more relevant to the interests of thousands of member companies and business associations in every part of the world.

Equally vital is ICC's role in forging internationally agreed rules and standards that companies adopt voluntarily and can be incorporated in binding contracts.

ICC provides business input to the United Nations, the World Trade Organization, and many other intergovernmental bodies, both international and regional.

Source: www.ICC.com

1.3　Traditional Payment Methods

There are four traditional methods of effecting payment for the international trade. They have been the accepted international payment techniques for over 100 years in western countries. The four traditional payment methods are: Cash in advance, Letter of credit, Documentary collection, and Open account. In addition to these four traditional methods, some new methods has been developed and used in an increased level. Table 1.1 and Table 1.2 describe these four traditional payment methods and two other non-traditional methods that are getting more popular. Table 1.1 notes the time of payment to the exporter, when the importer can gain control of the goods, and the risks to each party. The information in these figures runs from the exporters least risk at the top to most risk at the bottom of each list.

Table 1.1　Payments Terms/Methods: Definition[1]

Method	Method of Payment	Description
non-traditional	Credit Card or E-commerce	Self-explanatory. Be sure to comply with card issuers' rules as to notice of charge of payment.
traditional	Cash in Advance	Self-explanatory. This can include e-commerce solutions with or without bank intermediaries.
traditional	Letter of Credit	Any arrangement, however named or described, that is irrevocable and thereby constitutes a definite undertaking of the issuing bank to honour a complying presentation.
traditional	Documentary Collection	The banks of documents, in accordance with instruction received, deliver documents against payment and/or against acceptance.
traditional	Open Account	A payment method by which the exporter gives the importer open credit against a written or understood underlying payment arrangement.
non-traditional	Consignment	A shipment held by the importer until the goods have been sold, at which time payment is made to the exporter.

---

[1] John S. Gordon, *Export/Import Letters of Credit and Payment Methods: Making Payments in International Trade* (2009 Edition), Global Trainning Center, Inc. 2009, p1 – 8.

The following table, table 1.2 more fully describes each of these and how they impact the buyers and sellers who use them.

Table 1.2　Characteristics of Payments Terms/Methods[①]

Method of payment	Time of payments to Seller	Merchandise Available to Buyer	Risk to Seller	Risk to Buyer
Credit card	On receipt of order	Upon arrival	None	Reliance on seller to ship as ordered
Cash in advance	Prior to shipment	Upon arrival	None	Reliance to seller to ship as ordered
Sight letter of credit	After the documents that comply with the credit are presented to the bank	Upon settlement of the letter of credit obligation by the buyer to the issuing bank	Minimal, if all the terms and conditions of the letter of credit are met	Minimal, if buyer will receive the documents stipulated in the credit
Time letter of credit	By acceptance or discount of time bill of exchange	Upon the drawee banks' acceptance of the time draft drawn under the letter of credit	Minimal, if all terms and conditions of the letter of credit are met	Buyer will receive the documents stipulated in the credit
Sight draft for collection, or Document against payment (D/P)	Upon presentation of draft to buyer, and buyer's payment	After payment of the sight draft	Possible non-payment of draft. Goods are in-transit	Required to pay prior to receipt of goods
Time draft for collection, document against acceptance (D/A)	Upon maturity of time draft accepted by the buyer	Upon buyers' acceptance of the time draft	Possible non-payment of draft at maturity. Buyer has possession of goods	Minimal, not required to pay until after receipt and control of goods
Open account	When the buyer pays the invoice	Upon delivery	Full reliance on buyer to pay the invoice when due	None
Consignment	After goods are sold by consignee	Immediately after payment to consignee	Reliance on consignee to pay when goods sold	None

Risk and cost are the two main driving factors behind the trade-offs that must be made. A sale on open account is the least costly, but offers virtually no credit

---

① John S. Gordon, *Export/Import Letters of Credit and Payment Methods: Making Payments in International Trade* (2009 Edition), Global Trainning Center, Inc. 2009, p1 - 8.

protection for the exporter. On the contrary, cash in advance or a confirmed letter of credit well protects the exporter against risks, but is costly and relatively inflexible in implementation. To an exporter, the most risky payment methods are consignment, open account; the most advantageous payment methods are payment in advance. To an importer, it is just opposite. Table 1. 3 shows the risk level, from an seller's perspective, of each payment method.

Table 1. 3   Terms of Payment Risk Matrix (risk scale: 1=least risk, 7=most risk)

Type of Risk	Credit Risk	Foreign Exchange Risk	Transfer Risk	Policy Risk
Risk Scale	1 - 7	1 - 5	1 - 2	1 - 3
Cash in Advance/ Credit Card	1	1	1	1
Confirmed Irrevocable Letter of Credit	2	1	1	1
Irrevocable Letter of Credit, Unconfirmed	3	2	2	2
Sight Draft Documentary Collection	4	3	2	3
Time Draft Documentary Collection	5	4	2	3
Open account	6	4+	2	3
Consignment	7	5+	2	3

Because of the variety in timing and risk (and cost), it can be difficult for a buyer or seller to make a well-reasoned decision. Some sellers are arbitrary and choose open account or letter of credit because it is 'easy', or because the buyer wants it, or their bank says 'everybody does it', and so on. Well managed exporting companies make trade payment decisions only within the context of the needs of the company, the buyers country, credit analysis, market potential, and marketing strategy.

1.4 Factors in the Payment Decision

Payment decision is one of the most important decisions for both exporter and the importer. Every exporter and importer has to consider a number of factors in order to arrive at the appropriate terms of payment for a product or service. From the buyer's perspective, the factors that influence the payment decision are:

1. The credit standing of the buyer. Well established and profitable companies

can command more attractive payment terms than lesser companies. Companies that operate in a relatively unstable environment may be considered less credit-worthy.

2. The amount involved. Smaller sized transactions sometimes do not even cover the banking fees and administrative costs associated with a transaction (for example, letter of credit), while large sized transactions probably call for increased scrutiny of the buyer and greater caution in the payment arrangements. Often the cost of administering a letter of credit file may exceed the gross margin on the sale(s).

3. Availability of foreign exchange in the buyers country. The foreign exchange shortages in Russia in 1992, in Mexico in 1994 – 1995, and in South East Asia in 1997 all demonstrate that the buyer or its bank could face difficulty in obtaining foreign exchange to make payment. So the exporter should consider which currency to use in the payment.

4. Political conditions in the buyers country. Unstable political conditions create financial uncertainty, the exporter should pay a close attention on the political stability of the importer's country, the less the stability, the safer methods should be taken by the exporter.

5. Type of merchandise to be shipped. Most of manufacturing products can easily find another market if the buyer fails to perform while some of the agriculture products, say fresh vegetables and fruits, may be difficult to change the buyers in case of the buyer's default, therefore, the later need more safer payment methods.

6. Customs in the trade. Some industries may have payment terms unique to it, "accepted practices". These terms give an exporter little flexibility if it hopes to compete for buyers and markets.

7. Market conditions: a buyer's or seller's market. In a seller's market, due to price or demand, you can dictate payment terms. In a buyer's market, due to the size of the market, the buyers control over the market, or the number of competitors (excess supply), exporters may have to give concessionary payment terms in order to close sales.

8. Payment terms offered by competitors. What kind of payment terms the competitors are offering is also an important factor that an exporter should be taken into consideration.

1.5　Payment Methods

1.5.1　Credit card

Many international sales are for moderate amounts which origin from replacements, repairs, restocking, and parts orders. From a cost and administrative standpoint, cash in advance or open account are the preferred payment methods for these moderate sized transactions. There is another alternative that frequent exporters should consider. That alternative is Credit Card, Whether American Express, Visa, or MasterCard. Using a credit card for smaller transactions is simple, quick, and cost effective.

1. 5. 2 Consignment

Consignment is a business practice used for the development of a market or disposal of excess goods. It is not often thought of as a method of payment for export transactions.

Consignment is the practice of delivering your product to the buyer's place of business, placing the goods under the buyer's control, and requiring payment only after the goods have been sold. Consignment is less certain as to timing of payment than open account.

The consignee in a consignment sale is not to be confused with the consignee on a bill of lading. The consignee on a consignment sale becomes the holder of the goods at its pleasure, and assumes no responsibility for the handling, condition, insurance, or storage of the goods. These responsibilities can be contracted out, or provided by the consignee for a fee.

Consignment sales should be used in limited circumstances. One such circumstance is for the development of a new market, or for the introduction of a new product line or new model into existing distribution channels. An established distributor or reseller may not be willing to pay for a product with unproven performance, but may appreciate having the product available to demonstrate. In this way the distributor can learn about the product, and will be encouraged to add it to the line in a timely manner.

1. 5. 3 Cash in advance

Cash in advance is self-explanatory. Under this payment term, the exporter requires that the buyer pay for the goods either at the time of the order or prior to loading onto an inland carrier under a combined transport bill of lading, or prior to loading on the ocean carrier if a port to port bill of lading.

Under this method of payment there is no risk to the exporter if down payments and progress payments are received in a timely manner and prior to initiation of the work covered by the advance or progress payments.

For the buyer, this option is expensive and unattractive. There is no assurance of shipment, timely performance cannot be enforced, and quality cannot be controlled. An exporter that requires cash in advance must have a product or service that warrants this degree of discomfort by the buyer.

The document evidencing the transaction is the commercial invoice. Goods are shipped and the commercial invoice is sent to the buyer. The commercial invoice should be marked "Paid". Exporters should not invoice for less than the value of the goods being shipped. If a down payment or advance deposit was made, with the balance received before shipment, the commercial invoice should reflect the total value of the shipment, the advance payment or deposit, and the balance that was paid. In this way the customs authorities in the importing country will have a true accounting of the transaction.

1.5.4   Letter of credit

The letter of credit has been the traditional instrument for payment in international trade transactions for centuries. While the role of letters of credit in international trade is diminishing somewhat as alternatives become more popular, they (L/Cs) remain the single most important payment method.

A letter of credit provides the exporter with an assurance of payment by a bank, a third party assumed to be reliable and not otherwise involved in the underlying commercial transaction, if the exporter performs in accordance with the terms of the credit. With this assurance of payment, the exporter can purchase raw materials, parts, supplies, manufacture to order. This assurance is conditional. The condition is that the exporter must provide the negotiating bank with the stipulated documents, consistent with the requirements of the letter of credit, and internally consistent, on or before the expiry date of the letter of credit.

Properly handled, a letter of credit can be an effective payment mechanism for both exporter and the importer.

1.5.5   Documentary collection

The last of the traditional payment methods for international transactions is the documentary collection. A documentary collection is one in which the exporter sends the shipping documents and demand for payment to its bank, for presentation to the foreign buyer for payment. About one half of all US short term trade transactions (six months or less) use this payment method.

1.5.6   Open account

Open account is an arrangement between exporter and importer whereby the goods are manufactured and delivered before payment is required. Open account sales transactions are evidenced only by the invoice. Because there is no evidence of indebtedness by the buyer, the exporter must be assured of the buyers' goodwill and trust he will be paid at the agreed date. It provides the least risk for the buyers, and the greatest risk for the seller.

1.6　Decision Making and Payment Methods

What is the best payment term to use? How do exporter/importer make their decisions? Sometimes the importer or its government will make it for you. If you are an exporter, your bank or government may make it for you. An importer may issue a letter of credit because the seller or the buyer's government requires it. An importer may be required to arrange for a letter of credit because the exporter's bank demands a sure source of payment, or because the country of export requires a letter of credit to assure foreign exchange will flow to a commercial bank. Every exporter should make an effort to determine the most appropriate method of payment for every buyer, based on a number of factors: the country, the amount, the stage of the relationship, the amount and quality of credit, information on hand, and more. One other decision factor is the exporter's own financial condition.

For some exporters, those in weak financial condition or with heavy demands on all available cash flows, a letter of credit may be one of only two acceptable payment options. Letters of credit, and cash in advance, are two payment methods that convert sales into cash in a timely and (relatively) risk free manner. Some exporters have no option, so the decision criteria are quite simple.

Some exporters do not use any deliberative or analytical process to make a term of payment decision. Most do; most of the over 2,000,008 exporters in the United States go through some evaluation and decision making process to establish the most appropriate payment methods for the markets that have been selected or targeted. This analytical process includes some form of evaluation of some or all of the following issues:

- What are the corporate marketing and sales objectives for this (each) market?
- What is the credit standing of the buyer?
- What risk does the country impose?
- What are traditional payment terms for the products and the industry?
- What is the cost structure of the company?

Key Words

International Settlement，Consignment，Cash in Advance，Open Account

Questions

1. Please describe the evolution of the international settlement.

2. What are the factors an exporter should consider when making decisions on payment methods?

3. What are the traditional trade payment methods?

CHAPTER 2 NEGOTIABLE INSTRUMENTS

Learning Objectives

- To understand the concepts and characteristics of negotiable instruments
- To understand the functions of negotiable instruments
- To learn related negotiable instrument laws
- To understand and compare the parties to a negotiable instrument

2.1 General Introduction

2.1.1 What is a negotiable instrument?

A negotiable instrument, known as commercial paper, is an instrument the rights on which can be transferred easily from one person to another. In a broad sense, it refers to any commercial title ownership, including bills of exchange, promissory notes, cheques, dividend warrants, bearer bonds, bills of lading, in surance policies, warehouse warrants, treasury bills, certificates of deposits, etc., all of which have two characteristics in common:

- Representing a unilateral promise to pay a fixed amount of money to the instrument's legitimate holder, and
- being transferable or negotiable.

In a narrow sense, however, a negotiable instrument is a written document that contains an unconditional promise by the drawer to pay the payee or an unconditional or derby the drawer to the drawee to pay the payee a fixed amount of money at a definite time.

This chapter is talking about the narrow sense negotiable instruments, i.e., bills of exchange, promissory notes, and cheques.

2.1.2 Characteristics of negotiable instruments

Negotiability

Although it may or may not be circulated, a negotiable instrument is usually capable of being transferred or negotiated. The title to a negotiable instrument can be passed from person to person by mere delivery or by endorsement followed by delivery. The title here means the rights embodied in a negotiable instrument.

If payable to bearer, a negotiable instrument may be transferred by mere delivery; when payable to a named person or order, a negotiable instrument may be transferred by endorsement and delivery ; and if the payee is restricted to a named person only, a negotiable instrument will lose its capability of being transferred and the payer will only pay the named payee.

Unconditional promise or order to pay

No matter whether it is a bill of exchange, a promissory note, or a cheque, it must contain an unconditional order or promise to pay a fixed amount in money at a certain time. For instance, the drawer of a bill of exchange unconditionally orders the drawee to pay a fixed amount in money to the payee at a certain time; the drawer of a note unconditionally promises to pay the payee a fixed amount in money at a specified time; and the drawer of a cheque unconditionally orders the drawee bank to pay a fixed a mount in money to the payee at a certain time.

Requisite in form

A negotiable instrument must be in the form of a document containing certain required items. Different countries have different laws on negotiable instruments and hence different requirements for the form of a negotiable instrument. Despite of the differences, the requisites in form are to a great extent very similar. In general, as a written document of settling debts, a negotiable instrument must contain the following necessary items:

- The name of a negotiable instrument, say, " bills of exchange ", " promissory note ", or " cheque ";
- Unconditional promise or order to pay ;
- A fixed amount of money, representing the value of the instrument ;
- Issuing date and due date;
- Names and places of the drawer, the payee, and the drawee; and;
- The signature of the drawer.

Non-causative nature

A negotiable instrument exists in dependent of the commercial relations from which it originated or which occasioned its transfer.

It is obvious that there should be a certain reason for a negotiable instrument to be made out. For instance, when a drawer draws a draft on a drawee, there must be a commercial or funds relationship between the drawer and the drawee (with the accommodation bills as an exception), say, the seller and the buyer. When the payee transfers the draft to a transferee, the transferee will not mind how the instrument was generated and his only concern is that the instrument must be in a qualified form and contain the essential items required by the relative negotiable instrument law. Just because of the non-causative nature, a negotiable instrument possesses the characteristic of negotiability as its name shows.

In addition to above four characteristics, a negotiable instrument represents money or asset ownership, and the contents and scope of an instrument will be determined by a literal reading of the instrument.

2. 1. 3   Functions of negotiable instruments

The major function of a negotiable instrument is to serve as substitute for money. In noncash international payments, for example, bills of exchange, promissory notes or cheques are usually used as payment instruments to settle debts among traders from different countries.

A negotiable instrument itself has no value, but the parties to it provide the credit basis for it to serve as a payment instrument. For instance, that an accepted draft can be discounted in money market is because both the drawer and the accept or guarantee the payment for the instrument when due. If the acceptor is credit worthy, the draft will be even more desirable. Thus, a draft is not only a means of payment but also a credit instrument.

2.2　Negotiable Instrument Laws

Negotiable instrument laws in a broad sense refer to all the laws relating to negotiable instruments, but we are here talking about those laws directly dealing with negotiable instruments.

By the end of the 19th century, France, Germany, and the United Kingdom all had established their respective laws on negotiable instruments, thus constituting three different bodies of laws on negotiable instruments then.

The first established law on negotiable instruments was the French law. Many countries such as Belgium, the Netherlands, Portugal, and Latin American countries were under its influence. The German law was developed many years later, and countries such as Austria, Hungary, Switzerland, Sweden, Denmark, Japan, Norway, Poland, ex-Soviet Union, Turkey and Yugoslav were under its influence. The British law covered countries such as Canada, India, the United States, Australia and New Zealand.

Since the existence of different laws on negotiable instruments caused inconvenience for those dealing with cross border trade, a conference on forming a uniform law on negotiable instruments was held in Genevain in 1930. Delegates from about 30 countries participated in it, but most of them came from the continent of Europe. The result of the conference was the passage of the Geneva Uniform Law. Since then, countries under the influence of both Germanand French laws have adopted the Geneva Uniform Law by revising their domestic claws accordingly. The United Kingdom did not send any delegates to the conference, and has not yet joined the Geneva Convention. Therefore, there still exist two different bodies of laws on negotiable instruments, and the two representative documents are the Uniform Law for Bills of Exchangeand Promissory Notes of Geneva of 1930 and the UK Bills of Exchange Act of 1882.

The United States has its own law relating to negotiable instruments, i. e., the Article 3 of the US Uniform Commercial Code of 1962. Due to the economic importance of the United States, its negotiable instrument law has been attached great attention by international traders and bankers.

China has not participated in the Geneva Convention. In international trade settlement, China always refers to the Geneva Uniform Law although it has its own negotiable instrument law — the Negotiable Instrument Law of the People's Republic of China.

Having recognized the inconvenience caused by the existence of different negotiable instrument laws, the United Nations has been trying to bring the two bodies of laws on negotiable instruments together, and has drafted the Convention Providing a Uniform Law for International Bills of Exchange and International Promissory Notes and the Convention Providing a Uniform Law for International cheques. The United Nations has formally filed the two documents to different countries for comments.

Box 2.1

A Comparison Between Two Negotiable Instruments Laws

The United Kingdom in 1882 promulgated the Bill of Exchange Act. The United States and most members of the Common wealth such as Canada, India and so on developed their own negotiable instruments law on its basis, which formed the Anglo-American negotiable instrument law. In 1930, over 20 European continents based countries, like France and Germany, convened in Geneva to unify the International Law of Negotiable Instruments, and signed the "Geneva Convention on the Unification of the Law Relating to Bills of Exchange and Promissory Notes". In 1931, these countries signed the "Geneva Convention Providing a Uniform Law of Cheques". The two conventions collectively were known as the Geneva Uniform Law. Since then, and some non-civil law countries developed their Negotiable Instruments Law with reference to the Geneva Uniform Law (such as China's Law of Negotiable Instruments). Thus formed the civil common law bills, which is different from the Anglo-American law system.

In 1982, United Nations Commission on International Trade Law issued Draft Convention on International Bills of Exchange and International Promissory Notes, envisaging two Negotiable Instruments systems would be unified within the scope of the Convention, but failed to implement because of too few signatory states. Therefore, today there is still the coexistence of the two Negotiable Instruments system. Countries of each system have each Negotiable Instruments law basis, and moved to convergence within each system.

1. On the perspective of legislative configuration, the Anglo-American countries adopted bill generalist, while civil law countries have adopted the bill separatists. "UK Act" combined three bills into one, and dealt with promissory notes and checks as special form of bills of exchange (similar to China's Law of Negotiable Instruments). Geneva Negotiable Instruments separated these types and defined them separately.

2. Two Negotiable Instruments are different when give definitions. "Geneva Law" only defined the bills by regulating the necessary items, unlike the English Act, which has rigorous textual definition.

3. Notes are comply type securities; "Geneva Law" particularly stressed its compliance. The notes are only effective after meeting legal requirements as to format and recorded matters. Notes made in non-compliance ways don't have legal effects, and will result in bills invalid (China's Law of Negotiable Instruments stressed it too).

In regard to the necessary items:

(1) "Geneva Law" stressed there should be the name of the bills on it, which indicated that it is a bill of exchange or promissory note or check (China's Negotiable Instruments Law also has this regulation). "British law" has no such requirement.

(2) If the amount in capital letters and in small letters are inconsistent, both laws regulated the capital amount shall prevail (China's Negotiable Instruments Law regulated such instrument is invalid). "Geneva Law" also stipulates that if there are two uppercase amounts inconsistent, the small amount shall prevail.

(3) About the payee name, English Act provides three kinds of bills can use both name and anonymous (China's Law of Negotiable Instruments shall not use anonymous).

(4) The date of issue, in the "Geneva Law" is considered a necessary item (China's Negotiable Instruments Law has the same requirements). But in English Act, without date of issue, the bills still valid.

There are a number of different provisions in other recording areas. English Act regulates that the drawer and endorser can use recourse-free clauses to waive the responsibility when the notes were refused to pay and recourse. In Geneva Law, the drawer can only be exempted from the responsibility of guarantee of acceptance, not the responsibility of guarantee of payment. (China's Law of Negotiable Instruments regulates this responsibility shall not be waived)

4. The notes, in addition to the requirement in the format and content, behavior also needs to comply. The Negotiable Instruments Law has detailed and strict rules about all notes behavior. This can bring bill disputes to a minimum, thus ensuring a smooth flow of notes.

(1) "British Act" stipulates that endorsement restricted endorsee doesn't have rights to transfer the bill. "Geneva Law" thinks endorsement cannot be transferred, while the bill still can be transferred by the endorsee. The transfer person is only responsible for direct receiver, no obligation to the following ones (China's Law of Negotiable Instruments Negotiable Instruments agrees with the British Act).

(2) The bill rights are acquired in good faith, which means there should be no malice or gross negligence. "British Act" uses "actual knowledge" principle in regard to whether is aware of the prior owner's defects. "British Act" thinks that the holder is free of confrontation when he is only in good faith and paid the price. "Geneva Law" doesn't care whether he paid the right price (China's Law of Negotiable Instruments

Law agrees with English Act).

(3) Bills should be presented in time.   The "Geneva law" stipulates that bills must be presented for payment within 1 year from the date of issue; fixed period after sight drafts must be presented for acceptance within 1 year from the date of issue; long-term notes must be prompted for payment in the due date or the two business days as of the due date. "British Act" stipulates that sight draft must be prompted for payment within a reasonable time; fixed period after sight drafts must be presented for acceptance within a reasonable time . Usance draft must be prompted for payment in the due date. (China's Law of Negotiable Instruments stipulates that sight draft must be presented for payment within 1 month from the date of issue. Usance draft must be prompted for payment within 10 days from the due date). If the bearer does not prompt instrument within the prescribed time, then he loses the right to right of recourse from Prior party. However payment acceptor still have responsibilities for ticket holders. Limitation of liability, "Geneva law" provisions for 3 years from the due date, "United Kingdom law" provisions for 6 years from acceptance (China's Bill law for 2 years from the due date).

(4) Aging of Acceptance, "British Act" requires acceptance for payment to be made within habits time (24 hours). The "Geneva law" provides within 2 days (our country's Bill law within 3 days).

(5) Geneva law regulated the payer doesn't need to validate the endorsement. " British Act " requires the verification of the endorsement for payment (China's law agrees with English)

(6) If holder was bounced, according to "British Act" only international money orders need the public notary to make the rejection certificate. The "Geneva law" allows that court decisions can replace rejection certificate if the payer on the Bill is broken (similar to our country's Bill law).

(7) "British Act" does not have "guarantee" notes, "Geneva law" allowed "guarantee" notes (our country's Bill law agrees with "Geneva uniform law").

2.3   Parties to a Negotiable Instrument

Drawer

The drawer is the party that gives a promise or order to pay. In the case of a promissory note or a cheque, the drawer is also called the maker.

When drawing an instrument, the drawer engages that, on due presentment, the instrument will be accepted or paid as specified and that, if it is dishonoured, the drawer will compensate the holder or any endorser who is compelled to pay the instrument, provided that the requisite proceedings on dishonor is duly taken.

Drawee

The drawee is the party that is directed by the drawer to pay. The drawee of a promissory note is the drawer itself, the drawee of a bill of exchange is the person to whom the payment order is given, and the drawee of a cheque is the drawee bank. In the case of a usance bill, if the drawee refuses to accept the bill, then the drawee is not obliged to pay. That is, before acceptance, the drawee is not liable to any holder though he maybe personally liable to the drawer if he dishonours a bill properly drawn upon him.

Payee

The payee is the party to whom the drawee is directed to make payment. The payee has the right to ask the drawee to pay. As the only oblige on the instrument, the payee has the right of recourse to the drawer if he is refused by non-payment or non-acceptance. When an instrument is payable to order or bearer, the payee may transfer the instrument by end or sement and delivery or by merely delivery.

The drawer, the drawee, and the payee are the three basic parties to a negotiable instrument. Bills of exchange and cheques are three party instruments while promissory notes two party instruments.

Sometimes, the same party may take on the roles of more than one party. For example, when one makes a cheque out to oneself, then the person is the drawer as well as the payee. Another example is that when a bill is drawn payable to the drawer, then the drawer and payee are identical to each other.

Endorser

The payee or holder of a negotiable instrument may sign his name on the back of the instrument and transfer it to another party. The payee or holder who has signed his name on the back of the instrument and has transferred it is called an endorser, and the person to whom the instrument is transferred is called an endorsee. To an endorsee, all the endorsers on the instrument before him are called its prior parties, and to an endorser, all the endorsees after him are called its subsequent holders.

By endorsing an instrument, the endorser guarantees to the endorsee or endorsees that at the time of its endorsement the instrument is valid, that he has good title to the bill, that on due presentment it shall be accepted or paid as specified, and that if it is dishonoured he will compensate the holder or subsequent endorser who is compelled to pay it, provided that the requisite proceedings on dishonours be duly taken.

Acceptor

The acceptor is the drawee that has accepted ausance bill. By accepting a bill, the drawee signs his name on the face of the instrument, and engages that he will pay it as stated in the instrument or as accepted. Once a bill has been accepted, the drawee,

i. e. , accepter, becomes the party primarily on the bill.

Guarantor

A guarantor is the person who guarantees the payment or acceptance of an instrument. Typically, he is not a party already liable to the instrument and the party guaranteed can be any obligor on the instrument.

Holder

The holder is the person who possesses an instrument. He maybe the payee, endorsee or bearer.

The holder for value is a person who possesses an instrument for which value has been given by himself or by some other person prior to him. In other words, once value is given for a bill, the holder giving value and all subsequent holders are holders for value. The value can be given in the forms of money, goods, or services. If a person has a lien on the instrument, the person is also deemed to be a holder for value.

The holder in due course refers to an individual who acquires a negotiable instrument in good faith. Good faith means the observance of honourable intent in business relations and the avoidance of any attempts to deceive in assuming and performing contractual obligations. To make it easy to understand, a holder in due course should meet the following four requirements:

- The instrument should be complete and regular on its face ;
- The instrument is before maturity and the holder did not notice its previous dishonour, if any;
- The holder took it in good faith and for value;
- The holder did not notice any infirmity in the instrument or defect in the title of the person negotiating it.

A holder in due course is also called a bona-fide holder. A holder for value may or may not be a holder in due course, but a holder in due course must be a holder for value. The following example will illustrate the position of a holder in due course and the difference between a holder for value and a holder in due course.

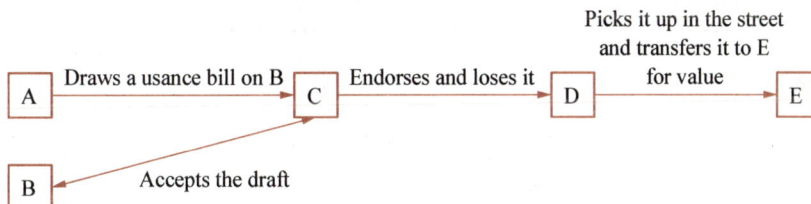

In this example, A, as a drawer, draws a usance bill on B to C, the payee. C presents the bill to B, the drawee, for acceptance, and B accepts the bill and delivers it to C. C, after endorsing it blankly, loses the bill in the street. By chance, D picks it up and transfers it to E for value. E obtains the bill in good faith and for value without noticing the defect of D's title to the bill. When the bill becomes due, E, as the holder and only obligee of the bill, has the right to present it to B, the accept or, for payment. In the event of dishonour, E has the right to sue A, B, C and D. The defect in the title of this instrument was on the part of D. E's title should not be affected because E took it in good faith and for value.

In the same example, suppose E gives the bill further to his daughter, F, as a present. Since F does not give any value for the bill to E, F is not a holder in due course, but a holder for value, for her prior party E gave the value for the bill. In the event of dishonour, F would have the right to sue A, B, C, D, but not E.

2.4 The Relationship of the Parties to a Negotiable Instrument

Subsection 2.3 has discussed both basic and derivative parties relating to a negotiable instrument. This subsection will illustrate the relationship of these parties.

Sight bill

In this sight bill, D, the holder, is the only obligee. A, B, C, E, F are all obligors, among whom, A, the drawer, is the principal obligor, i. e., the party primarily liable for the payment of the bill, and B, C, E, F are the secondary obligors, i.e., the parties secondarily liable for the payment of the bill. It is noted that E can be any obligor's guarantor, in this case C's, though.

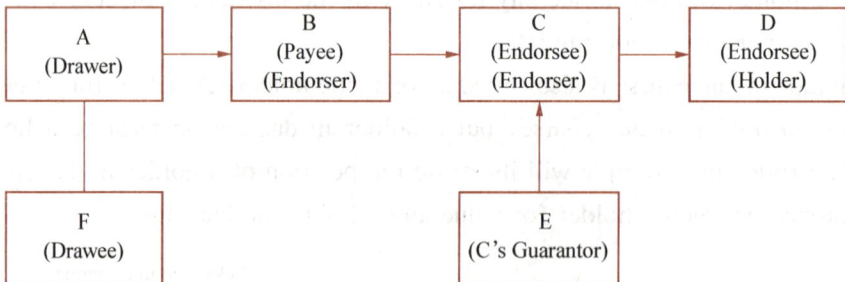

Usance bill

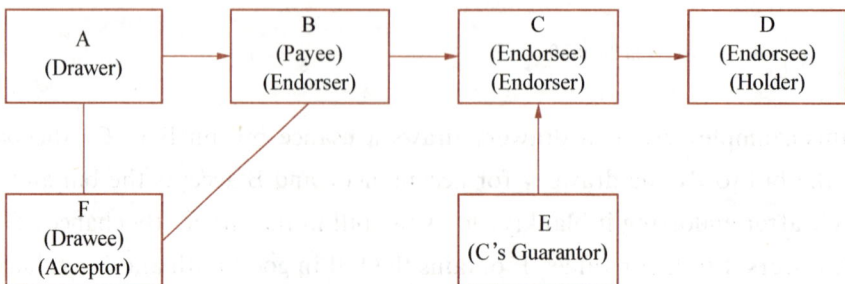

In this usance bill, D, the holder, is the only obligee. Before acceptance, F, the drawee, is the secondary obligor, and A, the drawer, is the principal obligor. After acceptance, however, F, the acceptor, becomes the principal obligor, and A, B, C, and E are secondary obligors. Although after acceptance F becomes the principal obligor, if he dishonours the accepted bill, the obligee has to enforce his right of recourse against C, E, B, and finally to A for payment.

Promissory note

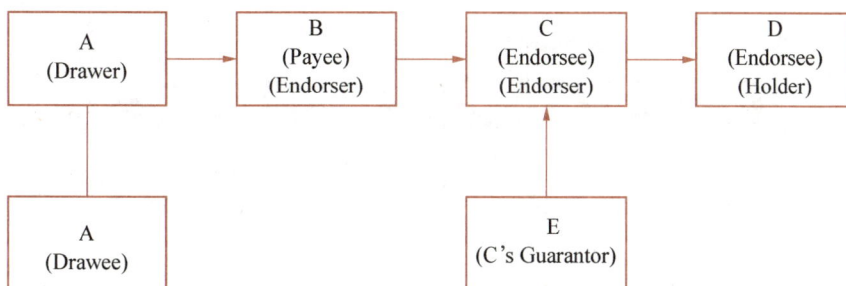

| A (Drawer) | → | B (Payee) (Endorser) | → | C (Endorsee) (Endorser) | → | D (Endorsee) (Holder) |

A (Drawee)   E (C's Guarantor) → C

In this promissory note, D is the holder, the only obligee. A, as both the drawer and the drawee, is the principal obligor, and B, C and E are secondary obligors.

Check

| A (Drawer) | → | B (Payee) (Endorser) | → | C (Endorsee) (Endorser) | → | D (Endorsee) (Holder) |

F (Drawee bank)   E (C's Guarantor) → C

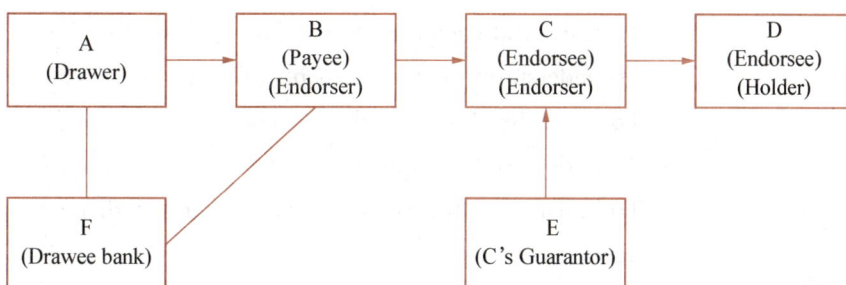

In this cheque, D is the holder and the only obligee, F is the drawee bank, one of the secondary obligors, A, B, C and E are all secondary obligors, and there is no principal obligor in the case of a cheque. If the cheque is certified by a bank, however, the certified bank will become the principal obligor and all other obligors liabilities' will be discharged.

Key Words

Negotiation, Drawee, Drawer, Endorser, Guarantor, Holder, Sight Bill, Usance Bill

Questions

1. What is a negotiable instrument?
2. What are the characteristics of a negotiable instruments?

CHAPTER 3   BILLS OF EXCHANGE

Learning Objectives

- To master the definitions and classification of bills of exchange
- To learn and compare the parties to a bill of exchange
- To understand the requirements of a bill of exchange
- To learn the acts of a bill of exchange
- To understand the application of a bill of exchange in financing
- To understand the risks and advantages of different payment methods

3.1 Definitions of Bills of Exchange

As defined in the Bills of Exchange Act 1882 of the United Kingdom, a bill of exchange is unconditional order in writing, addressed by one person to another, signed by the person giving it, requiring the person on whom it is addressed to pay on demand or at a fixed or determinable future time a sum certain in money to or to the order of a specified or to bearer.

3.2 Parties to a Bill of Exchange

3.2.1 Basic parties

There are three basic parties to a bill of exchange: the drawer, the drawee, and payee.

1. The Drawer

The drawer is the party who draws and signs a draft on the drawee and delivers it to the payee. He is a debtor to the draft. Before the bill is accepted by the drawee, he is primarily liable to the payee or holder of the instrument. In the event that the drawee dishonors the bill by non-acceptance or by non-payment, the drawer must redeem and pay the bill. However, when the bill is accepted, his liability becomes secondary.

2. The Drawee, also called Payer

The drawee is the party on whom the bill is drawn and he is the party to honor the bill at the order of the drawer. In other words, he is the party who will effect payments to the payee. In this sense, he can also be called the payer and he is another debtor to the bill. He is called a drawee because the draft is drawn on him. However, when the bills is presented to him, the drawee can make a choice whether to honor it (agree to make acceptance and payment) or dishonor it (refuse to make acceptance and payment) because he can not prevent any party to whom he owes no debt from drawing a draft on him. This means that before the drawee agrees to honor the draft, he is not yet a debtor to the bill, and if he agrees, he acknowledges his indebtedness to the bill and in the case of a time bill, he becomes an acceptor.

3. The Payee

The payee is the party to receive payment. He is the first creditor to the bill and the first legal owner of the instrument. He can either daim payment against the bill or transfer (negotiate) the draft to another party. If the bill is transferred, he is called the original holder/transferer because the bill is taken away from him while the transferee, the person who takes the bill, becomes the new holder.

3.2.2 Other parties

There are also other important parties who probably involve in the process of payment, transfer, negotiation, and so on.

1. Acceptor

An acceptor is the party who sign on a Time Bill with his assent to the order given by the drawer. He engages, by signing his name on the bill of exchange that he will pay when it falls due.

2. Endorser

An endorser is a payee or a holder who signs his name on the back of a bill for the purpose of negotiation. Because the payee is the first holder, he will be the first endorser. When the payee becomes the endorser, he transforms himself from a creditor to a debtor because he obligates himself that he will be liable to the endorsee and his subsequent parties. In the process of negotiation, we will have the first endorser, the second endorser, the third endorser and so forth and the list can go on and on.

3. Endorsee

An endorsee is the party to whom the instrument is transferred. He becomes the new holder to the instrument and is the creditor to the instrument. An endorsee can also become an endorser if he wishes to transfer the instrument to another party by signing his name on its back. And by doing so, he transforms himself into a debtor. If the process of negotiation creates a sequence of endorsers, similarly, it will also bring about a series of endorsees.

4. Holder

A holder is a party who is in possession of the instrument. A holder can be the payee/ bearer or the endorsee. The payee will always be the original holder. A holder is a creditor to the bill. The holder can be further classified as a holder for value and a holder in due course. The perfect title to a bill will be accrued to the holder in due course.

(1) Holder for value

As we have mentioned, value refers to anything which is sufficient to support a simple contract and may be given in the form of goods, services or money. A holder for value is the holder of a bill for which value has been given either by himself or by his prior parties. In the former case, we usually refer to the payee. In the latter case and according to Bills of Exchange Act, a holder for value usually refers to the holder when the value is given by his prior parties rather than by himself. For example, if a bill is drawn by A on B payable to C and accepted by B; C endorses the instrument and gives it to D as a gift. Although D gives no value for the instrument by himself, he is qualified as a holder for value for the reason that the value has already been given by C, his prior party.

A holder for value is the creditor to the bill. He enjoys the same rights but is subject to the same defects in title, if any, of the transferor. That is to say, the rights of a holder for value can not be superior to his direct prior party.

(2) Holder in due course

A holder in due course can also be called bona-fide holder. According to Bills of Exchange Act, a holder in due course is the person who is in possession of an instrument that is: ①Complete and regular on its face (A complete and regular bill is the one that contains all the essentials required) ②Taken before maturity ③Taken in good faith and for value ④Taken without notice of its previous dishonor and without notice of any infirmity in the instrument or defect in the title of the person negotiating it.

"Good faith" is defined as: "A thing is deemed to be done in good faith where it is in fact done honestly, whether it is done negligently or not." For example, if a holder is a ware of some fraud or illegality in connection with the instrument or if he has actual or constructive notice of a defect in the title on the part of his transferor, consequently, he can not be a holder in due course because he has not taken the instrument in good faith.

5. Guarantor

A guarantor is another third party who guarantees the acceptance and the payment of a bill of exchange. The guaranteed can be the drawer, endorser, acceptor or acceptor for honor. The obligations of the guarantor are the same as those of the guaranteed.

3.3 Requirements of a Bill of Exchange

In conformity with the Uniform Law on Bills of Exchange and Promissory Notes 1930 of Geneva, a bill of exchange must fulfill the following requirements: ①The word "Exchange" ②An unconditional order ③Place and date of issue ④Time of payment ⑤Amount ⑥Name of the drawee and place of payment ⑦Name of the payee ⑧Drawer's name and signature (see Figure 3.1)

Figure 3. 1

ACCEPTED 12 th April, 2008 Payable Bank Ltd. London 　　For Bank of Europe, 　London signature	Due 11th July, 2008 ① 　　　　⑤ 　　　　③ Exchange for GBP 5000.00, Beijing, 5 th April, 2008 ④ 　　　　② 　　⑦ At 90 days after sight pay to C Co. or Order ⑤ The sum of five thousand pounds To Bank of Europe, London ⑥ 　　　　　　　　　　For A Company, Beijing 　　　　　　　　　　signature 　　　　　　　　　　⑧

1. The word "Exchange"

The word "Exchange" should be indicated on a bill of exchange, such as "Exchange for GBP 5, 000", but it is not definitely required in the Bills of Exchange Act 1882 of the United Kingdom.

2. An unconditional order in writing

A bill of exchange must be an unconditional order in writing (including "printed" and "typewritten"). For example, "Pay to A Co. or order the sum of one thousand US dollars." If these words such as "Please pay on demand US $1, 000 to John Smith provided the goods are up to standard" or "Pay US $400 to Mary Hawkins 30 days after her marriage to John Smith" are written on an instrument, it is not a bill of exchange, for such expressions cannot be regarded as an order nor as unconditional. A drawn clause added on a bill of exchange, such as "Pay to A Bank or order the sum of ten thousand US dollars. Drawn under L/C No. 12345 issued by × Bank, New York dated on 15 th August, 20 _____", which is in illustration of a transaction resulting in the use of the bill, is permitted and is not considered as conditional.

3. Date and place of issue

The issuing date of a bill of exchange is a legal requirement. It is used to ascertain that the date of presentation or the date of acceptance is not before it, and also to compute the date of payment if the bill is payable after date. If the bill issued undated, any holder may fill therein the true date of issue and the bill shall be paid accordingly. If the holder fills in a wrong date by mistake, the bill shall be paid as if the date so filled was the true date. A bill should not be considered as invalid only by reason that it is, ante-dated or post-dated or that it bears a date on Sunday.

The place of issue is very important especially to an international bill of exchange. The validity of the bill is normally judged in conformity with the law of the place of issue.

4. Tenor

A bill of exchange may be payable on demand or at a fixed or determinable future time.

(1) Payable on demand

a. The words "on demand" or "at sight" or "on presentation" are indicated on the bill. For example,

"At sight pay to the order of AB . . ."

"On demand pay AB only . . ."

"On presentation pay bearer . . ."

b. No time of payment is stated on the bill. For example,

"Pay to the order of AB . . ."

(2) Payable at a future time

a. At a fixed time after date (issuing date). For example,

"30 days after date pay to the order of . . ."

"Two months after the date herein pay to the order of . . ."

b. At a fixed time after sight (accepting date). For example,

"At 90 days after sight pay to the order of . . ."

"At 3 months after sight pay to the order of . . ."

c. On a fixed date. For example,

"On Sept. 30th, 2012 pay to the order of . . ."

d. At a fixed time after the happening of a specified event. For example,

"At 60 days after bill of lading date pay to the order . . ."

"At 60 days after presentation of documents pay to . . ."

"At three months after the death of XY pay to the order . . ."(Here death is also a specified event which will certainly happen.)

In case, a bill is payable after sight, presentment for acceptance is necessary in order to fix its due date. In case a bill is payable at a fixed rote-after date or on a fixed date or at a fixed time after the happening of a specified event, it is not obligatory to present it for acceptance. The holder may present it for payment on its maturity date. As a rule, however, he does present it for acceptance in order to make acceptor so that it could be made possible for him to discount the bill. Moreover, if the drawee refuses to accept the bill, the holder will then have an immediate right of recourse against his prior parities.

As regards the computation of the time of payment, the following basic points should be kept in mind:

(1) If the date of payment falls on a non-business day, the bill shall be payable on the succeeding business day.

(2) If a bill is payable at a fixed time after date, after sight or after the happening

of a specified event, the time of payment is calculated by counting in the date of payment but counting out the accepting date or the issuing date or the date of the happening of a specified event.

(3) The word "month" on a bill means a calendar month.

(4) Three days of grace as stipulated in the Bills of Exchange Act 1882 imply that three days should be added to the time of payment of a bill payable at a determinable future time. The Bills of Exchange Act enacted in most countries, however, has no such stipulations. With the enactment, of the Banking and Financial Dealings Act 1971 of the United Kingdom, days of grace were then abolished for all the bills drawn on or after January, 16th, 1972.

5. Amount

The amount must be expressed as a sum certain in money both in words and in figures, so a document ordering the delivery of 200 shares of AB Company or 2 tons of steel cannot be considered as a bill of exchange.

If a discrepancy exists between the sum in words and that in figures, the former shall be the amount payable. However, it is a regular practice in some countries that whichever of the two is the smaller should be considered as the amount payable.

The amount payable may be paid (1) with interest, (2) by state installments, or (3) according to an indicated rate of exchange. In that case, the interest rate or the rate of exchange must be definitely indicated on the bill. For example,

"Pay to the order of A Co. the sum of one thousand US dollars plus interest."

"Pay to the order of A Co. the sum of one thousand US dollars plus interest calculated at the rate of 6% per annum from the date of hereof to the date of payment."

"Pay to the order of A Co. the sum of one thousand US dollars plus interest calculated at the rate of $x\%$."

"Pay to the order of A Co. the sum of one thousand US dollars converted into sterling equivalent."

"Pay to the order of A Co. the sum of one thousand US dollars converted into sterling equivalent at current rate of exchange."

6. Drawee and place of payment

Drawee and place of payment must be reasonably clear and definite. A bill of exchange may be addressed to two or more drawees jointly no matter whether they are partners or not, but if addressed to either of the two drawees or more drawees alternatively, it is not valid. For example, a bill of exchange drawn on "AB & CD" is valid but drawn on "AB or CD or EF" is invalid. In case the drawer and the drawee on the bill are the same person or the drawee is a fictitious or insolvent person, the holder may treat the instrument at his option, either as a bill of exchange or as a promissory note.

If the place of payment is required on a bill of exchange, but is not indicated thereon, the location where the drawee resides should be considered to be the place of payment.

7. Name of the payee

Unless a bill of exchange is payable to bearer; the payee must be named with reasonable certainty. A bill may be made payable to two or more payees jointly, or to either of the two payees, or to one or some of several payees alternatively. A bill may also be made payable to the drawer himself, if the payee is a fictitious or non-existing one, the bill may be treated as payable to bearer.

As specified in the Bills of Exchange Act 1882 of the United Kingdom, the name of a payee may take one of the following three forms:

(1) Restrictive order. A bill may be payable to a named person only or to a named person not transferable. For example,

"Pay to John Davids only."

"Pay to John Davids not transferable."

(2) Demonstrative order. A bill may be payable to the order of a particular person or to a particular person without any words indicating the prohibition of transfer. For example,

"Pay to the order of A Co."

"Pay to A Co. or order."

"Pay to A Co."

(3) Payable to bearer. A bill may be payable to bearer with no specified person as a payee thereon. A bearer bill can be transferred simply by delivery; in his case there needs no endorsement. For example,

"Pay to bearer."

"Pay to A Co. or bearer."

8. Drawer and his signature

The drawer's signature serves as a means of authenticating a bill of exchange. No bill is valid if the drawer has not signed thereon. Forged or unauthorized signature of the drawer makes the bill invalid, too.

3.4 Acts of a Bill of Exchange

3.4.1 Issue

To issue a draft comprises two acts to be performed by the drawer. One is to draw and sign a draft, the other is to deliver it to the payee.

Delivery means transfer of possession of the draft from one person to another. The legal title to the draft can be transferred only when the act of delivery is performed. Delivery without endorsement is not recognized as an act of delivery by the Common Law.

After the draft is drawn and delivered to the payee, it becomes irrevocable and in the meantime the drawer engages that the drawee will accept and pay it. If it is dishonoured by non-acceptance or by non-payment, the holder has the right of recourse against the drawer who is primarily liable thereon.

3.4.2 Endorsement

Endorsement is an act of negotiation. When the payee or the holder of a draft wants to transfer and pass its title to another person, he should endorse it first. When the holder sells or discounts it, he must also make an endorsement thereon before delivering it to the party purchasing the draft.

Kinds of endorsements:

1. Special endorsement. It is also called an endorsement in full. A special endorsement is one that specifies an endorsee to whom or to whose order the draft is to be paid, addition to the signature of an endorser. Thus, if a draft is endorsed "Pay to AB" or "Pay to the order of AB" above the endorser's signature, no one except AB can transfer the draft or receive its payment. An endorsement made by such an endorsee is necessary for further transfer of the instrument. The special endorsement not only shows a chain of endorsers but also gives the holder full right of recourse against all the prior endorsers.

Any holder may change a blank endorsement into a special endorsement by writing above the endorser's signature such a directive as "Pay to" or "Pay to the order of" himself or some other person.

2. Blank endorsement or endorsement in blank. It is also called a general endorsement. An endorsement in blank is one that shows an endorser's signature only and specifies no endorsee. A draft so endorsed becomes payable to bearer.

3. Restrictive endorsement. Restrictive endorsement is an endorsement which is prohibited further transfer of the draft. For example,

"Pay to A bank only."

"Pay to A Bank not transferable."

"Pay to A Bank not to order."

4. Conditional endorsement. A conditional endorsement is a special endorsement adding some words thereto that create a condition bound to be met before the special

endorsee is entitled to receive payment. The endorser is liable only if the condition is fulfilled. For example,

Pay to the order of B Co.

On delivery of B/L No. 125

For A Co. , London

Signature

5. Endorsement for collection. Endorsement for collection is an endorsement with the purpose of collection. Normally the creditor just put the words of "for collection" before or after the text "Pay to the order of B Bank" to distinguish it from a general endorsement.

For example:

"For collection pay to the order of B Bank"

"Pay to the order of A Bank for collection"

3. 4. 3   Presentment

A draft must be duly presented for payment if it is a sight bill or duly presented for acceptance first and then presented for payment at maturity if it is a time bill.

If the holder does not present the bill for acceptance or for payment within a reasonable time, then he loses right of recourse against his prior parties. That is to say, the drawer and all the prior endorsers are discharged of their liability on the bill. In determining what is a reasonable time, one should regard the nature of the bill, the usage of trade with respect to similar bills and the concrete conditions in a particular case.

Presentment must be made at the proper place specified on the bill. If no place is specified except that of the drawee or the acceptor, the bill, shall presented at the drawee's or acceptor's place.

3. 4. 4   Acceptance

Acceptance of a bill of exchange is a signification by the drawee of his assent to the order given by the drawer. He engages, by signing his name across the face of the bill that he will pay when it falls due. As a rule, the act of acceptance cannot be considered complete, however, until the bill has been delivered (handed back) to the person presenting it for acceptance. That is to say, after the drawee accepts the bill he should\return it to the holder, who will present it for payment at maturity.

A valid acceptance require: (1) The word "accepted" must be followed by the signature of drawee without additional words is also justified. (2) It must not be expressed that the drawee will carry out his promise by any other means than the payment of money.

When the drawee has signed his acceptance, he is known as the acceptor instead of the drawee and becomes primary liable for the payment of this bill. He may also add such words as "payable at Midland Bank, Blankton", which imply his account. Most banks, after accepting a draft, would always issue a notice of acceptance indicating its due to the holder in due course. In such case, the draft is kept in the hands of the banks, and will be paid on due date accordingly.

How should the time for acceptance be treated? (1) Acceptance is generally to be made at a reasonable hour on a business day subsequent to the presentment of the bill before it is overdue. However, the drawee is allowed to have a reasonable time to deliberate whether accepting it or not. (2) Acceptance is also to be made immediately after the bill has been dishonoured by a non-acceptance. (3) When a bill payable after sight is first dishonoured, by non-acceptance and then accepted by the drawee, the holder, in the absence of any dissent, is entitled to treat the bill as accepted as of the date of first presentment to the drawee for acceptance.

Acceptance can be divided into general acceptance and qualified acceptance.

1. General acceptance

A general acceptance is an acceptance by which the acceptor assents without qualification to the order given by the drawer. This is a most usual acceptance.

2. Qualified acceptance

A qualified acceptance is an acceptance by which the acceptor varies in express words the specified terms on the bill. There are five kinds of the qualified acceptance.

(1) Conditional acceptance

A conditional acceptance is one by which the payment to be made by the acceptor will depend on the fulfillment of some condition as stated. For example,

ACCEPTED

1　June, 2001

Payable on delivery of

Bills of Lading

For A Bank Ltd, London

Signature

(2) Partial acceptance

Partial acceptance is one by which the acceptor will pay only part of the amount for which the bill is drawn. For example, the whole amount stated thereon is USD1000.00

ACCEPTED

3　June, 2001

Payable on amount of

USD800.00 only

For A Bank Ltd, London

signature

(3) Local acceptance

It is an acceptance by which the acceptor will effect payment only at a particular specified place. For example,

ACCEPTED

5　June, 2001

Payable at The Hambros

Bank and there only

For A Bank Ltd, London

signature

If it is

ACCEPTED

5　June, 2001

Payable at The Hambros Bank

For A Bank Ltd, London

Signature

Then it is not a qualified acceptance but a general acceptance.

(4) Qualified acceptance as to time

It is another kind of a qualified acceptance. If a bill drawn payable three months after date is "Accepted payable at six months after date", it is a time qualified acceptance.

ACCEPTED

5　June, 2001

Payable at 6 months after date

For A Bank Ltd, London

signature

3.4.5　Payment

Act of payment is performed when a bill of exchange is paid. The so-called payment in due course signifies the payment made in good faith on or after the maturity date of the bill to the holder thereof without realizing that his title thereto is effective.

Payment may be made in the national currency of the drawee's country or in the currency stated on the draft, depending upon the foreign exchange regulations, enforced in the drawee's country.

It is important to observe that payment in due course should be the payment made to the holder. If the drawee of the acceptor does pay some person other than the holder, it does not constitute payment in due course, and so he will be compelled to pay again to the true owner. But if he does pay the holder, whether the latter is the true owner or not, he will no longer be liable to any other party, for he has obtained the paid draft as a receipt.

Discharge of a bill

1. A bill is discharged by payment in due course only when such payment is made by or on behalf of the drawee or the acceptor.

2. When a bill is paid by the drawer or an endorser it is not discharged, for he may claim payment from the drawee or the acceptor.

3. When an accommodation bill is paid in due course by the party accommodated the bill is discharged.

3.4.6　Dishonour and notice of dishonour

Act of dishonour is a failure or refusal to make acceptance on or payment of a bill of exchange when presented. When a bill duly presented for acceptance is not accepted within the customary time, the presenting person must treat it as dishonoured by non-acceptance. When a bill is duly presented for payment and the drawee refuses to pay, the holder must treat it as dishonoured by non-payment. When a bill is dishonoured by non-acceptance, an immediate right of recourse against the drawer and the endorsers accrues to the holder, and presentment for payment is not needed. If the drawee or the acceptor only assents to the payment of part to the stated amount on the bill, the holder can take or refuse it at his disposal.

A notice of dishonour is a notice on which default of acceptance or of payment by the drawee or the acceptor is advised, to be given by holder of a bill of exchange to the drawer and all the endorsers whom he seeks to hold liable for payment. According to the British Bills of Exchange Act, if the notice of dishonour is not given, the holder shall be discharged of the right of recourse against the drawer and all the endorsers.

For a holder in due course, however, his recourse claim shall not be prejudiced by such an omission. According to the Geneva's Uniform Law, the right of omission of the holder shall remain unless the drawer or the endorsers do suffer loss due to his omission of giving the notice, in which case the holder must compensate for the loss.

A notice of dishonour must be given by or on behalf of the holder or an endorser on the next business day after the dishonour of the draft.

If the holder gives the notice of dishonour to his prior endorser only, the latter shall do so in quick succession till it is given to the drawer. The notice may be given in writing or by personal communication. The return of a dishonoured draft to the party liable thereon may be deemed to be an appropriate notice of dishonour.

Suppose A is the drawer, B the payee, C, D, E, F and G the endorsers, H the holder and X the acceptor. When X dishonours the draft presented to him by H, H should send a notice of dishonour to each endorser and the drawer separately in order to retain their liability. But if he merely advises G, then G gives a notice to F, F to E, E to D, D to C, C to B and B to the drawer A, the result is the same. In practice the latter method is generally adopted since it is fairly certain that each prior party will pass on the notice. Any party failing to do so shall remain liable to the holder and lose his own right of recourse against all his prior endorsers and the drawer. If the holder H gives the notice direct to the payer B, this implies that B remains liable not only to H but also to H's prior endorsers C, D, E, F and G. This does not mean, however, H need not give the notice to his prior endorsers if he wishes to retain their liability to himself. If a bank fails to advise the dishonour of a draft in time, it may imply that the holder (the bank's customer) being ignorant of the act of dishonour, fails to pass on the notice and so is discharged of the right of recourse against his prior parties. If he suffers any loss financially therefrom, the bank will have to recoup him.

3. 4. 7　Protest

Protest is a written statement under seal drawn up find signed, by a Notary Public or other authorized person for the purpose of giving evidence that a bill of exchange has been presented by him for acceptance or for payment but dishonoured.

After a bill is dishonoured, by non-acceptance or by non-payment, and a notice of a dishonour is sent, the holder may hand the bill to a Notary Public who will present it again for acceptance or for payment as the case may be, so as to obtain a legal proof of the act of dishonour. As it is dishonoured again, the Notary Public then draws up a protest, i. e. , an official certificate evidencing the act of dishonour and stating the reason for the protest, demands made on the drawee(or the acceptor)and the response received. A copy of the bill has to be attached to the certificate on which is also clearly stamped the same amount as that on the bill. Only foreign bills should be protested or noted for non-payment or for non-acceptance, whereas domestic bills need not be according to the British Bills of Exchange Act. If it is not protested the drawer and endorsers are then discharged of their liability thereon. It may be protested on the very day. The protest fee is to be borne by the drawer and will be charged to him at the time that compensation for the amount of the bill is claimed. If the drawer is not willing to bear the protest fee, he must write on the bill such words as"protest waived" or "please do not protest if dishonoured". In that case, if the holder still wants the Notary Public to draw up a protest, he himself will pay the protest fee.

3.4.8　Right of recourse

The term "recourse" is used to signify the right of a holder of a bid of exchange to compel his prior endorsers to perform their legal obligations by effecting the payment, thereof if dishonoured by the drawee or by the acceptor. In other words, in the event of a bill being dishonoured, the holder has a right of recourse against the other parties thereto, that is, a right to claim compensation from the drawer or any endorser.

The recourse claim, not excluding an action at law against the parties liable should be enforced within the legal limit of time, which are six years according to the British Bills of Exchange Act or three years according to the Geneva's Uniform Law.

It is often a practice in most countries that the drawer, or any endorser of a draft can write thereon the words "without recourse" which will discharge the drawer and the endorser of their liability in the event of the instrument being dishonoured.

3.4.9　Acceptance for honour supra protest

Acceptance for honour supra protest is an act performed by the acceptor for honour, who accepts the bill supra protest, for the honour of any party liable thereon or for the honour of person for whose account the bill drawn. A bill may be accepted for honour only a part of the sum drawn payable.

A valid acceptance for honour supra protest is one signed by the acceptor for honour, indicating clearly on the bill that it is an acceptance for honour. If the acceptance for honour does not expressly state for whose honour it is made, it is deemed to be an acceptance for the honour of the drawer. If the bill so accepted is payable after sight, its maturity is calculated from the date of the protest, not from the date of acceptance for honour. The acceptor for honour engages that he shall pay the bill on its presentment on due date provided it is not paid by the drawee and is duly protested for its non-payment. The acceptor for honour is liable to the holder and all other parties subsequent to the one for whose honour he has accepted the bill.

3.4.10　Payment for honour supra protest

Payment for honour supra protest is an act similar to acceptance for honour supra protest in the sense that it vindicates the honour of a party liable on a bill of exchange. When a bill has been protested for non-payment, any person who is not a party liable thereon may intervene and pay it supra protest for the honour of a party liable thereon or for the honour of the person for whose account the bill is drawn. When a bill has been paid for honour, all parties subsequent to the one for whose honour it is paid are discharged of their liability thereon. If the holder refuses to receive payment supra protest, he shall lose his right of recourse against the party for whose honour the payment is to be made. Any person can act as a payer for honour without the consent of the holder. As soon as the payer for honour pays the bill, he becomes the holder and has the right to reimburse from the party for whose honour he pays the bill as well as from all prior parities thereon.

3.4.11 Guarantee

Act of guarantee is performed by a third party called guarantor, who engages that the bill will be paid on presentation if it is a sight bill or accepted on presentation and paid at maturity if it is a time bill. That is to say, the guarantor stands surely for a debtor such as the drawer, endorser or acceptor and assumes his indebtedness to the holder. If the bill is dishonoured by non-acceptance or by non-payment the guarantor shall pay it, hold it and have the right of recourse against the acceptor or the drawer.

Box 3.1

Cancellation, Modification and Forgery of Bills

Bills cancellation

Bills cancellation refers to the behavior of people to erase the signature or other recorded items on the bills in certain way. Bills cancellation usually is done by people who have the appropriate permissions. The cancellation is limited to the removal of the recorded content on the bills. The adding of the recorded content doesn't belong to it.

There are two types of cancellation: statutory cancellation and arbitrary.

1. The statutory cancellation

The statutory cancellation refers to the cancellation where Negotiable Instruments Law clearly stipulates the legal effect. Under normal circumstances, the statutory cancellation does not affect the effectiveness of the bills. But depends on the specific content of cancellation, cancellation may have different effects.

There are three types of statutory cancellation.

(1) Cancellation of endorsement. Cancellation of endorsement is the behavior to eliminate the recorded endorsement of the bills. Cancellation is usually done by the endorsee himself, but also by the other rights owners.

Possible cancellation of endorsement:

- The holder erased the draft of endorsement record before handing down to the receiver.
- The endorsee erased the endorsement when he gained the bills after receiving recourse notes.

- The applicant bought back the discounted bills from the bank, and eliminated own previous endorsement for discount.

Obliteration of wrong endorsement:

Endorsee obtain the notes by flipping the next holders' endorsement, other than a second endorsement. The Negotiable Instruments Law regulates the cancellation of endorsement as no records, that the endorsement is invalid. But the cancellation does not affect the effectiveness of the notes and other records on the bills.

(2) Cancellation of the acceptance. The cancellation is to wipe clean all the recorded bill acceptance behavior. It can only be cancelled by the drawer or acceptor who accept the acceptance notice or record the textual. The cancellation shall be after acceptance is recorded while the bills haven't been handed over.

If the bill has been delivered, the acceptor can no longer cancel its acceptance.

The cancellation of the bills' acceptance, can remove completely the acceptance records thus suggesting that the payer withdraw the acceptance, but it does not affect the effectiveness of other records.

(3) The cancellation of the scribe on the check. It is to eliminate the scribe on the check. Negotiable Instruments Law does not recognize the cancellation of the scribe, even though the check is cancellation, still be deemed not cancelled. In other words, the special scribed check won't change to general scribed check due to cancellation. The general scribed check won't change into ordinary due to the cancellation. The effect of cancellation of transfer check is the same.

2. Arbitrary cancellation refers to the cancellation whose legal effect wasn't clearly defined in the Negotiable Instruments Law, which shall be determined in accordance with other relevant provisions.

(1) The cancellation with the bills' effect maintained. If the erased items are not necessary records, it does not affect the effectiveness of the bills itself. The holder can claim the rights with the context of bills after cancellation. If the necessary recorded matters were erased, as long as the holder can prove that such cancellation is not deliberate and can prove the actual content, then he can require the bills' rights.

(2) The cancellation with bill invalid. If cancellation was don deliberately. The erased part of the rights on the bill expired. If the cancelled part is necessary recorded matters, all the notes right expired.

Bills modification

The modification refers to the authorized person changes or revises the recorded contents of the bills. Modification includes not only the cancellation of the original recorded content, but also to add new content. As there are strict format requirement for the bills, the Negotiable Instruments Law also have strict requirements on bills modification. Depending on the effectiveness of the bills after modification, it can be divided into two types:

(A) Modification with loss of the bills effectiveness.

The Negotiable Instruments Law in general does not allow modification in the substantial content, which leads to invalid bills. China's Negotiable Instruments Law regulates: The amount, date, payee name cannot be changed, and the modified bills are invalid.

(B) Modification with bills effectiveness unchanged.

Modification can be made to less important content. China's Negotiable Instruments Law states, the recorded items, other than the amount, date, payee, can be changed by the original recorder. However, modification can be done with the original recorder's seal. In this case, not only the bills are still valid, but modified content is valid.

Forgery

Forgery is the behavior to issue bills under the guise of others' name. The counterfeiter can forge the bills by imitating the handwritten signature of others, making other's seal, and stealing other's seal and so on. The forged one is normally a real person.

If only the signature is forged, the bills are with full form. It then is valid in the form. According to the independent rule of bills, the forged signature doesn't affect the effectiveness of the bill. The real signer can't waive the bills responsibility because of forged signature.

If the person being forged doesn't have gross fault in the forgery, the holder can't claim any rights towards the person being forged, and can only claim damage towards the counterfeit. If the person being forged has gross negligence, and the holder obtained it with good will, then the holder can claim bills' rights.

The bills holder is responsible of proving the bills signature is genuine, either proving it is indeed signed by himself, or the seal is his true seal.

Since the forgery of signature wasn't the intention of the holder, he bears no responsibility for the bills. However, he has to prove the seal was stolen. If he has gross negligence, then there occurs the exception.

The counterfeiter shall hold responsible for the forgery and bear responsibility for the damages of victims. He also bears criminal responsibility. China's Negotiable Instruments Law stipulates that the counterfeit of bills or intentional use of counterfeited bills is a fraud. The behavior shall be prosecuted for civil liability and criminal liability.

3.5 Application of a Bill of Exchange in Financing

3.5.1 Discounting of a bill of exchange

Discounting of bill is to sell a time bill already accepted by the drawee but not yet fallen due, to a financial institution at a price less than its face value. The difference between the amount paid and the face value represents the implied interest up to the maturity date, to be received by the discount institution. Suppose an exporter draws a bill payable at three months after sight on an importer abroad. At the time that the accepted bill is returned, he finds that there are still two months and twenty-four days to go before it becomes due. If he needs the money right now, he will discount the bill.

The process of discounting a bill of exchange is as follows: (1) issue a bill, present it for acceptance (2) accept it (3) discount it (4) pay the amount (i. e. less than the face value) (5) present it for payment at maturity (6) pay the face value.

For example, suppose an accepted bill for US $10,000 falls due on Sep. 18th, 2012 the exporter takes it to a discount bank on Jun, 30th. 2012. This should be calculated in actual days, that is, thirty-one days in both July and August and eighteen days in September, altogether eighty days. If the discount rate is 10%, the discount interest is calculated as follows:

$$D = (V \times t \times d) / 360$$

Where: $D = discount\ interest$
$V = face\ value\ of\ the\ bill$
$t = tenor\ (days)$
$d = discount\ rate\ (\%p.a.)$

Hence

$$D = (10,000 \times 80 \times 10\%) /360 = US\$ 222.22$$
$$Net\ proceeds = US\$ 10,000 - US\$ 222.22 = US\$ 9,777.78$$

The exporter is to be paid US $9,777.78 by the discount bank, which may retain the bill till maturity, then present it to the acceptor for payment and receive the full amount (face value). The discount bank obtains a profit of US $222.22. According to the European and American computation the basic days for a year are 360 days but according to the British computation actual are to be calculated, i. e. 365 days for a year and 366 days for a leap year.

3.5.2   Accommodating of a bill of exchange

Because the credit standing of a small size firm is not strong enough, he will find that a draft drawn on and accepted by himself will be difficult to be discounted in the discounting market. Then, accommodating provides him an alternative by which he can "borrow" the credit standing of a first class bank to get financed.

1. Definition

Accommodating is another way to get financed by making use of a bill of exchange. The bill drawn in such a way is called an accommodating bill. In simple words, an accommodating bill is drawn by a firm on a financial institution payable to himself. That is to say, when a firm or a trader wants to raise funds this way, he will make himself the drawer and the payee of a time bill and invite a financial institution to be the drawee and later the acceptor of the bill. Thus the firm obtains a banker's accepted bill which will be easily discounted in the discount market and get financed. The word "invite" indicates the special feature of an accommodating bill because it is drawn on a financial institution when the drawer (the firm) gives no value to him. In other words, the accommodating bill is established for the purpose of raising funds, not drawn on the basis of trade. In accommodating, the financial institution simply lends its creditworthiness for a fee to the firm and he is the accommodating party and the firm is the party accommodated. Accommodation is a finance to a company (the party accommodated) by a financial institution's (the accommodating party) consent to be the drawee of the accommodating bill drawn by the company.

The financial institution (the accommodating party) which specializes in accepting a time bill drawn on himself for the pure purpose of financing is called an accepting house. In London there are 17 accepting houses and they are members of the London Accepting Committee. The difference between a discount house and an accepting house is that the former acts as an endorsee and the latter acts as a drawee, though the purpose of both is to provide finance to traders. Another difference to be noted is that only the discount house will get involved in discounting whereas in accommodating, both the accepting house and the discount house will be included for the trader to receive funds.

2. Procedure

① The trader draws a time bill on an accepting house payable to himself and presents the bill to the drawee for acceptance.

② The accepting house accepts the bill and returns it to the payee.

③ Before maturity, the payee discounts (sells) the bill to the discount house.

④ The discount house discounts (buys) the bill and makes the payment to the

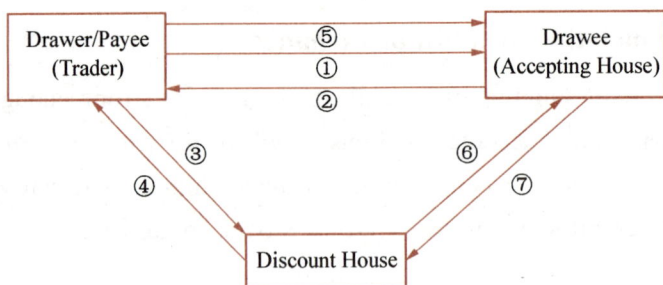

payee at an amount less than the face value of the bill.

⑤ The trader provides funds to the accepting house just before maturity so that the drawee can honor the bill at maturity.

⑥ At maturity, the discount house, as the new holder of the bill, presents the bill to the accepting house for payment.

⑦ The drawee makes payment to the discount house at the face value.

3.6 Classification of Bill of Exchange

1. According to the tenor:

(1) Sight bill: It is a bill payable on demand or at sight or on presentation.

(2) Time bill or usance bill: It is a bill payable at a fixed or determinable future time.

2. According to the drawer:

(1) Banker's draft or bank draft: It is a draft drawn by a bank on another bank.

(2) Trade bill: It is a bill issued by a trader on another trader or on a bank.

3. According to the acceptor:

(1) Banker's acceptance bill: It is a time bill drawn on a bank and accepted by this bank. This kind of bill is more preferable and negotiable than the trader's acceptance bill and is more acceptable in the discount market.

(2) Trader's acceptance bill: It is a time bill drawn on a trader and accepted by him.

4. According to the currency denominated:

(1) Local currency bill: It is a bill on which the amount is denominated in local currency.

(2) Foreign currency bill: It is a bill on which the amount is denominated in foreign currency.

5. According to the place of issue and place of payment:

(1) Inland bill or domestic bill: It is a bill drawn and payable in the same country.

For instance, if both drawer and drawee are residents in U. K. , it is apparently an inland bill.

(2) Foreign bill: It is a bill drawn in one country and payable in another country. If a London exporter draws a bill on his Paris importer payable in Paris, it is a foreign bill. If a London exporter draws a bill on his Paris importer payable in London, it is an inland bill. Having been dishonoured by nonacceptance or by nonpayment, a foreign bill is usually to be protested, whereas in the case of an inland bill protesting is optional except in certain circumstances.

6. According to whether or not the shipping documents are attached:

(1) Clean bill: It is a bill without shipping documents attached thereto.

(2) Documentary bill: It is a bill with shipping documents attached thereto.

Key Words

Bills of Exchange, Endorsement, Acceptance, Payment, Dishonour, Protest Acceptance for Honour Supra Protest, Recourse, Discounting of a Bill of Exchange, Clean Bill

Questions

1. What is a bill of exchange?
2. What are the requirements of a bill of exchange?
3. Describe the types of bills of exchange

CHAPTER 4 PROMISSORY NOTE & CHEQUES

Learning Objectives

- To understand the definitions and requirements of a promissory note
- To compare the difference between a bill of exchange and a promissory note
- To learn the major forms of promissory notes
- To understand the definitions and requirements of a cheque
- To learn the types and risks of cheques
- To compare the difference between a bill of exchange and a cheque

4.1   Promissory Note

4.1.1   Definitions and requirements of a promissory note

As defined in the Bills of Exchange Act 1882 of the United Kingdom, a promissory note is an unconditional promise in writing made by one person(the maker) to another(the payee or the holder) signed by the maker engaging to pay on demand or at a fixed or determinable future time a sum certain in money to or to the order of a specified person or bearer.

In conformity with the Uniform Law on Bills of Exchange and Promissory Notes 1930 of Geneva, a promissory note must fulfill the following requirements: ① The word "Promissory Note" ② An unconditional promise to pay ③ Payee or his order ④Maker's signature ⑤ Date and place of issue ⑥ Period of payment ⑦ A certain amount of money⑧Place of payment (Figure 4.1).

Figure 4.1

```
        ①                    ⑦                  ⑤
   Promissory Note for GBP 800.00                     London, 8th Sept., 2000
                           ⑥                        ②
                    At 60 days after date we promise to pay
                           ③
                    Beijing Arts and Crafts Corp. or order      the sum of
   ⑦
   Eight hundred pounds

                                                      ⑧
                                              For Bank of Europe,
                                                   London
                                                 signature ④
```

4.1.2   Difference between a bill of exchange and a promissory note

The nature of a promissory note has much in common with that of a bill of exchange. However, there is some difference between these two instruments, which lies in:

1. A promissory note is a promise to pay, whereas a bill of exchange is an order to pay;

2. There are only two parties to a promissory note, namely the maker and the payee (or the holder in the case of a bearer note), whereas there are three parties to a bill of exchange, namely the drawer, the drawee and the payee;

3. The maker is primarily liable on a promissory note, whereas the drawer is primarily liable, if it is a sight bill and the acceptor becomes primarily liable, if it is a time bill;

4. When issued, promissory note has an original note only, whereas a bill of exchange may be either a set bill or a bill in set, i. e. a bill drawn with second of exchange and third of exchange in addition to the original one.

4. 1. 3　Major forms of promissory notes

1. Trader's Note

Trader's note is a promissory note whose maker is a firm or trader. By issuing a trader's note, the firm can raise funds from the public. However, because of its low credit worthiness, trader's note is acceptable only when it is guaranteed by the firm's or trader's bank. For this reason, a trader's bill is generally replaced by a letter of guarantee.

2. Banker's Note

The promissory note has found its wide application in banks. A banker's note made by a bank payable to a specified person can be deemed as cash. But the bearer promissory notes payable on demand issued by banks are equivalent to bank notes of large denomination, an uncontrolled issue of banker's sight bearer order notes by commercial banks will certainly disturb a country's monetary system. Therefore, commercial banks can only issue notes payable to a specified person. Banker's sight bearer order notes are put under special statutory basis and can be issued by the central bank or the authorized banks only.

3. International Money Order

International money order is usually denominated in US dollars with the maximum amount not exceeding USD2,500. It is issued by clearing banks in New York for the payee's convenience when he is traveling outside the U. S. It can also be used to settle payments in international trade when the amount is small. International Money Order is favorable to the maker because the clearing bank can take hold of the capital from the time of the purchase of the note by the payee to the time that the note is exchanged in for collection.

4. Traveler's Cheque

A traveler's cheque can be either considered as a promissory note or a cheque. It is a promissory note because it is drawn by the issuing bank upon itself payable to a traveler. However, a customer who wishes to obtain a traveler's cheque should first make payment equivalent to the face value to the issuer of the cheque. Then as a payee, the customer can cash the cheque or make use of the cheque to pay for the commodities he bought and services he enjoyed in a foreign country. To the customer, to purchase a traveler's cheque is similar to deposit money into the issuing bank while to cash it is like to withdraw the money from the issuing bank or his agents. So it can also be called a cheque. Similar to the international money order, the major advantages for the traveler's cheque are that it is easy to carry and safe to use because they are replaceable. It has gained a large popularity.

The denominations of a traveler's cheque can be $10, $20, $50, $100, $500 and $1,000. To prevent fraud, the customer is required to sign his/her name on the cheque in the presence of the issuer or his selling agent at the time of purchase. The customer will also be required to countersign the cheque in the presence of the cashier at the time when the cheque is cashed or used to pay for the commodities he bought or the services he enjoyed. The amount he receives will be less than the face value because a small commission will be deducted which will be earned by the banks. An additional benefit to the issuing bank is that he can hold the capital from the time the cheque is purchased by the customer to the time the cheque is exchanged in by the cashier to claim compensation.

5. Treasury Bill

It is also referred to the government bond with the maker to be the Ministry of Finance. In Britain, it is a short-dated government security. Treasury bills bear no formal interest, but are promises to pay in 91 days time. It is issued at a discount on their redemption price. The amount of purchase is to be calculated as follows:

The amount of purchase = net proceeds
$$= principal - (principal \times tenor \times redemption\ rate)/365$$

For example, suppose a Great Britain treasury bill at GBP100,000 payable 91 days after date with the redemption rate at 7.5%, the purchase amount would be:

$$The\ purchase\ amount = 100,000 - (100,000 \times 91 \times 7.5\%)/365$$
$$= GBP\ 98,130.14$$

4.2   Cheque

4.2.1   Definitions and requirements of a cheque

According to the Bills of Exchange Act 1882 of the United Kingdom, a cheque is an unconditional order in writing addressed by the customer (the drawer) to a bank (the drawee) signed by that customer authorizing the bank to pay on demand a specified sum of money to or to the order of a named person or to bearer (the payee).

A cheque is mostly payable on demand.

Follow the rules of "the Uniform Law on Bills of Exchange and Promissory Notes" of Geneva, a cheque must fulfill the following requirements: (1)The word "Cheque". (2)An unconditional order to pay. (3) The name and address of the paying bank. (4)Drawer's name and signature. (5)Date and place of issue. (6)the word "at sight". (7)A certain amount of money. (8)Name of payee or his order (see Figure 4.2).

Figure 4.2

31st Jan., 2000	① ⑤
Payee	Cheque London, 31st Jan., 2000 NO. 652156
Tianjin Economic	③
& Development	BANK OF EUROPE
Corp	LONDON
	② ⑥ ⑧
	Pay to Tianjin Economic & Development Corp.
	or order the sum of Four hundred / ⑦ £450.0
£450.0	and fifty pounds
	For Sino—British Trading Co., London ④
	signature
652156	
	652156 60…2116 02211125 000045000

4.2.2 Types of cheques

Crossed Cheques

Crossed cheques are cheques bearing two parallel lines on the face. A crossing on a cheque is in effect an instruction by the drawer or holder to the drawee bank to pay the fund to a bank only, so a crossed cheque will not be paid over the counter of the drawee bank, but must be presented for payment through a collecting bank. The drawee's bank will also act as the collecting bank if both the drawer and the payee maintain current accounts with the drawee's bank. Cheques bearing no crossing are called uncrossed cheques or open cheques.

General crossing   A general crossing is to mark two parallel transverse lines across the face of a cheque. No name of the collecting bank is indicated on the cheque which means the cheque can be collected through any bank. The forms of a general crossing cheque are as follows:

a.

Since there is no name of the bank is indicated here, any bank can be the collecting bank.

b.   **Not Negotiable**

When the term "not negotiable" is added to a crossed cheque, it has the effect that, if transferred, the transferee gets no better title than the transferor.

c.   **A/C Payee**

"A/C Payee" is an instruction to the collecting bank to collect only for the payee's account.

d.   **Not Negotiable**
      A/C Payee

This kind of crossing means it is not negotiable and must be paid through the payee's account.

Special crossing A special crossing usually contains the name of a bank and means that it can only be collected by through the named bank. In practice, only one name of a bank is allowed, but the named bank can collect the fund through another bank by making another special crossing. However, a cheque only can bear no more than two special crossings. The forms of special crossing are as follows:

a.   Mildand Bank Ltd.

The effct of such a crossing is that the cheque can only be collected through the Midland Bank Ltd.

b.   Midland Bank Ltd.
        A/C Payee

Such a special crossing means that the cheque can only be collected through the Midland Bank Ltd. and the money must be paid directly to the payee's account.

c.   Midland Bank Ltd.
        Not Negotiable

This apecial crossing means that the cheque can only be collected through the Midland Bank Ltd. and it is not negotiable.

d.   Midland Bank Ltd.
        Not Negotiable
        A/C Payee

The effect of such a crossing is that the cheque can only be collected through the Midland Bank Ltd. , it is not negotiable and it must be paid to the payee's account.

The chief aim in crossing a cheque is to make more certain for the right holder to obtain its payment, and more difficult for a wrongful holder to negotiate it or obtain the sum stated in the cheque. The holder of a crossed cheque cannot encash it at the drawee bank and must either deposit it in the drawee bank crediting his account or have the drawee bank pay the sum to another bank crediting his account through the local clearing.

If a cheque is crossed specially, only the bank mentioned in the cheque, can receive payment from the drawee bank.

As for crossing a cheque, there are following points for attention:

(1) A cheque is crossed generally, the holder may add some words specially crossed cheque.

(2) Where a cheque is uncrossed, the holder may cross it generally or specially.

(3) Where a cheque is crossed generally, the holder may add some words therein to make it a specially crossed cheque.

(4) Where a cheque is crossed generally or specially, the holder may add the words "not negotiable" therein.

(5) Where a cheque is specially crossed to bank, this bank may again cross it specially to another bank for collection.

(6) Where an uncrossed cheque or a cheque crossed generally is handed to a bank for collection, the bank may cross it specially to make himself the payee.

4.2.3   Countermand of payment and wrongful dishonour of a cheque

Countermand of payment denotes the cancellation by the customer (the drawer) of his mandate to the bank represented by the cheque, but in order to be effective the countermand must actually come to bank's notice. Mere constructive countermand, is not enough. If a bank pays a "stopped" cheque it commits a breach of its customer's cancellation mandate and can incur a dual liability. (1) For paying the "stopped" cheque (2) For wrongfully dishonouring other cheques. The drawer is the only person who can instruct his bank to stop payment on particular cheque. Sometimes the holder of a cheque may inform the bank that the cheque has been stolen, in which case, the bank should seek the instructions of the drawer.

If a bank wrongfully dishonours a cheque, the customer (the drawer) can sue it for damages. The damages are not measured against the nominal amount of the cheque but against the injury to the drawer's credit worthiness so as to get reasonably compensated.

Cite a case. A cheque for £20 drawn by a bookmaker to pay his supplier is wrongfully dishonoured by the bank with the words "not sufficient" (because the bank has exhausted the balance in the book maker's current account by paying a stopped cheque), it is held that the words are libellous and so the bookmaker obtains £250 damages.

4.2.4　Difference between bill of exchange and cheque

The differences between a bill of exchange and a cheque are as follows:

1. A bill of exchange may be drawn upon any person, whereas a cheque must be drawn upon a banker.

2. Unless a bill is payable on demand, it is usually accepted, whereupon the acceptor is the primarily liable party. A cheque need not be accepted and the drawer is the party primarily liable.

3. A bill must be presented for payment when due, or else the drawer will be discharged. A cheque must be presented for payment within a reasonable time or within a certain time, such as 20 to 70 days according to the regulations of the country concerned. The drawer of a cheque is not discharged even though it has not been presented for payment within the stipulated time unless the delay in presentation incurs losses to the drawer.

Key Words

Clean Bill, Promissory Note, Cheque, Countermand of Payment, Crossed Cheque

Questions

1. What are the differences between a bill of exchange and a promissory note?
2. What are the differences between a bill of exchange and a cheque?

CHAPTER 5   COLLECTION

Learning Objectives

- To understand definitions of collection
- To learn and compare the parties to a collection
- To learn collection procedure and the types of collection
- To understand the risks of collection methods to the exporter and financing under a collection

5.1 Definitions of Collection

After the exporter has shipped the goods or rendered services to his customers abroad, he draws a bill of exchange on the latter with or without shipping documents attached thereto and then gives the draft to his bank together with his appropriate collection instructions. Thus, a collection is usually processed through banks acting as the intermediary. There are outward collection and inward collection. Outward collection is a banking business in which a bank acting as the remitting bank sends the draft with or without shipping documents attached, relevant to an export, to an appropriate overseas bank, namely, the collecting bank to get the payment or acceptance from the importer. Inward collection is a banking business in which a bank acting as the collecting bank receives the draft with or without shipping documents attached as well as the instructions from a bank abroad, namely, the remitting bank, on whose behalf the collecting bank endeavors to collect the payment or obtain the acceptance from the importers and to which the collecting bank remits the proceeds.

Collections serve as a compromise between open account and advance payment in settlement of international transactions concluded by the importer and the exporter. This service facilitates a creditor in one country to obtain settlement from a debtor in another at a minimum cost.

5.2 Parties to a Collection

1. Drawer or principal

It is the exporter or the seller who entrusts the collection items to his bank.

2. Remitting bank

It is the bank to which the drawer entrusts the collection items. Having received the collection items from the exporter, the bank forwards them to the collecting bank, in accordance with the collection instructions given by the principal.

3. Collecting bank

It is the bank entrusted by the remitting bank to present the collection items to the drawee. The collecting bank is generally a correspondent or an agent of the remitting bank.

4. Drawee

It is the buyer or the importer to whom the collection items are to be presented for acceptance or payment.

5. Presenting bank

The presenting bank is usually the collecting bank which presents the collection items to the drawee and then credits the remitting bank's account with the proceeds. If the drawee's residence or place of business is not in the same city as that of the collecting bank, the draft and the shipping documents may be sent to the collecting bank's branch or directly to the drawee's bank there if known, in order to be presented for acceptance or for payment. In that case, the collecting bank is not the presenting bank, it is another bank actually presenting the shipping documents and the draft to the drawee for acceptance or for payment.

6. Representative in case of need

It is the representative appointed by the principal to act as case of need in the event of non-acceptance and/or non-payment, whose power should be clearly and fully stated in the collection order.

Box 5.1

URC 522

URC 522 (ICC Uniform Rules for Collections ICC Publication No. 522) forms an internationally accepted code of practice covering documentary collections. URC are not incorporated in national or inter-national law, but become binding on all parties because all bank authorities (especially the collection order) will state that the collection is subject to URC. URC will apply unless the collection order states otherwise or the laws in one of the countries concerned specifically contradict them.

There are 7 parts, 26 articles in URC 522. It includes General Provisions and Definitions, Form and Structure of Collections, Form of Presentation, Liabilities and Responsibilities, Payment, Interest, Charges and Expenses and other Provisions.

According to URC 522, "Collection" means the handling by banks of documents as defined in sub-Article 2 (b), in accordance received, in order to: I. obtain payment and/or acceptance, or II. deliver documents against payment and/or against acceptance, or III. deliver documents on other terms and conditions.

"Documents" means financial documents and/or commercial documents: I. "Financial documents" means bills of exchange, promissory notes, cheques, or other similar instruments used for obtaining the payment of money. II. "Commercial documents" means invoice, transport documents, documents of title or other similar documents, or any other documents whatsoever, not being financial documents.

Source: ICC Uniform Rules for Collections ICC Publication No. 522

5.3 Types of Collections

1. Clean collection

Clean collections are collections on financial instruments without being accompanied by commercial documents, such as invoice, bill of lading, insurance policy, etc.

A bill of exchange drawn by the exporter on the importer will be handed to a bank for collection, when the shipping documents are sent by the exporter to the importer directly.

The payee or holder of a cheque drawn by someone abroad may request his bank to send the cheque abroad for collection. Traveler's cheques are usually sent by the bank buying them to their issuing bank abroad for collection.

Promissory notes may also be sent by the bank for collection so as to get its payment from the overseas maker.

2. Documentary collection

Documentary collections may be described as collections on financial instruments being accompanied by commercial documents or collections on commercial documents without being accompanied by financial instruments, that is commercial documents, alone without a bill of exchange. A documentary collection can be defined as the collection of a sum due from a buyer, by a bank against delivery of certain documents.

Basic forms of documentary collections are:

(1) Documents against acceptance (D/A)

The presenting bank may release the documents against the buyer's acceptance of a draft, for instance, drawn payable 60 - 180 days after sight or due on a definite date. After acceptance, the buyer gains possession of the goods before the payment is made and is able to dispose of the goods as he wishes. The seller, however bears the risk of buyer's non-payment.

If the seller intends to have the shipping documents released against acceptance, he must be sure that the buyer will be in a position to pay the long bill at maturity because he will lose control of the goods and rely on the credit worthiness and integrity of his overseas customer to pay on due date.

(2) Documents against payment (D/ P)

Practice has shown that some buyers prefer to delay the take over of the documents and effect the payment until the goods arrive, unless a respective clause "payment should be effected on first presentation" should be included in the collection order.

(3) Collection with acceptance, release of documents only against payment (Acceptance D/ P).

Bills of exchange under documents against payment are usually sight bills. But sometimes, the drafts under D/P may be payable on a certain date in the future. This means that the drawee must accept the bill upon presentation. The accepted bill is kept at the collecting bank together with the documents which will be released to the drawee as soon as he makes payment. If the drawee refuses to accept the bill, the exporter will have time to take appropriate measures or possibly to look for another customer for the goods.

5.4 Collection Procedure

A collection procedure usually involves seven steps:

1. The principal presents the collections to the remitting bank.

As soon as the goods are shipped, the exporter (the principal) prepares the documents with or without a draft drawn on the overseas importer and presents then, to his bank (the remitting bank) for collection,together with his complete and precise instructions.

2. The remitting bank forwards the collections to the collecting bank, what step should the remitting bank take when receiving a customer's documents prior to sending them abroad for payment? The remitting bank has a moral, though not legal, responsibility to examine the documents so as to ensure that there will be no problem with respect to receiving payment from the overseas buyer.

Document are to be examined in respect of the following points:

● Endorsements made on the bill of lading, on the insurance policy or certificate as well as on the bill of exchange are correct.
● The bill of lading is in complete set.
● The bill of exchange is properly drawn.
● The documents are consistent with one another.
● The documentary requirements set lay the customs authorities of the importing country are fully met. Failing to meet them, the goods will not be cleared in through the customs in that country or the importer may get the goods subject to a higher rate of import duty.

Having examined the documents, the remitting bank will forward them together with a collection order to a collecting bank by choice if the exporter has not been asked by the importer to have the collections, presented through the latter's bank.

The collection order must contain the following information or instructions:

- Name and address of the collecting bank.
- Release of the documents to the drawee against payment or against acceptance. Without such instructions, documents will be released against payment.
- Tenor of the draft: at sight or after sight. If it is after sight, how many days or how many months after sight must be stated.
- Presenting the collections to the importer immediately for payment or for acceptance by the collecting bank unless otherwise instructed. This ought to be done as the importers in many countries are in the habit of deferring payment or acceptance of bills until the arrival of the goods.
- Bank charges for account of the drawer or the drawee. Waiving such cost or not if it is refused by the drawee.
- Protesting the bill or not if it is dishonoured by non-acceptance or by non-payment.
- Full name and address of the case of need and his precise power to be exercised so as to assist the settlement in case of default of payment.
- Action to be taken by the collecting bank to protect the goods after its arrival (such as warehousing it, insuring it against fire on behalf of the exporter, etc.) in case of dishonour by non-acceptance or by non-payment.
- The way of remitting the proceeds after the payment.
- Amount of the draft, name of the principal as well as name and address of the drawee.
- Signature of the remitting bank.
- Number of copies of each commercial document.
- Partial release of the goods against partial payment to be allowed or not.
- Overdue interest to be collected at such-and-such rate from the drawee.
- Discount at such-and-such rate on payment effected before the due date of the draft in question to be given or not.

3. The collecting bank presents the collections to the importer.

Upon receipt of the collection order, the collecting bank will verify, if the documents received are the same as listed in the collection order and then notify the drawee to take away the documents either against: payment or against acceptance in accordance with the instructions of the remitting bank.

4. The importer accepts or pays the collections to the collecting bank.

Having checked the documents, the drawer pays or accepts the draft. Partial payment in respect of clean collections can be accepted if it is permitted by the law in force in the place of payment. As far as documentary collections are concerned, partial payment will only be accepted if it is allowed in the collection order. However, release of the documents can only be done at the time of making full payment, unless otherwise specified in the collection order.

5. The collecting bank advises the remitting bank of the acceptance or payment.

6. The remitting bank receives the advice of acceptance or payment and notifies the principal.

7. The principal receives payment or the advice of acceptance.

5.5 Risks of Collection Method to the Exporter

There are a number of risks which may be, incurred to the exporter. In order to avoid or minimize these risks, first, the exporter should always make sure that the overseas importer is of good reputation and of good financial standing. Otherwise, an importer without satisfactory credit-worthiness may reject the goods on some pretext after its arrival, in the hope of driving the seller into a price reduction. Failing to take delivery of the goods promptly upon its arrival at the final destination will result in substantial storage and insurance costs, as well as damages especially to those perishable goods, to be borne by the exporter. Secondly, the exporter should take into account the economic and political conditions in the importing country. For instance, if the market price of the imported goods falls, the importer may also find a pretext to refuse to make payment. Thirdly, the exporter should also pay attention to the foreign exchange regulations in the importing country so that the outward payment made by the importer will present no problem.

Furthermore if the payment is to be effected in a currency other than that of the exporter's country, the exporter will have to bear the risk of conversion of a foreign currency into his national currency. And also, the exporter will generally not get paid until payment on collection is really received by his bank, so that the turnover of his working fund will be more or less affected. This is another risk.

5.6 Financing under a Collection

1. Negotiation as a means of financing

If a bank negotiates an outward collection, it is buying its customers' bill drawn on an overseas buyer at the time that the collections are to be sent abroad. The bank buying the bill will look to the overseas buyer as a source of payment. By negotiation the bank becomes a holder for value because of its lien on the bill or it may become a holder in due course. In both cases the negotiating bank will take a hypothecation certificate as a pledge from its customers. In the event of non-payment or delayed payment, the negotiating bank will exercise the right of recourse against its customer, the drawer.

2. Advance against collections

An advance against collections can be described as being equivalent to a partial collection and a partial negotiation. The remitting bank may lend to its principal a proportion of the amount of each bill presented, leaving the balance to be financed with the latter's own resources.

3. Accommodating bills for discount

(1) For the exporter

The exporter should draw a time draft on a bank or an accepting house for the agreed proportion of the face value of the documentary collections with maturity slightly later than the expected time of receipt of proceeds from the overseas buyer.

After the draft is accepted by the drawee's bank or by the accepting house, it is discounted and the proceeds so obtained are to finance the exporter. The proceeds of the documentary collections received before the due date of the time draft are sufficient to provide the bank or the accepting house with funds in time to meet its own acceptance.

(2) For the importer

The importer can draw a draft on a bank or an accepting house at the required usance when he receives documentary collections abroad. After acceptance the bill is discounted and the proceeds are remitted through the collecting bank to the overseas exporter. In this case, a written pledge will be required of the importer and the shipping documents will be released to the importer against a trust receipt upon the arrival of the goods. The importer will pay the proceeds to the bank or accepting house before the maturity of the draft.

4. Trust receipt (i. e. T/R)

When the collecting bank intends to release the documents of title or the goods to the importer while still retaining its security interest in the goods and/or the proceeds of sale, the bank may obtain a completed trust receipt from the importer. This is an acknowledgement of the pledge of the goods to the bank and an undertaking of the importer to deal with the goods as a trustee for the bank. That is, the importer holds the goods or it proceeds, as the case may be, on behalf of and in trust for the bank, whereas the bank holds legal title to the goods.

The obligations of the trustee are:

- To arrange for the goods to be warehoused and insured in the bank's name.
- To pay all the proceeds of sale to the bank or to hold them on behalf of the bank.
- Not to put the goods in pledge to other persons.

- To return the goods or the proceeds to the bank at anytime when request.
- To settled claim of the bank before liquidation in the case of the trustee's bankruptcy.

It should be noted that this may involve some risk to the bank, as the protection afforded by the trust receipt against a dishonest customer is slight, owing to the fact that the letter of trust does not prevent the passing of title to a purchaser who buys the goods from the importer for value and without notice of trust.

Key Words

Collections, Clean Collections, Documentary Collections, Trust Receipt

Questions

1. Write out the full names of the following abbreviations:

D/P   D/A   T/R

2. Compare the advantages and disadvantages among the different types of remittance.

3. What are the risks of documentary collections?

CHAPTER 6   LETTERS OF CREDIT

Learning Objectives

- To learn the basic elements and characteristics of letters of credit
- To compare the benefits and costs of letters of credit
- To understand the basic procedures of a freely negotiable documentary letters of credit
- To learn different types of common and special letters of credit

6.1 Introduction to the Letters of Credit

Letters of credit are a payment mechanism, particularly used in international trade. The Seller gets paid, not after the Buyer has inspected the goods and approved them, but when the Seller presents certain documents (typically a bill of lading evidencing shipment of the goods, an insurance policy for the goods, commercial invoice, etc.) to his bank. The bank does not verify that the documents presented are true, but only whether they "on their face" appear to be consistent with each other and comply with the terms of the credit. After examination the bank will pay the seller (or in L/C terms the beneficiary of the letter of credit).

6.1.1   The concept of letters of credit

In its simplest form a letter of credit is a letter written by a bank to another party, the beneficiary, informing that beneficiary that the bank will pay a sum certain in money to the beneficiary if the beneficiary of the letter provides the bank with certain described pieces of paper within a proscribed time frame. From the 1920s banks have created, modified, and regularly amended the rules they use to handle letters of credit. These rules are called the Uniform Customs and Practice for Documentary Credits, and the revision dated 2007 is the seventh in the line of updates. It is accepted by most banks in the world as the standard for handling letters of credit. Shorthand for these rules is UCP 600.

Said in another way, a letter of credit is a letter from a bank promising to pay on certain specific conditions. Note that the letter of credit is a conditional promise and it is not a guarantee. Another more structured definition offered by the International Chamber of Commerce Commission on Banking Technique and Practice is "The Documentary Credit or letter of credit is an undertaking issued by a bank for the account of the buyer or for its own account, to pay the Beneficiary the value of the Draft and/or documents provided that the terms and conditions of the Documentary Credit are complied with".

The value in a letter of credit to the beneficiary (the exporter, seller, supplier) is that the payment commitment is made by a third party, and the third party is a bank. Most banks, in most countries, are responsible and reliable organizations, generally believed to adhere to ethical business practices and to exercise prudence in their commercial dealings. The bank is not involved in the commercial transaction.

This is the principal reason that an exporter will ask for a letter of credit. The exporter believes that it has an unimpeachable source of payment, if the exporter provides the correct documents to the right place on time. There can be other reasons why an exporter might demand a letter of credit from a buyer. These include the following, among others:

1. The exporter has no funds to manufacture or acquire the goods to be exported, and the letter of credit serves as collateral acceptable to the exporters bank in support of loans to acquire goods, manufacture, etc.

2. The exporter cannot borrow unless it can demonstrate that there are sufficient sales to pay back the loan.

3. The exporter has an export sales policy that requires all sales be made on a letter of credit or cash in advance.

4. The value of the letter of credit to the buyer is significantly more limited. The ability to obtain a letter of credit expands the buyers' purchasing power; a buyer that cannot obtain a letter of credit is generally not creditworthy and cannot buy. There may be other benefits.

6.1.2   Parties to the letter of credit

Every letter of credit covering an export or import transaction involves at least three different parties. They are the applicant, the beneficiary, and the issuing bank.

1. Applicant

Applicant is the buyer of the goods or services supplied by the seller. Letters of credit is opened by the issuing bank as per applicant's request. However, applicant does not belong one of the parties to a letter of credit transaction. This is because of the fact that letters of credit are separate transactions from the sale or other contract on which they may be based. Many sellers assume that the buyer has placed cash with the issuing bank in order to purchase or collateralize the letters of credit. This is usually not the case.

2. Beneficiary

Beneficiary is the seller of the goods or the provider of the services in a standard commercial letter of credit transaction. Letters of credit is opened by the issuing bank in favor of the beneficiary.

3. Issuing Bank

Issuing Bank is the bank that issues a letter of credit at the request of an applicant or its own behalf. This bank is also called the "opening bank" or the "buyers' bank". The issuing bank is obligated to the beneficiary. Issuing bank undertakes to honor [1] a

---

[1] Honor means: a. to pay at sight if the credit is available by sight payment. b. to incur a deferred payment undertaking and pay at maturity if the credit is available by deferred payment. c. to accept a bill of exchange ("draft") drawn by the beneficiary and pay at maturity if the credit is available by acceptance.

complying presentation of the beneficiary without recourse.

4. Advising Bank

The advising bank is a bank in the seller's country that receives the letter of credit from the issuing bank, determines it is authentic, and informs the seller that the letter of credit is available (it advises). The advising bank is selected by the issuing bank. Exporters should note that unless the letter of credit specifies otherwise, the beneficiary is not required to present documents to or through the advising bank.

5. Confirming Bank

Confirming bank is the bank that adds its confirmation to a credit upon the issuing bank's authorization or request. Confirming bank may or may not add its confirmation to a letter of credit. This decision is up to confirming bank only. However, once it adds its confirmation to the credit confirming is irrevocably bound to honor or negotiate as of the time it adds its confirmation to the credit. Even if the issuing bank fails to honor, confirming bank must pay to the beneficiary.

6. Nominated Bank

The nominated bank is selected by the issuing bank. It is the bank to which the beneficiary is directed to present documents for payment, acceptance, or a deferred payment undertaking.

7. Negotiating Bank

The negotiating bank is any bank that is authorized by the issuing bank to give value to the beneficiary for documents presented in compliance with the terms and conditions of the letter of credit. The nominated bank is also the negotiating bank.

8. Reimbursing Bank

Reimbursing Bank shall mean the bank instructed and/or authorized to provide reimbursement pursuant to a reimbursement authorization issued by the issuing bank. For example, a Japanese bank issues a letter of credit in USD (the abbreviation for U.S. Dollars used throughout the book) to a beneficiary in Ohio. When payment is made, the reimbursing bank pays the negotiating bank with USD drawn from the Japanese banks USD account. Most U. S. reimbursing banks are in New York, Chicago, or Los Angeles. They charge a fee for this reimbursement function.

6.1.3　Letters of credit characteristics

1. Negotiability[1]

Letters of credit are usually negotiable. The issuing bank is obligated to pay not

---

[1] Negotiation means the purchase by the nominated bank of drafts (drawn on a bank other than the nominated bank) and/or documents under a complying presentation, by advancing or agreeing to advance funds to the beneficiary on or before the banking day on which reimbursement is due to (to be paid the nominated bank).

only the beneficiary, but also any bank nominated by the beneficiary. Negotiable instruments are passed freely from one party to another almost in the same way as money. To be negotiable, the letter of credit must include an unconditional promise to pay, on demand or at a definite time. The nominated bank becomes a holder in due course. As a holder in due course, the holder takes the letter of credit for value, in good faith, without notice of any claims against it. A holder in due course is treated favorably. The transaction is considered a straight negotiation if the issuing bank's payment obligation extends only to the beneficiary of the credit. If a letter of credit is a straight negotiation it is referenced on its face by "we engage with you" or "available with ourselves". Under these conditions the promise does not pass to a purchaser of the draft as a holder in due course.

2. Irrevocability

Letters of credit must be irrevocable under the Uniform Customs Practice for Documentary Credits (UCP 600).

A revocable letter of credit may be revoked or modified for any reason, at any time by the issuing bank without notification. A revocable letter of credit cannot be confirmed. If a correspondent bank is engaged in a transaction that involves a revocable letter of credit, it serves as the advising bank. Once the documents have been presented and meet the terms and conditions in the letter of credit, and the draft is honored, the letter of credit cannot be revoked. The revocable letter of credit is not a commonly used instrument. It is generally used to provide guidelines for shipment. If a letter of credit is revocable it would be referenced on its face.

The irrevocable letter of credit may not be revoked or amended without the agreement of the issuing bank, the confirming bank, and the beneficiary. An irrevocable letter of credit from the issuing bank insures the beneficiary that if the required documents are presented and the terms and conditions are complied with, payment will be made. If a letter of credit is irrevocable it is referenced on its face.

3. Independence

A credit by its nature is a separate transaction from the sale or other contract on which it may be based. Banks are in no way concerned with or bound by such contract, even if any reference whatsoever to it is included in the credit. Consequently, the undertaking of a bank to honour, to negotiate or to fulfil any other obligation under the credit is not subject to claims or defences by the applicant resulting from its relationships with the issuing bank or the beneficiary. A beneficiary can in no case avail itself of the contractual relationships existing between banks or between the applicant and the issuing bank.

6.1.4 Payments under letters of credit

There are three terms for the manner in which a payment is made on a letter of credit (bankers usually say 'under'). There is also one variation on these three terms.

1. Payment by payment means that the bank authorized to pay will pay the beneficiary within a specified time frame, usually with 7 – 15 banking days after presentation of the documents that comply with the terms and conditions of the Credit. A letter of credit may or may not require a draft. If a draft is required, a draft is a "document". A letter of credit will state that it is "available by payment on presentation of … in accordance with …" or words to that effect.

2. Payment by acceptance means that the letter of credit calls for a draft with a payment term at other than sight. This is called a time draft, and the Credit is called a usance credit. The tenor (term or mode) of the draft is usually within 180 days, and stated something like "90 days sight" or "120 days bill of lading date" or any other term that is not simply "sight".

3. Payment by deferred payment means that the letter of credit does not call for a draft and payment is at some time other than sight. The beneficiary of a deferred payment credit presents documents to the nominated bank. If the bank determines that the documents comply with the terms and conditions of the credit, the bank gives the exporter a "deferred payment undertaking", a promise to pay at a fixed date in the future.

4. Payment by negotiation. The nominated bank reviews the documents presented by the beneficiary and determines if they comply with the terms and conditions of the Credit. If the documents comply with the terms and conditions of the Credit, the negotiating bank pays the exporter with or without recourse and claims reimbursement from the issuing bank through the reimbursing bank. Payment can be by payment of the documents (with or without draft), by acceptance of a time draft, or by a deferred payment undertaking.

6.2 Cost and Benefits

6.2.1 Benefits for the exporter

Properly executed, a sale on a letter of credit provides an exporter with a reasonable assurance of payment and minimal risk of non-payment. The benefits that a letter of credit transaction afford an exporter, in the absence of other issues presented elsewhere in this book, are the following:

1. Assurance of payment by a third party. This is the paramount benefit to the exporter. The seller has replaced the uncertainty of the buyer with the relative certainty of a third party bank. Under the international rules for handling letters of credit, the Uniform Customs and Practice for Documentary Credits, ICC Publication 500 (known as the UCP 600), the obligation of a bank for its letter of credit is absolutely independent of the relationship between the buyer and the beneficiary, i.e. Article 3.a. of the UCP 600 states "... banks are in no way concerned with or bound by such contact(s) [sales or other], even if any reference whatsoever to such contract(s) is included in the Credit". Note that the UCP refers to a letter of credit as "Credit". The terms Credit and letter of credit will be used interchangeably throughout this material.

The Uniform Commercial Code is the law that governs letters of credit in the United States. There is a significant body of case law that reinforces the concept that the issuing banks' payment obligation is separate from the commercial transaction. To paraphrase one Arkansas court case "The most fundamental principle of modern letter of credit law is that the credit is separate and distinct from the underlying contractual transaction between the issuer's customer and the beneficiary. Thus .... the merits of customer's underlying contractual dispute with ... the beneficiary would not be considered".

2. Certainty as to the performance requirements in order to obtain payment. The seller receives a letter that states the specific documents that must be presented to the bank in order to be paid, and the time frame in which the documents must be presented. The letter of credit provides the seller with all the information necessary to obtain payment.

3. Some certainty as to the timing of receipt of the payment for the sale. Unlike Open Account, Documentary Collection, and Consignment, a letter of credit offers some certainty as to when payment should be received by the exporter.

4. Some protection from political or economic risk in the buyer's country. Banks that engage in international trade finance and letters of credit transactions are very protective of their good name and reputation. Most of these banks, regardless of home country, will make every reasonable effort to pay a beneficiary even if their home country is experiencing financial difficulty. This is a fairly strong form of protection from home country political or economic risk. However, it is not perfect or assured.

5. Perfect or assured comes with a confirmed letter of credit, and the confirmation by a bank that is not related to or owned by or affiliated with the issuing bank or the country of the issuing bank. As noted earlier, the payment obligation of the issuing bank is taken on by the confirming bank.

6. 2. 2   Costs to the exporter

While a letter of credit provides the exporter with a basic level of comfort and assurance of payment, there are some important costs, in financial and operating terms, that should be understood. These costs are:

1. The out of pocket costs of each letter of credit transaction. Exporters pay a number of fees to hire banks for every letter of credit handled. Exporters across the United States report they pay bank fees of between USD 200 and USD 400 per letters of credit. These fees include:

(1) An advising fee, to tell the exporter about the Credit. If the exporter chooses to use more than one advising bank, the exporter will pay an advising fee to each advising bank. It is not necessary to use more than one advising bank.

(2) An amendment fee, if the Credit is amended for any reason.

(3) A negotiation or document review fee, for review of the documents by the bank, and for payment. Some banks charge "transit interest" when crediting an exporters account with the proceeds of a negotiation. Transit interest is payable to the bank for a set number of days at a pre-determined rate, to compensate the bank for being out-of-funds from the date the exporters account was credited and the date the banks account was credited by the reimbursing bank in settlement of the claim for reimbursement. Banks report transit interest is charged for 12 days at the prime rate as the minimum. An exporter may elect to have documents reviewed by its own bank, even if it is not the nominated or negotiating bank, in order to have a "friendly" review of the documents. This will result in additional document review fees.

(4) Discrepancy fee, which is a fee the bank charges for identifying errors in the documents submitted by the exporter. Practice varies some banks charge one fee for all discrepancies, other banks charge a fee for each discrepancy found.

(5) A fee to credit the exporters account with the payment.

(6) If there is a time draft, there could be acceptance commissions and discount fees, in addition to the fees in above.

(7) A confirmation commission or fee. This will vary by the credit quality of the issuing bank and its country. A low fee could be $100, while bankers report that in some cases confirmation fees have been as high as 8% of the amount of the letter of credit. This spectacular fee included the cost of foreign credit insurance used by the confirming bank to support its confirmation commitment.

(8) The reimbursing bank's fee, if so stated in the Credit.

2. The administrative burden of preparing documents that conform to the terms and conditions of the letter of credit. All documents required by the letter of credit

must be consistent with each other, and comply with the Credit. Failure to present documents that comply with the credit can result in non-payment.

6.2.3   Benefits for the importer

There is one principal benefit of a letter of credit for an importer, one secondary benefit, and other reasons why a letter of credit may be required for the import transaction. These are:

1. Principal benefit. The ability to obtain a letter of credit demonstrates the buyer's capacity to obtain credit; in other words, it shows the buyer's credit-worthiness. The importer would rather purchase on some other term of payment.

2. Secondary benefit. A letter of credit assures the buyer that it will receive specific documents that conform to the stipulations of the buyer, as represented by the letter of credit. Unless controlling documents are required, such as inspection certificates, a letter of credit does not assure the buyer that the goods covered by the letter of credit have been shipped. UCP 600 Articles 15 - 18 hold banks harmless if fraudulent documents are presented and the issuing (and confirming bank if any) negotiates the documents as if they were valid. Compliant documents do not in themselves guarantee that the goods exist or are in good condition.

3. Extended payment terms. If the buyer is located in a country with high inflation, or banking and financial markets that lack liquidity, and the buyer can negotiate a usance letter of credit with both its bank and with the seller, the extended payment terms of this type of letter of credit give the buyer purchasing power that would otherwise be unavailable in the local financial markets. With the time draft, the buyer will have an extended period of time before payment to the issuing bank is due. This time period may be interest free or at an interest rate lower than that charged in the local market. Another variation: in the mid 1990s some South Korean banks issued letters of credit with very long time draft payment terms, and included a provision that acceptance commissions and discount charges would be for the buyers account, turning this into a sight draft transaction for the exporter.

4. Many countries require imports on letter of credit terms in order to control monetary outflows, capital flight, fraud, and external demands on foreign exchange reserves. Similar to an import license requirement, a requirement that all imports be done with letters of credit places the control of hard currency outflows in the hands of banks which can (usually) be readily monitored and controlled (Russia is one of a number of startling exceptions).

6.2.4   Costs to the importer

A letter of credit places some fairly significant cost burdens on the importer. If the importer is in the United States, these costs can be readily determined with a few judicious telephone calls. Outside the United States the fee structures will vary by country and by bank. Some regions of the world charge very high fees. A few exporters tell of buyers stating they "had to pay letter of credit fees of about 20% of the letter of credit amount." This could happen. It's hard to verify. The costs that an importer has to deal with on its letter of credit purchase include the following:

1. The issuing fee, for the issuing bank to issue the letter of credit.

2. An amendment fee, if an amendment is required.

3. A payment fee, for the issuing bank making the payment to the advising bank.

4. A document review or negotiation fee, charged by the issuing bank for its review of the documents presented under the Credit (separate from that paid by the exporter).

5. A possible charge for clearing discrepancies with the importer.

6. A reimbursing bank fee (passed on from the reimbursing bank).

In addition, unless the Credit stipulates otherwise, all bank charges are for account of the applicant.

6.3 Letters of Credit Procedure

6.3.1 The sales contract

The sales contract is the formal agreement between the buyer and seller specifying the terms of sale that both parties have agreed upon. The contract should include: a description of the goods; the amount; the unit price; the terms of delivery; the time allowed for shipment and presentation of documents; the currency; and the method of payment.

6.3.2 Application & agreement

The bank's letter of credit application and agreement forms, when executed, constitute a payment and reimbursement contract between the issuing bank and its customer. It is also the customer's instruction to the issuing bank. The letter of credit must be issued exactly in accordance with the customer's instructions; therefore, it is important that the application be completed fully and accurately, so as to avoid the inconvenience of having to have the letter of credit amended. The agreement constitutes an undertaking by the customer to reimburse the issuing bank for drawings paid in accordance with the terms of the letter of credit, and normally takes the form of an authorization to debit the customer's account.

6.3.3 Issuance of the letter of credit

The issuing bank prepares the letter of credit as specified in the application and forwards it by teletransmission or airmail to the advising bank (a branch or correspondent of the issuing bank). The issuing bank instructs the advising bank as to whether or not to add its confirmation, as per their customer's instructions.

6.3.4 Advising

The advising bank forwards the letter of credit to the beneficiary (seller) stating that no commitment is conveyed on its part. However, if the advising bank has been asked to confirm the letter of credit and agrees to do so, it will incorporate a clause undertaking to honour the beneficiary's drafts, provided the documents evidence that all terms and conditions of the letter of credit have been complied with.

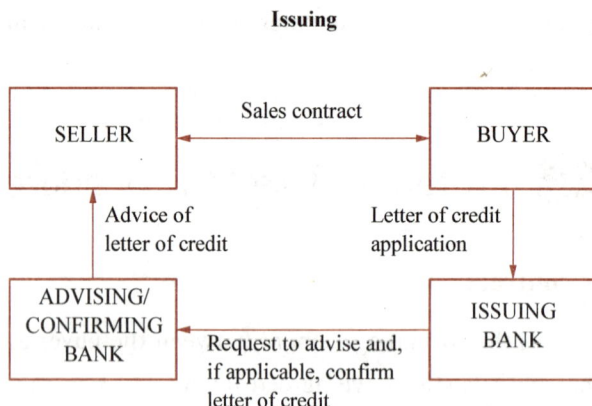

Issuing

| SELLER | Sales contract | BUYER |

Advice of letter of credit | Letter of credit application

ADVISING/ CONFIRMING BANK | Request to advise and, if applicable, confirm letter of credit | ISSUING BANK

6.3.5 Shipment of goods

Upon receiving the letter of credit, the beneficiary should examine it carefully and be satisfied that all the terms and conditions can be complied with. If this is not possible, the beneficiary should request the applicant to arrange an amendment to the letter of credit. Once completely satisfied, the beneficiary will then be in a position to assemble and ship the goods.

6.3.6 Presentation of documents by beneficiary

The beneficiary prepares an invoice in the number of copies required, with the description of goods shown exactly as stipulated in the letter of credit. The beneficiary obtains the bill of lading and/or other transport documents from the carrier and prepares and/or obtains all other documents required by the letter of credit. These are attached to the draft, drawn on the bank indicated and at the term stipulated in the letter of credit, and are presented to the advising/confirming/negotiating bank.

6.3.7   Sending documents to the issuing bank

The advising/confirming/negotiating bank checks the documents presented by the seller against the letter of credit. If the documents meet the requirements of the letter of credit, that bank will send them to the issuing bank, claiming reimbursement and paying the seller.

6.3.8   Delivering documents to the applicant

The issuing bank will also check the documents for compliance and then deliver them to the applicant either against payment or as an undertaking to pay on maturity of the drawing under the letter of credit.

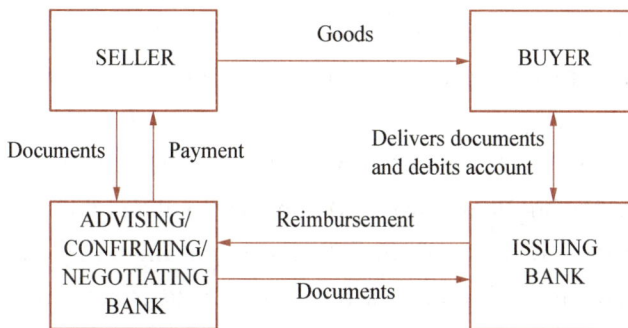

6.3.9   Payment

On presentation of the documents called for under the letter of credit, provided they are in compliance with its terms, the advising/negotiating bank, in the case of an unconfirmed letter of credit, may pay/negotiate the draft. In the case of a confirmed letter of credit, the confirming bank is obliged to honour the drawing without recourse to the beneficiary.

6.3.10   Reimbursement

The advising/confirming/negotiating bank will claim reimbursement from the issuing bank.

6.3.11   Settlement

On receipt of conforming documents, the issuing bank will also be responsible for checking documents and will charge the applicant's account under the terms of the letter of credit application and agreement forms, effecting reimbursement to the negotiating bank.

6.4 Types of Letters of Credit

6.4.1 Revocable and irrevocable

The two principal types of letters of credit are irrevocable and revocable. As mentioned in previous chapters, the type that is usual and customary to international trade is an irrevocable letter of credit. Even though Article 6 of the UCP 600 states that "in the absence of such indication (that a credit should clearly state it is revocable) the Credit shall be deemed to be irrevocable" exporters should always carefully review the advice and the letter of credit instrument itself to assure that the letter of credit is irrevocable. Because this is a "belt and suspenders" issue, exporters should never hesitate to ask the advising bank if there is any uncertainty about whether the credit is irrevocable.

Article 9 of UCP 600 states "An irrevocable Credit constitutes a definite undertaking of the Issuing Bank, provided that the stipulated documents are presented to the Nominated Bank or to the Issuing Bank and that the terms are conditions of the Credit are complied with ...", while a revocable Credit is not a definite undertaking of the issuing bank.

A revocable Credit can be canceled or amended by the issuing bank at any time and without prior notice to the beneficiary. Exporters must interpret this to mean that payment on the transaction covered by this type of credit is absolutely uncertain and outside its control. I strongly recommend that exporters never agree to ship against a revocable letter of credit. Now that I've said this and you've read it. If the exporter/seller operates in an industry where a revocable credit is the norm or accepted payment practice, industry practice may prevail. In that instance, use caution, and be sure that control of the asset(s) being sold remain with the seller until such time as payment is received.

Most of the letters of credit we will review have been issued in SWIFT format. SWIFT is the Society for Worldwide Interbank Financial Telecommunications. It is a bank owned and operated closed communications system, providing secure interbank communications for the conduct of payment related transactions. The letter of credit transactions are conducted in a SWIFT 700 message format. Exporters and importers familiar with electronic data interchange will appreciate the application of standards based inter-corporate messaging.

6. 4. 2 Confirmed and unconfirmed credits

An unconfirmed letter of credit has the binding obligation of the issuing bank to pay the beneficiary of the credit if all the terms and conditions of the credit have been met.

1. A confirmed Credit is one upon which a second bank makes an independent and preceding undertaking to pay against documents presented in accordance with the terms and conditions of the Credit. Again, the confirmer's obligation precedes the payment obligation of the issuing bank, if all terms and conditions of the Credit have been complied with. A confirmation is an exception. Some of the reasons an exporter might want a confirmation include:

a. Payment is quicker, usually

b. Country risk is removed, usually

c. It may be easier to catch problems with documents if the negotiation and payment obligation is in the U.S., rather than after submission to the issuing bank.

With an unconfirmed sight letter of credit, payment of funds flows from the applicant (buyer) to the beneficiary (seller).

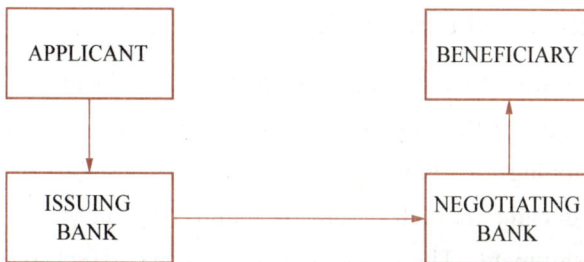

```
┌─────────────┐              ┌─────────────┐
│  APPLICANT  │              │ BENEFICIARY │
└─────────────┘              └─────────────┘
       │                            ▲
       ▼                            │
┌─────────────┐              ┌─────────────┐
│  ISSUING    │─────────────▶│ NEGOTIATING │
│  BANK       │              │ BANK        │
└─────────────┘              └─────────────┘
```

With a confirmed sight letter of credit, the payment of funds also flows from the applicant (buyer) to the beneficiary (seller). However, the payment made by the negotiating/confirming bank is made without recourse to the beneficiary.

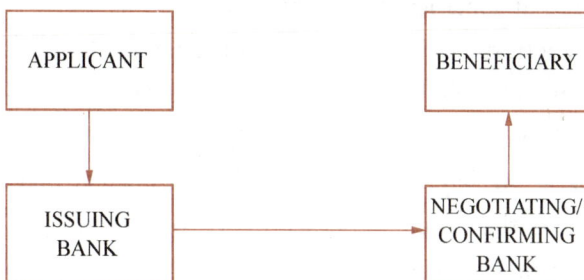

```
┌─────────────┐              ┌─────────────┐
│  APPLICANT  │              │ BENEFICIARY │
└─────────────┘              └─────────────┘
       │                            ▲
       ▼                            │
┌─────────────┐              ┌──────────────┐
│  ISSUING    │─────────────▶│ NEGOTIATING/ │
│  BANK       │              │ CONFIRMING   │
│             │              │ BANK         │
└─────────────┘              └──────────────┘
```

Exporters are encouraged to use caution when dealing with confirming banks that are owned by non-U.S. parents.

2. Branches. U.S. based branches of foreign banks have no capital requirements: their capital is that of the parent bank. Some states require that the parent bank operating a branch in the state (e. g. , NY) be in compliance with the risk-adjusted minimum capital requirements for international banks as agreed in the Basle Accords (an agreement among leading nations regarding minimum capital of commercial banks). Having noted this, the UCP states in Article 2 states that "For purposes of these Articles, branches of a bank in different countries are considered another bank", which means the exporter can look only to the assets and equity of the local bank for financial capability and responsibility.

3. Agencies. Agency office capital requirements vary by state. For example, in New York state, agencies of foreign banks have no minimum capital requirement, in California the minimum is $500,000, and agencies are not allowed in Illinois.

4. Subsidiaries. The minimum capital requirement for a foreign bank subsidiary incorporated in a state varies by state; in New York, the statutory minimum is $1,500,000, in California the legal minimum its $5,000,000, and in Illinois the minimum capital requirement is $5,000,000 - 6,000,000.

6.4.3　Documentary and clean credit

Letters of credit are either documentary or clean. A documentary letter of credit is used primarily to pay for the shipment of goods. Therefore, it is payable against the presentation of shipping or delivery documents. The seller must submit to the [nominated] bank documents such as bills of lading, invoices, and other documents which describe the shipment. The UCP applies with equal effect to both types of credit if the UCP 600 is included by reference in the body of the Credit.

1. A clean letter of credit calls for payment against presentation of a demand for payment, usually only a draft. The credit may call for a simple statement. There are many variations, the most widely known is called a standby letter of credit. Standby credits will be covered at some length in Chapter 8.

2. Documentary letters of credit. International trade transactions conducted on a letter of credit basis usually require a documentary letter of credit (documentary letters of credit are used for both domestic and international trade transactions with equal effect). This is because the buyer wants to receive documents that evidence shipment and transfer title, and the seller wants assurance of payment in exchange for the shipping and title documents. The documentary credit is a perfect instrument for this purpose.

Every documentary letter of credit (Credit) has four common elements. Each of these elements is important because they stipulate:

(1) When the Credit expires.

(2) Where the Credit expires.

(3) Where to present the draft (and documents).

(4) Who to draw the draft on (if a draft is required).

These elements are critical because a slight change in phrase or wording will have a significant impact on the exporters access to funds under the Credit (Credit and letter of credit are used interchangeably throughout this material). In the balance of this chapter we will look at a number of examples of documentary letters of credit, each slightly different.

6.4.4 Time letter of credit

1. Acceptance

On presentation of the documents called for under the letter of credit, provided they are in compliance with its terms, the beneficiary's bank, which may be the advising bank, will send the documents and the draft to the accepting bank for acceptance. The accepted draft may be held by the accepting bank until it matures or it may be returned to the beneficiary at the beneficiary's option, who may hold it until maturity or discount it at the best rate with any bank.

The chart below tracks the term draft and documents to the beneficiary's bank which, in turn, presents these items to the accepting bank for acceptance.

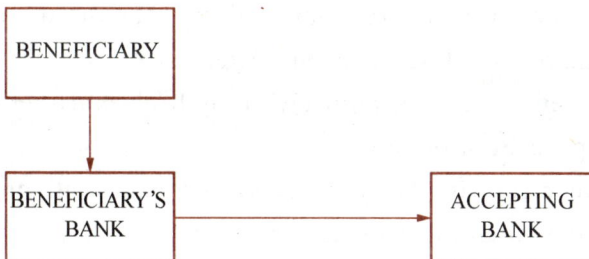

2. Payment

On maturity of the accepted draft, the accepting bank will pay the beneficiary or the discounting bank and claim reimbursement from the issuing bank who will charge the applicant's account and will remit the proceeds. The discounting bank would be any bank which had purchased the accepted draft at a discount.

The chart below tracks this procedure. The applicant (buyer) pays the issuing bank who in turn pays the beneficiary or discounting bank through the paying bank.

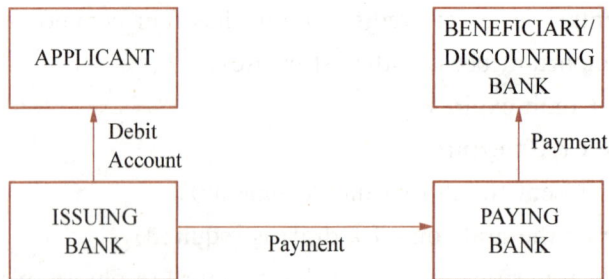

6.4.5　Straight, restricted, or freely negotiable documentary credit

(1) Straight letter of credit. A straight irrevocable documentary letter of credit is a credit advised directly to the beneficiary without use of an advising bank. This type of credit is relatively unattractive to exporters, so it is in very limited use today. However, it is used and will be experienced by exporters opening new markets or dealing with new and smaller or less sophisticated buyers.

The advantages of a straight Credit, often called a Direct Credit, are:

a. It is issued directly to the beneficiary.

b. It has not passed through an advising bank, so it is received by the beneficiary a few days quicker.

c. There are no advising fees.

d. There are no negotiation or document review fees.

The disadvantages of a straight credit are:

Its authenticity has not been verified. It may not be a valid letter of credit.

a. It expires in another country, which means that the documents have to be received at that bank on or before the expiry date.

b. Payment, when made, will probably be by bank draft, either on the issuing bank's U.S. correspondent or on itself.

c. If there are errors in the documents, the bank will probably return the documents noting the discrepancies. The exporter may have a difficult time resubmitting the documents prior to the expiry and last presentation date.

(2) Restricted letter of credit. Under a restricted credit, the issuing bank's engagement (called the engagement clause) may be extended to third parties who negotiate or purchase the beneficiary's draft (or documents) presented under the letter of credit. The important point is that the beneficiary is directed to present documents to a specific bank (the nominated bank). This bank may be the advising bank or issuing bank. A confirmed credit is a restricted credit.

A confirmed letter of credit is a restricted letter of credit, in that the beneficiary is required to present documents that comply with the terms and conditions of the credit to the confirming bank, wherever it maybe.

(3) Freely negotiable credits. A credit in which the beneficiary has some flexibility in where it may present documents for payment. This flexibility is conditioned by the wording in the letter of credit. In the letters of credit that have been reviewed thus far, the negotiation has been restricted to the advising bank, the confirming bank, or a nominated bank.

While you are encouraged to use your bank for an early review or review prior to presentation to the bank nominated to pay or negotiate, you do have to use that nominated bank.

There may be circumstances when you want the flexibility to use any bank, anywhere. How could this be? There are too many reasons to list. The point is that increased flexibility is better. It's a preferred situation for the exporter. The operative phrasing in a freely negotiable letter of credit is that this credit is available with any bank by negotiation.

Each of these letters of credit provides a different look at an important trade payment document. There are infinite variations in the conditions that may be stipulated in a letter of credit, so great care should be taken when reviewing each Credit. That is why the checklist is so important. Exporters must be certain they can comply with a letter of credit before they initiate the export.

Each of these letters of credit has some positive and some negative features. Letters of credit that are available with any bank by negotiation provide increased flexibility to the exporter. This stipulation is better than a credit that has payment or acceptance restricted to a specific bank in the exporters country or region. An exporter in Reno will not be pleased to have to deal with an unfamiliar bank in Chicago, New York, or Florida. Least attractive is the letter of credit which requires that documents be presented to the issuing bank for negotiation and payment / acceptance. This type of Credit increases the time delay between presentation and payment, and increases the uncertainty about payment because discrepancies can not be resolved in a timely manner.

Exporters will incur costs with each letter of credit received. These costs are associated with the advice, payment, negotiation or document review, amendment, and the inevitable discrepancies.

6.5　Special Types of Letter of Credit

6.5.1　Revolving letter of credit

A revolving letter of credit is a documentary letter of credit that by its nature eliminates the costly practice of requiring issuance of a separate letter of credit for each recurring 5 ~ 8 transaction between a buyer and seller.

When should you use a revolving Credit? Regular and repetitive transactions are amenable to a revolving letter of credit, one in which the amount of the Credit can be renewed or reinstated according to the terms and conditions of the original Credit, without the need for a specific amendment. This type of Credit may revolve: ① in relation to time, or ② in relation to value, or ③ in relation to quantity shipped.

(1) Time. A letter of credit that revolves in relation to time stipulates that the amount of the Credit is automatically available for each new period regardless of whether a drawing occurred in the prior period. This type of Credit can be cumulative or non-cumulative. In a cumulative revolving Credit, an amount not drawn in the current period is available in the subsequent period. In a non-cumulative Credit, an amount not drawn is no longer available. This type of Credit can be very attractive to exporters and importers trading under a continuing supply agreement or other arrangement calling for regular and repetitive shipments of similar or identical goods over an extended period of time, usually not to exceed one year. Here is an example of wording to provide for this revolving characteristic:

This letter of credit will automatically be reinstated to the original value of [amount] on the 25th day of each month for [number of monthly] periods.

(2) Value. A letter of credit that revolves in relation to value stipulates that the stated amount of the Credit is automatically reinstated on utilization, without relation to time: the Credit continually renews itself each time it is drawn. This can be a very unattractive Credit to an issuing bank, as its liability under the Credit can be infinite. Letters of credit that revolve in relation to value usually contain a clause (or clauses) that control the maximum amount available under the Credit. Here is an example of wording to provide for this revolving characteristic:

This letter of credit will automatically reinstate itself to its original value of [amount] five [5] working days after each drawing. This reinstatement will occur for a period of [period] of time in days, weeks, or months] months from the date of issuance of this letter of credit. In any event, drawings may not exceed [amount] in any one calendar month period.

(3) Quantity. A letter of credit that revolves in relation to value stipulates that the quantity of goods to be shipped under the Credit is automatically reinstated for each new period regardless of whether a shipment and drawing occurred in the prior

period. This type of Credit can be cumulative or non-cumulative. In a cumulative revolving credit, the quantity not shipped in the current period is available in the subsequent period. In a non-cumulative Credit, the quantity not shipped is no longer available. This type of Credit can be very attractive to exporters and importers trading under a continuing supply agreement or other arrangement calling for regular and repetitive shipments of similar or identical goods over an extended period of time, usually not to exceed one year. Here is an example of wording to provide for this revolving characteristic:

> This letter of credit will automatically be reinstated to the original quantity and value of [amount] on the 25th day of each month for [number of monthly] periods.

A revolving letter of credit can also be structured to provide for reinstatement subsequent to each shipment. The applicable wording would be similar to that immediately above.

6.5.2　Transferable letter of credit

A transferable letter of credit is one in which the value of the Credit is made available to another party by a transfer. This type of Credit is most often used by brokers, traders, trading companies, middlemen and agents, in order to provide a supplier with a letter of credit for the purchase of goods. The parties to a transferable letter of credit are:
(1) The buyer or applicant.
(2) The issuing bank.
(3) The advising or transfer bank (often but not necessarily the same).
(4) The first beneficiary (broker, trader, middleman, the seller).
(5) The second beneficiary or supplier.

A transferable letter of credit is another form of commercial documentary letter of credit, one of the infinite variety that exporters, importers, and their bankers can create to deal with particular circumstances. This Credit, if issued in this manner and so states, is subject to Article 48 of the UCP 600. Article 48 stipulates that a transferable Credit may be transferred only on the terms and conditions specified in the original Credit, with the exception that the following may be reduced or curtailed in the transfer to the second beneficiary (IEC) [the supplier]:
(1) The amount of the Credit.
(2) The unit price of the products / goods therein.
(3) The expiry date.

(4) The last day for presentation of documents.

(5) The date for shipment or period for shipment.

(6) In addition, marine insurance if required may be increased so that the coverage arranged by the second beneficiary will match the amount stipulated in the original Credit. Here's an example: If a letter of credit calls for insurance at 110% of the CIF value, and CIF is USD100,000, insurance must be USD110,000. The second beneficiary, recipient of a USD90,000 transfer, is then required to obtain marine insurance at 122.22% of its CIF invoice value. Even though not at 110% of CIF, the insurance will be acceptable due to Article 48.

Exporters and suppliers who are potential recipients of transfers of letters of credit need to be aware of some unique aspects of this variation on the letter of credit theme.

(1) A letter of credit is transferable if it says it is.

(2) A letter of credit can be transferred only once. Second beneficiaries cannot transfer on to a third beneficiary.

(3) The first beneficiary may elect that all amendments not be advised to the second beneficiary (IEC). This places the second beneficiaries at extreme risk.

(4) There can be multiple second beneficiaries if the Credit allows partial shipments.

On presentation by the second beneficiary of documents called for under the Credit, the transfer bank will contact the first beneficiary for substitution of documents. The documents that are specifically substitutable, according to Article 48, are:

(1) The commercial invoice.

(2) The draft.

Should the first beneficiary fail to provide its own commercial invoice and draft on first demand, the transfer bank may deliver to the issuing bank the documents received from the second beneficiary. This situation, performance by the first beneficiary, is of particular importance to suppliers that receive transfer credits for payment.

The obligation of the issuing bank to the second beneficiary, should the first beneficiary fail to present documents on first demand, is clear. The issuing bank must pay on the second beneficiary's presentation of compliant documents.

If however the first beneficiary timely presents documents that are found in error, the transferring bank is obligated to the second beneficiary to step in and assist in correcting the documents to assure payment. Larger and / or more sophisticated banks report that they do take on an added performance burden when acting as a transfer bank.

If the second beneficiary presents faulty documents, the transfer bank is under no obligation to correct them.

Exporters that utilize a local or less sophisticated bank to handle transfers of letters of credit should take care to assure that the documents they present strictly comply with the terms and conditions of the letter of credit.

A review of Article 48.1 suggests that the second beneficiary retains the right to present documents directly to the issuing bank in the event the first beneficiary fails to timely present conforming documents. The transfer bank, and the issuing bank, have a responsibility to the second beneficiary to pay against presentation of documents which comply with the terms and conditions of the credit: this responsibility is not clearly stated in the UCP. Bankers suggest that suppliers might have legal recourse to the transfer, confirming, or issuing bank under the Uniform Commercial Code (if the bank in question is subject to the UCC). In addition, bankers state that the second beneficiary should not be put at risk simply because the first beneficiary does not perform; the bank will present the second beneficiary's documents for payment under the Credit.

6.5.3 Red clause letter of credit

Under this letter of credit variation, the beneficiary is able to obtain advances or funds against (from within) the letter of credit in order to purchase or process merchandise or carry out other activities. The beneficiary does not have to borrow money to get money. The Credit, which contains a special clause that was historically set out in red ink, authorizes a bank to make advances or make funds available to the beneficiary prior to presentation of the shipping documents.

This type of Credit is used to provide a seller (a broker or middleman) with funds to obtain product or consolidate smaller purchases from multiple suppliers. One of its original uses was to provide Australian wool shippers with funds to purchase wool for shipment to British wool merchants.

The "red clause" enabled the Australian wool broker to obtain funds from a local bank to pay growers for wool. Repayment of the funds would be from negotiation of the documents under the letter of credit. In the event the beneficiary would fail to present documents under the letter of credit, the negotiating bank (the bank that funded the broker) will claim on the issuing bank, which in turn will recover from the applicant. A red clause reads somewhat as follows:

The negotiating bank is hereby authorized to make advances to the beneficiary up to lesser of the aggregate amount of / or the remaining unused balance of this credit, against the beneficiary's receipt stating that the advances are to be used to pay for the purchase and shipment of the merchandise for which this credit is opened and the beneficiary's undertaking to deliver to the negotiating bank the documents stipulated in the credit prior to the expiration date there of. The advances with interest are to be deducted from the proceeds of the drafts drawn under this credit. We (opening bank) hereby undertake the payment of such advances with interest should they not be repaid by the beneficiary prior to the expiration of this Credit.

There is one common variation to the red clause letter of credit. The advance (as in our example above) is repaid at the time the credit is drawn upon. This variation is called an "anticipatory drawing" and works as follows: at the time funds are disbursed to the beneficiary, the disbursing bank claims on the issuing bank and is reimbursed. The issuing bank is paid by the applicant to the Credit. In this way the disbursing bank remains whole.

6.5.4 Green clause letter of credit

A green clause letter of credit operates essentially the same as a red clause credit. Historically, the wording of the funding clause was printed in green ink. And the phrasing of the funding clause is different in that the beneficiary of the credit makes the drawing or draft for the advance coupled with warehouse receipts evidencing merchandise has been placed in a warehouse under third party control. The funding clause in a green clause letter of credit requires:

(1) Presentation of a draft.

(2) A statement as to the use of the funds as noted in the discussion of the red clause letter of credit.

(3) Negotiable warehouse receipts evidencing storage of goods and the valuation there of.

This type of letter of credit might be useful in a fishery, logging, or mining operation. The operator (fisherman, etc) tenders its catch to a processor or cold storage warehouse operator, and receives a receipt. The receipt is presented to the bank, along with a draft for an agreed percentage of the value of the receipt (s), and a statement as to the use of the funds. The funds are then used to operate the vessel in order to obtain more fish. When a full shipment is amassed, the receipts are converted to bills of lading, the credit is drawn down, the advances paid, and the balance paid to the beneficiary. The buyer has seafood (or logs, or minerals, what have you), and the supplier has its profit.

Both the red clause and the green clause are not in frequent use today. I find this interesting, particularly as it relates to resource oriented industries. Undercapitalized supplier scan by a green clause credit utilize the financial capacity of their customers. This lower cost or increased availability of funding can benefit both parties, in the near and the long term.

Buyers and account parties considering use of this type of Credit should take appropriate care prior to arranging for the issuance of a red or green clause letter of credit. Payment of the drawings and advances are the obligation of the account party, whether or not conforming documents are presented.

Exporters that require advance payments or down payments in order to begin production or other activity need to consider the timing of the payment when structuring the instructions for issuing letters of credit. If the advance or deposit is to be made prior to issuance of the Credit, the Credit could be worded to reflect the total contract amount, the deposit or advance, and the amount of the drawing. The invoice would state the total transaction amount, reflect the advance payment or deposit, and the balance due would reflect the amount due on shipment.

Or, if the advance is to be available from the letter of credit itself, the Credit should be structured to provide for two separate drawings:

(1) A drawing for the advance payment or deposit amount. This drawing would be available against a draft, and an invoice for the deposit marked paid.

(2) A drawing for the performance under the contract, i. e. shipment, shipping documents, etc.

Box 6. 1

Introduction of eUCP

The official name for this publication is "Supplement to the Uniform Customs and Practice for Documentary Credits for Electronic Presentation (Version 1. 1)". It uses the acronym "eUCP".

During the course of drafting UCP 600, ICC national committees indicated that, due to the limited usage of eUCP Version 1. 0, the eUCP should remain as a supplement to the UCP. Version 1. 1 has, therefore, been updated solely to reflect the changes made in UCP with regard to terminology and style of presentation.

The eUCP continues to provide definitions permitting UCP 600 terminology to accommodate the electronic presentation of the equivalent of paper documents and providing necessary rules to allow both sets of rules to work together. The eUCP allows for presentation electronically or for a mixture of paper documents and electronic presentation.

It is important for the eUCP reader to understand that many articles of the UCP are not impacted by the presentation of the electronic equivalent of paper documents and do not require any changes to accommodate electronic presentation.

When read together, the UCP and the eUCP provide the necessary rules for electronic presentation and are broad enough to anticipate developing practice in this area. Where specific words or phrases used in the UCP are defined in the eUCP, these definitions, unless otherwise stated, apply wherever the terms appear in the UCP.

eUCP Version 1. 1 is specific to UCP 600 and, if necessary, may have to be revised as technologies develop, perhaps prior to the next revision of the UCP. For that purpose, the eUCP is issued in version numbers that will allow for a revision and subsequent version if the need arises.

The eUCP has been specifically drafted to be independent of specific technologies and developing electronic commerce systems, i. e., it does not address specific technologies or systems necessary to facilitate electronic presentation. These technologies are evolving, and it is left to the parties to the credit to agree on the technology or systems to be used for presentation of electronic records in compliance with the requirements of the eUCP.

The eUCP has been created to meet the demands of the market for the presentation of electronic documents. The market has created a higher standard in anticipation of increased processing efficiencies when the electronic equivalents of paper documents are presented. In anticipation of this demand and to meet market expectations, several changes to the standards established by the UCP have been deemed necessary for an electronic presentation. These changes are consistent with current practice and the expectations of the marketplace.

All of the articles of eUCP Version 1.1 are consistent with UCP 600 except that they relate specifically to electronic presentations. Where necessary, changes have been made to address the unique issues related to presentation of the electronic equivalent of paper documents.

In order to avoid confusion between the articles of the UCP and those of the eUCP, the eUCP articles are numbered with an "e" preceding each article number.

Key Words

Letter of Credit, Revocable Letter of Credit, Conformed Letter of Credit, Document of Letter of Credit, Freely Negotiable Credits, Revolving Letter of Credit, Transferable Letter of Credit, Banker Acceptances

Questions

1. What are the characteristics of letters of credit?

2. What are the basic procedures of a freely negotiable documentary letter of credit?

3. Should the credit be confirmed by another bank? Are there any risks for exporters in dealing with that confirming L/C? Why?

CHAPTER 7   UCP 600 AND CASE STUDIES OF LETTERS OF CREDIT

Learning Objectives

- To learn about the background and comparisons of UCP 500 and UCP 600
- To grasp some case studies of letters of credit

7.1 UCP 600 and UCP 500

7.1.1 Background on drafting of UCP 600 and UCP 500

The Uniform Customs and Practice for Documentary Credits (UCP) is a set of rules on the issuance and use of letters of credit. The UCP is utilised by bankers and commercial parties in more than 175 countries in trade finance. Some 11% – 15% of international trade utilises letters of credit, totalling over a trillion dollars (US) each year.

Historically, the commercial parties, particularly banks, have developed the techniques and methods for handling letters of credit in international trade finance. This practice has been standardized by the ICC (International Chamber of Commerce) by publishing the UCP in 1933 and subsequently updating it throughout the years. The ICC has developed and moulded the UCP by regular revisions. The result is the most successful international attempt at unifying rules ever, as the UCP has substantially universal effect.

The new rules for Uniform Customs and Practice for Documentary Credits will come into force on July, 1st 2007. These rules are called the UCP 600. The previous version, UCP 500, had been operative since 1994. Historically, ICC does revision of UCP every 10 years to incorporate changes in international business practice. UCP 500 still contained discrepancies that seemed to hinder the smooth operation of documentary credit transactions. The Banking Commission in Paris in May 2003 established a Drafting group and a Consulting group to formulate UCP 600. After three years of rigorous review, UCP 600 was finalized, hoping to remove the discrepancies in the previous version. Coupled with the ICC Documentary Credit Dispute Resolution Expertise Rules (DOCDEX), there was much confusion amongst business persons and bankers regarding documentary credit transactions, resulting in 70% of the presentations not being honored due to discrepancies. The objective of UCP 600 is therefore to reduce dispute rates, lower rates of inquiries regarding interpretations of certain articles and reduce lawsuits resulting from such confusion.

7.1.2 The main comparison between UCP 600 and UCP 500

Whereas UCP 500 contained 49 Articles, UCP 600 now has 39 Articles that are clearer, more concise and more organized. Major amendments have been enacted in relation to various Articles of UCP 500 that used to induce the most number of inquiries. The major changes are best understood when comparison is made between the two versions, an outline is sketched below:

1. Application

UCP 500 Article 1	UCP 600 Article 1
No formal status was given, only stating that they would apply to documentary credit. However, courts would generally find that they would apply when expressly stated or by implication.	These Articles are now rules? Once they are referred to in the credit documents, they are binding on all parties, unless excluded or modified by the credit document. Probably this would reinforce the legal status of the provisions.

2. Definitions

UCP 500 Article 2	UCP 600 Article 2
Only the meaning of Credit was defined.	Article 2 introduces new definitions section. Particularly the meaning of honor, negotiation and presentation has been defined among others. This was a prime area of uncertainty in the previous version.

3. Interpretation

No corresponding Article in UCP 500	UCP 600 Article 3
	By Article 3 there is now a new section on interpretations. It clarifies certain procedural matters and interpretation of various commonly used yet misunderstood terms.

4. Examination of Documents

UCP 500 Article 13(b) and 14(d)	UCP 600 Article 14(b) and 16(d)
In UCP 500, the stipulated time was reasonable time not exceeding seven days? This created much confusion.	Under Article 14(b) Five Banking days are now the maximum for determining whether a presentation complies. Banks will now have to settle the issue within this period.

5. Standard for Examination of Documents

UCP 500 Article 13	UCP 600 Article 14
Referred to reasonable care and reasonable time, there was much uncertainty interpreting these terms.	The examination of documents and sets out new standards. Needless to say that this area has been a major source of problem, specially between the beneficiary and the confirming/nominating bank. Attempts have been made to reduce the problems usually arising out of wrong interpretation.

6. Original Documents

UCP 500 Article 20(b)	UCP 600 Article 17
Unless otherwise stipulated in the Credit, banks will accept as an original document, a document produced as a copy provided that it is marked as original and appears to be signed.	Under the new rule in Article 17, a document bearing an apparently original signature, mark stamp or label of the issuer would be accepted as original document.

7. Authorization to Discount

UCP 500 Article 10(d)	UCP 600 Article 12(b)
By nominating another bank, or by allowing for negotiation by any bank, or by authorizing or requesting another bank to add its confirmation, the Issuing Bank authorizes such a bank to pay, accept draft(s), or negotiate as the case may be, against documents which appear on their face to be in compliance with the terms and conditions of the Credit and undertakes to reimburse such bank in accordance with the provisions of these Articles.	As per Article 12(b), By nominating a bank to accept a draft or incur a deferred payment undertaking, an issuing bank authorizes that nominated bank to prepay or purchase a draft accepted or a deferred payment undertaking incurred by that nominated bank.

8. Consistency Requirement

UCP 500 Article 21	UCP 600 Article 14(d)
There must not be inconsistencies between data content of one document with another.	Article 14(d) states that data in the credit, other documents and international banking practice need not be identical but also must not conflict with each other.

9. Lost Documents

UCP 500 Article 16 (in part)	UCP 600 Article 35 (in part)
Banks assume no liability or responsibility for the consequences arising out of delay and/or loss in transit of any message(s), letter(s) or document(s), or for delay, mutilation or other error(s) arising in the transmission of any telecommunication.	Article 35 (in part) states that if a presentation is complying then if the documents are lost during transit between banks, the issuing or confirming bank must honour, negotiate or reimburse the credit. Admittedly, this is much more logical than the previous version.

10. Multimodal Transport Shipment

UCP 500 Article 26(a) (in part)	UCP 600 Article 19(a)
If the Credit called for a transport document covering at least two different modes of transport, then this section would apply.	Article 19 (in part) now gives different description of multimodal transport shipments. The credit need not call for a transport document to cover different modes of transport.

There is no doubt that UCP 600 has taken some serious steps to remove confusion and promote consistency in international business practice. The ICC has taken great care to ensure that experience gathered by bankers, importer, exporters and lawyers during the time of UCP 500 are put to good use in the new rules. With over 70% documents presented found to contain discrepancies, it is hoped that UCP 600 would be more successful than its predecessors in bringing in more uniformity in a field that is in die need of it.

7.2 Case Studies in Letters of Credit

Figure 7.1

The Montreal & Quebec Bank	
Quebec City, Quebec	
22, November, 2000	
Applicant:	Beneficiary:
Halifax Paper Mill Co.	Paper Equipment Supply Co.
351 Jacques Preview Drive, Quebec City, Quebec B2C6W3 Canada	1703 Main Street, Boise, ID83704, Canada

At hereby issue our Irrevocable Documentary Credit No. 73371 in your favour for account of the above mentioned applicant up to an aggregate amount of CAD150,000.00.

This credit is available by your draft (s) drawn at 60 days sight on ourselves accompanied by the following documents:

Signed commercial invoice in 3 copies

Packing List in 3 copies

Uniform Truck Bill of Lading consigned to Halifax Paper Mill Co., Halifax,

Nova Scotia marked "Freight Prepaid"

Inspection Certificate

Covering: One repair kit Model No. 77AB CPT Halifax, Nova Scotia

Expiry Date: 15 January, 2000

Partial Shipments: Not Permitted

Special Conditions:

1. All banking charges other than those of the issuing bank are for account of beneficiary.

2. Acceptance commission and discount charges are for applicant's account.

This Letter of Credit is subject to the Uniform Customs and Practice for Documentary Credits, International Chamber of Commerce Publication No. 500 (1993 Revision)

Documents maybe presented at our International Banking Department prior to 3 : 00 PM each banking day.

By _____

Authorized Signature

(1) Paper Equipment Supply Co. received the letter of credit in Figure 6. 1. It was routed to export order entry. What is the first question the company should have about this letter of credit?

(2) After Paper Equipment Supply resolved the first question (♯ 1 above), it shipped the goods on December 4 and presented documents to the bank on December 28, prior to the expiry of the letter of credit. The Montreal & Quebec Bank reviewed the document sand found they were in order. However, the bank refused to pay the beneficiary claiming the documents had been presented late. The bank advised that it would have to ask the importer for permission to pay against late presentation. Paper Equipment was upset and concerned that the bank had a problem with its clean presentation. They claimed that the applicant was not involved as the documents were in order and presented before the expiry date of the Credit. Who is correct? And why? Who? _____ Why (UCP Article)? _____

(3) Paper Equipment tried again, same letter of credit. Begin again: On receipt of this same letter of credit, Paper Equipment Supply contacted their bank, Boise Banking Co. for assistance and direction. Boise Banking Co. was very willing to assist, and advised Paper Equipment that when the documents were ready, the company could send them to Boise Banking Co. for an initial review and analysis. Paper Equipment also wanted instruction on preparation of the draft. Because Paper Equipment Supply was going to take its documents to Boise Banking Co. , they wanted to know who to draw the draft on? The bank told them _____ .

(4) Same letter of credit, different circumstances. Paper Equipment presented

documents to The Montreal & Quebec Bank on Thursday December 27 at 4 PM. The bank examined the documents and found them to be in order. However, the bank told Paper Equipment that the documents had been presented late and the bank would have to get the permission of the applicant the drawing. Paper Equipment strenuously objected, stating that the bank was closed on the latest day for presentation, and under UCP Article 44. a. the documents could be presented the next business day. The beneficiary went onto state that as "Boxing Day" is a bank holiday in Canada the documents could not be presented until December 27. "We made a timely presentation of the correct documents and we want to get paid" was the attitude of the exporter. The bank again refused to pay, claiming late presentation. Who is correct, and why? Who? _____ Why (UCP Article)? _____

(5) Under the letter of credit in Figure 7. 1, Paper Machinery presented documents and a draft drawn on the issuing bank for CAD 146 000. The bank found the document in compliance with the Credit, even though the draft was less then the Credit. Should the bank pay the beneficiary? _____ Why (UCP Article)? _____ .

Figure 7. 2 is Amendment No. 1 to the above letter of credit No. 73371 issued by The Montreal & Quebec Bank in favor of Paper Machinery Supply Co.

Figure 7. 2

The Montreal & Quebec Bank

Quebec City, Quebec

26 November 2000

Applicant:	Beneficiary:
Halifax Paper Mill Co.	Paper Equipment Supply Co.
351 Jacques Preview Drive	1703 Main Street
Quebec City, Quebec B2C6W3	Boise, ID83704

At hereby advise you of Amendment No. 1 to our Irrevocable Documentary Credit No. 73371 in your favour for account of the above mentioned applicant.

This letter of credit has been amended as follows:

The Amount is now CAD140,000

The latest shipping date is now December 25

The product description is now as follows:

One repair kit Model No. 83 - A - 45

CPT Halifax, Nova Scotia

All other terms and conditions remain unchanged. We require that you advise us immediately upon your acceptance of this amendment to this letter of credit. Thank you.

This Letter of Credit is subject to the Uniform Customs and Practice for Documentary Credits, International Chamber of Commerce Publication No. 500 (1993

Revision) By _____

　　Authorized Signature

　　(6) Paper Machinery received the amendment. The amendment letter requires that the beneficiary immediately accept or reject the amendments. The beneficiary did not respond. On December 18 the beneficiary shipped "One repair kit Model No. 77 AB". On December 27, Paper Equipment Supply Co. presented the following documents to the bank: a Beneficiary's draft for CAD 150,000, a signed commercial invoice in three copies, a packing list in three copies, a Uniform Truck Bill properly consigned and prepaid, and an Inspection Certificate. The documents complied with the Credit prior to the amendment. What happened? _____ Why(UCP Article)?

_____

　　(7) Same letter of credit, different circumstances: Paper Machinery received the amendment to the letter of credit in Figure 6. 2 above. The amendment letter required that the beneficiary immediately accept or reject the amendments. The beneficiary did not respond. Paper Equipment Supply Co. shipped "One repair kit Model No. 83 A 45". All other documents complied with the original Credit. The bank rejected the documents and held them available to the beneficiary. The exporter stated that they shipped the revised order as required, within the contracted shipping date and terms. The bank stated that they would have to obtain permission to pay, claiming the presentation was discrepant. On what basis was the presentation discrepant? _____ Why (UCP Article)? _____

　　(8) Newport Metal Works, Newport News, VA received a letter of credit from CDI Bank of Commerce & Trust Co. , Abidjan, Coted' Ivoire for USD2,500,000. The NMW salesman was excited about the sale. He knew if the shipment was made before month end he would get a big commission. He pushed for immediate shipment, stating there was "no risk" because the Credit was confirmed by a big New York bank, CDI Bank of Commerce & Trust Co. , New York Agency. The credit department at Newport Metal Works wasn't excited. Why? _____ Did this confirmation accomplish both of the basic reasons for requiring a confirmed letter of credit? _____ What are those two reasons?

　　Review Figure 7. 3 and answer the questions.

　　(9) This letter of credit calls for shipment of 470 metric tons of soy waste at USD120 / MT. The beneficiary shipped and presented a draft for USD54,600 and documents under the Credit. The commercial invoice revealed that shipment was 455 MT of soy waste. All other documents were in compliance with the Credit. Should this drawing be paid? Yes or No? _____ Why (UCP Article)? _____

　　(10) Same Credit (Figure 7. 3), different circumstances: Under this above letter of credit, the commercial invoice states the exporter shipped 480 MT of soy waste. All

other documents were in compliance with the Credit. Should this drawing be paid? Yes or No? _____ What article of the UCP applies to this situation? _____

(11) Same Credit (Figure 7.3), different circumstances: Soy Processors presented documents under the Credit to Washoe County Bank. The bank reviewed the documents, claimed reimbursement and forwarded the documents to the issuing bank. After ANZED Bank received the documents they contacted Washoe County Bank requesting a payment of the reimbursing payment made under its letter of credit AA-I-FAP-880013, claiming discrepancies. ANZED Bank claimed the documents were discrepant as exporter failed to present evidence that shipment was made via Blue Star Lines. Washoe Country Bank rejected this claim citing an Article of the UCP. Which bank was correct? _____ Which Article of the UCP 600 did Washoe County Bank cite in rejecting the claim of the issuing bank? _____

Figure 7.3

Name of Issuing Bank: ANZED Bank, Adelaide IRREVOCABLE Number: AA I FAP 880013 DOCUMENTARY CREDIT	

Place and Date of Issue: 000220 at Adelaide   Expiry Date and Place for Presentation of Documents

APPLICANT   Expiry Date: 000420
Food Additives Pty   Place for Presentation Negotiating Bank
12 Guernsey Lance, West   BENEFICIARY   Soy Processors
Auckland, NZ   3500 Food Court Park
   ADVISING BANK   Reference No.   Des Moines IA 30049
Washoe County Bank   A-4801
   First and Oak Streets
   Bridge City, Iowa
AMOUNT: US $56,400.00

Name of Issuing Bank: ANZED Bank, Adelaide   IRREVOCABLE
Number: AA I FAP 880013
                DOCUMENTARY CREDIT

Partial Shipments □ Allowed   □ Not Allowed   CREDIT AVAILAVLE
WITH: Any bank by negotiation
Transhipment □ Allowed □ Not Allowed   □ By payment at sight:
□ By deferred payment at:
× Insurance covered by buyers   □ By acceptance of drafts at
× By negotiation
SHIPMENT AS DEFINEDIN UCP ARTICLE46
From: U.S. West Coast Port   Against the documents detailed here in:
For transportation to: Auckland, NZ   and beneficiary's draft (s) drawn on: Issuing Bank
Not later than: 970310

Documents Required:

1. Signed commercial invoice in three copies

2. Full set of clean on board ocean bills of lading consigned to ANZED Bank and blank endorsed and marked "freight collect"

3. Packing list in four copies

4. Beneficiary's certificate as to quality and quantity

Description of Goods:

470 MT of soy waste at USD120 / MT as per proforma number SP10004546, FOB Vessel.

Additional instructions:

Beneficiary to use Air Sea Forwarders, 2890 Drury Lane, So San Francisco, CA.

Shipment to be made on Blue Star Lines vessel.

Reimbursement instructions:

Negotiating bank to claim reimbursement on our account at Big City Bank, Los Angeles, CA. Negotiating bank must send a copy of its reimbursement claim to us at the time of claim.

Negotiating bank must send the draft and documents to us in one mailing at Postal Slot R44, Western Station, Adelaide, NZ TT Reimbursement allowed.

Reimbursement is subject to URR525.

Documents to be presented within days after the date of shipment but within the validity of the Credit

We hereby issue this Irrevocable Documentary Credit in your favor. It is subject to the Uniform Customs and Practice for Documentary Credits (1993 Revision, International Chamber of Commerce, Paris, France. Publication No. 500) and engages us in accordance with the terms thereof. The number and the date of the Credit and the name of our bank must be quoted on all drafts required. If the credit is available by negotiation, cash presentation must be noted on the reverse side of this advice by the bank whether the Credit is available.

Lydany Bank House

This document consists of 1 signed page (s)   ANZED Bank. Adelaide

---

(12) Same Credit (Figure 7.3), different circumstances: What if the above letter of credit called for shipment of 470 boxes of office products and the exporter shipped 455 boxes. Is this acceptable? _____ Why or why not (UCP Article)? _____

(13) New situation: A letter of credit is received by an exporter of household appliances and other products. The letter of credit states the Credit covers the shipment of household appliances. The invoice presented under the credit states "refrigerators and stoves". The bill of lading states "household appliances-refrigerators and stoves, shippers load and count". The Packing List states "Household Appliances". Are these documents acceptable? _____ Why? _____

(14) New situation: A letter of credit is received by an exporter of household appliances and other products. The letter of credit covers the "shipment of washers, dryers and household appliances." The bill of lading covers shipment of "washers, dryers, ranges, ovens and televisions". Is the bill of lading discrepant? _____ Why [UCP Article (s)]? _____

(15) New situation: A letter of credit prohibits partial shipments. The amount of the letter of credit is USD200,000, and the credit calls for the shipment of 200 units at USD1,000 each. For each of the following determine if the drawing is in compliance with the Credit and state which UCP 600 article applies.

a. The exporter ships 200 units and draws under the Credit for USD 195,000. Yes or No? _____ Why (UCP Article)? _____

b. The exporter ships 195 units and draws under the Credit for USD 200,000. Yes or No? _____ Why (UCP Article)? _____

(16) New situation: A letter of credit calls for shipment of merchandise described as "hand tools and operating software". The commercial invoice presented under the Credit contains the following merchandise description: Hand tools, software, parts and supplies. Is the commercial invoice discrepant? _____ Why? _____

Box 7.1

URR 725

ICC announced that an updated version of its Uniform Rules for Bank-to-Bank Reimbursements under Documentary Credits (URR) will take effect on October, 1st 2008.

Also known as URR 725, the update was necessary to bring the URR rules into conformity with the UCP 600, ICC's universally used rules on letters of credit. An updated version of the UCP 600 took effect on 1 July last year.

First published in 1995 under the title URR 525, the URR rules are the most widely-referenced rules of their kinds. They clarify a number of issues in bank-to-bank reimbursements, such as expiry and conditions under which claims can be authenticated.

The updated rules were approved at a meeting of ICC's Banking Commission held on 16 April.

URR 725 will be used by practitioners who elect to incorporate the updated URR into their letters of credit. The updated rules contain several important technical changes that bring the language into line with the UCP 600, such as "express indication", and "operative reimbursement authorization".

The Uniform Rules for Bank-to-Bank Reimbursements under Documentary

Credits ("rules"), ICC Publication No. 725, shall apply to any bank-to-bank reimbursement when the text of the reimbursement authorization expressly indicates that it is subject to these rules. They are binding on all parties thereto, unless expressly modified or excluded by the reimbursement authorization.

URR 725 is now available as a four-page leaflet and is sold in sets of 10. A bilingual edition in English and French is available.

Key Words

UCP 600, UCP 500

Questions

1. What is the main difference between UCP 600 and UCP 500?

2. What is the maximum amount of drawings available under the credit (Figure 7.1)? Please list the types of L/C in Figure 7.1.

3. What is the expiration date for the credit (Figure 7.2)? Where must the Beneficiary present the documents required under the credit (Figure 7.2)?

CHAPTER 8 GUARANTEES AND STANDBY LETTER OF CREDIT

Learning Objectives

- To understand the concept, parties and types of guarantees
- To understand the concept and nature of standby letter of credit
- To learn the differences between guarantees and standby letter of credit

8.1　Banker's Letter of Guarantees

8.1.1　What is a banker's letter of guarantee

A bank guarantee is a written damand issued by a bank at the request of its customer, undertaking to make payment to the beneficiary within the limits of a stated sum of money in the event of default by the principal. It may also be defined as the irrevocable obligation of a bank to pay a sum of money in the event of non-performance of a contract by the principal.

In international trade, on one hand, the buyer wants to be certain that the seller is in a position to honor his commitment as offered or contracted. The former therefore makes it a condition that appropriate security be provided. On the other hand, the seller must find a way to be assured of receiving payment if no special security is provided for the payment such as in open account business and documentary collections. Such security may be obtained through banks in the form of a guarantee. A bank guarantee is used as an instrument for securing performance or payment especially in international business.

Distinguished from a letter of credit, a bank guarantee is an undertaking which will be brought into effect by the guarantor, namely the bank, only if the principal fails to pay or perform and so the bank is secondarily liable to the beneficiary. However, under a payment guarantee, it is stipulated that the bank undertakes to pay, provided the documents presented are in compliance with the terms and conditions of the guarantee. In that case, the issuing bank is primarily liable to the beneficiary.

8.1.2　Parties to a letter of guarantee

(1) Principal. The principal is the person at whose request the bank issues the guarantee. He is one of the parties of the contract who wants to provide security through the form of a guarantee. For instance, in tender bond the principal is the tenderer, in payment guarantee importing contract he is the importer, etc. If he is in breach of his obligations, he will be claimed after the bank makes the payment.

(2) Beneficiary. The beneficiary is the person in whose favor the guarantee is issued. He obtains the right to claim to the bank for compensation according to the terms of the guarantee. For instance, in tender bond the beneficiary is a party inviting tender, in import guarantee, he is the exporter, etc. He is secured against the risk of the principal's not fulfilling his obligations towards the beneficiary in respect of the underlying transaction for which the demand guarantee is given. He will obtain a

certain sum of money if the obligations are not fulfilled.

(3) Guarantor. The guarantor is a bank or a financial institution which issues a letter of guarantee undertaking to make payment to the beneficiary in the event of default by the principal against the presentation of a written demand and other specified documents. He is not required to decide whether the beneficiary and principal have or have not fulfilled their obligations under the underlying transaction with which the guarantor is not concerned.

(4) Instructing party. The instructing party is a bank or a financial institution or any other body or person which issues a counter guarantee acting on the instruction of a principal in favor of a bank or a financial institution located in the beneficiary's country instructing the latter to issue a letter of guarantee on behalf of the former's principal in favor of a specified party named therein.

A counter guarantee refers to any guarantee, bond or other payment undertaking of the instructing party given in writing for the payment of money to the guarantor on presentation in conformity with the terms of the undertaking of a written demand for payment and other documents specified in the counter guarantee. Counter guarantees are by their nature separate transactions from the guarantees to which they relate and from any underlying contract or tender conditions, and instructing partners are in no way concerned with or bound by the related guarantees.

8. 1. 3 Nature of demand guarantee

(1) The purpose of guarantee is to make payment. It assures the beneficiary that the principal's obligations will be fulfilled. If the principal is not able to honor the commitment, the guarantor may undertake to do it, but the principal must compensate him. It is the principal's duty other than the guarantor's to pay.

(2) Guarantees are payable on presentation of one or more documents as stipulated in the letter of guarantee and only put into effect when the principal is in breach of his obligations under the underlying contract. However, the guarantors are not concerned with the fact of default or the actual default by the principal in the underlying transaction but concerned only with documents. Where such documents do not appear on their face to conform to the terms of guarantee or appear on their face to be inconsistent with one another, payments shall be refused. The documents required under a guarantee vary widely, the most simply, only requiring a written demand without a statement stating the principal is in default, the most strictly, an arbitration award or a judgment form court.

(3) Guarantees by their nature are separate transactions from the contractor tender conditions on which they may be based and guarantors are in no way concerned

with or bound by such contract or tender conditions despite the inclusion of a reference to them in the letter of guarantee. In publication No. 325 there is no such clear indication. The disputes arising from the contract may involve a dispute in the guarantee. But Uniform rules for demand guarantee (ICC Publication No. 458) published in 1992 regulated that the duty of making payment by the guarantor or issuer under the new rules lies in the presentation of a written demand and any other documents specified in the guarantee, not conditional on proof of default by the principal in the underlying transaction. Under new rules, they stand by themselves. The obligation of the guarantor does not relate to the underlying contract.

8. 1. 4 Types of guarantees

A guarantee may be issued directly or indirectly to the beneficiary if the beneficiary is located in a foreign country. A direct guarantee occurs when the client authorized the bank to issue a guarantee directly to the beneficiary. It is as following Figure 8.1:

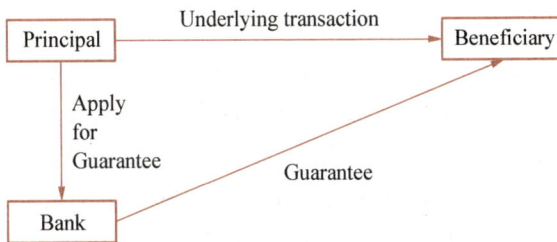

Figure 8.1 Direct guarantee

An indirect guarantee is a guarantee where a second bank is involved. This bank (usually a foreign bank located in the beneficiary's country of domicile) will be requested by the initiating bank to issue a guarantee in return for the latter's counter guarantee. Thus, the initiating bank protects the foreign bank from the risk of a loss which could result from the beneficiary submitting a claim under the foreign bank's guarantee. The initiating bank must formally pledge to pay those amount claimed by the beneficiary under the guarantee upon demand by the guaranteeing bank. Indirect guarantees are mainly used in connection with international business. It is as following Figure 8.2.

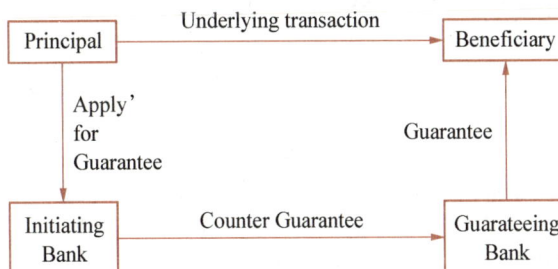

Figure 8.2 Indirect guarantee

There are various types of guarantees to be issued by the banks at the request of the importer or the exporter to serve different purposes. Some of them guarantee the performance of a contract; others guarantee the payment of importing goods under open account terms or under documents against acceptance collection; still others guarantee the payment under consignment. Most of them, however, are issued at the request of the importer to guarantee his effecting payment according to the sales contract terms. If the importer fails to pay wholly or partially, the guarantor bank undertakes to pay to the beneficiary the corresponding amount plus interest for the delayed payment. According to Uniform Rules for Contract Guarantees, International Chamber of Commerce publication No. 325, the main types of the bank guarantee are tender bond, payment guarantee and performance guarantee. But in practice there are also guarantees for compensation trade and processing assembly, etc.

(1) Tender guarantee. A tender guarantee is an undertaking given by a bank at the request of a tenderer in favour of a party inviting tenders abroad, whereby the guarantor undertakes, in the event of default by the principal in the obligations resulting from the submission of tender, to make payment to the beneficiary within the limits of a stated sum of money. The guarantor will pay the total amount stated in the guarantee on first demand, if the beneficiary of the guarantee informs him that the offer is withdrawn before its expiry date or the tenderer has failed to accept the contract awarded or the bid bond is not replaced by a performance bond after the contract has been awarded. The bank's liability depends upon the precise wording of the guarantee. In tender bond, the beneficiary is the party inviting the tender who is entitled to get compensation if the tenderer fails to meet his obligations arising from the submission of tender. The principal is the party tendering who will meet his obligations arising from the submission of tender, which is guaranteed by the bank. The guarantor is the bank, which should meet its commitment in compliance with the terms of the guarantee without becoming involved in possible disputes between the beneficiary and the principal resulting from the tender transaction. As a rule, the guaranteed amount is 1%-5% of the amount offered. The period of validity is usually between three and six months until the signing of the contract or issuing of a performance bond. Tender Guarantee is as following Figure 8.3:

To: _____   Issuing Date _____
                                               Bid Security for Bid No.

                                               _____
                                               For supply of _____
        This Guarantee in hereby issued to serve as a Bid Security of _____ (name of Bidder) (here in after called the "Bidder") for invitation for (Bid No. _____) for supply of (description of goods) to _____ (name of the buyer).
        _____ (name of issuing bank) hereby unconditionally and irrevocably guarantees and

binds itself, its successors and assigns to pay you immediately without recourse, the sum of upon receipt of your written notification stating any of the following:

(a) The Bidder has withdrawn his bid after the time and date of the bid opening and before the expiration of its validity period; or

(b) The Bidder has failed to enter into contract with you within thirty (30) calendar days after toe notification of contract award; or

(c) The Bidder has failed to establish acceptable Performance Security within thirty (30) calendar days after the receipt of the Notification of Award.

It is fully understood that this guarantee takes effect the date of the bid opening shall remain valid for a period four _____ calendar days thereafter, and during the period of any extension there of that may be agreed upon between you and the Bidder with notice to us, unless sooner terminated and or released by you.

Issue Bank _____

Signed by _____

(Printed name and designation of official authorized to sign on behalf of issuing bank)

Official seal _____

Figure 8.3   Tender guarantee or form for bid security

(2) Payment guarantee importing contract. It is issued at the request of the importer to guarantee his effecting payment in accordance with the terms and conditions of the relative contract. It is mainly employed to secure the payment on an open account basis. Should the importer fail to make payment wholly or partially within the time limit as stipulated in the contract, the guarantor plus interest, if any. For instance, a twelve-month contract has been signed by the buyer and the seller for the delivery of consumer goods or for the performance of services. Monthly deliveries on open account are to be paid by the buyer 10 days after his receipt of the invoice. If the monthly payment has not been effected by the buyer as stipulated in the contract, a claim can be made by the seller under the bank guarantee. Payment guarantee is as following Figure 8.4:

To: (Name of Seller)   Date _____

Re: Our Irrevocable Letter of Guarantee No. _____

With reference to Contract No. _____ for a total value of _____ signed between your goods sellers (hereinafter referred to as "the Seller") and China National Technical Import Corp., Beijing, China (hereinafter referred to as "the Buyer's") concerning the Buyer's purchase from the Seller of the Equipment for, we at the request of the Buyer, open our Irrevocable Letter of Guarantee No. _____ in favor of the Seller to the extent of covering 100% of the total value of the contract and under take that payment will be effected by the Buyer as follows:

1. 90% of the total Contract price, viz. _____ shall be paid by the Buyer after his having received from the Seller the following documents and has found them in order.

2. 5% of the total Contract price, viz. _____ shall be paid by the Buyer after his having from the seller one Certificate of Acceptance of the Contract Plant.

3. 5% of the total Contract price, viz. _____ shall be paid by the buyer after expiry of the guarantee period of Contract Plant and his having received from the Seller one Certificate of Expiry of the guarantee period.

In connection with the above, we undertake that if the Buyer fails to pay wholly or partially we will within 3 days after receipt of the Seller's written Notice pay the Seller relative amount plus simple interest at the rate of 7% per annum for delayed payment, which the Buyer is liable under the Contract, provided that Buyer is unable to submit any proof that the documents presented by the Seller are not in conformity with the stipulation of the Contract, our liability under this letter of guarantee shall diminish proportionally with the percentage of amount paid by the Buyer. The letter of guarantee shall effective on the date of issue and shall automatically become null and void after payment made as above stated.

For Bank of Asia

...

Signature

Figure 8.4　Payment guarantee

(3) Performance guarantee. A performance guarantee is an undertaking given by a bank (the guarantor) at the request of a supplier of goods or services or a contractor (the principal) to a buyer or an employer (the beneficiary), whereby the guarantor undertakes to make payment to the beneficiary within the limits of a stated sum of money in the event of default by the supplier or the contractor in due performance of the terms of a contract between the principal and the beneficiary. In performance bond, the beneficiary is the party awarding the contract, who is entitled to get compensation if the supplier or other contractors fail to perform the contract. The principal is the party to whom the contract has been awarded and who is guaranteed by the bank to perform the contract in compliance with its terms. The guarantor is the bank guarantees the principal to perform the contract in accordance with its terms. The guarantor is the bank which guarantees the principal to perform the contract in accordance with its terms. The guaranteed amount is usually 10% of the contract amount. The bond remains valid for the full amount until complete performance of the contract. The period of validity may be one year, two years or longer. Performance guarantee is as following Figure 8.5:

To: _____ (Beneficiary)

Dear Sirs,

This Bond is hereby issued as the performance bond of _____ (Applicant) (hereinafter called the supplier) for supply of _____ (the name of the goods) under the contract No. _____ to (the name of the beneficiary) _____.

The _____ (the name of the guarantor) hereby irrevocably guarantees itself, its successors and assigns to pay you up to the amount of _____ (the amount of the guaranteed value) representing _____ percent of the contract price and accordingly covenants and agrees as follows:

a. On the supplier's failure of faithful performance of the contract (hereinafter called the failure of performance), we shall immediately, on your demand in a written notification stating the effect of the failure of performance by the supplier, pay you such amount or amounts as required by you not exceeding _____ (the guaranteed amount) in the manner specified in the said statement.

b. The covenants herein contained constitute irrevocable and direct obligations of the guarantor, no alternation in the terms of the contract to be performed thereunder and no allowance of time by you or any other act or omission by you, which but for this provision might exonerate or discharge the bank shall in any way release the guarantor from any liability hereunder.

    c. This performance bond shall become effective from issuing date and shall remain valid until (the date of expiry). Upon expiry, please return this bond to us for cancellation.

Figure 8.5 Performance guarantee or form of performance bond for supply of

(4) Compensation guarantee. Compensation trade refers to such kind of trade that the importer pays for the equipment imported from an exporter with products produced by it. A compensation guarantee is an undertaking given by a bank at the request of the importer to the exporter. Should the importer fail to pay for the equipment with products produced by it as stipulated in the underlying contract, the guarantor bank undertakes to effect payment for the equipment delivered by the exporter plus interest.

(5) Processing assembly guarantee. This guarantee is an undertaking given by a bank (the guarantor) at the request of an assignee (the principal) of the underlying contract to a consigner (the beneficiary), whereby the guarantor undertakes to make payment to the beneficiary within the limits of a stated sum of money in the event of default by the assignee in the provision of finished goods to the consigner as stipulated in the underlying contract after receiving the raw materials or accessories in conformity with the contract.

8.1.5 Differences between a letter of guarantee and a letter of credit

(1) A letter of credit can only be applied to goods trade under payment against documents and provides payment guarantee to the exporter while a letter of guarantee can be applied to any types of economic contract and the guarantor undertakes to make payment to the beneficiary in the event of default by the principal.

(2) The undertaking of the issuing bank under a letter of credit is to pay, accept and pay draft or negotiate draft and / or documents, or to fulfill any other obligations under the credit provided documents presented are in compliance with the terms and conditions of the credit. A letter of guarantee is properly operative only if the principal failed to fulfill his obligations. Their purpose is different from that of a letter of credit.

(3) The documents required for payment under a letter of credit are commercial bills including shipment bills while those required under a bank of guarantee are certificate documents which can prove the default of principals.

(4) There is confirming bank, negotiating bank, paying bank, reimbursing bank, accepting bank as well as an issuing bank under a letter of credit. However, under a

letter of guarantee there is only an issuing bank.

（5）Under a letter of credit，a confirmed one bears not only the undertaking of the issuing bank but also that of the confirming bank. Documents will be presented either to the issuing bank or to the confirming bank. While the beneficiary of a guarantee can only present the documents to the issuing bank.

（6）UCP 600 does not stipulate the governing law and jurisdiction. If there is any dispute under a letter of credit，where the disputes shall be settled is a complex problem. Under a letter of guarantee publication No. 458 and No. 325，the governing law and jurisdiction are all clearly indicated，that is，the governing law shall be the place of business of the guarantor or instructing party. In case of more than one place of business，it is the place where the guarantee or counter guarantee is issued.

（7）A letter of credit is always used for financing the international trade while the beneficiary of a letter of guarantee cannot obtain financing through it.

Box 8.1

TENDER GUARANTEE

TO：_____　（BENEFICIARY）　　ISSUING DATE：_____
GUARANTEE NO. _____

WE HAVE BEEN INFORMED THAT RESPONDING TO THE TENDER NOTIFICATION NO. _____ （BID NO. _____ ）BY _____ （HEREINAFTER CALLED "THE PRINCIPAL"）WILL APPLY TO YOU FOR THE TENDER'S QUALIFICATION.

FURTHERMORE, WE UNDERSTAND THAT, ACCORDING TO YOUR REQUIREMENT, FOR OVERSEA APPLICANT APPLYING FOR THE TENDER'S QUALIFICATION, A TENDER GUARANTEE MUST BE PRESENTED.

AT THE REQUEST OF THE PRINCIPAL, WE （NAME OF BANK） _____ HAVING OUR REGISTERED OFFICE AT （ADDRESS OF BANK） _____ , HEREBY IRREVOCABLY UNDERTAKE TO PAY YOU ANY SUM OR SUMS NOT EXCEEDING IN TOTAL OF _____ （AMOUNT IN WORD）UPON RECEIPT BY US OF YOUR FIRST DEMAND IN WRITING AND YOUR WRITTEN STATEMENT STATING THE OCCURRENCE OF ONE OR MORE OF THE FOLLOWING CONDITIONS ONLY, WITHOUT STATING ANY REASON OF SUCH DEMAND.

　　1. THE PRINCIPAL WITHDRAWS HIS OFFER BETWEEN THE DATE OF

PRESENTATION OF HIS OFFER AND YOUR ANNOUNCEMENT OF THE BIDDING RESULT WITHOUT YOUR PRIOR AGREEMENT;

2. ON THE DATE THAT THE PRINCIPAL HAVING BEEN NOTIFIED BY YOU TO BE THE SUCCESSFUL BIDDER, FAILS OR REFUSES TO SIGN THE DEAL CONFIRMATION WITH YOU;

3. ON THE DATE THAT THE PRINCIPAL HAVING SIGNED THE CONTRACT WITH YOU, THE PRINCIPAL FAILS OR REFUSES TO EFFECT PAYMENT TO YOU FOR THE FIRST INSTALLMENT OF _____ .

THIS GUARANTEE WILL EXPIRE ON _____ AT THE LATEST. ANY DEMAND FOR PAYMENT IN RESPECT THEREOF MUST BE SENT TO US (ADDRESS: _____) ON OR BEFORE THAT DATE.

ALL BANKING CHARGES UNDER THE GUARANTEE ARE FOR ACCOUNT OF THE PRINCIPAL.

ISSUING BANK: _____
SIGNED BY: _____
OFFICIAL SEAL: _____

Source: http://www.docin.com/

8.2   Standby Letter of Credit

8.2.1   What is standby letter of credit

A standby letter of credit is issued by a bank on behalf of a customer to provide assurances of his ability to perform under the terms of a contract between the beneficiary and the customer. It serves a different function than the commercial letter of credit. The commercial letter of credit is the primary payment mechanism for a transaction. The standby letter of credit serves as a secondary payment mechanism. The parties involved with the transaction do not expect that the letter of credit will ever be drawn upon.

The standby letter of credit assures the beneficiary of the performance of the customer's obligation. The beneficiary is able to draw under the credit by presenting a draft, copies of invoices, with evidence that the customer has not per formed its obligation. The bank is obligated to make payment if the documents presented comply with the terms of the letter of credit.

In the United States and Japan，issuing a letter of guarantee （L/G） is not permitted by law. Banks in those countries are only allowed to issue a standby letter of credit instead of a letter of guarantee. A standby letter of credit is somewhat different from a letter of guarantee. It is actually a clean letter of credit which generally guarantees the payment to be made for an unfulfilled obligation on the part of the applicant. It is payable upon presentation of a draft together with a signed statement or certificate by the beneficiary that the applicant has failed to fulfill his obligation.

8. 2. 2　Common statements and examples of standby letter of credit

（1）Repayment standby. This one supports an obligation of the applicant to make repayment to the beneficiary as the latter has lent money to him. The statements are cited as below：

a. Beneficiary's signed statement in duplicate certifying that （name of borrowers） have failed to make repayment on or before the due date on the loan referred to below made to them by the beneficiary and that the amount drawn represents unpaid principal and accrued interest as agreed upon.

b. Beneficiary statement certifying that the amount drawn hereunder represents and covers the unpaid indebtedness due to your bank on or before （date） by （name of borrower）.

c. Beneficiary signed statement certifying that the amount drawn hereunder represents covers the unpaid indebtedness and interest thereon due to you arising out of your granting general banking facilities to （name of borrower）.

（2）Performance standby. This one irrevocably obligates the bank to pay a third party （beneficiary） when a customer （applicant） fails to execute a contract. Figure 8. 6 diagrams performance standby. The statements are cited as below：

a. Beneficiary signed statement certifying that （name of applicant） has defaulted in the performance of the terms and conditions of its Agreement with you （beneficiary） dated _____ .

b. Beneficiary written statement certifying that （name of applicant） has failed to carry out the terms and conditions of contract No. _____ , and a written statement by Mr. _____ certifying that the terms and conditions of the above mentioned contract has not been met.

8. 2. 3　Differences between a standby letter of credit and a letter of guarantee

1. From a legal viewpoint，standby credits and demand guarantees are capable of falling within two sets of rules，Uniform Customs and Practice for Documentary Credit and Uniform Rules for Demand Guarantee. The difference between standby credit and

NAME OF ISSUING BANK First Union Trust Bank of Dallas PLACE AND DATE OFISSUE Dallas, 20 July, 20 _____	IRREVOCABLE STAND BY CREDIT Date and place of expiry, Cairo, 30 Nov., 20 _____ NUMBER 45612
Applicant Ewing Oil Company Inc. 2425 John Ross Avenue, Dallas, Texas.	Beneficiary United Arab Pipelines Co., Farouk Palace Square, Alexandria, Egypt.
Advising Bank Bank of the Nile, Cairo.	Amount USD 1,000,000.00 (say U.S. dollars One million only)
Partial shipments ☐ allowed ☐ not allo. | Transhipment ☐ allo ☐ not allo.	Credit available with Bank of Nile, Cairo by PAYMENT ☐ ACCEPTANCE ☐ NEGOTIATION Against presentation of the documents detailed herein and of beneficiary's draft at sight drawn on Bank of the Nile, Cairo.
Shipment / dispatch / taking in Charge from at For transportation to	

Signed statement of United Arab Pipelines Co. that Ewing Oil Company Inc. failed to perform its contractual obligations under the agreement concluded on 30 June, 19—between Ewing Oil Company Inc. and United Arab Pipelines Co. in which Ewing Oil Company Inc. was the successful bidder.

Special Conditions:

It is agreed up on that we may be released from our liability under this Letter of Credit prior to the expiry date, only if we receive notification from Bank of the Nile by tested telex to the effect that Bank of the Nile been duly advised by United Arab Pipelines that the above agreement has been completely performed by the Ewing Oil Company Inc. Bank of the Nile has to advise the beneficiary adding its confirmation. We hereby authorise Bank of the Nile to draw on us by means of tested telex for the value of all drafts drawn under this Credit, provided the telex states that all terms and conditions have been complied with.

We hereby issue this Standby Credit in your favour, it is subject to the International Standby Practices.

For First Union Trust Bank of Dallas
<u>Signature</u>

Figure 8.6 Performance standby credit

demand guarantees not of law but of practice and business terminology.

2. The standby credit has developed into an all-purpose financial support instrument embracing a much wider range of uses than the normal demand guarantee. Thus, standby credits are used to support financial as well as non-financial obligations of the principal and to provide credit enhancement for the primary financial undertaking.

Box 8.2

STANDBY LETTER OF CREDIT

TO：_____BANK

FROM：_____

DATE：_____

STANDBY LETTER OF CREDIT

WITH REFERENCE TO THE LOAN AGREEMENT NO. _____ (HEREIN AFTER REFERRED TO AS "THE AGREEMENT") SIGNED BETWEEN BANK OF COMMUNICATIONS，_____BRANCH (HEREINAFTER REFERRED TO AS "THE LENDER") AND _____ (HEREIN AFTER REFERRED TO AS "THE BORROWER")，FOR A PRINCIPAL AMOUNT OF _____ RMB (IN WORDS)，WE HEREBY ISSUE OUR IRREVOCABLE STANDBY LETTER OF CREDIT NO. _____ IN THE LENDER'S FAVOR FOR AMOUNT OF THE WHICH HAS ITS REGISTERED OFFICE AT _____FOR AN AMOUNT UP TO UNITED STATES DOLLARS _____.(USD _____) WHICH COVERS THE PRINCIPAL AMOUNT OF THE AGREEMENT PLUS INTEREST ACCRUED FROM AFORESAID PRINCIPAL AMOUNT AND OTHER CHARGES ALL OF WHICH THE BORROWER HAS UNDERTAKEN TO PAY THE LENDER. THE EXCHANGE RATE WILL BE THE BUYING RATE OF USD/RMB QUOTED BY BANK OF COMMUNICATIONS ON THE DATE OF OUR PAYMENT. IN THE CASE THAT THE GUARANTEED AMOUNT IS NOT SUFFICIENT TO SATISFY YOUR CLAIM DUE TO THE EXCHANGE RATE FLUCTUATION BETWEEN USD AND RMB WE HEREBY AGREE TO INCREASE THE AMOUNT OF THIS STANDBY L/C ACCORDINGLY.

PARTIAL DRAWING AND MULTIPLE DRAWING ARE ALLOWED UNDER THIS STANDBY L/C.

THIS STANDBY LETTER OF CREDIT IS AVAILABLE BY SIGHT PAYMENT. WE ENGAGE WITH YOU THAT UPON RECEIPT OF YOUR DRAFT(S) AND YOUR SIGNED STATEMENT OR TESTED TELEX STATEMENT OR SWIFT STATING THAT THE AMOUNT IN USD REPRESENTS THE UNPAID BALANCE OF INDEBTEDNESS DUE TO YOU BY THE BORROWER，WE WILL PAY YOU WITHIN 7 BANKING DAYS THE AMOUNT SPECIFIED IN YOUR STATEMENT OR SWIFT. ALL DRAFTS DRAWN HEREUNDER MUST BE

MARKED DRAWN UNDER _____ BANK STANDBY LETTER OF CREDIT NO. _____ DATED _____.

THIS STANDBY LETTER OF CREDIT WILL COME INTO EFFECT ON _____ AND EXPIRE ON _____ AT THE COUNTER OF BANK OF _____.

THIS STANDBY LETTER OF CREDIT IS SUBJECT TO UNIFORM CUSTOMS AND PRACTICE FOR DOCUMENT CREDITS INTERNATIONAL CHAMBER OF COMMERCE PUBLICATION NO. 500.

Source: http://www.docin.com/

Key Words

International Settlement, Consignment, Case in Advance, Open Account Standby Letter of Credit, Repayment Standby, Performance Standby, Letter of Guarantee, Demand Guarantee, Direct Guarantee, Indirect Guarantee, Tender Guarantee, Payment Guarantee Importing Contract, Performance Guarantee, Compensation Guarantee, Processing Assembly Guarantee

Questions

1. What parties are involved in a letter of guarantee?
2. What are the contents of different types of guarantees?
3. What are the differences between a letter of guarantee and a letter of credit?
4. What are the differences between a standby letter of credit and a letter of guarantee?

CHAPTER 9   DOCUMENTS IN INTERNATIONAL PAYMENT

Learning Objectives

- To learn about different types of documentary bills
- To learn about various kinds of commercial invoices
- To understand transport documents

9.1 Documentary Bill

9.1.1 Draft under collection

Draft under collection can be defined as an unconditional order in writing addressed by the exporter to the importer, signed by the exporter giving it, requiring the importer to whom it is addressed to pay on demand or at a fixed determinable future time a sum certain money to or to the order of the exporter himself. The three immediate parties are:

(1) The Drawer

The drawer is the exporter.

(2) The Drawee

The drawee is the importer.

(3) The Payee

The payee can be the exporter/ the remitting bank/ the collecting bank.

When dealing with draft under collection, it should first remember that collection is a reverse remittance where the direction of the movement of the draft is opposite to that of the flow of funds. This is the reason why the draft is issued by the creditor (the exporter) on the debtor (the importer). Another point to be noted is that collection is a payment method based on trader's credit. For this reason, the drawee of this kind of draft will always be made on the importer. Normally, in the case of a documentary collection, the draft will also specify the type of collection to clearly indicate whether the documents are released against sight payment (D/P sight), deferred payment (D/P after sight) or acceptance (D/A).

9.1.2 Draft under letter of credit

Draft under letter of credit can be defined as an unconditional order in writing addressed by the exporter to the bank, signed by the exporter giving it, requiring the bank to whom it is addressed to pay on demand or at a fixed future time a sum certain in money to or to the order of the exporter himself or the exporter's bank.

Attached the form of the draft under letter of credit in the following Figure 9.1:

Figure 9.1   The draft under letter of credit (1)

Exchange for USD 100,000.00   Tampa, May 27,2005
        At sight of the bill of exchange pay to the order of
              Ourselves   the sum of
One hundred thousand U.S. dollars

continued

Drawn under The French Issuing Bank, Paris, France Documentary Credit
No. 12345 dated April 10, 2005.
Value received and charge same to account of
To The French Issuing Bank,   The American Exporter
        38 rue fuancois ler   Co. Inc. , Tampa
        75008, Paris, France   signature

The three immediate parties are:

(1) The Drawer

The drawer is the exporter.

(2) The Drawee

The drawee is a bank.

(3) The Payee

The payee is the exporter himself or his bank.

Similar to collection, letter of credit is also a reverse remittance. Therefore, the drawer of the draft under L/C will be the exporter instead of the importer. Unlike collection, letter of credit is a payment method based on banker's credit in the sense that the payment undertaking is giving by the bank on behalf of the importer. For this reason, the draft drawn under letter of credit should be drawn on a bank and can never be on an importer.

Sight payment credit and negotiation credit may or may not require a draft. In countries such as France, Spain and Sweden etc. , a simple receipt or a commercial invoice may take the place of a draft. A sight draft is normally required under sight payment credit and negotiable credit if a draft is required whereas a time draft is required under acceptance credit and draft is not applicable under deferred payment credit.

Draft drawn under letter of credit should be made in strict compliance with the terms and conditions of the credit. The following points deserve special attention:

(1) Drawn Clause

Under documentary credit, draft must contain a "drawn clause" indicating that the draft is established under a documentary credit. The drawn clause should be made in strict compliance with the stipulations in the credit and will usually indicate the name of the issuing bank, the issuing date and the credit No.

(2) The Amount

The draft amount is normally for the full 100% invoice value and should not be made exceeding the amount of the credit or the amount permissible under the credit. In the event that the invoice value exceeds the credit amount, the beneficiary should present a supplementary draft of the excess amount for collection. In certain special cases when commission charges are reflected on the credit, the draft amount will be made less than the invoice value with the balance being the commissions distracted from the invoice value.

The amount of the draft can also be made payable with interest at a certain percent per annum. The interest should be paid by the applicant.

Draft amount in words is exactly equal to its amount in figures and both amounts should indicate the currency as stipulated in the credit.

(3) Place of Issue

The place of issue should be made in consistence with the place of the issuer.

(4) Date of the Draft

The date of draft is the issuing date of the draft and is normally the negotiating date. It should be made no later than the latest date for presentation of documents stipulated in the credit but within the expiry date of the credit.

(5) Tenor of the Draft

The tenor of the draft indicates the time of payment and should be made in accordance with the terms of the credit on the following points:

∗ At sight

Payment should be effected immediately upon presentation or at sight.

∗ At ×× days after sight

Presentation is needed for acceptance as to the calculation of the due date. Payment will be effected at maturity. The word "after" is usually omitted in the credit and the accepting date is the date when the documents are found in compliance with the terms and conditions of the credit.

∗ At ×× days after date

Presentation is normally needed for acceptance in order to secure the drawee's liability on the draft.

∗ At ×× days after the date of shipment

In practice, the date of the draft is based on the date of shipment and the tenor of the date is normally made "30 days after the date of shipment".

∗ At ×× days after the B/L date

In practice, the B/L date is normally indicated on the tenor. For example, "at 30 days after B/L date dated 16/03/200×".

∗ At a fixed future date

Presentation for acceptance is normally required to secure the drawee's liability on the draft.

Attached the form of the draft under letter of credit in the following Figure 9.2:

Figure 9. 2　The draft under letter of credit（2）

Exchange for USD 100,000.00   03，July，2005
　　　① At thirty days date pay this first bill of exchange
or　　　② At thirty days after bill of lading date 15/6/05 pay this first bill of exchange
　　　（second unpaid ）to the order of ourselves the sum of USD one hundred thousand
　　　Drawn under ...
To Mellon Bank International，
　　New York

                                                          For seller/exporter
                                                          Hong Kong

（6）Payee

Generally speaking, the payee of the draft is either the beneficiary or the exporter's bank（the negotiating bank）.

When the payee is the beneficiary himself, the beneficiary will endorse the draft and present the drafts and documents to the negotiating bank for negotiation. In this case, endorsement should be made according to the stipulations of the credit. The endorsement in full will usually take the following form：

Pay to the order of

Overseas United Bank，Singapore

The ABC International Pte. Ltd. Singapore

<u>Signature</u>

After negotiation, the bank will become the holder in due course. If the negotiating bank chooses not to negotiate the drafts and documents, no endorsement is required and the bank will not be the holder in due course.

The advantage of making the negotiating bank the payee is that no endorsement is required. However, if the negotiating bank simply examines the documents without negotiating（giving value）, the beneficiary should better make himself the payee.

（7）The Drawee

Under documentary credit, the drawee should be made on a bank as required in the credit. The drawee can never be made on the applicant. Any draft drawn on the applicant will be considered as an additional document.

Under sight payment credit or acceptance credit, the drawee bank is the nominated paying or accepting bank. Under negotiating credit, the draft should be drawn on another bank rather than the negotiating bank. Normally, negotiating credit will stipulate the draft "drawn on us", which means that the drawee bank is the issuing bank.

（8）The Drawer

As letter of credit is a reverse remittance, the drawer should be the exporter/

beneficiary.

(9) Full Set

Drafts usually are made in duplicate to make a full set. In order to guard against lost in transit, the two parts will be sent separately with the first part indicating "Pay this first bill of exchange (Second bill of exchange being unpaid)" and the second part indicating "Pay this second bill of exchange (First bill of exchange being unpaid)".

(10) Other Terms

The endorsement should not be made in restrictive order and there should be no indication of "without recourse" either on the face or the back of the draft unless it is under special authorization to do so.

9.2 Commercial Invoice

9.2.1 Commercial invoice and its major items

A commercial invoice is the accounting document prepared by the seller to claim payment from the buyer for the value of goods and/or service being supplied. It gives the details of the goods, the payment method, the delivery terms and detailed breakdowns of the monetary amount due.

A commercial invoice serves as a basic document against which other documents such as drafts, transport documents, insurance documents and packing list are established. Commercial invoice can either take the form shown below or be made on the seller's letterhead with the wordings "commercial invoice" clearly indicated. It contains the following major items:

(1) Name and Address of the Seller

If the invoice is made on the seller's letterhead, this item can be omitted. The name and address in either form should be the same as those called for in the credit.

(2) Name and Address of the Buyer

The invoice must be made out to the L/C applicant with the name and address being in accordance with those appeared in the credit.

(3) The Issuing Date

The commercial invoice should be made no later than the latest date for presentation and within the expiry date of the credit, and it can be made earlier than the issuing date of the credit. In practice, the issuing date of the commercial invoice can be the earliest one compared with other documents.

(4) Description of Goods

Complete description of goods will normally include the quantity, packing and specification that should be made in compliance with those in the credit. Detailed description about the goods will be found in commercial invoice whereas the information will only appear in general terms in the credit and other documents.

For example: the goods is described as "Chunlan air-anditioner" in the credit, such description shall be shown exactly the same in the invoice. However, descriptions like "air-conditioner" will do in all other documents.

(5) Price and Price Terms

Price should be broken down into unit price and the seller should work out the total amount which represents the invoice value payable by the importer. Invoice value, unit price and quantity should agree with the credit stipulations. Banks are not responsible for checking the mathematical calculation.

The invoice value normally is the draft amount and is within the credit amount. In the event that the invoice value exceeds the credit amount, the draft amount will be made equal to the credit amount and thus be smaller than the invoice value. The difference between the invoice value and the draft amount will be collected through collection.

The words "about", "approximately" or similar wordings in connection with the amount, quantity or unit price stated in the credit are to be understood as allowing a difference not exceeding 10% less than the corresponding items they refer.

Price terms refer to the incoterms such as FOB, CIF and CIP, etc. The price term should be clearly indicated as different terms will affect the actual price of a transaction.

(6) Port of Loading and Port of Discharge

(7) Shipping Mark

Shipping mark is made for the purpose of easy handling and recognition by the carrier and the consignee. It normally contains a mark, the name of the port of discharge, package No and the country of origin and it should be subject to the stipulations on the credit, if any. There may not be a shipping mark for a certain shipment, and the column "marks and number" will be entered with "N. M. (No marks)" or simply be left blank. However, when a shipping mark is used, the same shipping mark will also appear in other documents such as packing list or bills of lading in order to tie them up.

(8) Payment Method

Payment method such as D/P, D/A or documentary credit should be indicated in the invoice. In the case of settlement by documentary credit, the same of the issuing bank, the L/C No. and the issuing date of the credit should be indicated in the commercial invoice.

(9) Name of the Vessel, Cost of Freight and Insurance

The name of the vessel should be entered in the blank after s. s/M. V. _____ . If the goods are consigned to air transportation, the name of the airliner and the flight number may be included.

The commercial invoice may also bear the breakdowns of the costs of freight and insurance. However, it is not always necessary for the seller to supply this information.

(10) Signature of the Exporter

Unless otherwise stipulated in the credit, invoice needs not to be signed.

9. 2. 2   Other types of invoice

1. Proforma invoice

The proforma invoice is a form of quotation made by the seller to a potential buyer. It is often required by the buyer so that an importer licence and / or foreign exchange permit will be approved by the authorities concerned. It differs from a commercial invoice in that the word "proforma" will appear thereon. Such invoice may serve as an invitation to the buyer to a place a firm order. It normally indicates the price and sales terms so that once accepted by the buyer there will be a firm contract to be made in accordance with the contents in the proforma. Details in the accepted proforma must be transposed identically to the commercial invoice, which is to be issued in due course. Quite frequently the seller is required to certify on his commercial invoice "that goods are in accordance with proforma invoice NO. ..."

Proforma invoices are also used where settlement is to be made.

(1) For advance payment i.e. cash payment is required before shipment.

(2) On consignment where goods are exported without a firm sales contract but placed in the hands of an agent to whom the proforma invoice will serve as a guide for his offer to the potential buyer.

(3) Subject to tender, where the proforma invoice will enable the buyer to make a salescontract at reasonable price and sales terms among a number of competitive suppliers.

2. Certified invoice

A certified invoice is an ordinary signed commercial invoice specifically certifying:

(1) That the goods are in conformity with a specific contract or a proforma invoice.

(2) That the goods are (or are not) from a specific country of origin.

(3) Any statement to be required by the buyer.

A certified invoice may be certified by the seller, or the chamber of commerce in the exporting country.

To serve different purposes, there are also other invoices, such as sample invoice, consignment invoice, receipt invoice, detailed invoice, etc. All of them are to be issued by the seller if and when the buyer needs them. However, there is another kind of invoice, namely the manufactures' invoice, to be issued in domestic currency by the manufacturer to the seller, which will be discussed in Chapter Fourteen.

9.3 Transport Documents

Transport documents mainly refer to marine bills of lading, seaway bills, airway bills, combined transport documents, inland transport way bills and parcel receipts.

9.3.1 Marine bills of lading

1. What is a marine bill of lading?

Put simply a bill of lading can be defined as a transport document which is signed by the carrier or his agent acknowledging the goods have been received for shipment to a particular destination and stating the terms on which the goods are to be carried. In addition to evidencing receipt of the goods and the contract of carriage, the marine bill of lading is also a document of title. The carrier will only release the cargo in exchange for the surrender of the original bill of lading.

2. Functions of a Bill of Lading

(1) A Receipt of Goods

A bill of lading serves as a receipt for goods shipped, acknowledging that the goods have been received in said quality, quantity and in apparent good order for the purpose of shipment on board a vessel. It is the responsibility of the carrier to deliver the goods accordingly to the consignee named in the bill(s) of lading.

(2) An Evidence of the Contract of Carriage

A bill of lading is a contract of carriage made between the carrier and the shipper. The detailed provisions will be made on the reverse of the document which stipulate the rights and responsibilities of the two parties. On one hand, it is the responsibility of the carrier to transport the goods by sea and make the delivery to the consignee. On the other hand, the obligation of the shipper is to consign the goods in apparent good order and in agreement with packing requirements of the shipment.

(3) A Document of Title

A bill of lading is a title document in the sense that the legal owner of the bill of lading is the legal owner of the goods. The carrier will only release the goods against the production of the original bill of lading. Original bills of lading are usually issued in sets of two, three or four (the number of originals should be indicated on the bill of lading). As any one original B/L will enable the possessor to obtain the goods, possession of a full set is required before ownership of the goods is secured. When a bill of lading is transferred, the ownership over the goods has also been transferred. As a result, constructive delivery has come into being on the basis that bills of lading have become title documents.

3. Parties of a Bill of Lading

The carrier and the shipper are the two parties on the bill of lading and they are the basic parties to such a document. In addition to these two, other parties will include the consignee, the notify party and the transferee/holder.

4. Contents of a Bill of Lading

A bill of lading normally contains the following items:

(1) The name of the shipping company (the carrier).

(2) The name of the shipper, who is usually the exporter or the exporter's agent.

(3) The name of the consignee.

(4) The notify party.

When a B/L is made out to order without the importer shown as the consignee, information of the importer or his agent should be shown in the notify party, otherwise the notify party should be left blank.

(5) The name of the carrying vessel and the voyage No.

(6) The two ports.

One port is called the port of receipt, the port of loading or the port of shipment and the other port is referred to as the port of destination, the port of discharge or the port of delivery. When a B/L is made for port to port shipment, the name of the two ports only will serve the purpose. On other occasions, however, a B/L may be made for combined transport shipment where door to door service is provided. In this case, a place of receipt, usually the premises of the exporter and a final place of delivery, usually the premises of the importer, are mentioned in addition to the two ports.

(7) Marks and numbers.

The marks and numbers should be made consistent with those on the other documents such as the invoice or the packing list. The same marks and numbers will appear on the boxes, cartons or cases where the goods are contained so as to indicate that they are covered by the same bill of lading.

(8) Description of goods.

A general or a brief description of goods will do. If the transaction is under L/C, the credit number, the name of the issuing bank and the credit issuing date should be indicated here.

(9) Total packages.

This shows how many boxes/cartons/cases into which goods are packed.

(10) Freight charges.

Freight charges can be made as prepaid or collects. Freight prepaid indicates that the freight costs have already been paid by the exporter, which is usually the case under the incoterms like C&F and CIF. Freight collect means that payment of the sea-freight is due to the importer and it is to be collected on arrival at the destination, which is usually the case under FOB.

(11) Number of original B/L.

This indicates how many original bills of lading will make a full set. In practice, full set may contain 2,3 or 4 originals. An original bill of lading is one which is signed by the ship's master, or by an agent of the shipping company. If it is an original, the very word "original" should be clearly indicated thereon so as to distinguish itself form a copy. Shipping companies often issue unsigned copies of bill of lading for record purposes, these unsigned copies are not documents of title.

(12) The signature of the carrier.

For a bill of lading to be original, it should be signed on behalf of the shipping company. Shipping companies often issue unsigned copies of the bill of lading for record purpose. These unsigned copies are not title documents and can not be taken as original bills of lading.

(13) The B/L issuing date.

This is the date when the shipping company receives the goods foe shipment and/or when the goods are loaded on board the ship.

If the transaction is under L/C, the B/L date should be made consistent with the stipulations of the credit and is usually be made between the invoice date and the latest date of shipment.

5. Types of Bill of Lading

There are many different types of bill of lading according to different criteria:

(1) Shipped on board bill of lading

It is a bill of lading evidencing that the goods have been actually shipped on a named vessel. Most bill of lading forms are already printed as shipped bill of lading and commence with the wording "Shipped in apparent good order and condition ...", which confirms the goods are actually on board the vessel. The date of issuance of the bill of lading will be deemed to be the date of loading on board and the date of shipment.

(2) Received for shipment bill of lading

It is a bill of lading merely confirming that the goods have been handed over to the ship owner and are in his custody. The cargo may be in his dock warehouse or even inland and so the word "shipped" does not appear on the bill of lading. It is just a receipt, not a document of title to the goods.

(3) Direct bill of lading

It is issued when the goods are shipped by one vessel direct from the loading port to the destination port without transshipment on the route.

(4) Transhipment bill of lading

It is usually issued by the shipping company if there is no direct service between two ports, but the shipowner is prepared to transship the cargo from one vessel to another at a named transshipment port at his expense.

(5) Through bill of lading

A through bill of lading resembles a Combined Transport Document except that a through bill of lading is issued by the first carrier who will only be responsible for his part of the journey only.

(6) Clean bill of lading

The wording "in apparent good order and condition" is usually stated on each bill of lading. If this statement is not modified by the shipowner, such a bill of lading is regarded as "clean" or "unclaused", that is, it does not bear any clause declaring a defective condition of the goods or its packaging.

(7) Unclean bill of lading

If the shipowner does not agree with any of the statements made in the bill of lading he will add a clause to this effect, thereby causing the bill of lading to be termed as "unclean", "foul" or "claused".

(8) Liner or regular bill of lading

The liner bill of lading is issued by a shipping company in respect of the goods carried on regular line vessels with scheduled runs and reserved berths at destination.

(9) Charter party bill of lading

When a vessel, usually a "tramp" steamer, is leased by a shipper for a voyage or for a round voyage or for a designated time, it is referred to as "chartered" in shipping terms. Charter party bill of lading is issued when a vessel is chartered by a hirer and this vessel does not necessarily adhere to a very strict schedule and may make unscheduled calls at various ports on the way to the ultimate destination.

(10) Named consignee bill of lading

A straight bill of lading indicated consigned to a named consignee.

(11) Bearer order bill of lading

A bearer order bill of lading is made out to bearer. It is also referred to as open bill of lading. This type of bill of lading is negotiable by mere delivery without endorsement. In practice, it is rarely used because of its higher degree of risk.

(12) Order bill of lading

An order bill of lading refers to the demonstrative order bill of lading. This type of bill can be made to order, to the order of shipper, to the order of the issuing bank and to the order of the importer. An order bill of lading can be transferred by endorsement and delivery.

6. Bill of lading Act (Maritime Law)

There are two acts playing an important role in the development of bills of lading: one is the Bill of Lading Act, 1985 and the other is International Convention for the Unification of Certain Rules of Law Relating to Bills of Lading signed at Brussels by 26 countries on August 24, 1924, namely The Hague Act or Rules, which is now applicable to more than fifty countries. The Bills of Lading Act, 1855 established the principle of transferability, permitting the transfer of a bill of lading from the holder to a person to whom the property in the goods passes, together with any rights and liabilities incorporated in the document. Visby Rules signed at Brussels in 1968 somewhat amended The Hague Rules and came in force in 1977 applicable to 16 countries. As the Hague Rules are apparently partial to the interests of the carrier, the shippers propose to amend it. In 1978 a meeting was held in Hamburg where "U. N. Convention on the Carrier of Goods by Sea 1978" namely the Hamburg Rules, was passed. It will come into force when approved by the government of the twentieth country. The responsibility and liability of the carrier in The Hamburg Rules are increased and so the interests of both the shipper and the carrier are more or less impartially protected. The bill of lading clause stipulated by China Ocean Shipping Company is mainly subject to The Hague Rules, such as "The responsibility of the carrier shall commence from the time when the goods are loaded on board the ship and shall not be liable for loss of or damage to the goods before loading and after discharging from the vessel", whereas under the Hamburg Rules "The responsibility of the carrier for the goods covers the period during which the carrier is in charge of the goods at the port of loading, during the carriage and at the port of discharge. From the time he has taken over the goods until the time he has delivered the goods."

9.3.2 Airway bill

1. What is Airway bill?

The air carrier bill of lading is known as an airway bill or a consignment note, which is a document evidencing shipment or dispatch or receipt of goods. Each airline furnishes its own distinctive airway bill but in general, all airway bills are similar in contents, showing the name and address of the consignee.

2. Functions of AWB

Similar to a seaway bill, an air transport document only performs two functions, both as a receipt of goods and as a contract of carriage. For this reason, there is no such a thing as a bill of lading with regard to air transport and the only air transport document can be issued is an airway bill or an air consignment note.

3. Contents of AWB

(1) Date of dispatch

(2) Signature of carrier or agent

(3) Transhipment

(4) Full set of originals

4. International Rules of AWB

The liability of the carrier in most countries is governed by the Convention for the Unification of Certain Rules Relating to International Carriage by Air, signed at Warsaw, Poland in 1929, popularly known as the Warsaw Convention. The carrier is liable for the loss of, or damage to the goods unless he can prove that he and his agent have taken all necessary measures to avoid the loss or damage, or that the loss or damage was due to the negligent pilotage or handling of the aircraft or the negligence in aerial navigation.

9.3.3   Railway bill

When the goods are sent by railway, a railway bill or cargo receipt will be issued. It is subject to the International Convention for the Transport of Goods by Rail (CIM) established in some form in 1893 with additional protocol made in 1970 after various revision to meet the needs of the international trade of the modern time.

A railway bill will contain the following major items:

(1) Date and place of issue

(2) Name and address of the shipper, consignee and carrier

(3) Place of the original railway station and the place designated for delivery

(4) General description of goods with their packing method, quantity in weight or in measurement

(5) Carriage charges

(6) Instructions for customs and other formalities

(7) Signature of the carrier or its agent

Box 9.1

CDCS

Introduction

CDCS is benchmarked at Level 3 and is the professional certification that will enable documentary credit practitioners to demonstrate specialist knowledge and application of the skills required for competent practice. The CDCS program has been developed in consultation with industry experts to ensure that the certification reflects best practice. It has been developed in partnership by the Institute of Financial Services and the BAFT – IFSA. It is endorsed by the International Chamber of Commerce.

Benefits

- To improve one's practical knowledge and understanding of the complex issues associated with documentary credit practice
- As part of one's continuing professional development
- To enhance one's career
- To increase one's expertise and professional value
- To gain access to the professional designation CDCS
- To demonstrate a level of expertise that is accredited worldwide

Requirements

There are no entry requirements to undertake the CDCS examination, however, it is strongly recommended that candidates have a minimum of three years documentary credit experience. Candidates who wish to become Certified and use the professional designation "CDCS" must submit a letter of recommendation from an individual in a senior position to verify their experience. Membership in the Institute, BAFT – IFSA or any other organization is not required.

Key Words

Documentary Bill, Commercial Invoice, Certified Invoice, Proforma Invoice, Marine Bills of Lading, Airway Bill, Railway Bill

Questions

1. What are the differences between a normal draft and a Draft under L/C?

2. What are the main items should be contained in a commercial invoice?

3. What are the functions of a bill of lading?

4. What documents must the Beneficiary present in order to receive payment under the credit?

CHAPTER 10 FORFAITING AND FACTORING

Learning Objectives

- To Learn the concept and characteristics of forfaiting
- To understand the advantages and disadvantages of forfaiting
- To learn the corcept and the procedure of factoring
- To compare the difference between forfaiting and factoring

10.1 Forfaiting

10.1.1   What is forfaiting

Basically, forfaiting is the purchase without recourse of debt instruments due to mature in the future and arising from the provision of goods and services. The English term "forfaiting" comes from the French "a forfeit" meaning "outright" or "all in" conveying the idea of some sort of package deal. It also conveys the idea of "forfaiting" —meaning the giving up of all rights to a payment under a debt instrument.

In practice, forfaiting is a specific form of export finance which enables the exporter to offer his client medium term fixed term financing with which to fund the order. At the same time it offers the exporter a means of immediate cash payment as soon as he has fulfilled his contract, passing on all risks of non-payment to the purchaser.

In short, forfaiting is possibly one of the most flexible and efficient means of finance available to exporters today. However, it is remarkable that despite the numerous advantages this service provides to both buyer and seller, forfaiting has yet to be fully developed in the United States even though that country is one of the largest commercial markets in the world with one of the most advanced financial markets.

Any estimate of the size of the forfaiting market is no more than a guess. Whilst the market has grown considerably over the past years only a small portion of the total medium-term finance provided world wide is based on forfaiting. Perhaps there exists some USD10 billion of forfaiting paper today, of which some 30% is being traded at any one time.

10.1.2   History of forfaiting

Forfaiting, as it is known today, began to develop after the Second World War and made rapid progress in the 1950's and 1960's when the seller's market for capital goods gradually changed to the buyer's market as importers began to demand credit periods exceeding 90 or 180 days.

In addition, this period saw the development of trade barriers and the Cold War era. The resurgence of trade between the West and the Eastern European nations coupled with growing importance of developing nations in Africa and South America created financial problems for the West European exporter, where by the existing banks were unable to offer the services that the exporters of the day required.

The Swiss banking community, pioneered forfaiting to finance the purchase of grain sold mainly by the United States to East European Countries. It soon became clear that forfaiting was a rapidly developing field requiring its own specialist departments within the traditional banking framework.

The pre-eminence of the Swiss in forfeit finance has continued, however, the business has spread throughout Western Europe, whereby the United Kingdom, Germany and Italy play a major role in the forfaiting market.

Historical factors resulting in the growth of forfaiting are:

(1) Developments/changes in world trade in the 1950's and 1960's.

(2) Shift from a seller's market to a buyer's market.

(3) Need for medium term finance (previously 90 to 180 days).

(4) Industrialization in developing nations.

(5) Establishment of trade barriers "Cold War".

(6) Inability of banks to meet financing needs of exporters.

10. 1. 3   Characteristics of forfaiting

Characteristics of forfaiting are no recourse to the exporter/endorser, fixed rate financing, bank guarantee and simple straightforward documentation. The above four characteristics are the keys to forfaiting and should be looked into in certain depth. Firstly, however, it is beneficial to look at the prerequisites of a forfaiting transaction. Basically, if the following circumstances prevail, forfaiting may be applied:

(1) The exporter has agreed to extend his customer credit for a period of any time from 90 days to 10 years.

(2) The exporter has agreed to stage payments over the credit period.

(3) A security, the exporter has called for a bank guarantee or letter of credit or avalised bills of exchange or notes.

(4) The amount of the transaction is more than say USD100,000.

Box 10.1

A Simplified Forfaiting Transaction

The buyer and seller conclude a contract covering a used printing machine sales price at USD1,000,000. The buyer requires 2 year financing but is able to repay the financing in four installments of USD250,000 each every six months. As security for the transaction, the buyer requires a bank aval/guarantee. Therefore, the transaction can be structured as following:

The structure of bills of exchange

4 single avalised bills of exchange at USD 250,000 to mature at 6 month intervals		
Bill No. 1	USD250,000	Maturity 6 months from shipment
Bill No. 2	USD250,000	Maturity 12 months from shipment
Bill No. 3	USD250,000	Maturity 18 months from shipment
Bill No. 4	USD250,000	Maturity 24 months from shipment

Each bill being avalised by a prime bank.

The exporter approaches a bank seeking "a forfeit" finance. The bank agrees to purchase — without recourse to the exporter — the avalised bills of exchange at a fixed interest rate, say 8% p. a. straight.

The seller draws the bills of exchange and sends them to the buyer for acceptance. After accepting the bills, the buyer obtains the required bank aval and returns the aval and returns the avalised bills to the seller.

After shipment, the seller presents the bills along with evidence of shipment to the bank discounting the bills and pays the discounted proceeds to the exporter straight away. The exporter can then close his books on this transaction. The forfeiter will then, on his own account, present the bill at maturity to the guarantor for payment.

(1) Size of the transaction. It is wrong to believe that forfaiting can only be applied to high value transactions. This view is maintained due to forfaiting's association with capital goods. It is easily possible to obtain financing for transactions of no more than USD100,000, yet as a general rule, the financing charges (in percentage terms) for a smaller transaction will often be higher than those of larger transactions. This merely reflects the "cost" of processing smaller transactions whereby the actual paper work is almost identical for a small or a larger transaction. Also, it is common practice to be charge a "flat fee" on a smaller deal.

(2) Instruments used in forfaiting. Probably the most common forfeting instrument is the avalised bill of exchange — the instrument itself is simple and the laws relating to the instrument are clear. Other instruments seen in forfeting are promissory notes, bank guarantees and letters of credit. Book receivables can also be discounted a forfeit.

(3) Risk elements in forfaiting. In any cross border export transaction, the seller enters into a number of risks, and it is quite surprising that many exporters are not fully aware of the risks that they actually take on. The risks connected with any type of export are usually defined as follows:

a. Political risk. Extraordinary state measures or political incidents like war, revolution, invasion or civil unrest can lead to losses for the exporter.

b. Exchange risk. One of the risks in forfaiting is that of payment in a currency other than the exporter's local currency. Movements in exchange rates can have the effect of changing the exporter's contract value over night.

c. Transfer risk. This risk covers the inability or unwillingness of states or government to effect payment in the currency agreed upon — including the risk of moratorium.

d. Commercial risk. This risk covers the inability or unwillingness of the obligor guarantor to pay and applies to all forms of credit as well as forfaiting. The danger that commitments will not be honoured requires in each case an evaluation of the creditworthiness of the guarantor.

e. Interest risk. This risk covers the potential losses that may arise as a result of a movement in interest rates.

(4) Types of trade financed via forfaiting. As stated, forfaiting developed shortly after the Second World War. At the start debts for commodities such as grain were forfeited but this soon developed into the forfaiting of payment obligations for capital goods.

Commodity transactions are still regularly forfeited for periods of up to 12 months, however, capital goods can be forfeited for periods exceeding 5 years. It must also be remembered that payments for services can also be financed via forfaiting. Indeed, it is virtually true that any term sale can be forfaited.

10. 1. 4   Advantages and disadvantages of forfaiting

(1) Advantages to the exporter

①A forfeit finance is a fixed rate finance. ②Finance is provided by the forfeiter without recourse to the exporter. ③The exporter receives immediate cash payment upon delivery of the goods or services provided. Hence, greater business liquidity, reducing bank borrowings or freeing financial resources for reinvestment or other purposes. ④The exporter does not need to monitor the debt outstandings or administer the transaction after he has received the discounted proceeds. ⑤The forfeiter, not the exporter, bears the risks of currency and interest rate movements, transfer risk and default. ⑥ A forfeiter finance is negotiable for each of the exporter's trade transactions; he does not need to commit any particular volume of business as with factoring. ⑦The exporter can ascertain very quickly indeed whether forfeit finance is available for a particular transaction. In fact, assuming that the guarantor is acceptable to the forfeiter, the forfaiting terms can be established in a matter of hours. ⑧Documentation is very simple and straightforward. ⑨Forfaiting transactions are "confidential", unlike commercial loans where "tombstone" advertisements are commonplace. ⑩The exporter can obtain an option to finance at a fixed rate from the forfeiter. He can therefore build financing costs into his contract price and, if necessary, the costs of any foreign exchange cover he need to take a swap into his own currency.

(2) Advantages to the importer

①Documentation for the transaction is simple and can be quickly arranged. ②The importer obtains fixed rate extended credit. ③Borrowing to pay for his purchase as what he receives will utilize credit facilities; although he must arrange for a bank guarantee/aval which will also be allocated against a credit facility that is usually weighted lower.

(3) Disadvantages to the importer

①The bank aval/guarantee will be allocated against the buyer's credit line.②The importer will have to pay a guarantee fee. ③ As bills of exchange are abstract instruments giving an absolute obligation to pay, any dispute regarding the contracted goods will be irrelevant to the payment. ④ Forfaiting can be more expensive than various Government financing schemes.

(4) Advantages to the forfeiter

①Again, documentation is simple and can be easily compiled; there are no 30 page loan agreements as in commercial lending. ② There exists a strong "secondary market" for forfaiting paper. Thus, a forfeiter is able to sell down transactions in order to free up limits for new business, whilst earning fees/interest on the difference between the purchase and sales price of a transaction. ③The assets purchased are easily transferable as to title so that trading them in the secondary market is possible. ④As the forfeiter absorbs all the risks involved in the transaction, the margins charged are usually attractive from the forfeiter's point of view.

(5) Disadvantages to the forfaiter

①The forfeiter has no recourse to anyone else in the event of default. ② The forfeiter must be familiar with the laws and regulations governing the validity of bills of exchange, avals and guarantees in the various countries with which his export clients will be doing business. ③ The forfeiter must check the creditworthiness of the guarantor. ④ The forfeiter bears the funding/interest rate risk throughout the transaction.

10.1.5 Types of instrument

When looking at forfaiting transaction, it is easiest to refer to bills of exchange and promissory notes as the debt instruments involved in forfaiting. However, there are a number of other types of instrument which can be used for forfaiting. The important point to remember is that whatever the debt instrument forfeited, the forfeiter will insist that to any underlaying contract upon whose performance payment is contingent. Any contract disputes affect the exporter and importer and forfeiter cannot be involved. He must be able to receive payment without dispute or delay.

(1) Bills of exchange / Promissory notes. Whereas a bill of exchange is drawn by the seller on the buyer, a promissory note is a promise by the buyer to pay the seller. Apart from the simplicity of both instruments, there is one other reason to explain the predominant use of these two debt instruments in forfaiting, namely the establishment of the International Convention for Commercial Bills at the Geneve Conference of 1930. This convention agreed a legal framework regarding bills and notes which is basically a code of practice adopted by the signatory nations. Not all countries, however, were signatories — the United Kingdom for instance — but the practical implications of this for UK traders or bankers are of little significance. The important point is that the Convention added to the domination of bills and notes as debt instruments.

Both bills and notes are simple documents, easily transferable and almost universally accepted. Promissory notes will sometimes have a slight advantage over bills of exchange, since in the case of the latter it may prove difficult for the drawer to release himself from liability under the bill A promissory note, on the other hand, may simply be endorsed by the exporter as "without recourse".

Both documents and instruments have the major advantage in forfaiting in that each repayment can be evidenced by way of a separate document.

Going back to the process of transferring the instrument from the drawer (the exporter) to the forfeiter, both bills and notes are transferred by way of endorsement. This simple process of signing the reverse of the instrument is accompanied by adding the words "without recourse". The intention of the exporter/endorser in doing this is to free himself from any liability under the bill or note. If the exporter did not use these words, or others to the same effect, the endorser would certainly remain liable as a guarantor of the obligation.

Article 9 of the Geneve Convention states that the drawer guarantees both acceptance and payment. He may release himself from guaranteeing acceptance, but any stipulation by which he release himself from guaranteeing payment is deemed not to be written. Thus the drawer may not be liable on a bill as endorser but will always be liable as its drawer. This article does not apply to promissory notes. Indeed under the Convention, the endorser of a promissory note has the legal right to free himself of any liability by the use of the words "without recourse".

(2) Letters of credit. Usance letters of credit account for a large proportion of for feting transactions. Basically, any usance letter of credit with a maturity from say 30 days to say a number of years and with an amount of more than USD 100,000 may be suitable for a forfaiting transaction. Here, a forfeiter must be particularly careful that the payment obligation given by the issuing bank is "clean" and that once credit conform documents have been presented and taken up, payment will be forthcoming without any further conditions having to be fulfilled for example compliance certificates/test completion certificates etcetera.

(3) Avals/Guarantees. Since the exporter is released from all risks in a forfaiting transaction, the forfeiter must seek some form of security that the obligation to pay will be honoured. The most usual forms of security involved in a forfaiting transaction are bank guarantees and bank avals. An aval is an irrevocable and unconditional undertaking issued by a bank or financial institution (the buyer's banker) which is written on the actual instrument itself and binds the avalist to payment. The avalist takes the place of the party which has committed itself to make payment.

10.1.6 "Without Recourse" clause

It is essential when looking at forfaiting to look at the meaning of the words "without recourse" and how far these absolve the seller of responsibility. Essentially these words are the basis of the contract between the seller of the transaction and the forfeiter. A lawyer therefore tends to say that the subject matter of the sale, the bill, is irrelevant and looks at the words as a standard form of exclusion clause applied to the contract of sale.

The meaning and legal implications of the expression "without recourse" is very broad indeed, yet legal decisions have shown that these words do not totally absolve the seller of all his obligations under the instrument. The obligation of the exporter in a forfeit transaction is to sell a valid claim relating to a valid transaction and the words "without recourse" do not limit this obligation.

For example, were the seller of an instrument to claim that the bill was trade backed, i.e. export related, when in fact it was a financial transaction, the words "without recourse" would not absolve the seller of misrepresentation.

When the words do is exclude any liability on the drawer of the bill and any seller of the bill if the bill is not honoured at maturity because the acceptor or guarantor are insolvent and unable to pay or if payment is prohibited by exchange control or government regulations imposed subsequent to the conclusion of the transaction.

10.1.7 Discounting methods

The first thing to clarify when looking at discounting methods is the difference between "straight discount" and "discount to yield", which are two types of discounting methods used in forfaiting. A simple example best illustrates this:

Straight Discount

Straight Discount	10% per annum
Amount	USD1,000,000.00
Maturity	360 days
Interest	USD100,000.00
Discounted sum	USD900,000.00

If the bill is repayable in one year time, this represents a yield of 100/900 or 11.11% p.a. compounded annually.

Hence, a straight discount of 10% p. a. can be termed as "a discount at a rate corresponding to a yield of 11.11% compounded annually" or more simply "a discount to yield of 11.11%".

Straight discount involves dividing the principal amount into equal amounts, according to the repayment plan and then calculating the interest on the declining balance over time.

The above shows a simple yield calculation. In more complex transactions of the discount to yield are much more sophisticated and are normally computed by using software programmes. The formular is however worth nothing:

$$D = \frac{V \times (S+G)}{100} \times \frac{d}{N}$$

D=discount	G=number of grace days
V=face value of bill	d=interest rate
S=number of days to maturity	N=days in year(360)

10.2 Factoring

Factoring is the sale of an account receivable to a third party, called a "factor". This type of trade finance has been used long and extensively in the garment industry with in the U. S. In the factoring model, the seller provides the factor with a list of its clients. The factor approves (or not) the names on the list, for certain transaction amounts or limits, within the payment term structure of the industry or as agreed between the seller and the factor. The seller ships, invoices, and sells the invoices to the factor, with or without recourse. The invoice directs the buyer to pay to the factor, or to a mail box controlled by the factor. At maturity of the invoice the factor pays the seller the face amount less the factoring fee. If the seller needs to finance the invoice, the factor will make a loan against the invoice or discount the invoice. The factoring fee still applies. Or, the seller can finance this factored invoice with another financial institution.

The factor will provide its service either with recourse or without recourse. Under "with recourse" factoring the factor retains the right to claim back on the seller in the event the buyer does not pay. This is somewhat similar to expensive accounts receivable finance.

Under "without recourse" factoring, the factor buys the account receivable after it has determined that the goods conform and have been accepted, and the buyer has both the intent and the capacity to pay. The factor looks at four hurdles client risk, the seller is viable and capable of performance, debtor risk, that the buyer has the capacity and intent to pay, transaction risk, that performance did occur and the client really has a right to payment, and default risk, a procedure to assure the remittance is sent to the factor.

International or export factoring uses the same logic. The exporter gets approval of accounts prior to exporting. The sale is made on open account or documentary collection terms. The factor purchases the account receivable with recourse or without recourse to the exporter. In effect, the factor is financing the buyer. Export factoring activity has been increasing at large and smaller commercial banks and finance companies, because of improved information on foreign companies (the debtors), and improved understanding of the risks involved. Export factoring is similar to the sale of accounts receivable mentioned above. However in concept the factor is financing the buyer and makes its decision based on the credit worthiness of the buyer rather than the seller.

10.2.1 Definition of export factoring

Export Factoring is basically a service provided to sellers, whereby the exporter, having closed a commercial contract with a domestic or overseas buyer, will submit his invoices to the factoring company, who will in turn advance against the invoices to the exporter.

Thus the "factor" is collecting the debt in accordance with the terms of the transaction and at the same time providing the exporter with cash flow. Factoring can either bear ranged on a with recourse or a without recourse basis.

The advantages of export factoring are in some respects similar to the advantages gained in forfaiting. However, whereas forfaiting tends to be related to one-off deals, factoring is an ongoing "package service". To exporters, factoring performs three functions:

(1) Debtor administration and collection.

The factor will assume all debtor administration and collection responsibilities on behalf of the exporter. This includes: book keeping, including regular reporting to the exporter; collection of outstanding receivables and, if required, legal procedures.

(2) Financing.

The factor will advance between 80% and 90% of all agreed invoices upon presentation of the invoices by the exporter to the factor. The balance will be remitted to the exporter upon receipt of the proceeds by the factor at maturity.

(3) Credit risk protection.

The factor will allocate "credit limits" to the exporter on a buyer basis, up to which amounts the exporter is covered in the event that the buyer fails to pay the invoiced amount at maturity. Hence, factoring provides the exporter with a type of credit insurance.

10. 2. 2   The cost of factoring

Factoring charges are calculated based upon the turnover of the exporter; the payment terms granted by the exporter; the number of invoices raised by the exporter and the quality of the debtors. On average, the factor will charge the exporter a factoring fee of between 1% and 3% of the invoice value on top of the refinancing cost to the factor.

10. 2. 3   Types of factoring program

There are two basic types of factoring program:

(1) Maturity factoring.

The client does not draw funds in advance of the maturity date of accounts receivables sold to the factor.

a. Collected fund basis. Proceeds are to be remitted on a pay as paid basis, or as collected by the factor to the client.

b. Average due-date basis. Funds are to be remitted to the client on a fixed date based upon previous collection experience with each account. This method of settlement is adjusted regularly based on performance.

(2) Discount factoring.

With financing available, the client can draw advances against accounts receivables sold to the factor prior to maturity date.

10. 2. 4   Factoring working procedure

A factoring agreement will be signed after the assessment of the exporter has been made by the factor based on the written information including the business conditions, the balance sheet and other required information presented by the exporter and the investigation made by the factor.

In a factoring business, the factor assumes financial and administration responsibility for the invoice, including credit cover against customer's in solvency. Generally 80% of the invoice face value is immediately available to the seller. The balance is payable within a fixed number of days after the invoice date or when the customer makes his payment. The procedure usually adopted is as following Figure 10.1:

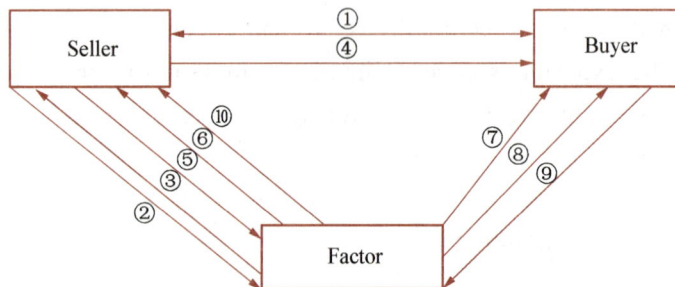

Figure 10.1   Factoring working procedure

① contract concluded between the buyer and the seller on open account terms.
② application forced it approval.
③ credit assessment of customer and credit limit/cover agreed.
④ goods delivered and invoice made out.
⑤ copy of invoice forwarded.
⑥ sales ledger updated and up to 80% of invoice value available.
⑦ status of credit or notified.
⑧ collection activity when invoices fall due.
⑨ payment.
⑩ sales ledger updated and balance paid.

10.2.5   Advantages to the seller

(1) The seller gets access to finance linked to his current levels of business. By contrast, the amount of money available under a traditional overdraft arrangement is based on the historic balance sheet ratios. When accompany is up against its overdraft limit and yet confident of its sales prospects, the factoring can finance a higher level of sales, without requiring any injection of new equity from external sources or any additional guarantees from the management.

(2) The seller can get assistance from the factor by latter's providing an assessment of the credit worthiness of the overseas buyers as well as by latter's offering credit protection and collection service.

(3) The seller will be able to offer competitive open account selling terms in the highly competitive market.

(4) Seller's bad debts will be eliminated.

10. 2. 6　Functions of factoring

(1) Finance

In the factoring contract the factor agrees to pay the seller a substantial proportion, say 80% of the value of the qualifying Account Receivables (A/R) as soon as they come into existence. The seller will receive the balance when the factor has collected from the buyer.

The advantages of factoring finance are as follows:

a. Injection of working capital to finance expansion;

b. More finance available than from bank borrowing;

c. Suppliers can be paid promptly so the seller can double benefit from reducing costs by taking advantage of prompt payment discounts and improving his standing with suppliers;

d. No loss of equity and no formal funding limit.

(2) Sales Ledger Administration

The factoring will take the buyer accounts onto his book and will update these accounts with all transactions-invoices, credit note payment, etc..

(3) Collection of A/R

The factor's administration system is designed to prompt the buyers for payment systematically by letter and to give the collection staff the necessary information to seek payment from the buyer.

(4) Credit Cover

If the buyer defaults in his payment, the factor will pay the seller normally 100% of the credit covering A/R when the buyer is insolvent or the A/R is 90 days past the due date on the invoice. This arrangement is referred to as "without recourse".

Box 10.2

Invoice Factoring Case Study

Imagine your business has the chance to sign a new customer that would double your revenue, but you don't have enough cash to hire the new employees required to support the customer.

This is the exact problem recently faced by a client of ours, Florida Staffing, a U. S. staffing company. (While this factoring case is real, Florida Staffing is a fictitious company name, in accordance with a privacy agreement with the real company).

Florida Staffing originally came to Factor King when they were presented with the opportunity to take on a new customer that would increase their overall revenue from 150K to 300K/month. Since allowing the potential business to simply slip away was not an option Florida Staffing knew they needed help.

After Florida Staffing completed our easy approval process, their customer was contacted and subsequently agreed to terms of net 30 and to be billed at the end of each month.

Using Factor King allowed Florida Staffing to factor the first invoice the same day they sent the invoice to the customer. This enabled Florida Staffing to receive the money they would have had to wait up to 60 days for-further enabling them to pay employees for the next 30 days. This would have been impossible without Factor King's services.

After the first invoice it was smooth sailing. Each and every month Florida Staffing received advances that allowed them to be cash positive. Additionally — and most importantly-they were able to grow because they could continue to take on new business knowing that Factor King would be buying the invoice, paying Florida Staffing the cash, and handling all collections for them. Florida Staffing never had any issue paying their employees as business grew.

What factoring did was to allow Florida Staffing to keep their employees happy and their customers free from burdening collection calls … all while growing the staffing company on a continuous basis.

Factor King has now been working with Florida Staffing for a little over a year. And when they started with FK their receivables were about 150k/month. Now, Florida Staffing brings in over 650K/month! And they now take on new customers that no so long ago would have been out of the question.

What this factoring case study proves is that factoring is not only for businesses that run into a cash crunch, but more often for small and medium sized businesses, it provides a way for them to seize business opportunities that allow them to grow in ways they would have never thought possible.

Key Words

Forfaiting, Without Recourse Forfaiter, Factoring, Maturity Factoring, Discount Factoring

Questions

1. What is forfaiting and what is factoring?
2. What does the "without recourse" clause mean?
3. What functions does factoring perform?
4. What is the working procedure of factoring?

CHAPTER 11 OTHER FINANCE AND SETTLEMENT METHOD

Learning Objectives

- To understand the means of import trade finance: shipping guarantee and trust receipts
- To understand the means of export trade finance: packing loan and bill discount
- To understand the defination and procedure of a traveler's cheque and credit card

11.1 Import Trade Finance

11.1.1　Shipping guarantee

It is rather common for the goods to arrive at importer's country earlier than the documents by mail if the distance between trade countries is not far. The importer then needs a shipping guarantee issued by the bank to take over the goods. The importer will get the documents from the issuing bank by returning the shipping guarantee.

By issuing the shipping guarantee, the bank will bear the risk of non-payment and losing the goods title, and stand the loss claim from the shipping company due to its goods releasing without obtaining the Bill of Lading.

Therefore the bank must require the importer to fulfill his obligations as follows before issuing such shipping guarantee:

(1) Transfer the fund as per the invoice in copy into an escrow account of the issuing bank.

(2) Present copies of Bill of Lading and invoice to the issuing bank.

(3) Waive the right of rejecting the documents even if there are discrepancies.

(4) Redeem the shipping guarantee from the shipping company by original Bill of Lading to return to the bank within 7 working days after the arrival of the original Bill of Lading.

(5) Be fully responsible for any loss of the shipping guarantee issued by the bank. Yet, all these above mentioned can not fully ensure the bank to bee free from risks, because there is a possibility that the third party who holds the original Bill of Lading to take goods does not make a presentation or the bank does not receive the Bill of Lading from the negotiating bank.

11.1.2　Trust receipts (T/Rs)

A trust receipts is a kind of import financing facility provide by a bank. A issuing bank is obliged to pay upon the documents that complied with the letter of credit. Yet sometimes importers have shortage of cash to effect payment to get the documents to take the goods. However the importers require the issuing bank to lend the Bill of Lading to him and take the goods under the goods title held by the bank. The importer will fulfill his obligation fir payment under the letter of credit after he sells the goods.

A trust receipts is a kind of credit line granted by the bank to the importer. The bank bears risk of losing the goods while it grants authority to the importer to handle the goods on its behalf. Thus, the bank must check the creditworthiness of the importer and take measures for risk mitigation in the operation of trust receipt. And the operation of trust receipt is on case basis. For example, T/R allows the importer to clear the customs and the goods. T/R is used in the way that the goods are transported by air. The bank will issue a release order for importer to take goods from the airline company in the case when the goods arrive earlier than the documents.

When the bank prepares the trust receipt for the importer, it must specify the amount of the goods clearly, because the importer may have the same kind of goods financed by some other bank. In addition, the bank should ask the importer to provide his financial statement and copies of packing lists and invoices. In the receivable items, the importer should clarify his receivables under each letter of credit issued by different banks.

Upon the legal sense of a trust receipt, it is regards as the combination of mortgage transfer and indirect agency. The bank will entrust the importer to handle the goods under its name and the importer gets the right to sell the goods with the trust receipt.

11.2 Export Trade Finance

11. 2. 1   Packing loan

Packing loan refers to an export financing provide by banks for exporters preparing goods before shipment. Usually the exporter gets loan from the bank upon the letter of credit pledged by the bank so as to prepare shipment of the goods. The exporter must present its documents to the bank from which he gets the loan, and the bank will negotiate the documents and deduct the amount for the purpose of packing goods. Normally the period of packing loan provide by the bank will last from the date of getting the loan to the date of negotiating or no longer than 21 days after the expiry date of the letter of credit. The amount for packing loan is in the proportion of 40% to 80%. The bank should take the following points into account before making a packing loan to his customer:

(1) Credits investigation on issuing bank and importer

One of the risks of packing loan comes from the issuing bank and the importer. We need to have good knowledge of the issuing bank in terms of credit rating, bank ranking, funding capacity, business status, operation style and discrepancies caviling. Reputation of an importer is also important. The bank should know if the importer and exporter is long-term cooperators and friends or initial business parents, and if there had been any bad records on payment.

(2) Careful study on letter of credit

Before the packing loan is made, the bank should make a careful study on the characteristics, quality and quantity of commodity, be sure that the goods can be shipped within its latest delivery time and documents presented for negotiation can meet the requirement of the letter of credit. The bank can only make a packing loan after these unfavorable clauses are amended.

(3) Be careful of transferable credit

The bank must be careful when it makes a packing loan for a transferable letter of credit. A case demonstrate that a bank was put into dilemma after it provide a packing loan under a transferable credit in the amount of USD800,000. After the first beneficiary got the packing loan from a bank, the letter of credit is transferred to the second beneficiary. The bank that provided the packing loan to the first beneficiary negotiated the documents of the second beneficiary and purchased its bill so as to off-set the packing loan of the first beneficiary. Unfortunately, due to their discrepancies the documents were rejected by the issuing bank. The bank then required the second beneficiary to repay the loan, but he said:"the bank has no evidence to show that I have got the fund from it." Actually the first beneficicuy directed the fund for other purposes.

(4) Know the trade and the market

The bank should always keep an eye on the trade background and its market under letter of credit. The bank must check the sales contract, supply contract and transportation contract incorporating the letter of credit before the packing loan is made. The quality of the exported products and production or performance capacity of the supplier should be taken into account by the bank because all these have close relationships to the completion of a letter of credit.

The bank should also be kept informed about the market, because the market is changeable, and the operation of a letter of credit will last more than one month. When the margin of the exporting goods is rather small or even none, the exporter will probably not execute the letter of credit. In addition, the foreign exchange rate is also a factor affecting the gain of the export.

(5) Supervision and risk mitigation

A letter of credit itself can be regarded as a security for refund, but it is not the sole one, due to its many uncertainties. With the complicated and changeable international financial market, a bank must establish its warning and mitigating mechanism for trade finance. Legal and effective mortgage or pledge and qualified guarantors are needed. The second source of repayment must be ensured before a packing loan is provided. In the operation, by signing maximum amount of lending contract with a borrower or guarantor, a guarantee can be used repeatedly in the fixed time so as to simplify the procedure and save time.

Supervision is an important step to control the risk of packing loan. The bank should keep an eye on the capital flow of each packing loan under the letter of credit to avoid the packing loan being used for other purposes. The bank should try to reduce the proportion of loan in the amount stated in the letter of credit. The bank may also supervise the shipment to avoid passing off sham as genuine if necessary.

11. 2. 2   Bill discount

Bill discount is an act of bill, and is kind of financing. The bill to be discounted must be a time bill, and it can be discounted after its acceptance.

When a bank starts an operation for export bill discounting, it must examine the information about the application carefully including his account, acceptor's name, address, maturity and amount. Under a usance letter of credit, the bank has to check the documents to see if they are in compliance with the credit. The bank can only discount the bill when the documents are in conformity with the letter of credit and the bill is accepted by a reputable bank. Bill discounting belongs to a kind of financing with recourse. Usually the bank and the exporter will sign an agreement to define the liability and responsibility of each party.

Discount rate for export bill will be made by the bank. Usually banks like to make the discount rate on the base of Libor plus certain point. In some countries with developed international financial market, the discounted bills can be rediscounted by the central bank or sold in the market.

11.3 Traveler's Cheque

11. 3. 1   Definition

A traveler's check is a specially printed form of check issued by a financial institution, leading hotels, and other agencies in preprinted denominations for a fixed amount to a customer for use when he is going to travel abroad. The issuer commits himself to pay the stated sum to any payee and undertakes to repay the purchaser if the check is lost or stolen before it is cashed. A traveler's check is actually a draft on a bank or other agency, which is self-identifying and may be cashed at banks, hotels, etc., either throughout the world or in particular areas only.

11. 3. 2   Parties

There are five parties to a traveler's check, namely, the issuer, the selling agent or office, the purchaser or the holder, the paying agent or the person who encases the traveler's check and the transferee.

(1) Issuer.

The issuer is the financial institution, leading hotels or other agencies issuing the traveler's check. If the issuer is a bank, it is called the issuing bank or the drawee bank, for the check is drawn on the issuer. The name and address of the issuer usually appear on the upper part of the check. A valid traveler's check should bear the printed facsimile of the issuer's authorized signature.

(2) Selling agent or office.

The selling agent or office is one that sells the traveler's check. If the issuer sells the check by itself, then it is acting as the selling agent or office. If the issuer dispatches its traveler's checks to its branches or correspondents in other countries for sale, the latter is acting as its selling agents. All dispatches of the traveler's checks are to be advised to their selling agents by the issuer. Receipt is to be acknowledged by the selling agent, usually on a form attached to the advice of dispatch. If the traveler's checks do not reach the selling agent in due time, he must inform the issuer by cable. The selling agents shall keep separate accounts to record the total amount or checks that they have received and sold. The sales proceeds must be remitted to the issuer at once.

(3) Purchaser or holder.

The purchaser is a person who buys a traveler's check from the issuer or his selling agent. When purchasing the check, he must sign his name thereon at the counter of the issuer or his selling agent, thereby making himself a holder or the instrument. Any unused checks may be returned to the issuing bank or the selling agent for refund.

(4) Paying agent.

The paying agent is one that undertakes by arrangement with the issuer to pay the latter traveler's checks when presented by the holder. The paying agent, on honoring a check, pays the holder in local currency at the current rate of exchange, then sends the check forward for collection and instructs the issuing bank to pay the proceeds either to its account or to some other bank for credit to its account.

(5) Transferee.

The transferee is one to whom the traveler's check is transferred. If the purchaser or the holder makes use of the traveler's check to pay a bill of any hotel or restaurant or an invoice of any shop, the hotel, restaurant, or shop becomes the transferee.

11.3.3　Procedure

(1) Purchase.

a. The traveler first fills in an application form in which the total amount and denominations needed are indicated, requesting the issuer or his selling agent to sell him the traveler's checks.

b. The clerk or the bank teller then takes out the checks from the inventory and records the number (each traveler's check is number) of the check to be sold on the purchaser's purchase receipt along with the purchaser's name and address.

c. The purchaser signs his name on the face of each check in a designated place in the presence of the clerk or the teller and pays the amount equivalent to the total value of the checks plus a small commission, usually one percent or less.

d. The purchaser receives the checks, together with a list of the checks' serial number of which it is advisable to be carried separately from the checks.

(2) Encashment.

a. Whenever the traveler desires to cash one or more of the traveler's during a trip, he or she countersigns on each check in a designated place in the presence of the cashier of a store, a hotel or a bank.

b. The cashier then compares this signature with that already singed thereon. If the two signatures are identical with each other, the cashier encases the traveler's check. If the counter-signature differs slightly from the initial signature, the holder may be requested to endorse his name on the back of the check in the presence of the cashier. The encashment by the paying agent is subject to the presenter's passport or some other official identity with his photograph affixed may be required.

(3) Claims.

One of the most important features of the traveler's check favorable to the purchaser or the holder is that in case the checks are lost or stolen, they will be replaced. Once the checks are lost the loser should notify the issuer either directly or more often through one of its local selling agent. The issuer will replace the lost checks as quickly as possible, frequently within hours. If the losers fail to keep a separate listing of their check numbers, they may encounter a delay in time in obtaining the replaced checks, for the issuer will seek to identify the missing check numbers from computer records.

11. 3. 4 Advantages

(1) Traveler's checks are safer than foreign bank notes and coins. The issuer will soon replace the lost or stolen checks that have not been encased.

(2) Traveler's checks are readily encasable at banks, hotels, railway stations, airports and many commercial firms abroad because of their wide acceptability.

(3) Different denominations of traveler's checks facilitate their use by the traveler to meet his needs during a trip.

(4) Traveler's checks are not as bulky as an ordinary wallet full of bank notes for the same total amount.

(5) No time limit is set to the circulation of the traveler's checks, for in general, no expiry date is specified in the check.

11.4 Credit Card

11.4.1 Definition

Credit cards are instructions issued by banks to carefully selected customers with a line of credit ranging from several hundred to several thousand dollars based on the latter's financial status for use in obtaining, on credit, consumer goods, services and other necessities. They may be used, in effect, as a substitute for money. By using these cards commodities can be bought, hotel bills paid, and airfares met without paying any cash in many regions of the world.

In other words, credit cards are a short-term small amount consumer's credit extended by a bank. Those who have a current account with the card issuing bank and whose credit is good often use credit cards. A credit card is a small plastic with the name of the bank printed on it, a specimen of the user's signature, account number of the card and the expiry date, embossed with the card holder's name, his signature, account number and an expiry date for card.

The best known cards in the world are American Express Card, Diners Club Card, Visa Card, Master Card, Federal Card, etc.

11.4.2 Parties

(1) Issuing bank. The bank that extends a small amount of short term credit to its customers, first by careful selection and evaluation of the customers and then issuance of a line credit.

(2) Cardholder. The customer who has a current account with the card-issuing bank and whose credit is good, and who based on his financial status can obtain, on credit, consumer goods, services and other things when necessary.

(3) Merchant. Store, hotel or restaurant that is bound to have a prearrangement with the card issuing bank and is willing to accept the credit card for payment of commodities sold or services rendered.

11.4.3 Procedure

Credit cards provide control and also smooth the relationship between the issuing bank, cardholder and the merchants. The procedure goes as follows:

(1) The process of the issuance of cards.

a. The client fills in an application form according to the requirements and

b. The bank investigates and examines the annual income and the credit standing of the client before approving the issuance of cards. An entrance fee and / or annual membership dues may be charged to the cardholder. Some credit cards are given to the holders free of charge.

(2) Setting up relations with merchants and authorization.

Credit cards have to be widely accepted by what is called the merchant or assigned merchant, i. e. shops, hotels, restaurants, airports that agree to accept credit card prior to an agency agreement signed between the bank and the merchant. This agreement is a promise made by the merchant. Rights, duties and obligations shall be expressly stipulated in the agreement. Staff members of the merchant are to be trained by the bank and the merchant as to the essential steps of handling credit cards.

Authorization is an important step by which the bank controls the credit of the card holder in the process of its circulation and a means by which the bank bridges the relations between the individual and the merchant through the consumption of goods or services by the card holder. In the agreement between and the bank, a credit limit is usually set out for the customer. Much larger limits can be granted to selected customers. The cardholder is expected not to exceed the ceiling limit in using the card, otherwise the merchant has to contact the acquirer and obtain permission to accept the largest amount.

(3) Clearing and settlement.

The bank is the center dealing with the clearing and settlement between the cardholder, merchant and the bank. Steps necessary in the actual use of the card as follows:

a. When the cardholder purchases goods or services from the merchant, he should sign a sales slip and hand it together with his card to the merchant. Sales ships are provided to record all the details of each transaction. A part of the required information is hand-written on the sales slip and the remaining obtained by processing the credit card and sales slip through an imprinter provided by the card-issuing bank. While processing, the imprinter will record on the sales slip the cardholder's name and account number, card expiration date, merchant's name and account number. Other information such as date, description of merchandise purchased or services rendered, total amount, etc., is filled in by the clerk.

b. The merchant examines the card carefully to determine whether the card is a valid or a forged one, and whether it is expired or not. If the card is valid, the merchant then delivers the goods to the card holder.

c. The merchant presents to the bank the sales slip bearing the signature of the cardholder.

d. The bank effects payment of the amount on the slip, less a discount ranging from one to several percent allowed to the bank. The discount depends on the volume of the credit card sales generates by the merchant, the types of goods sold or services rendered and competitiveness among banks in the area.

e. The bank issues monthly bills to the cardholder for his purchases.

f. The cardholder repays the amount to the bank. He has the option of paying the bill in full within a grace period (usually 25 days) without interest or drawing revolving credit with an interest usually higher than a 90 day commercial paper discount rate.

11.4.4　Functions

Credit cards have been in fashion for decades and are currently issued in various countries that are active in tourism. They contribute to the development of new contrivances for the benefit of consumers, tourism and business travels and for the generation of foreign exchange. As is well known to all, a credit card is one of the most popular banking instruments in the conduct of retailing banking business nowadays. Specifically, a credit card avoids the need of carrying too much cash or bulky traveler's checks, allows cash to be drawn at banks as and when required without planning it beforehand, and serves as a useful "back-up" if traveler's checks or bank notes are lost or stolen.

Box 11.1

The History of Credit Card

The concept of using a card for purchases was described in 1887 by Edward Bellamy in his utopian novel Looking Backward. Bellamy used the term credit card eleven times in this novel.

The modern credit card was the successor of a variety of merchant credit schemes. It was first used in the 1920s, in the United States, specifically to sell fuel to a growing number of automobile owners. In 1938 several companies started to accept each other's cards. Western Union had begun issuing charge cards to its frequent customers in 1921. Some charge cards were printed on paper card stock, but were easily counterfeited.

The Charga-Plate, developed in 1928, was an early predecessor to the credit card and used in the U.S. from the 1930s to the late 1950s. It was a $2\frac{1}{2}$ in $\times$ $1\frac{1}{4}$ in rectangle of sheet metal related to Addressograph and military dog tag systems. It was embossed with the customer's name, city and state. It held a small paper card for a signature. In recording a purchase, the plate was laid into a recess in the imprinter, with a paper "charge slip" positioned on top of it. The record of the transaction included an impression of the embossed information, made by the imprinter pressing an inked ribbon against the charge slip. Charga-Plate was a trademark of Farrington Manufacturing Co. Charga-Plates were issued by large-scale merchants to their regular customers, much like department store credit cards of today. In some cases, the plates were kept in the issuing store rather than held by customers. When an authorized user made a purchase, a clerk retrieved the plate from the store's files and then processed the purchase. Charga-Plates speeded back-office bookkeeping that was done manually in paper ledgers in each store, before computers.

In 1934, American Airlines and the Air Transport Association simplified the process even more with the advent of the Air Travel Card. They created a numbering scheme that identified the Issuer of card as well as the Customer account. This is the reason the modern UATP cards still start with the number 1. With an Air Travel Card passengers could "buy now, and pay later" for a ticket against their credit and receive a fifteen percent discount at any of the accepting airlines. By the 1940s, all of the major domestic airlines offered Air Travel Cards that could be used on 17 different airlines. By 1941 about half of the Airlines Revenues came through the Air Travel Card agreement. The Airlines had also started offering installment plans to lure new travelers into the air. In October 1948 the Air Travel Card become the first internationally valid Charge Card within all members of the International Air Transport Association.

The concept of customers paying different merchants using the same card was expanded in 1950 by Ralph Schneider and Frank McNamara, founders of Diners Club, to consolidate multiple cards. The Diners Club, which was created partially through a merger with Dine and Sign, produced the first "general purpose" charge card, and required the entire bill to be paid with each statement. That was followed by Carte Blanche and in 1958 by American Express which created a worldwide credit card network (although these were initially charge cards that acquired credit card features after BankAmericard demonstrated the feasibility of the concept).

However, until 1958, no one had been able to create a working revolving credit financial instrument issued by a third-party bank that was generally accepted by a large number of merchants (as opposed to merchant-issued revolving cards accepted by only a few merchants). A dozen experiments by small American banks had been attempted (and had failed). In September 1958, Bank of America launched the BankAmericard in Fresno, California. BankAmericard became the first successful recognizably modern credit card (although it underwent a troubled gestation during which its creator resigned), and with its overseas affiliates, eventually evolved into the Visa system. In 1966, the ancestor of MasterCard was born when a group of banks established Master Charge to compete with BankAmericard; it received a significant boost when Citibank merged its proprietary Everything Card (launched in 1967) into Master Charge in 1969.

Early credit cards in the U. S. , of which BankAmericard was the most prominent example, were mass produced and mass mailed unsolicited to bank customers who were thought to be good credit risks. But, "They have been mailed off to unemployables, drunks, narcotics addicts and to compulsive debtors, a process President Johnson's Special Assistant Betty Furness found very like 'giving sugar to diabetics' ." These mass mailings were known as "drops" in banking terminology, and were outlawed in 1970 due to the financial chaos they caused, but not before 100 million credit cards had been dropped into the U. S. population. After 1970, only credit card applications could be sent unsolicited in mass mailings.

The fractured nature of the U. S. banking system under the Glass - Steagall Act meant that credit cards became an effective way for those who were traveling around the country to move their credit to places where they could not directly use their banking facilities. In 1966 Barclaycard in the UK launched the first credit card outside of the U. S.

There are now countless variations on the basic concept of revolving credit for individuals (as issued by banks and honored by a network of financial institutions), including organization-branded credit cards, corporate-user credit cards, store cards and so on.

Although credit cards reached very high adoption levels in the US, Canada and the UK in the mid twentieth century, many cultures were more cash-oriented, or developed alternative forms of cash-less payments, such as Carte bleue or the Eurocard (Germany, France, Switzerland, and others). In these places, adoption of credit cards was initially much slower. It took until the 1990s to reach anything like the percentage market-penetration levels achieved in the US, Canada, or UK. In some countries, acceptance still remains poor as the use of a credit card system depends on the banking system being perceived as reliable. Japan remains a very cash oriented society, with credit card adoption being limited to only the largest of merchants, although an alternative system based on RFIDs inside cellphones has seen some acceptance. Because of strict regulations regarding banking system overdrafts, some countries, France in particular, were much faster to develop and adopt chip-based credit cards which are now seen as major anti-fraud credit devices. Debit cards and online banking are used more widely than credit cards in some countries.

The design of the credit card itself has become a major selling point in recent years. The value of the card to the issuer is often related to the customer's usage of the card, or to the customer's financial worth. This has led to the rise of Co-Brand and Affinity cards, where the card design is related to the "affinity" (a university or professional society, for example) leading to higher card usage. In most cases a percentage of the value of the card is returned to the affinity group.

Source: http://en. wikipedia. org/wiki/credit-card

Key Words

Traveler's Check, Credit Card

Questions

1. What are the advantages of Traveler's Check?
2. What are the parties of Credit Card?